with Visual Basic® 4

Joel P. Dehlin and
Matthew J. Curland

Microsoft® Press

PUBLISHED BY
Microsoft Press
A Division of Microsoft Corporation
One Microsoft Way
Redmond, Washington 98052-6399

Library of Congress Cataloging-in-Publication Data pending.

Printed and bound in the United States of America.

1 2 3 4 5 6 7 8 9 QMQM 1 0 9 8 7 6

Distributed to the book trade in Canada by Macmillan of Canada, a division of Canada Publishing Corporation.

A CIP catalogue record for this book is available from the British Library.

Microsoft Press books are available through booksellers and distributors worldwide. For further information about international editions, contact your local Microsoft Corporation office. Or contact Microsoft Press International directly at fax (206) 936-7329.

Acquisitions Editor: Casey Doyle
Project Editor: Erin O'Connor
Technical Editor: Jean Ross

This book is dedicated to my wife, with whom I've spent the last six years, and to the two little boys who continually entertain, infuriate, and enliven us. I can't wait to get to know Lani, Benjamin, and Jonathon again. And this book is dedicated to my father, David Dehlin, who bought an Apple II back in the Ice Age and encouraged me to quit spending so much time playing games and start learning to program. In Basic.

—Joel

On the home front, this book is dedicated to my beautiful bride, Lynn, whom I hope to see more often in the second year of our marriage. It's my turn to wait for her to finish "ten more minutes" of writing several hours after midnight. On the Visual Basic front, this book is dedicated to anyone who has ever said, "You can't do that in Visual Basic!" I've always taken that statement as a personal challenge. You can do that in Visual Basic—and much more.

—Matt

CONTENTS SUMMARY

APPENDIXES

TABLE OF CONTENTS

PART TWO Objects and Visual Basic

APPENDIXES

PREFACE

In 1994, Joel was traveling around the world, meeting with customers in Fortune 500 companies. His evangelical message to developers frequently focused on convincing them to use Visual Basic and Microsoft Office for Windows as their principal development platform. Clients were willing, but their follow-up question, "Can you recommend a good, comprehensive book on how to program Office objects from VB?" had to be met with a resounding "Uh, no. There really isn't one." Thus the idea for this book was born.

At the same time, Matt was looking for opportunities to spread the tips and tricks he'd accumulated in the course of writing many thousands of lines of Visual Basic and Microsoft Excel macro code. And he was looking for a way to release the object browsing tool he was writing.

We put our heads together and joined forces to write this book. Matt brought the hardcore developer preoccupations and Joel the IS perspective to the effort. The book evolved. We added some beginner chapters on Visual Basic. Matt's object browser blossomed and became *Object Navigator*. And now here it is.

This book focuses, as we wanted it to, on the new object-oriented features of Visual Basic 4 that enable you to achieve the tightest integration possible between Visual Basic and Microsoft Office for Windows 95. We hope you learn as much reading it as we did along the way.

ACKNOWLEDGMENTS

Much love and many thanks to my wife, Lani, and to my boys, Benjamin and Jonathon, who have been so patient and understanding this last year while I've stolen nights, weekends, and early mornings to work on this book. Special thanks to Matt for working so hard, for being so smart, and for enduring my endless questions.

I can't get away without at least mentioning folks I've worked with in the past. Thanks to Pieter Knook, who gave me the first real encouragement to go forward with the book, and to John Neilson and Juan Vegarra, who gave their approval. And regards to my old teammates, "the guys from CATM"—Pat, Jonathan, Charles, and Mark—and the OTS team at Arthur Andersen & Co. Thanks (I guess) to Jim Holzer, who made me write my first VB program (for MS DOS).

Thanks to my father, David, who inspired me to get into computers in the first place, and to Nan, Don, Cathy, Gina, John, Julianne, Tom, John, Margi, Genny, and Robert for just being cool.

Many thanks to the folks at Microsoft Press, who did a ton of work. Casey Doyle got us into the project and guided us through the initial process. The editor, Erin O'Connor, showed tremendous patience and really improved the quality of the work. Jean Ross sorted out a number of difficulties in both the text and the code and helped us with the setup disk. Lisa Theobald fussed over our prose. Peggy Herman and Sandra Haynes made it look good, and Travis Beaven perfected the art. That much we know, and we suspect that at least a dozen other people at MS Press contributed their expertise.

Glenn Hackney reviewed our early chapters and made innumerable invaluable suggestions. Dan Berlin kept us on our toes early on. We want to thank David Boctor, John Tafoya, Marcus Aiu, Michael Mathieu, Charles Sterling, Peter Loforte, Mike Risse, and everybody we've forgotten to mention, too.

—Joel

A great many people have contributed to this book, either during its writing or while we scraped together the programming tidbits contained in it. These are a few of the people who stand out in my mind.

Special thanks go to my wife, Lynn, who has shown incredible patience, support, and love during the last year of seemingly interminable work. A little less in the way of thanks goes to Joel Dehlin, who got me into this in the first place. If we'd known what it took to write a book, we might have reconsidered.

My thanks go to Marjorie Grove and Arthur Fisher from the Early Entrance Program at the University of Washington, who taught me how to write. I appreciate their excellent training more every year, although I didn't exactly enjoy it at the time. Thanks to my parents, Jill Elmer and William Curland (deceased), who taught me the value of hard work.

The book team was rock solid. Our acquisitions editor, Casey Doyle, took a chance in giving us the opportunity to write this book. Our manuscript editor, Erin O'Connor, worked with us on many early drafts before the style solidified and the pages started rolling in. Jean Ross, our technical editor, diligently checked every line of text and code in the book and banged hard on every sample program. And I can't say enough about the contributions of Glenn Hackney, who meticulously reviewed many of the chapters. Glenn has served as the initial sounding board for many of my programming ideas over the years and has frequently brought my errant understanding of difficult concepts back in line.

Thanks go to Brett Burris and Paul Bryant for encouraging me to set my programming sights higher; to Betty Chinn for allowing me to let off steam when the going got tough; to Chris Dias for knowing the answer to every obscure question; to Martin Cibulka and Matt Shulman for putting up with my weird hours while I finished this book; and to Mark Chace for answering all the hardest OLE questions. I'm also grateful to John Norwood, Kennth Lassensen, Scott Swanson, Doug Franklin, and Bruce McKinney.

For help with the *Object Navigator,* thanks go to Steven Mitchell, who gave me most of my usability feedback. An "I don't get it" from Steven always meant hours of late night toil. Thanks also go to Brent Aliverti for graphics advice and to Jim Cash for his work with me on add-ins in Visual Basic.

—Matt

INTRODUCTION

Microsoft has spent several years evangelizing the idea that OLE technology can be leveraged to seamlessly integrate multiple applications into one custom software solution, but the task can be far from trivial. The immediate availability of reusable objects has been a strength in Microsoft's push for componentized applications, but it has also been the source of many programming potholes. The very fact that objects are easy to use also means that they are just as easy to misuse. This book will steer you away from the potholes on the road to successful object programming.

The ability of applications in the Microsoft Office for Windows 95 suite to expose objects through the magic of OLE Automation, allowing one application to control another, is great technology. As you start your journey, you'll find the object road to be pretty smooth, but the road gets rougher as your programs increase in complexity. As soon as you get serious about combining all of these objects into a useful custom solution, you'll find that you're missing some objects you need to complete your program. There's no quick fix. Your missing objects won't be the same as someone else's because you're writing a different program for a different audience.

This is where the object-oriented design of Visual Basic 4 steps into the picture. Visual Basic 3 was able to control OLE Automation objects from the sidelines by dispatching instructions to other objects. Visual Basic 4 has moved onto the playing field, right into the middle of the object fray. And Visual Basic 4 enables you to introduce new players whenever you want—that is, to bring in custom objects to fill the inevitable gaps in the Microsoft Office object lineup as you need to. Helping you create and integrate custom objects is the central theme of *Object Programming with Visual Basic 4.*

What's in the Book?

The first three chapters in *Object Programming with Visual Basic 4* have nothing to do with object programming. In fact, every line of code in Part One would have felt right at home in Visual Basic 1. Part One is a rapid overview of the

Visual Basic design environment and the event-driven programming model, a model fundamental to any Visual Basic program. If you're an experienced VB programmer, you can skim this part of the book or just skip it altogether. If you're new to VB, read Part One to get acquainted with how easy it is to use the leading RAD (rapid application development) tool on the market.

Part Two addresses defining and creating Visual Basic custom classes. We walk through coding a class module to define a class, creating instances of the class (objects), and exposing our classes to be used and instantiated by external applications. Along the way, we take a close look at the most efficient ways to call the methods and set the properties of a running object. We evaluate the cost of each call to an object and how that cost changes for objects exposed by other applications. We also take a look at the in-place activation capabilities of Visual Basic 4, which allow you to easily use graphical objects from Microsoft Office for Windows 95 applications in your programs, with little or no code.

Part Three looks in depth at programming Microsoft Excel with Visual Basic. Although the focus in this section is on Microsoft Excel, the concepts can be applied universally to program objects exposed by any of the Microsoft Office for Windows 95 applications, or any other object servers, with Visual Basic. We start with a discussion in Chapter 8 of using the Visual Basic for Applications language in Excel. We look at the most common objects in Excel's object model both from within Excel macros and from Visual Basic programs. We look at lots of Excel macro code snippets as we go, especially at code for the often confusing Range object. Chapter 9 on performance-tuning is short but important. If you want to double or even quadruple the speed of your Excel macros, it's required reading.

As we move through the last two chapters in Part Three, we concentrate as much on program architecture as on writing code. Once you've mastered the techniques in Chapter 9, you'll find that writing solid object code is similar for all object models. The tricks for great performance lie in putting your code in the right place. Simply moving code from one component application to another—say, from Visual Basic to Microsoft Excel—often makes the difference between a useful program and one destined for the trash can. By the time we're through, you'll have a Visual Basic form integrated directly into the Microsoft Excel shell. Excel uses a custom Visual Basic object to launch the modeless Visual Basic form. The Visual Basic form then uses the custom VB object to notify Excel of user-generated events.

In Part Four, we look at using Visual Basic to control two other Microsoft Office applications, Microsoft Word and Microsoft PowerPoint. WordBasic, the macro language in Microsoft Word, is not compatible with Visual Basic for Applications, so we look at the differences between writing to WordBasic directly in Word and controlling the WordBasic object through VBA code. Microsoft Power-

Point for Windows 95 is the first PowerPoint release to support OLE Automation. PowerPoint now exposes an extensive object model that can be controlled by Visual Basic.

VBA Language Concepts

In Appendix A, you'll find an in-depth look at selected Visual Basic for Applications topics such as branching and looping, scoping, collections, and so on. Cross-references in the main text point to Language Concepts topics so that you can refer to this appendix in the contexts in which you might need to.

The Object Navigator

You can use the Object Navigator tool included on the companion CD to view the structure of any object library and to locate elusive functionality across multiple object libraries with full substring search capabilities. The Object Navigator lets you graphically build complex code expressions, complete with parameter values, that can be pasted directly into VBA code. The Object Navigator greatly reduces the time it takes to learn object programming by helping you find your way through the maze of complicated object models you'll encounter. Appendix B documents the features of this powerful programming tool.

Object Models and Visual Basic Notation

For your convenience, we've put graphical representations of the Microsoft Access/DAO, Microsoft Excel, Microsoft PowerPoint, and Microsoft Word object models into an appendix. We've also included an appendix that shows the Visual Basic adaptation of Charles Simonyi's Hungarian naming conventions.

PART ONE

A Taste of Visual Basic

IN THIS PART

If you're reading this, you've probably programmed the line "Hello, World!" before. You won't encounter that beginner's favorite again in this book, but we did design the following three chapters to give you a brief overview of Visual Basic to clear the cobwebs if you've used VB before, or to bring you up to speed if you haven't. If you find the text too elementary, just skip ahead. But if you detect a few spiders crawling around after the next three chapters, you might consider consulting a more basic VB book before you go on in this one.

Cross-Reference Mike Halverson's *Microsoft Visual Basic 4 for Windows 95 Step by Step* (Microsoft Press, 1995) includes hands-on exercises and step-by-step instructions for using VB.

Chapter 1 - Visual Basic Building Blocks

In Chapter 1, we'll look at some basic concepts an experienced Visual Basic programmer will probably already know about: Visual Basic objects, events and event procedures, and properties. We'll also move around in the VB environment a little. If you're inexperienced in VB programming, read through this chapter to get a foundation for your work in the rest of the book. If you're pretty experienced, you'd do well to skip ahead to Chapters 2 and 3.

Chapter 2 - *QuickEdit,* Your First Visual Basic Program

In the second chapter, we'll design our first sample program, *QuickEdit.* We'll take up fundamental program architecture considerations and create all of the objects necessary for our sample program. At the end of this chapter, you should be ready to move from the mouse to the keyboard and start writing Visual Basic code in Chapter 3. If you're familiar with adding controls and menus to a form and setting run-time properties from VB code, you might go straight to the end of Chapter 3 and study the code listing to verify that you understand what's going on.

Chapter 3 - Let's Write Some Code

In the third chapter, we'll add the guts to our *QuickEdit* program. We'll look at all of the code in detail as we write it. And we'll debug some code in Visual Basic. We'll finish with a few enhancements to make the *QuickEdit* sample more user friendly.

1

Visual Basic Building Blocks

We'll get started in this chapter by looking at the most elementary aspects of Visual Basic programming. And we'll even create a rudimentary program.

Graphical User Interface

GUI (pronounced goo-ee). Graphical user interface.

The GUI acronym may sound like an ice cream flavor, but in the world of computers it stands for a powerful mechanism that enables a user to interact with a computer intuitively. At the bare minimum, a computer program must be friendly enough that it doesn't raise a user's blood pressure. And what's the secret of such friendly behavior? Communication. GUI is the language, if you will, that allows us to easily communicate with our computers.

Windows Communication

Not only does a computer need to be able to speak to the user in a language that he or she intuitively understands, but the user must be able to respond accordingly. The explosive popularity of the Microsoft Windows operating system is largely due to its easy to learn and use language, its *GUI*.

Microsoft Windows has revolutionized the personal computing world because it has made PCs easy to use by means of a graphical language that's quickly learned and easily understood.

Just to refresh your memory—if you're an old-time computer user, what used to look like this on screen

```
Output:
Holzer, James, Carolyn, Kristin, (515)555-1212, Des Moines, IA
Please press any key to continue...
```

now looks more like the window shown in Figure 1-1.

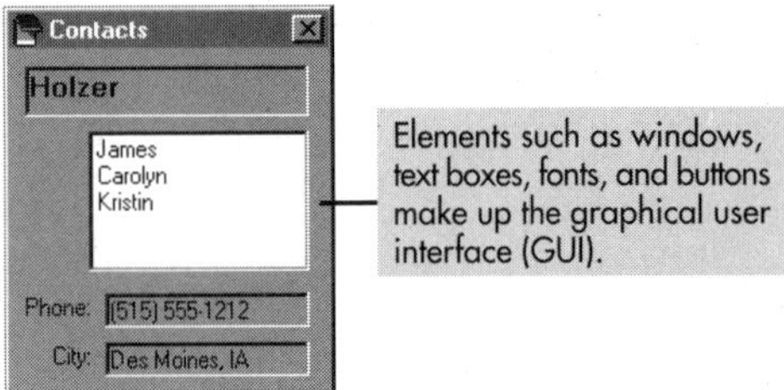
Contacts
Holzer
James
Carolyn
Kristin
Phone: (515) 555-1212
City: Des Moines, IA
Elements such as windows, text boxes, fonts, and buttons make up the graphical user interface (GUI).

Figure 1-1. *An example of the Windows graphical user interface.*

Why Go GUI?

Windows is certainly not the first GUI environment (nor will it be the last), so why is Windows so popular? Can you spell A-P-P-L-I-C-A-T-I-O-N-S? Customers can choose from thousands of applications for Windows. No other graphical operating system can boast the number of applications that have been written for Windows.

Of course, some of the older, nongraphical, operating systems such as MS-DOS and UNIX might have even more applications than Windows, but the problem with those operating systems is that each program that runs on one of them typically has its own unique look and feel. Each program's interface differs from the interfaces of other programs. For example, a user follows one key sequence to save files in Lotus 1-2-3 for MS-DOS and a different key sequence to save files in WordPerfect for MS-DOS. But in almost every Windows-based program you save a file in the same way: from the File menu, you choose Save.

Windows Does GUI

When communicating verbally, we use different parts of speech to make up a sentence. Nouns, verbs, and adjectives, plus other parts of speech, help us to express concepts clearly.

The Windows GUI language also has "parts of speech" that facilitate communication between a computer user and an application. We'll look briefly at the Windows GUI parts of speech here, and then in the next section we'll consider how Visual Basic helps you create programs that speak the Windows GUI language.

Objects

Windows *objects,* such as windows, menus, and buttons, are the nouns of the GUI language. Like nouns in a sentence, Windows objects get *done to* and *do.* However, Windows objects are passive until they're instructed to do something by the user or by Windows. For example, a button on the screen will do nothing until the user clicks it, or an animated picture might not move until Windows sends it a timer message.

Once it is told to act, an object performs its assigned task, which may include instructing another object to do something as well. Going back to our examples: we could instruct the button to trigger the animation when the button is clicked rather than have Windows trigger the animation. In this example, the button would be getting *done to* (by being clicked) and *doing* (by instructing the picture to animate itself).

Events and Event Procedures

A computer user uses the mouse and the keyboard to communicate with the computer. User actions, such as clicking a menu item, maximizing a window, double-clicking in a list box, and dragging an icon, generate *events.* Objects themselves can act like users by generating events in other objects. Objects (whether part of Windows or part of an application) respond to events with *event procedures.*

Events and event procedures are the verbs of the GUI language. Remember it this way: Something that happens to an object is an event. The object's response to the event is an event procedure.

Properties

Finally, *properties,* such as Height, Width, BackColor, and Caption, are the adjectives of the GUI language. They describe objects.

NOTE The GUI language allows the user to communicate with the computer. Instead of nouns, verbs, and adjectives, *objects, events* and *event procedures,* and *properties* make up the GUI language.

Working with Visual Basic Elements

Visual Basic allows you to quickly master the different parts of the GUI language. It allows you to create objects, assign properties to objects, and instruct the objects how to respond to events with coded event procedures. Once the basics of the GUI language are on the tip of your tongue (or should we say at your fingertips?), you can quickly turn your programs into powerful orators as well as good listeners.

Let's look in more detail at how Visual Basic helps you create programs that work with the elements of the Windows GUI language: objects, events and event procedures, and properties.

The Object

One reason the Windows GUI is so much friendlier than the old-style character-based interfaces of the past is its repeated use of familiar, visually represented objects. Users can expect to see the same basic objects whenever they launch a new Windows program. Standard menus, buttons, scroll bars, check boxes, and the like have made Windows programs easier to use and quicker to learn.

Whenever a user sees a familiar object, he or she usually knows what actions will make it perform. For example, if a user sees a button on the screen, he knows that he's supposed to simulate pushing the button by clicking it with the mouse.

You, the programmer, benefit from this consistency across Windows-based programs because the user has already learned how to click buttons, scroll the contents of a window, and click menu items by the time he or she runs your program. The time that used to be associated with learning how to use a new program is considerably shortened.

Creating an object

With Visual Basic, you can easily add Windows objects to your own application. Let's get right down to it.

1. Double-click on the Visual Basic icon, and up comes a template for your first program. This simple template contains one object: the form. See Figure 1-2.

   Believe it or not, this default form object is your first VB "program." A user could now run your program even though you haven't even written any code! Let's leave design mode and see what would happen when a user ran your program. (See the "Visual Basic Modes" sidebar on page 10 for more information on design, run, and break modes.)

2. Press F5 (or from the Run menu select Start) to enter run mode. You'll see your form rendered on the screen. In run mode, the user can resize the form, minimize it, maximize it, and move it around. See Figure 1-3.

3. Click the *close* button in the upper right corner of the form to exit the program and return to design mode.

OK, so your first program isn't all that useful, but it does have the same behavior as a standard window. VB has given you all of the default windowing functionality for free.

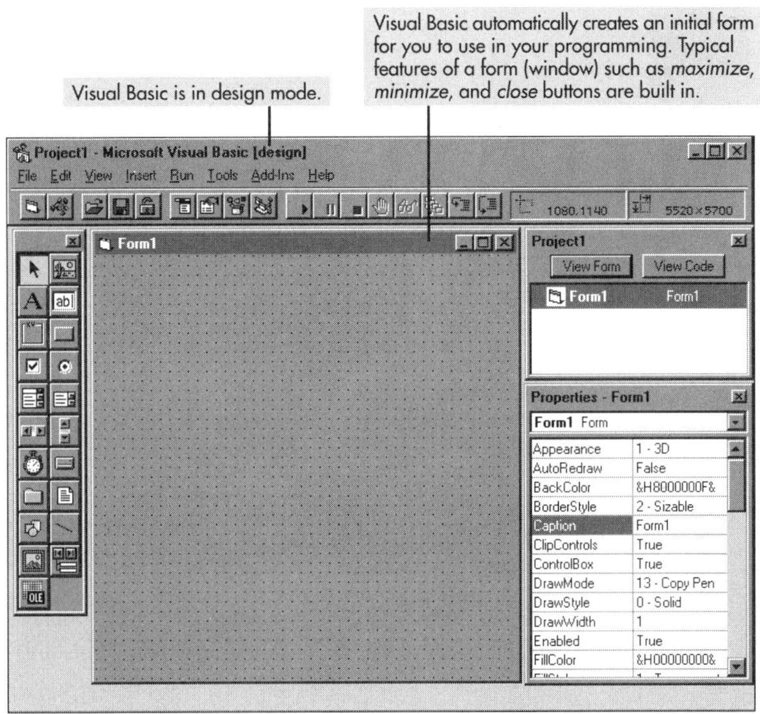

Figure 1-2. *Visual Basic in design mode. A default form (*Form1*) comes up on the screen.*

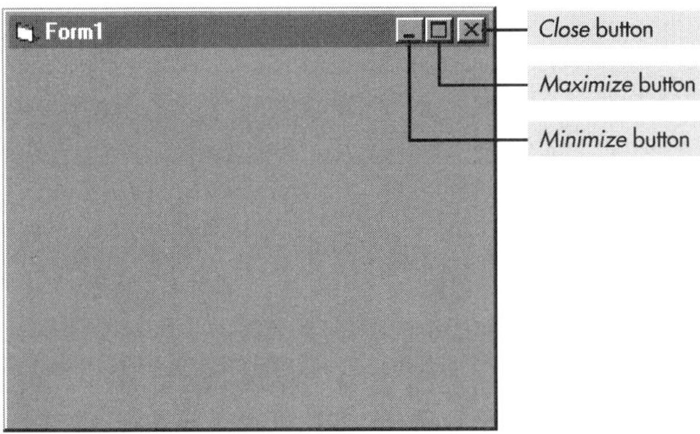

Figure 1-3. *The default Visual Basic form in run mode.*

FYI

Visual Basic Modes

Visual Basic has three distinct modes, all of which you'll frequently use as you develop a program. As you use VB, you'll switch among the *design, run,* and *break* modes.

You'll use *design mode,* indicated by *[design]* on the VB title bar, to create the initial GUI of your program. In design mode, you decide what types of objects your program needs in order to communicate effectively with the end user, and you define event procedures to respond to user-generated events.

You'll use *run mode,* indicated by *[run]* on the VB title bar, to simulate how your final program will run. In run mode, you can only run your program as a user would. You can't make modifications to code or to objects in your program in run mode. You can enter run mode to see how your program runs at any time by pressing F5. You can return to design mode from run mode by clicking a program's *close* button, by clicking the *stop* button on the toolbar, or by selecting End from the Run menu.

You'll use *break mode,* indicated by *[break]* on the VB title bar, to debug your code while your program is running. In break mode, you can make many modifications to your code without stopping the program. However, there are some code modifications you can't make in break mode. For example, in break mode you can't modify or add to the objects you defined in design mode. If you try to make a change that isn't allowed in break mode, VB will prompt you to cancel the change or return to design mode. If you are in run mode, you can move to break mode by pressing Ctrl-Break. Here's a chart to help you get to each mode.

Method	Design	Break	Run
Keystroke		Ctrl-Break	F5
Toolbar	*Stop* button	*Pause* button	*Run* button
Menu	Run-End	Run-Break	Run-Start

The Event

In this section, we'll look at user-, Windows-, and program-generated events.

User-generated events

Windows users are familiar with GUI objects such as windows, status bars, menus, buttons, and scrollbars because they have had to do things to them. A user's doing something to an object is an *event.* For example, a user can *resize* a form or *click* a button. The resizing and the clicking are examples of user-generated *events.* The user is providing a trigger, an event that signals an object to perform some action.

User-generated events are the actions performed by the end user to communicate with your program. It is your responsibility as the programmer to prepare your objects to respond to user-generated events. You do this by providing your objects with code for the *event procedures* that respond to events initiated by the user.

Let's look at an example. A user comes into Windows and loads your program. The first thing the user does is click a button on your form. At that point, Visual Basic wakes up and says, "Hey, Program, a user just clicked a button! What do you want to do about that event?" You can create an event procedure to respond to this user action. It might look something like this:

```
Private Sub Button_Click()
    MsgBox "You clicked a button."
End Sub
```

This piece of code will display a message box each time a user clicks the button in your program. We'll look at how VB helps you write the code for this event procedure later. Just note here that the real key to creating a good Windows program lies in customizing your objects' procedures to respond effectively to user-generated events.

In order to respond to an event, an object must have an event procedure that will be called by VB whenever the corresponding event occurs. In this book, a procedure with an underscore (_) in its name is an event procedure, a procedure that is triggered by the firing (techno-talk for "causing to happen") of an event. The designation *<object>_<event>* refers to the event itself, while

FYI

Multiple Events

Sometimes a familiar event, such as clicking a button or double-clicking an item in a list box, can appear to the user to be a single event. But what appears to be a single event can actually be made up of multiple events, many of which are not evident to the user. For example, your program might interpret the user's simple mouse action as several events: dragging a box to another location on the screen as *MouseDown* event followed by multiple *MouseMove* events and then a *MouseUp* event, for instance.

<object>_<event>() refers to the corresponding event procedure in the program code. So *Form_Load* is an event, and *Form_Load()* is the event procedure that responds to the *Form_Load* event.

In such an "event-driven" environment, your program will catch whatever events the user may throw at it and will respond to them. By responding to user-generated events, your program communicates with the user.

Fortunately, a VB programmer doesn't have to provide an event procedure for every user event. The objects themselves provide a default response for each event. For example, a button object will appear to be pushed when it's clicked even if the programmer doesn't provide code for the event procedure for the click event.

You, the programmer, can determine which user events require customized responses from your program objects. An event that doesn't require a customized response from your program objects is handled for you by VB and doesn't require you to write code.

When we ran your first program, *Form1,* we saw a perfect example of an object's default responses to events. VB has provided your form object with the ability to display, resize, minimize, maximize, and close a window. Let's run *Form1* again.

1. Press F5 to switch to run mode.
2. Drag a border of the window to resize the window.
3. Close the *Form1* window.

Notice that you didn't have to write any code so that Windows would know what to do when you dragged the border to resize the window. In run mode, the user can resize, minimize, maximize, and close the form object. And you didn't have to write a single line of code!

Now, instead of letting VB do everything, let's try having our program respond to an event with a customized event procedure. We'll customize the form object's *Form_Load()* event procedure. This is where the fun starts.

1. To add code to an event procedure, be sure VB is in design mode and double-click anywhere in the client area of the form—that is, anywhere except in the sizing border or in the title bar.

   You'll see a code pane on the screen. See Figure 1-4. By default, the *Form_Load()* event procedure is displayed in the code pane. VB provides the *Private Sub Form_Load()* and *End Sub* lines that make up the beginning and the end of the *Form_Load()* event procedure. If you wanted something special to happen each time the form loaded itself, you would insert code into this procedure. For this exercise, however, we'll insert code into the *Form_Resize()* event procedure instead.

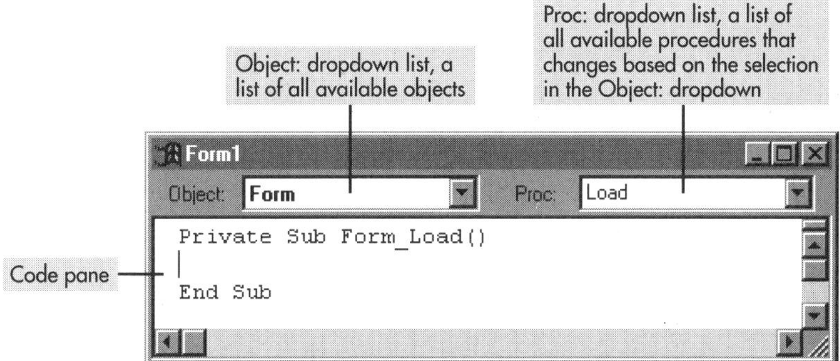

Figure 1-4. *The Visual Basic code pane. The event procedures in the Proc: dropdown list belong to the object in the Object: dropdown list. All available event procedures for that object are listed in the Proc: dropdown.*

2. Be sure Form is selected in the Object: dropdown. Select Resize from the Proc: dropdown. See Figure 1-5.

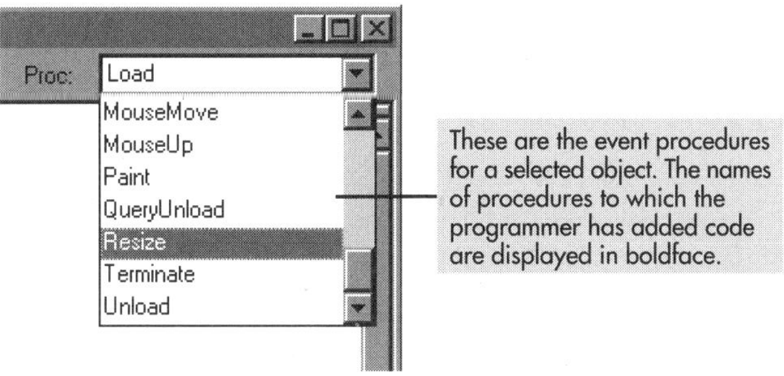

Figure 1-5. *The Proc: dropdown list for the form object.*

You'll see the following stubbed-out event procedures in your code pane:

```
Private Sub Form_Load
End Sub
Private Sub Form_Resize()
End Sub
```

NOTE Your code pane will show both procedures only if you have the Full Module View option turned on. You can find the check box for this option on the Editor tab of the Options dialog. (From the Tools menu, select Options.) Otherwise, you will see only one procedure at a time—the one you've selected from the Proc: dropdown.

3. Add code to the *Form_Resize()* event procedure to display the new height and width of the form whenever it is resized. (Note that VB shows keywords in a different color on the screen. You can set or change these colors on the Editor tab of the Options dialog.)

```
Private Sub Form_Resize()
    Cls
    Print Height, Width
End Sub
```

NOTE VB will remove any event procedure you leave empty (in this case, the *Form_Load()* event procedure) the next time you go from design mode to run mode. If you have the Full Module View option turned on, you'll see the empty procedures disappear from the code pane.

Because it contains code you provided, the name of the *Form_Resize()* event procedure will now appear in boldface when you view it in the Proc: dropdown.

Windows- or program-generated events

Now let's look at events that the user doesn't initiate.

1. Press F5 to go to run mode.

   Notice that even before a user can resize the window, the *Form_Resize()* event procedure has been called and has printed the height and width of the form in the upper left corner of the form, just below the caption bar. This introduces an important concept, namely that events can be fired not only by the user, but also by Windows or by a program. In this case, Visual Basic has provided default code in your program to fire the *Form_Resize* event each time the program starts, and you, the programmer, have added code to the *Form_Resize()* event procedure to print the height and width of the form. The user can also fire the *Form_Resize* event by dragging a border of the window or clicking the *maximize* or *minimize* button, which will cause the *Form_Resize()* event procedure to be called again.

2. You can simulate a resize event by having another event procedure call the *Form_Resize()* procedure directly. For example, if you want your program to execute the code in the *Form_Resize()* event procedure before the form is visible, you can have the *Form_Load()* event procedure call *Form_Resize()*:

```
Private Sub Form_Load()
    Form_Resize
End Sub
```

NOTE The code we added to the *Form_Load()* event procedure above doesn't actually make the window look any different when we run the program since all it does is execute the code in *Form_Resize()* that is already being executed, in effect making *Form_Resize()* execute twice before the window is displayed. This is just an example to show that one event procedure can call another.

Form events

A form object has many event procedures associated with it. There is the *Form_Load()* event procedure, which, as we saw above, responds to the *Form_Load* event that is fired when the form object first loads; a *Form_Unload()* event procedure, of course; and many event procedures in between. There is even a *Form_QueryUnload* event, which responds to the event that is fired before the *Form_Unload* event in order to give the programmer the opportunity to provide code that will run each time a user tries to unload a form. The programmer might put code into the *Form_QueryUnload()* event procedure to warn the user to save data before closing the program or to allow the user to cancel the *Form_Unload()* operation.

It is beyond the scope of this book to fully examine every possible event and responding event procedure provided by VB, but we strongly encourage you to explore more objects and their event procedures in the VB help file as well as to create small sample programs in order to understand what user action causes each event procedure to be called.

The Property

Let's pursue our grammar analogy a bit longer. The part of speech that describes a noun, or an object, is an adjective, or a *property*. A property is any setting that defines the appearance and status, and sometimes even modifies the behavior, of an object. For example, the form object we have been looking at has a Caption property that is set to *Form1*. (See the top of the window in Figure 1-3 back on page 9.) Other form properties include Height and Width.

As you'll see in later chapters, you can give these properties initial values at design-time and have your program set the values dynamically at run-time.

When an object is created, it receives a set of default values for each of its properties. For example, a form object has—by default—values for a sizeable border, a control box, a *maximize* button, a *minimize* button, and a title bar. The values of the form object's ForeColor and BackColor properties are determined by the system settings. To allow the programmer to change the values of the object's properties to nondefault settings, VB provides a *property sheet* that can be used for any object. Using the property sheet, you can set most of the object's property values at design-time. It is also possible to change most object property values at run-time. We'll look at setting properties at run-time in Chapter 2.

Using the property sheet

The easiest way to get to know your way around the property sheet is to step through setting different types of property values. After you have set each of these values in design mode, you can rerun the program to view the effects of the changes to the property settings you've made.

1. Click on the form.
2. Press F4 (or select View-Properties) to bring up the form object's property sheet. See Figure 1-6.
3. Scroll up and down the rows in the property sheet to view the properties of the form object.
4. To get help on a property, select the row and press F1.

Let's go through the steps for changing a text or a numeric property value:

1. Click on the Caption property.
2. Type *A Better Caption*
3. Press Enter to commit the change.

Now let's change an enumerated property value:

1. Select the MousePointer property.
2. Click the down arrow at the right edge of the MousePointer row to open the dropdown list of possible MousePointer values.
3. Select *2 - Cross* from the list.

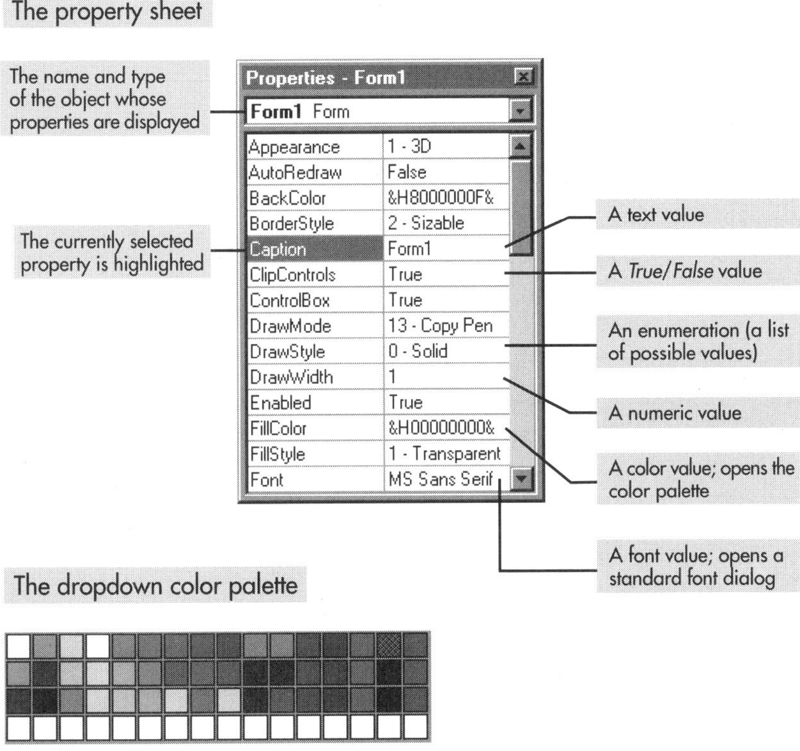

Figure 1-6. *The property sheet and the dropdown color palette.*

Let's change a *True/False* property value:

1. Select the MaxButton property.
2. Click the down arrow to open the dropdown, and choose *False* from the list.

Let's change a Color property value:

1. Select the ForeColor property.
2. Click the down arrow to open the color palette.
3. Click the square in the color palette that contains your favorite color.

Now we'll change a Font property value:

1. Select the Font property.

2. Click the ellipsis (. . .) button at the right edge of the Font row to open the Font dialog. See Figure 1-7.

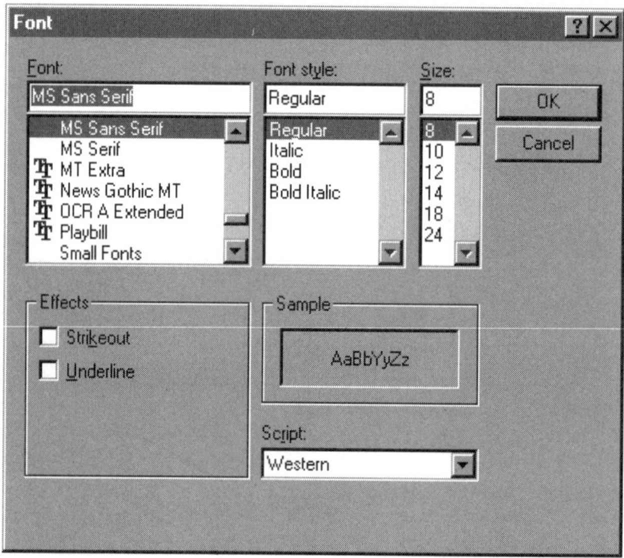

Figure 1-7. *The Font dialog box.*

3. Change the font style to *Bold* and the size to *14.*
4. Press Enter or click OK to close the dialog and commit the change.

Finally let's change one of the picture type properties (Icon, Picture, DragIcon, MouseIcon):

1. Choose the Icon property.
2. Click the ellipsis (. . .) button to get a standard File-Open dialog.
3. Choose an icon from the Microsoft Visual Basic\Icons directory structure. (If you haven't installed the icon library, you can skip this step.)
4. Press Enter or click Open to activate the icon, close the dialog, and commit the change.

NOTE To remove a picture property value, select the text in the right column of the property sheet—*Icon,* for example—and then press Delete.

Now let's see what we've done. Press F5 to run the form.

If you've set all of the properties as indicated, you'll notice that some properties on the form have changed. The caption has changed to *A better caption*, the mouse pointer is a cross instead of an arrow, the *maximize* button is no longer available, and the height and width properties printed by *Form_Resize()* are now in a larger font size, in boldface, and in your favorite color. The icon of the form has changed as well, which you can see in the upper left corner of the window, or by minimizing the form.

NOTE Double-clicking in the property sheet provides a shortcut for many operations. A double-click does the following to various property types: an enumeration value is incremented to the next item in the list, *True/False* values are toggled, a font or file dialog opens for font and picture properties, and the color palette drops down for color properties.

Taking Control

Visual Basic has given the object-oriented catchword "reusability" new meaning. If you've programmed before, you've undoubtedly created an input box, drawn a shape, or created the functionality for finding a file on disk. VB wraps many common functions like these, along with their graphical representations, in objects called *controls*.

A *control* is a special object that, like a form object, has a visual representation, has properties that can be set at design-time or run-time, and has a set of events that can be fired. VB provides a rich set of *standard controls* that are available to all VB programs. Microsoft and other vendors also provide *custom controls* for programs whose requirements are more complex than these standard controls can meet. Custom controls can be used in programming environments besides Visual Basic, including Microsoft Visual C++, Microsoft Access, and Microsoft Visual FoxPro.

The programmer can affect a control object's visual representation by setting its properties at design-time with the property sheet or at run-time with code. Control properties such as Height, Width, Left, and Top can be used to size and move the control at both design-time and run-time. Other properties, such as Name and Index, are used to refer to a control in code and cannot be set or changed at run-time. Just as you can with a form object, you can add code to event procedures corresponding to the events to which you want the control object to respond.

The Visual Basic Toolbox

In Figure 1-8, you see the VB *toolbox,* a special window containing graphical representations of the controls available for use in your VB programs. The VB toolbox always contains the standard VB controls listed below. It can also contain custom controls and insertable objects, which we'll look into later. Any control or insertable object represented in the toolbox can be dragged and dropped onto a VB form to create a new object.

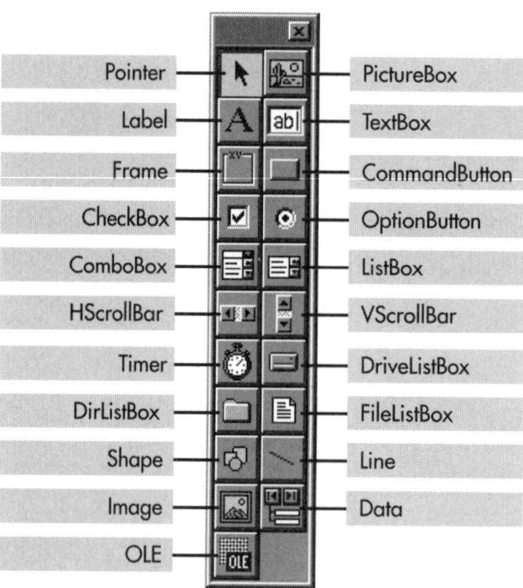

Figure 1-8. *The Visual Basic toolbox contains controls that can be placed on forms at design-time.*

Here's a short description of each of the standard toolbox controls that come with Visual Basic.

Control	Description
Pointer	Technically, is not a control. Provides a way to move and resize forms and controls.
PictureBox	Displays pictures, icons, and metafiles. Used as a container to group other controls. Also used to display formatted text and to render graphics.
Label	Used to place text that can't be edited by the user.
TextBox	Allows the user to enter and display text data.
Frame	Used as a container to group other controls.
CommandButton	Clicked to execute code.
CheckBox	Indicates the setting of an option.

Control	Description
OptionButton	Provides the user a choice of mutually exclusive options.
ComboBox	Acts as both a TextBox and a ListBox.
ListBox	Displays lists of data items.
HScrollBar	Scrolls horizontally.
VScrollBar	Scrolls vertically.
Timer	No graphical representation at run-time. Provides a *Timer* event to allow your code to perform a task at preset intervals.
DriveListBox	Displays a list of available local and network drives.
DirListBox	Displays a list of the subdirectory structure of a given drive and directory.
FileListBox	Displays a list of files in a given directory.
Shape	Displays simple geometric objects.
Line	Displays a line on the form.
Image	Used to display and stretch pictures, icons, and metafiles. More efficient than a PictureBox, but does not have drawing methods such as *Circle* and *Line*.
Data	Binds directly to a database.
OLE	Allows the programmer to display, manipulate, and activate OLE objects.

Adding Custom Controls to the Toolbox

You can make custom controls available for use in your program by adding them to the VB toolbox. To add a control to the toolbox, select Custom Controls from the Tools menu to display the Custom Controls dialog. (See Figure 1-9 on the next page.) Controls that are already in the toolbox will be checked. Check any controls you want to add to the toolbox, and uncheck any you want to remove. If you know you have a control on your hard drive that doesn't appear in the list of available controls, use the Browse button to find the control.

NOTE If a control doesn't run correctly, it may be registered incorrectly. To remedy this problem, use the Browse button in the Custom Controls dialog to locate the .OCX file that contains the control. When you click the Open button in the Add Custom Control dialog, the .OCX file will be re-registered.

You can also just double-click on the .OCX file from either File Manager or the Windows 95 Explorer to register the control.

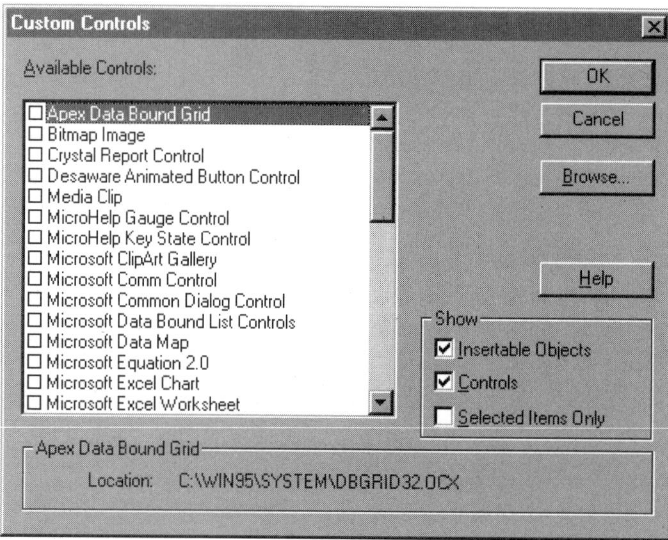

Figure 1-9. *The Custom Controls dialog box shows a list of the custom controls and insertable objects currently installed on your system that are available for use by your program. You can filter the items shown in the Available Controls: list using the Show part of the dialog.*

The Custom Controls dialog displays two types of objects: custom controls and insertable objects. Once it is added to the toolbar, a custom control acts just as a standard control does.

Insertable objects

Unlike other controls, an insertable object doesn't have object-specific events associated with it, so event procedures can be written only for the limited number of events that are provided by VB for these objects: *DragDrop*, *DragOver*, *GotFocus*, and *LostFocus*. Similarly, insertable objects have no custom properties.

A Microsoft Excel worksheet is a good example of an insertable object. It can be placed on a form, displayed, and activated by VB at run-time, but activating a cell on the worksheet does not generate a VB event. When using an insertable object in your program, you simply turn control of the object over to the object server that implemented it. We'll deal more with insertable objects during the discussion of in-place activation in Chapter 7.

The custom controls and insertable objects that will be visible in the toolbox may be different for each project and are saved in the project file. If a project doesn't use a custom object, you can remove it from the toolbox.

Each control object has its own unique set of events and properties that make it easy to customize the control's behavior. For example, the Visual Basic Text-Box control fires a *Change* event to tell the program that the user has changed the text. The TextBox control also provides all of the functionality the user needs to enter, select, scroll, cut, copy, and paste text. Other controls will have different sets of functionality.

Using Controls

To add a TextBox (or another) control to your form:

1. Select View-Toolbox.
2. Click the TextBox (or other) control button. See Figure 1-10.

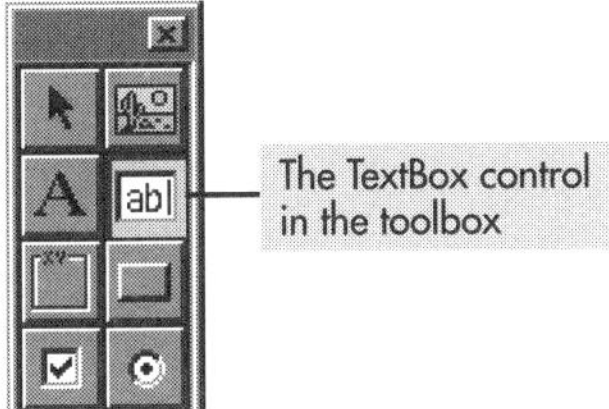
The TextBox control in the toolbox

Figure 1-10. *The TextBox control as it appears in the VB toolbox.*

3. Click in the form, hold down the mouse button while you drag the control to the size you want it to be, and then let go of the button. Your form should look something like the one shown in Figure 1-11.

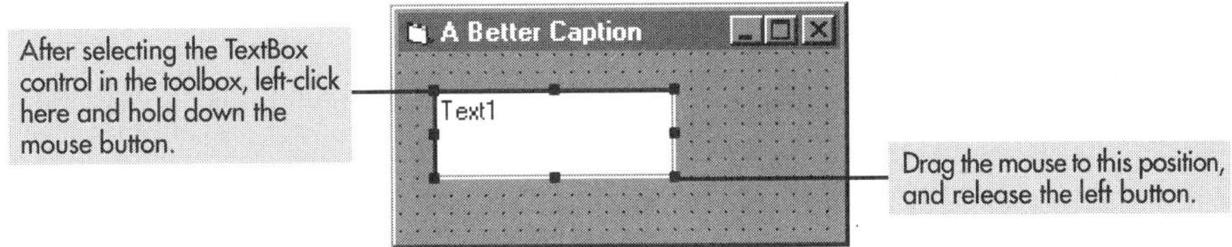
After selecting the TextBox control in the toolbox, left-click here and hold down the mouse button.
A Better Caption
Text1
Drag the mouse to this position, and release the left button.

Figure 1-11. *A new textbox on a form.*

NOTE Double-clicking a control in the toolbox will place the control in the middle of the form with a default size.

4. Press F5 to run the program.
5. Type in the textbox, replacing *Text1* with your name.

The functionality required to process and display keystrokes such as letters, numbers, delete, and backspace, as well as to interpret mouse input, is inherent in the TextBox control. As a Visual Basic programmer, you don't need to concern yourself with the internal TextBox implementation. VB provides all of the default behavior required from a TextBox control and requires no additional effort from the programmer. Just use the control—and be thankful for the work you didn't have to do.

SUMMARY

- The basic components of a Windows program created in Visual Basic are objects, events and event procedures, and properties. We used analogies with various parts of speech to understand the functionality of the different VB components for Windows programs.
- In the GUI language, objects are similar to nouns.
- Windows-, program-, and user-generated events and their corresponding default and customized event procedures are the verbs.
- Properties are like the adjectives that describe nouns.
- The VB toolbox contains controls you can use in your VB program.
- You can add a control to a form by dragging and dropping it.

In Chapter 2, we'll make use of the knowledge from this chapter floating around in our heads as we start creating a real program.

2

QuickEdit, Your First Visual Basic Program

OK. On to our first Visual Basic program. The *QuickEdit* program will be a weak replica of the NotePad text editor that comes standard with Windows. When we've completed our new program, a user will be able to open, edit, and save simple text files. If you feel confident in your abilities as a Visual Basic programmer, you might skip over this chapter. Or you could just skip to the code listing at the end of Chapter 3 to make sure you understand what's going on.

Creating Useful Programs

Writing programs is easy. Writing good programs takes effort. Take care to make your programs functional, efficient, and easy to use while at the same time giving them a standard Windows look and feel.

Functionality

Every program is created to perform a specific task or a set of tasks. A user should be able to do everything necessary to perform the task or tasks from within your program. If your program fails to perform the tasks for which the user bought it, it will be doomed to the recycle bin. You've probably used applications yourself that didn't live up to your expectations. You've probably thought to yourself on occasion, "Whoever wrote this program sure doesn't understand what I really want to be able to do . . . "

Don't let people say that about you and your programs! Think about what tasks your users need to perform, and provide all of the means necessary to complete those tasks.

Efficiency

Speed is of the essence! Visual Basic gets a bum rap sometimes: people say that VB programs are slow. While a C++ program is naturally going to be faster than a VB program, a lot of very inefficient VB code has been written and accounts for most of VB's bad publicity. As with any programming language, good implementation can dramatically improve performance. There are certainly programmers who use VB and don't take full advantage of the language features available to enhance program speed. On the other hand, a handful of programmers at Microsoft make a living just looking at other people's VB code and making it more efficient. It can be done!

Usability

Your program can have all of the functionality and efficiency a user might ever need, but if the user can't figure out how to use a feature, you have failed as a GUI programmer. Ultimately, your program, not your documentation, is responsible for making tasks easy to accomplish. Standard interface features have a lot to do with that. The look and feel of the user interface should make the user feel at home. Keep that in mind as you write your programs. If you can't make a particular feature easy to use, omit the feature.

Aesthetics

Finally your programs should be visually attractive. Users want a program that is aesthetically pleasing. That doesn't mean you should go overboard on graphical effects and visible objects, however. Too much clutter can interfere with usability and handicap the user with a long, flat learning curve and excessive eye strain.

NOTE For more information on creating solid programs, see Christine Solomon's book, *Developing Applications with Microsoft Office,* 2d Ed. (Microsoft Press, 1996).

QuickEdit Design Considerations

Before we start programming *QuickEdit,* let's clearly define what we need to accomplish. We'll apply the general program guidelines we just defined to the specific *QuickEdit* application.

QuickEdit Functionality

In order to design *QuickEdit,* we must first figure out the functionality we want it to have. *QuickEdit* needs to perform the set of simple tasks mentioned at the very beginning of this chapter. It needs to allow a user to open, edit, and save simple text files. Given our modest goal, it seems safe to say that *QuickEdit* doesn't need to be able to open arbitrarily large files or files that include text formatting. As you become more experienced, figuring out which features you want at the beginning of a programming project will help you gauge approximately how much time you should spend coding and what features you should include (or leave out).

QuickEdit Efficiency

Your goal as a programmer should be to keep noticeable delays in the performance of your program to a minimum. Start by optimizing the operations the user will perform most frequently. In the *QuickEdit* case, File-Open, typing in text, editing text, and File-Save will probably be the most common operations and should thus be optimized for speed.

QuickEdit Usability

QuickEdit needs to be friendly. If the user tries to open a nonexistent file, the program should let the user know, in a friendly way, that the file doesn't exist. If the user tries to open a second file or to exit the program without saving the current file, *QuickEdit* should display a warning and offer an opportunity to save the current file. *QuickEdit* should have the look and feel of a standard Windows text editor. The menu should contain the standard commands. The name of the current file should be clearly displayed on the title bar. When the window is resized, the visible text should be resized accordingly.

QuickEdit Aesthetics

As *QuickEdit* is not required to perform any task beyond opening, editing, and saving a simple text file, any user interface that went beyond these simple requirements would be overkill.

QuickEdit Object Creation

Before we add code to the *QuickEdit* project, let's create all of the objects necessary for the GUI part of our program. We need a *form* object to act as the main window for our program, a *textbox* object for displaying and editing a file, and a *file menu* object to control opening, saving, and closing the file. We should also give our new program a name and save the files we created to build the program.

The Project File

For our purposes, the project file isn't an object, but it is an integral part of any Visual Basic program, and it comes first. The *project file* maintains a list of all the files VB needs in order to define and manipulate the objects in our VB program. Let's create the *QuickEdit* project file by opening a new project, giving the project a name, and saving the project file and the default form file.

1. From the File menu, select New Project to create a new project. When a new project is created, you always start with a default form object called *Form1*.
2. Select Tools-Options and activate the Project tab of the Options dialog. (See Figure 2-1.)

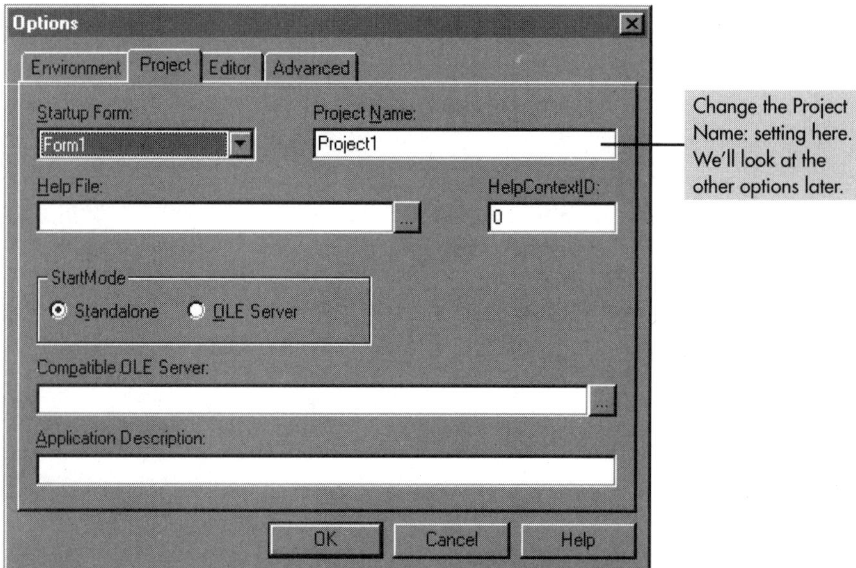

Figure 2-1. *The Project tab of the Options dialog box.*

3. Change the Project Name: setting to *QuickEdit*.
4. Click OK to close the Options dialog.

NOTE If you want to be prompted to save all files in your project when you switch from design mode to run mode, modify the File Save option on the Environment tab of the Options dialog. Don't Save Before Run is the default setting. If you select Save Before Run, Prompt, VB will ask you whether it should save files before you enter run mode. If you select Save Before Run, Don't Prompt, VB will save your files automatically when you enter run mode.

5. From the File menu, select Save Project to save the project.
6. A Save File As dialog will prompt you to save *Form1*. We don't want to save the default form yet, so cancel this dialog.
7. You'll see a dialog like the one shown in Figure 2-2.

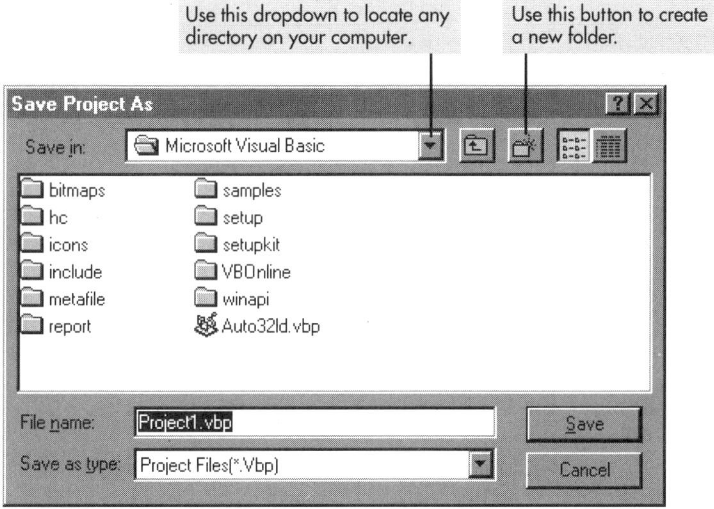

Figure 2-2. *The Save Project As dialog box.*

8. Use the Save in: dropdown to locate a directory in which to create a new folder.
9. Click the Create New Folder button. Replace the words *New Folder* with the name *QuickEdit.*
10. Double-click on the new QuickEdit folder to make it current.
11. Type the word *QuickEdit* in the File name: textbox.
12. Click the Save button. VB will automatically add the extension *.Vbp*, for Visual Basic Project, to our project name.

NOTE The project name QuickEdit.Vbp contains 12 characters. Windows 95 and Windows NT both support long file names, which makes keeping track of files much easier. You could name your project *My favorite VB Project that I love to play with* if you wanted to.

A reminder

It happens every day. Somewhere, in the middle of the day, someone screams. Everybody in the entire hallway rushes down to his office to find out what's wrong. Somebody calls 911. The screamer has lost several hours' worth of work because his program made his computer lock up. Here's a word of advice: Be wise. Save early, and save often.

The Form Object

In Chapter 1, we dealt extensively with the form object. In this section, we'll extend a form object to create the *QuickEdit* program. When we created our new *QuickEdit* project, we received a default form object. Let's modify the form object and save it in a file.

1. If the form isn't visible, you need to activate it. If the Project window isn't visible, select View-Project. Select Form1 in the Project window.
2. Click the View Form button on the Project window to activate the form.
3. Position and size the form exactly as you want users to see it when they run the program.
4. Press F4 to activate the form object's property sheet. (See Figure 2-3.)

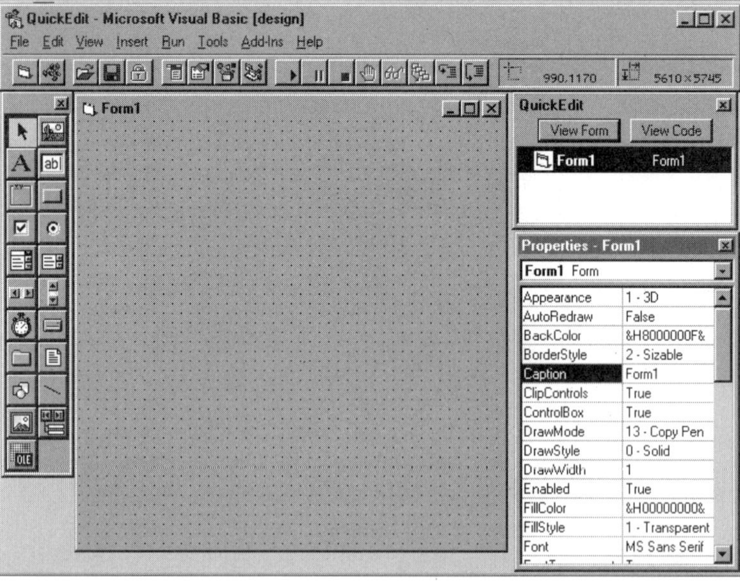

Figure 2-3. *The* QuickEdit *project with the form object's property sheet activated.*

5. Change the form object's Caption property to *QuickEdit*.
6. Change the form object's Name property to *frmQuickEdit*. This will change the name of the form object in the right column of the Project window.
7. From the File menu, select Save File.
8. Type *QuickEdit* as the name of the file, and press Enter. VB will create a QuickEdit.Frm file on disk. The left column of the Project window will be updated to indicate the new file name.

The TextBox Object

So far, our form isn't very interesting. It comes up and displays a custom caption. Whew! Heavy stuff.

In the next few sections, we'll accelerate the pace a little and make the form much more compelling. One of the ways we'll do that is by adding controls to the form.

1. From the toolbox, select TextBox.
2. Position the mouse pointer on the form and, holding down the left mouse button, drag the mouse pointer to size the textbox. When you release the left mouse button, the form should look like the one shown in Figure 2-4.

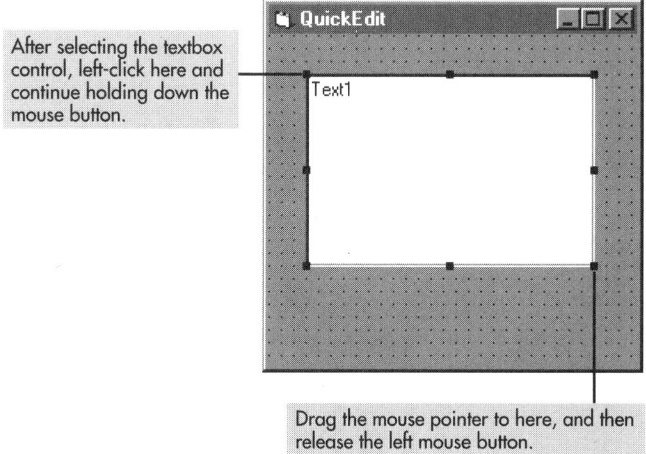
QuickEdit
After selecting the textbox control, left-click here and continue holding down the mouse button.
Text1
Drag the mouse pointer to here, and then release the left mouse button.

Figure 2-4. *The* QuickEdit *form with a textbox control on it.*

3. Press F4 to bring up the textbox object's property sheet.
4. Change the textbox object's Name property to *txtFile*.

NOTE The lowercase three-letter prefix *txt*, in *txtFile*, follows a standard naming convention referred to as *Hungarian* notation in programming circles. Although it may take some time to get used to, this naming style improves code readability if not pronounceability. By using Hungarian notation, a programmer can communicate the scope and type of a variable in its prefix.

VB Hungarian conventions are shown in Appendix D. The idea is that a programmer prefix a variable name with one-letter to three-letter abbreviations to indicate the type and/or the scope of the variable. For example, a form object name starts with *frm*, and a textbox object name with *txt*. Objects in our *QuickEdit* program will be called *frmQuickEdit, txtFile, mnuFile, mnuFileNew*, and so on.

Now let's make some further adjustments to our textbox object.

1. Delete the contents of the Text property so that the textbox comes up blank.
2. Change the Multiline property to *True*. This will enable the textbox to contain multiple lines.
3. Change the ScrollBars property to *3 - Both*. Notice that there are now both vertical and horizontal scrollbars in the textbox.
4. When the user enters changes in the textbox, we'll handle them with code we'll insert into the *txtFile_Change()* event procedure. To view the empty *txtFile_Change()* event procedure in the code pane, double-click on the textbox. The procedure is empty now, but we'll fill it in soon.

The Menu Object

You may notice that all of the applications coming out of Microsoft, and many other applications for Windows, feature similar menu bars. For example, File, Edit, View, and Insert are the first four menu items in all of the Microsoft Office for Windows 95 products. This consistency makes it easier for a user to learn new programs by reducing the need to menu-surf to find menu items. If the user knows where to find an item in one application, he or she will know where to find the item in another application. In the next two sections, we'll create menus and talk about how to associate event procedures with our menu items.

QuickEdit menu

For simplicity's sake, our *QuickEdit* application will have only a File menu with several items to allow the user to manipulate a text file: New, Open, Save, Save As, and Exit. VB provides a dialog to help us create menu objects. Let's create the File menu and its menu items.

1. Select the *QuickEdit* form by clicking on the form's title bar.
2. From the Tools menu, select Menu Editor.
3. In the Caption: field, type in *&File.* The & character designates the *F* as the accelerator key for the menu. So File will appear on the menu bar, and Alt-F will open the File menu. (To put an actual & character in a menu name, use *&&*.)
4. In the Name: field, type in *mnuFile.*
5. Click the Next button, and then click on the *right arrow* button to indent the next menu item. The next menu name you type in will appear as a menu item in the File menu.
6. In the Caption: field, type in *&New.*
7. In the Name: field, type in *mnuFileNew.*
8. Here's a table to help you finish the entries for the File menu.

Caption	Name	Indented
&File	mnuFile	No
&New	mnuFileNew	Yes
&Open . . .	mnuFileOpen	Yes
&Save	mnuFileSave	Yes
Save &As . . .	mnuFileSaveAs	Yes
–	mnuFileSep1	Yes
E&xit	mnuFileExit	Yes

NOTE You put *File* in all of the menu names to identify the captions as parts of the File menu. This precaution prevents name duplications (especially for separators). More important, this naming discipline will result in a grouping of all of the File menu objects in the Object: dropdown list.

When you've finished, the dialog box should look like the one shown in Figure 2-5 on the next page.

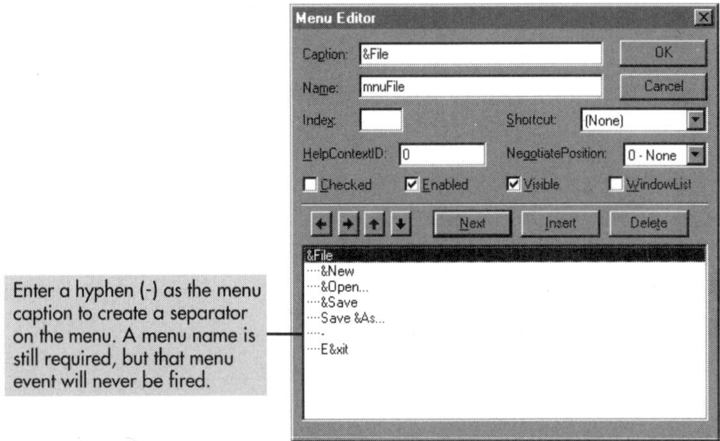

Figure 2-5. *The Menu Editor dialog box lets us define the menus that will show up in the* QuickEdit *program. The letter preceded by an ampersand (&) will become the shortcut key for that particular menu item.*

Event procedures for menu items

If you ran our program now, you could see and open the File menu. The menu items are useless right now, however, because we haven't provided event procedures to respond to menu click events.

A menu object has one event associated with it: the *Click* event. (Have you ever tried to double-click a menu item?) To view the *mnuFileExit_Click()* event procedure, just select the File-Exit menu item on the form in design mode. You can also select mnuFileExit in the Object: dropdown in the code pane. The empty event procedure for File-Exit should look like this:

```
Private Sub mnuFileExit_Click()
End Sub
```

In Chapter 3, we'll actually add code to the event procedures.

Creating an Executable

Let's take a step back for a minute. The ultimate goal of creating a Visual Basic program is to be able to run the program without the VB design environment. In other words, we want to create an executable file, or .EXE. Let's make and run an executable for the *QuickEdit* project. The running .EXE should look exactly the same as the *QuickEdit* project did in run mode, but it will not be tied in any way to the VB design environment. Let's make an .EXE now.

1. First, let's save the form. From the File menu, select Save File.
2. Now from the File menu select Make EXE File. You'll see a dialog like the one shown in Figure 2-6.

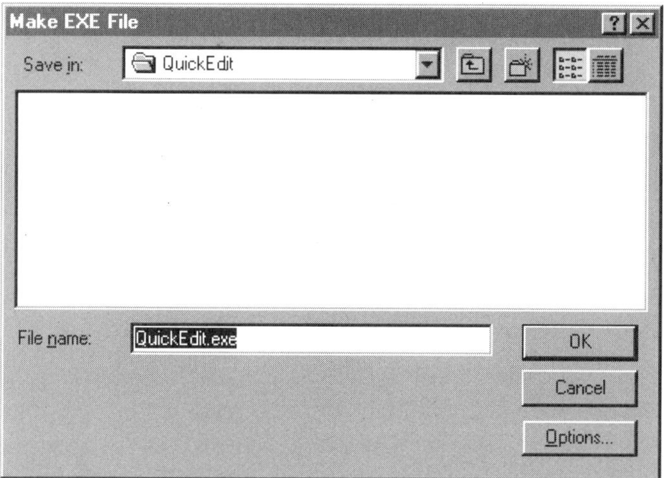

Figure 2-6. *The Make EXE File dialog box.*

3. Click OK.

You now have an executable QuickEdit.Exe that can be run from an icon on your desktop or from Windows 95 Explorer. Let's test the waters.

1. Bring up the Windows 95 Explorer (or File Manager), find the QuickEdit Application entry (QuickEdit.Exe), and double-click on the name to launch *QuickEdit.* (See Figure 2-7 on the next page.)

NOTE If you are running Windows 95 Explorer, you can set an option that lets you see the file extensions in the file names. Select View-Options. In the Options dialog that comes up, select the View tab and deselect Hide MS-DOS file extensions for file types that are registered.

2. Type something into the textbox. The program should work exactly as it did in run mode.
3. Click the *close* button to end the program.

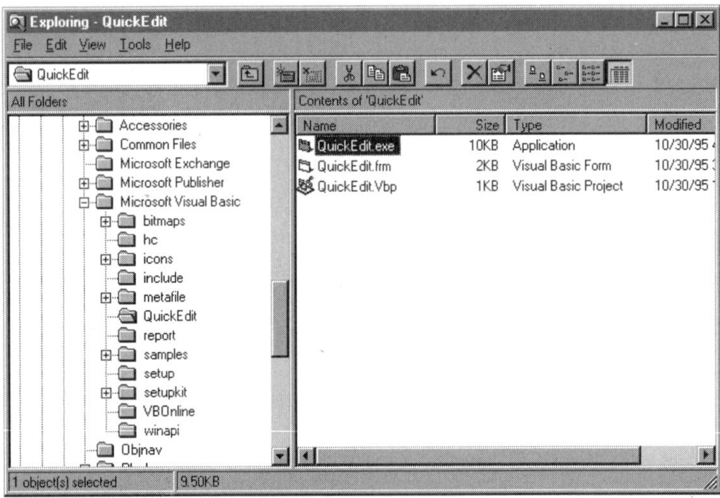

Figure 2-7. *Launching* QuickEdit *from the Windows 95 Explorer.*

Setting Properties at Run-Time

Although you can generate a rather complex form just by setting properties via the property sheet at design-time, most programs also have to set properties at run-time in response to events. For example, the caption of the *QuickEdit* window should change when the name of the currently open file changes. You can set properties at run-time by writing code. In Chapter 3, we'll look at where you write the code, but for now just get a feel for the syntax.

You change a property at run-time by means of the *object.property* syntax. You specify an object property in code by listing the object first, followed by a dot (.), followed by the property that will change. If you are setting the property, you put an equal sign (=) after the name of the property, followed by the new property value. (See the example shown in Figure 2-8.)

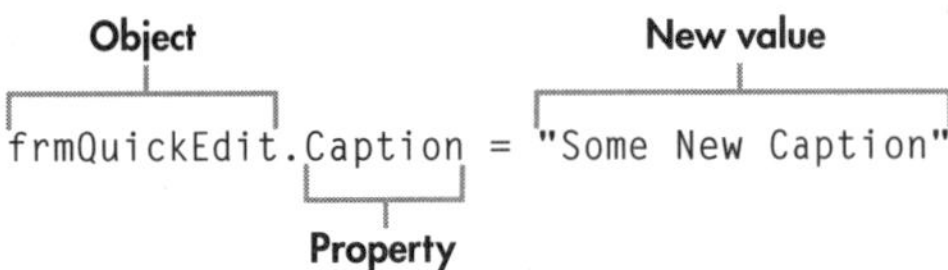

Figure 2-8. *The* object.property *syntax for changing a property of an object at run-time.*

For example, if you wanted to set the caption of the form to QuickEdit - New File any time the user selected File-New, you could put the following code into the click event procedure of the mnuFileNew menu object:

```
Private Sub mnuFileNew_Click()
    frmQuickEdit.Caption = "QuickEdit - New File"
End Sub
```

If you want to read the value of the property, you put the *object.property* element to the right of the equal sign. (See the example shown in Figure 2-9.)

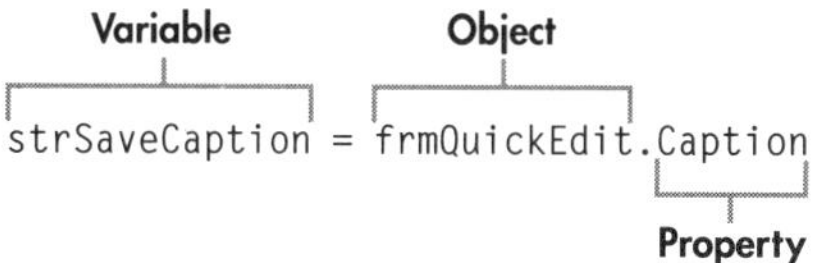

Figure 2-9. *The syntax for reading the value of an object property.*

In Chapter 1, we looked at several different types of properties—text, True/False (Boolean), enumerated, and so on—and at how to change their values at design-time by means of the property sheet. Now let's look at how to change the values of properties belonging to each of these property types at run-time by means of the *object.property* syntax. Remember that in the following chapters we'll consider where we actually put this code. For now, we'll concentrate on familiarizing ourselves with the syntax.

Numeric and Text Properties

Numeric and text properties are the easiest to change. The only difference between changing numeric properties and changing text properties is that string literals (as opposed to string variables) require quotation marks (") whereas numeric values do not. Both numeric and text properties can be represented by variables, as shown in the examples below.

```
frm.Caption = "A Better Caption"

frm.Caption = txtNewCaption.Text

frm.DrawWidth = 3

frm.DrawWidth = intNewNumber
```

Enumerated Properties

VB also makes it very easy to change enumerated properties at run-time because the enumerated values are built-into VB. For example, setting the MousePointer property to *2 - Cross* at design-time is equivalent to setting it to *vbCross* at run-time, as shown in the example below.

```
frm.MousePointer = vbCross
```

Boolean Properties

Setting a True/False (Boolean) property at run-time is very easy. Just set MaxButton, for instance, to *False*.

```
frm.MaxButton = False
```

That wasn't very nice of us. This code won't even compile because MaxButton can be set only at design-time. This was just a demonstration that not all properties can be set at run-time.

Here's code for setting a Boolean property at run-time that actually works.

```
frm.Visible = False
```

Color Properties

Several function procedures in VB help you set color properties at run-time.

- The *RGB()* function lets you set the color with the values *0* through *255* for red, green, and blue. VB will combine the colors for you.

  ```
  frm.ForeColor = RGB(255, 0, 0)     'Bright Red
  ```

- The *QBColor()* function lets you choose from 16 predefined colors.

  ```
  frm.BackColor = QBColor(7)     'Light Gray
  ```

- The system color constants provided by VB let you match a system color.

  ```
  frm.ForeColor = vbWindowBackground     'Stay in sync with Control
                                         'Panel settings.
  ```

NOTE To see a list of available color constants, search VB online Help for "color constants."

Font Properties

In order to set a font's properties at run-time, you need to access the individual properties of the font object. These properties include Name, Bold, Italic, Size, StrikeThrough, Underline, and Weight. Here's an example of setting the font's size and setting it to appear in boldface.

```
frm.Font.Size = 14
frm.Font.Bold = True
```

Picture Properties

The last type of VB property is the picture property. Several different properties can actually fall into this class of property, including Picture, Icon, DragIcon, and MouseIcon. From the property sheet, these properties are set by clicking an ellipses (. . .) to open a Load Icon or Load Picture dialog.

At run-time, a picture property can be set by specifying a file with the *Load-Picture* function, as in the example of setting an Icon property shown below.

```
frm.Icon = LoadPicture("C:\Microsoft Visual Basic\Icons\Misc\Bridge.Ico")
```

To clear a picture property, use *LoadPicture* with no arguments.

```
frm.Icon = LoadPicture     'Clear the icon.
```

NOTE A picture property can also be set at run-time by means of the *LoadResPicture* function. To use this function, you need to generate a resource file and add it to your project. More on this in Chapter 11.

SUMMARY

- A programmer should consider functionality, efficiency, usability (especially the standard look and feel), and aesthetics as he or she designs a program. The programmer should make the program attractive but not clutter the interface with unnecessary objects and graphics.
- Work on a new VB project starts in design mode with the creation of a project file by means of the Project tab of the Options dialog.
- A VB program is further developed by modifications to the default form object every new project receives. At design time, a VB programmer gives the form an individual identity (caption, name, file name, controls, menus, and so on) by means of the form's object property sheet.
- It's a good idea to use Hungarian notation to communicate the type and scope of a variable in a prefix to its name. See Appendix D for more information on the Hungarian conventions.
- The VB programmer makes run-time changes to the form's properties by means of the *object.property* syntax. To set a property, the programmer puts the *object.-property* element on the left side of the equal sign. To read a property, the programmer puts the *object.property* element on the right side of the equal sign.

In this chapter we've learned about architecting the objects in a program, and we've created a VB project, adding controls and menus to a form object. We also learned how to set properties at run-time. Now we have all of the tools we need to start adding code to the *QuickEdit* program to actually make it do something.

We're going to end the chapter here to give our brains a rest. All of the code for *QuickEdit* will be introduced in Chapter 3. Save your work, and review to make sure you understand all of the concepts so far. If you're ready to keep going, forge ahead with Chapter 3.

3

Let's Write Some Code

In this chapter, we'll finally write and debug some real Visual Basic code. In Chapter 2, we set up the form, control, and menu objects necessary to build the *QuickEdit* program. Now we'll look at a few other Visual Basic for Applications programming elements and then add the event procedures and support routines necessary to make our program work. Let's take a systematic approach to building our program. We'll break the work down into the following steps:

1. Get up to speed on additional elements of the VBA programming language.
2. Create support routines and variables to help event procedures respond correctly.
3. Establish basic form functionality. This includes correct loading and unloading of the form as well as positioning and sizing controls.
4. Hook up the events to the support routines we've written by generating event procedures for the objects we created in Chapter 2.
5. Debug and use the program. In the "Debugging" section of this chapter, we'll learn some basic debugging techniques. We'll walk through the code we've written in the earlier sections of the chapter.

Procedures

Before we proceed, let's define a few terms. A *procedure* is a unit of code instructions that are interpreted by Visual Basic. A procedure is delimited at its beginning by **Sub**, **Function**, or **Property**, and at its end by (surprise!) **End Sub**, **End Function**, or **End Property**. (We'll look at property procedures in Chapter 4.)

A procedure performs a specific task. If you write several small procedures as sub-tasks to break down the larger task, your code will be more readable and easier to debug.

For an introduction to procedures, let's look at a familiar example. The task at hand is to get into your house. Several steps, expressed here in code, are required to accomplish this task:

```
Sub GoInHouse()
    FindDoor
    TurnHandle
    OpenDoor
    WalkIn
End Sub
```

Subs and Functions

A *subroutine* (we'll use *sub* for short) is a procedure that doesn't return a value. A *function* procedure is just like a sub procedure except that it returns a value. The value generally indicates the status—such as the success or failure—of the function procedure. Most of the tasks in our *GoInHouse* subroutine are guaranteed to succeed. For example, it's unlikely that you'll be unable to find the front door. Hence, *FindDoor* is a sub, not a function. However, if the door is locked, *TurnHandle* will fail, so we should make *TurnHandle* a function and return *True* if it succeeds and *False* if it fails.

```
Sub GoInHouse()
    FindDoor
    If Not TurnHandle Then
        UnlockDoor
        TurnHandle
    End If
    OpenDoor
    WalkIn
End Sub
Function TurnHandle() As Boolean
    'Do some stuff
    TurnHandle = True
End Function
```

This code is a little smarter than our first attempt at *GoInHouse*. It still makes a lot of assumptions, however. For example, we assume that *UnlockDoor* always works correctly. And if *UnlockDoor* always succeeds, we can assume that *TurnHandle* will be successful the second time it is called, so it isn't necessary to check the return value again. In the second case, *TurnHandle* acts just as a sub would because we ignore the return value.

To give the *TurnHandle* function the return value, we assign the value to the name of the function as follows:

```
TurnHandle = True
```

Arguments

Sometimes a procedure needs to be qualified with some extra information. *TurnHandle* once again makes a good example. The qualification *TurnHandle* needs is the direction in which to turn the handle.

Now let's modify *GoInHouse* and *TurnHandle* again. This time, we'll give *UnlockDoor* a return value—that is, we'll make it a function. The return value will tell us whether we should try to turn the handle a second time or give up on getting into the house.

```
Sub GoInHouse()
    FindDoor
    If Not TurnHandle("Left") Then
        If Not TurnHandle("Right") Then
            If Not UnlockDoor Then Exit Sub
            TurnHandle Direction:="Both"
        End If
    End If
    OpenDoor
    WalkIn
End Sub
Function TurnHandle(Direction As String) As Boolean
    'Do some stuff
    TurnHandle = True
End Function
```

Let's pull a few more tips on VBA syntax from this last coding example before we move on.

- When you have your program call a function that returns a value, enclose the whole argument list in parentheses. For a sub or a function for which you ignore the return value, don't enclose the arguments in parentheses.
- You can assign argument values by name if you like. For example, this argument setting:

  ```
  Direction:="Both"
  ```

  is used in the third *TurnHandle* call and is called a *named argument,* as opposed to the *positional arguments* used in the first two calls to *TurnHandle.* If you must pass multiple arguments and have a hard time remembering the order of the arguments, use named arguments. You can pass named arguments in any order. You can't mix named and positional arguments in the same procedure call, though.

NOTE Arguments are sometimes called "parameters."

- You can leave a procedure at any time using the *Exit Sub*, *Exit Function*, or *Exit Property* statement. (We'll look at property procedures in Chapter 4.)

Support Routines

You're already familiar with event procedures, procedures that correspond to and have the task of responding to specific events. But not all procedures in Visual Basic are event procedures. In Chapter 1, we called *Form_Resize()* from the *Form_Load()* event procedure. Although *Form_Resize()* is an event procedure, we were able to call it just as we would any ordinary sub or function procedure. The only difference between an event procedure and an ordinary procedure is that the event procedure can be called by VB in response to an event.

In code, calling ordinary procedures is just like calling event procedures directly. Some procedures are not called directly by an object (by a form or a control, for instance) as the result of an event but are called by you, the programmer. Procedures called by the programmer are known as *support routines*.

Modules

The VB code pane allows you to view modules. A *module* is a code listing that consists of one or more event procedures, support routines, and/or module-level variables. Each form object has a code module consisting of one or more routines and/or module-level variables associated with it. It is also possible to have a "code module" that doesn't belong to a form or to another object. Such a module is used to provide *support routines* that need to be called from procedures in more than one module. A module that is not associated with a form or with any other object is saved in your project with a .Bas extension.

Since the lack of a form and other objects precludes the need for event procedures, a .Bas module can contain only support routines. Support routines are listed in the Proc: dropdown of the code pane when the Objects: dropdown is set to <General>.

A module-level variable is any variable that can be read and modified by all of the procedures in a module. To create a module-level variable, place the variable declaration at the beginning of the module, in the <General> section, outside and above all the procedures in the module. We prefix module-level variables with *m_* to distinguish them from local (procedure-specific) variables. You'll find the right section of the module for module-level variables by selecting Objects:<General> and Proc:<declarations> in the code pane.

If a variable must be visible from all procedures in a program, not just within a single module of the program, it needs not only *module-level scope,* but *global scope.* To give a module-level variable global scope, declare it with the *Public* keyword. Variables with global scope must be in a .Bas module.

Cross-Reference See VBA Language Concepts: Scoping

FYI

Adding Support Routines to a Module

You can add a new support procedure to a module at any time by selecting Insert-Procedure when focus is on the code pane. The Insert Procedure dialog shown in Figure 3-1 lets you choose a name, a type (Sub, Function, or Property), and a scope (Public or Private) for your new procedure and places a procedure outline for you in the code pane. You will have to fill in arguments and a return type yourself.

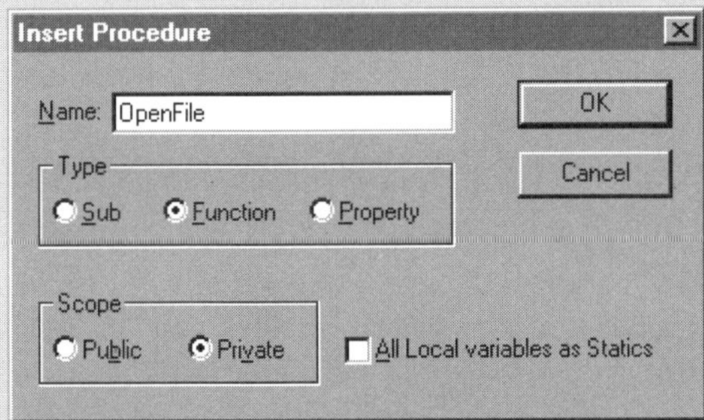

Figure 3-1. *The Insert Procedure dialog box.*

You can also add a new support procedure to a module by creating your own procedure outline. To create a procedure outline, put the insertion point on any blank line not already included in an existing procedure outline. Type *Sub foo,* and press Enter. VB will provide you with the *End Sub* line for free. If you are not in Full Module View, you will jump to a view that shows nothing but your new procedure outline.

Now that we have an understanding of VBA language procedures, let's get on with the code for our *QuickEdit* application.

QuickEdit Support Routines

In *QuickEdit,* four support routines will do most of the work for the program: *OpenFile, SaveFile, CheckFileDirty,* and *SetCaption.* In addition, we'll define two module-level variables, *m_strFileName* and *m_fFileDirty,* that will be used by all of the support routines.

The *OpenFile* Function

```
Private Function OpenFile(FileName As String) As Boolean
Dim FNum As Integer
    On Error GoTo OpenFileError
    FNum = FreeFile
    Open FileName For Input As FNum
    txtFile.Text = Input(LOF(FNum), #FNum)
    Close FNum
    m_fFileDirty = False
    m_strFileName = FileName
    OpenFile = True
    Exit Function
OpenFileError:
    MsgBox Err.Description, vbExclamation
    OpenFile = False
    Close
End Function
```

The *OpenFile* function takes a file name as an argument and tries to open the file. If the file opens successfully, *OpenFile* returns *True*; otherwise, it displays an error message and returns *False.* Reasons this function might fail and return *False* include:

- *FileName* is not a valid file.
- The file is too large for the *txtFile* textbox.
- There are already too many files open on the system.

Since any of these scenarios is possible and each will produce an error, we turn error trapping on.

Cross-Reference See VBA Language Concepts: Error Trapping

Other things to note about the *OpenFile* function:

- As we saw in Chapter 2, the line

  ```
  OpenFile = <value>
  ```

  sets the return value for the function to *<value>*.

- The *Input* function is used to read the whole file into memory in one statement. The data that is read in is assigned directly to the Text property of *txtFile*. This is the fastest way to read character data out of a file and meets the efficiency criterion of our *QuickEdit* design criteria in Chapter 2.
- Since an error is possible after the file has been successfully opened, our code could potentially go straight to the error handler, OpenFileError, but fail to reach our *Close* statement. The error handler needs to close any open files just in case. The *Close* statement without an argument specifying the file to close is used to close all open files. In the error handler, we use the catchall *Close* statement instead of *Close FNum* because closing a specific file in the error trap would generate another error if the file designated by *FileName* had not been successfully opened earlier in the procedure. An untrapped error in an error handling routine causes the program to terminate.
- Setting *m_strFileName* to the name of the file is a pretty obvious step if the file opened successfully. *m_strFileName* is used later in the *SetCaption* support procedure to insert the name of the file being edited into the *QuickEdit* window caption. Setting *m_fFileDirty* is not so obvious a step. We want to be able to tell at any time whether or not a file has changed. We use the *m_fFileDirty* flag to do this. If its value is *True*, then the file in memory has changed. If its value is *False*, then the file hasn't changed. As we'll see later, any time the *txtFile_Change()* event procedure is called, we flag the file as dirty.
- Programmatically assigning text to the Text property of a textbox fires the change event of the textbox. We'll examine this phenomenon in the "Event Hookup" section a little later in this chapter.

The *SaveFile* Function

```
Private Function SaveFile() As Boolean
Dim FNum As Integer
    On Error GoTo SaveFileError
    FNum = FreeFile
    Open m_strFileName For Output As FNum
    Print #FNum, txtFile.Text
    Close FNum
    m_fFileDirty = False
    SaveFile = True
    Exit Function
SaveFileError:
    MsgBox Err.Description, vbExclamation
    SaveFile = False
End Function
```

The *SaveFile* function looks very similar to the *OpenFile* function. The main difference is that in the *SaveFile* function the file is opened for output instead of input, meaning we'll write out to the file instead of reading in from it. Once again, we leave error trapping on for the whole routine. An error might occur if the user doesn't have write permission on the file or if the disk is full. Similar to *OpenFile*, *SaveFile* writes the entire content of *txtFile* to the file with a single statement, making this an optimally efficient routine.

The *CheckFileDirty* Function

```
Private Function CheckFileDirty() As Boolean
    If m_fFileDirty Then
        Select Case MsgBox( _
          "'" & m_strFileName & "' is not saved.  Save now?", _
          vbYesNoCancel Or vbDefaultButton3 Or vbQuestion)
            Case vbYes
                If Len(m_strFileName) Then
                    CheckFileDirty = Not SaveFile
                Else
                    mnuFileSaveAs_Click
                    CheckFileDirty = m_fFileDirty
                End If
            Case vbNo
            Case vbCancel
                CheckFileDirty = True
        End Select
    End If
End Function
```

The *CheckFileDirty* function uses *m_fFileDirty* to see if the file is "dirty," or in other words, if the user has made any changes to the file. If the file is dirty, the user is prompted to save the file on disk. If the user decides to save the file and the file is saved successfully, or if the user decides not to save the file, the *CheckFileDirty* function returns *False*. If the user chooses to cancel the action, or if the file is not saved successfully, the *CheckFileDirty* function returns *True*. Note that if the user chooses No in response to the screen query "Save now?" then *m_fFileDirty* is *True*, but *CheckFileDirty* returns *False*. Any time you call *CheckFileDirty* when the current file is dirty, it will prompt the user to save the dirty file.

Other things to note about the *CheckFileDirty* function:

- The *MsgBox* function is used both to display the warning message and to get the user's response. Extensive use is made of the constant values built into VBA to make the code readable. The use of constants saves the programmer the headache of having to remember or look up numeric values. Someone reading this code can deduce a lot about the type of message box to be displayed. Based solely on the use of the vbYesNoCancel, vbDefaultButton3, and vbQuestion options, the perception that the message box will have Yes, No, and Cancel buttons with the third (Cancel) button as the default and that it will show a question mark bitmap should be clear.

- *CheckFileDirty* takes advantage of the code already written in the *SaveFile* support routine. However, if a file name has not been chosen, *CheckFileDirty* defers to the *mnuSaveFileAs_Click()* event procedure since a file can't be saved without a name. The *mnuSaveFileAs_Click()* event procedure corresponds to the user action of selecting Save As in the File menu, which forces the user to enter a file name if he or she would like to save the file. We'll examine the *mnuSaveFileAs_Click()* event procedure in the "Event Hookup" section later in this chapter.
- We use the *Len* (string length) function to check if *m_strFileName* contains a value. If *Len* returns a *0*, then *m_strFileName* is empty and *mnuSaveFileAs_Click()* needs to be called to get a file name.

Cross-Reference See VBA Language Concepts: Library Constants, Branching and Looping: Select Case

The *SetCaption* Sub

```
Private Sub SetCaption()
    If Len(m_strFileName) Then
         Caption = App.Title & " - " & m_strFileName
    Else
         Caption = App.Title
    End If
End Sub
```

SetCaption is the most straightforward of our support routines. It is used to set the caption of the form to reflect the name of the current file. The value returned in *App.Title* comes from the Project Name: setting on the Project tab of the Options dialog. In Chapter 2, we set this value to *QuickEdit*. Using *App.Title* instead of the literal string "QuickEdit" allows us to change our project name at any time without making changes to our code.

These four support routines provide tools you can use when you code *QuickEdit*'s event procedures. In the next sections, we'll start responding to events fired by the objects we created in Chapter 2.

Basic Form Functionality

In this section, we'll discuss four very simple event procedures that will give our form the correct look and feel. This minimal functionality includes correctly loading the form, sizing the form, and unloading the form. Responding to the *Form_Load*, *Form_Resize*, *Form_QueryUnload*, and *mnuFileExit_Click* events will become very familiar because most VB programs require a response (that is, an event procedure) for all of these events.

The *Form_Load()* Event Procedure

```
Private Sub Form_Load()
    If Len(Command$) Then OpenFile Command$
    SetCaption
End Sub
```

Form_Load() is called when the form is initially loaded. For *QuickEdit*, *frm-QuickEdit* is the startup form, so the *Form_Load()* event procedure will be the first procedure called when the program starts. *Form_Load()* checks for a command line parameter to enable opening a file when the program first starts. If a file is specified, then the program calls the *OpenFile* routine to open the file. This allows someone using our program to enter in a file name at the command line. *QuickEdit* will bring up that file when the program starts. To emulate a command line parameter when using the VB design environment, set the Command Line Arguments on the Advanced tab of the Options dialog.

SetCaption must be called at the end of *Form_Load()* to bring the caption of the form in sync with the currently open file, if any.

NOTE frmQuickEdit is the first form loaded in our program because it is listed as the *Startup Form* on the Project tab of the Options dialog. When we build projects with multiple forms, we can choose which form will be loaded when the program starts. *Startup Form* can also be set to *Sub Main*. If this option is chosen, *Sub Main* must be a defined procedure in a .Bas module in our project.

The *Form_Resize()* Event Procedure

```
Private Sub Form_Resize()
    txtFile.Move 0, 0, ScaleWidth, ScaleHeight
End Sub
```

As we saw in Chapter 1, the *Form_Resize()* event procedure is called whenever the form is resized by the user. It will also be called by VB when the form first loads. We want the *txtFile* control to cover the whole client area of the form. We get it to do this by resetting the height and width of *txtFile* to match the dimensions of the new client area of the form.

ScaleWidth and ScaleHeight (as opposed to Width and Height) are the dimensions of the client area of the window. The client area doesn't include a window's borders, menus, or title bar. Invoking the *Move* method for *txtFile* (we'll look at methods in the next chapter) is equivalent to setting the Left, Top, Width, and Height properties of *txtFile* individually but is much faster because VB sets all four properties at one time. To avoid forcing the user to watch a control move and size itself four times (once each for Left, Top, Width, and Height), use the *Move* method.

The *Form_QueryUnload()* Event Procedure

```
Private Sub Form_QueryUnload(Cancel As Integer, _
    UnloadMode As Integer)
    Cancel = CheckFileDirty
End Sub
```

Form_QueryUnload() is called to give you, the programmer (and subsequently the user if you decide so), an opportunity to block the form unloading operation. If Cancel is *True* when the *Form_QueryUnload()* procedure ends, then the form will not unload. Now, notice that we did something tricky here. We don't want to unload the form if the file hasn't been saved (that is, if it's "dirty"), so the *Form_QueryUnload()* procedure calls *CheckFileDirty* to see whether the form unload operation should proceed. Recall that *CheckFileDirty* prompts the user to save a dirty file and returns *True* if the currently open file should not be overwritten. We just set Cancel to the return value of *CheckFileDirty*. If the value of Cancel is *True*, then the file isn't saved and we don't want to unload the form. If the value of Cancel is *False*, then the file is clean (or the user doesn't care) and we can proceed safely with unloading the form.

The *mnuFileExit_Click()* Event Procedure

```
Private Sub mnuFileExit_Click()
    Unload Me
End Sub
```

The user's selecting Exit on the File menu should always correspond to the user's choosing Close on the system menu or otherwise ending the program (by exiting Windows, for example). To this end, *mnuFileExit_Click()* does nothing more than unload the form. Any status checks and cleanup are left to the *Form_QueryUnload()* and *Form_Unload()* event procedures.

We have now achieved the look and feel specified in our design for *QuickEdit*. All necessary event procedures for the form object have been completed. All that's left to do is to wire the support routines into a few more event procedures.

Event Hookup

Now that we have all of our support routines and the basic functionality of the form in place, we can proceed to make the *QuickEdit* program fully functional by hooking up the rest of the code we've written in this chapter to the objects we created in Chapter 2.

Remember, to get an event procedure outline for an object, double-click on the object in the design environment and select the event procedure you want from the Proc: dropdown in the code pane. To bring up the event procedure outline for a menu, just select the menu item in the design environment.

The *txtFile_Change()* Event Procedure

```
Private Sub txtFile_Change()
    m_fFileDirty = True
End Sub
```

The *txtFile_Change()* event procedure is called whenever the user enters a new keystroke in the *txtFile* textbox. This event procedure is also called when the Text property is set in code. If you wonder why setting the Text property fires the *txtFile_Change* event, realize that setting the Text property in code replaces all of the existing text. This is equivalent to putting the new text on the clipboard, selecting all of the old text in the textbox, and pressing Shift-Insert to paste the new data into the textbox.

Since the change event of a textbox is called pretty frequently, the amount of code in the *txtFile_Change()* event procedure should be limited. In our case, we need to remember only that the file has changed and is consequently dirty. We do this very efficiently by setting the module-level *m_fFileDirty* variable to *True*. Now if we need to know in other places in the code if the text in the textbox has been modified, we can just check the *m_fFileDirty* flag.

The *mnuFileNew_Click()* Event Procedure

```
Private Sub mnuFileNew_Click()
    If Not CheckFileDirty Then
        txtFile = vbNullString
        m_fFileDirty = False
        m_strFileName = vbNullString
        SetCaption
    End If
End Sub
```

The *mnuFileNew_Click()* event procedure has a simple task: provide a clean slate in *txtFile* in which the user can type in a new file. This little service would be no problem if *QuickEdit* didn't have much consideration for the user. However, *QuickEdit* does prompt the user to save the current file before it opens up a new one. Fortunately, the *CheckFileDirty* routine already provides this cordial behavior.

The *mnuFileNew_Click()* event procedure calls *CheckFileDirty* at its very beginning to prompt the user to save a dirty file. If *CheckFileDirty* returns *True*, either the file was not saved successfully or the user clicked Cancel; in either of these cases, we don't create a new file. If *CheckFileDirty* returns *False*, the *Not* causes the expression between *If* and *Then* to evaluate to *True*, so the *If* clause in the code is executed.

If *CheckFileDirty* returns *False*—that is, if the file isn't dirty or was saved successfully, or the user didn't care about it—then all history of the current file is removed from memory. In order to return a clean slate to the user, we need to set *txtFile.Text* to an empty string and reset the Caption. We also need to forget the old file name and reset the dirty flag.

NOTE You might have noticed that the code says *txtFile = vbNullString*, not *txtFile.Text = vbNullString*. No, we didn't blow it. These two syntaxes are functionally equivalent. If an object (in this case a textbox) has a *default property* (the Text property for a textbox), then the name of the object in an expression is equivalent to the default property.

The *mnuFileOpen_Click()* Event Procedure

```
Private Sub mnuFileOpen_Click()
Dim strNewFile As String
    If CheckFileDirty Then Exit Sub
    strNewFile = InputBox$("Enter file path.")
    If Len(strNewFile) Then
        If OpenFile(strNewFile) Then
            SetCaption
        End If
    End If
End Sub
```

The *mnuFileOpen_Click()* event procedure provides more functionality than *mnuFileNew_Click()* does. To open a file, we not only need to void the existing data, but we also need to get new data. Once again, all the work is done by our support routines. The steps our program needs to take in order to open a new file are shown on the next page.

1. Call *CheckFileDirty*, which tries to save the file if it's dirty. If the current file remains dirty, that is, unsaved, then exit the event procedure with *Exit Sub.*
2. Get a new file name by means of the *InputBox* function.
3. If a file name was entered, try to open the file by means of *OpenFile.*
4. If the file opens successfully, then call *SetCaption.*

The *mnuFileSave_Click()* Event Procedure

```
Private Sub mnuFileSave_Click()
    If m_fFileDirty Then
        If Len(m_strFileName) Then
            SaveFile
        Else
            mnuFileSaveAs_Click
        End If
    End If
End Sub
```

The *mnuFileSave_Click()* event procedure is relatively simple. As with all of the other event procedures we've looked at thus far, the major part of the work will be delegated to the support routines.

If the file is dirty and there is a current file name, then the *SaveFile* routine is called. If there is no current file name, then we move execution along to the *mnuFileSaveAs_Click()* event procedure, which prompts the user for a name for the file. This is an admission by the event procedure that it really should not have been called in the first place and that the procedure for a Save As event is the appropriate one.

The *mnuFileSaveAs_Click()* Event Procedure

```
Private Sub mnuFileSaveAs_Click()
Dim tmpFileName As String
    tmpFileName = m_strFileName
Retry_mnuFileSaveAs:
    m_strFileName = InputBox$("Save File As...", , _
                    m_strFileName)
    If Len(m_strFileName) Then
        On Error Resume Next
        If Len(Dir$(m_strFileName)) Then
            If Err = 0 Then
                If vbNo = MsgBox("'" & m_strFileName & _
                                 "' already exists.  " & _
```

```
                                "Replace existing file?", _
                                vbYesNo Or vbDefaultButton2 Or _
                                vbExclamation) Then
                        GoTo Retry_mnuFileSaveAs
                    End If
                End If
            End If
            On Error GoTo 0
            If SaveFile Then
                SetCaption
            Else
                m_strFileName = tmpFileName
            End If
        Else
            m_strFileName = tmpFileName
        End If
    End Sub
```

The *mnuFileSaveAs_Click()* procedure is the most complicated of the *QuickEdit* event responses. Take a deep breath. Here are the basic steps this procedure goes through:

1. Save the current file name in the *tmpFileName* variable in case things go wrong.
2. Get the new file name.
3. Prompt the user if a file of that name already exists. Return to step 2 if necessary in response to the user's input.
4. Let *SaveFile* try to save the file.
5. Let *SetCaption* set the form caption if *SaveFile* succeeded.
6. Restore the old file name if *SaveFile* failed.

A single *MsgBox* function is again used to present the user with a Yes/No prompt for an overwrite and to return the user's choice (*vbYes* or *vbNo*) to the program. The *MsgBox* function is very useful when we need to get the user to make control flow decisions.

Notice the *GoTo* statement? That's in there to keep you on your toes. *GoTo* statements have become taboo in programming because they tend to generate spaghetti code. But *GoTo*s are useful when you need to jump out of nested statements to retry a chunk of code. If you end up with more than one *GoTo* per routine, however, you're probably using too many.

Cross-Reference See VBA Language Concepts: Branching and Looping

Take a hard look at everything you've learned so far in this chapter. Read the code, particularly, and make sure you understand what's going on. Refer to the "VBA Language Concepts," Appendix A, or another VB book if you have questions.

This is also a good time to press F5 to run the project and try out the program features. Click the *close* button on the title bar when you're done.

Playing the User

In this section we'll take a high-level look at what happens when a user actually uses our *QuickEdit* program. This exercise should help you connect the programming concepts you've just studied with what's happening from the user's perspective.

Our program begins with the *Form_Load* event. If the user has typed in a file name on the command line, then *QuickEdit* opens that file and resets the form caption. Otherwise, *QuickEdit* does nothing. When the *Form_Load()* event procedure finishes executing, our program just sits and waits for the next event to be fired. Here's a summary of the possible user-generated events, with *QuickEdit*'s responses:

The user types some text. As soon as the user types something into the textbox, the *m_fFileDirty* flag is set to *True*, and hence the file's status is dirty. The TextBox control automatically handles grabbing the text, displaying it, and allowing for user operations such as Copy and Paste.

The user resizes the program window. The *txtFile* textbox is resized to fit the new client area.

The user selects File-Exit. The *QuickEdit* program tries to unload the form. The *Form_QueryUnloadForm* event is fired. The program checks to see if the file is dirty and tries to save it if it's dirty. If the save succeeds, the program exits. Otherwise, the program goes back to waiting for a user-generated event.

The user selects File-New. *QuickEdit* saves the current file if it's dirty, blanks out the textbox and the file name, and then resets the form caption.

The user selects File-Open. *QuickEdit* saves the current file if it's dirty. Next, it asks the user what file he or she wants to open and puts the file name data into the textbox. Finally, it sets the form caption and the file name.

The user selects File-Save. *QuickEdit* saves the current file if it's dirty.

The user selects File-Save As. *QuickEdit* checks to see if a file is currently loaded. If a file is already loaded, *QuickEdit* asks the user under what file name he or she wants to save the file and then saves the current file under the new file name.

Debugging

Visual Basic provides an integrated environment with very powerful debugging tools. In this section, we'll take a brief look at the debugging commands.

F5 (Run, Continue)

Any time you'd like to run the program you're developing, press F5. You'll also use this key any time you want to continue running your program—after stopping on a breakpoint, for instance, which we'll get to. (See the "Visual Basic Modes" box in Chapter 1, page 10.)

F8 (Step)

F8 is one of the most-used keys for debugging Visual Basic programs. It allows us to step through our code one line at a time to discover where things aren't working right.

Let's try it. (If you closed VB to take a break, load the *QuickEdit* project first.) Press F8. You'll be in break mode, and the code pane should look like the one shown in Figure 3-2.

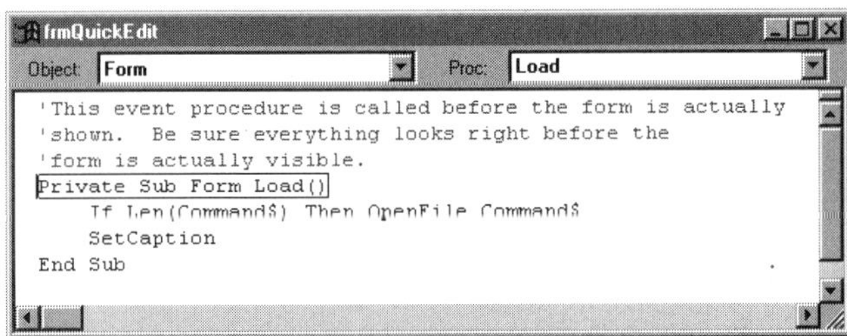

Figure 3-2. *Pressing F8 in design mode brings you to break mode and the first line of your code.*

Since the first thing our program does is load our form, the *Form_Load()* event procedure comes up in our code pane. Notice that there's a box around the first line. As you continue to press F8 to step through the lines of our code, that box will move, indicating which line of code is about to be executed.

Press F8 until that box is resting on the line that calls *SetCaption.* If you push F8 once more, you'll jump into the *SetCaption* code.

Continue pressing F8 until you reach the *End Sub* line of the *Form_Resize()* event procedure. Press F8 one more time. Notice that the box indicating the next line of code to be executed has disappeared. You've stepped right out of our code. You are now in run mode, but since you pressed F8 (Step) instead of F5 (Continue) to leave the *Form_Resize()* event procedure, execution of the program will break again at the top of the next event procedure that's called by VB. To see this, click on the form and type a letter into the textbox. VB will jump back into break mode, with the box around the line at the top of *txtFile-_Change()*. If you get tired of running the program one step at a time with F8, press F5 to make the program continue to run without interruption.

NOTE If your program is in run mode and you want to break at the top of the next event procedure, press Ctrl-Break to go to break mode, and then immediately press F8. This will leave VB in the same state as when you pressed F8 to step out of the *Form_Resize()* event procedure and stop at the next event procedure, which in our example was *txtFile_Change()*.

Shift-F8 (Step Over)

Often, you won't want to step through all of the procedures in your code to get to where you want to go. The Shift-F8 command allows you to "step over" procedures you don't want to view.

1. In run mode, from *QuickEdit*'s File menu, select Exit to close the program and return to design mode. Don't save the text you typed in.
2. From design mode, press F8 to restart the program, and continue pressing F8 until the box is around the line in the *Form_Load()* event procedure that calls *SetCaption*.
3. Press Shift-F8. Notice that you skipped over the code in the *SetCaption* procedure altogether.

Ctrl-F8 (Step to Cursor)

Let's say that you know exactly where you want to go in your program. You can have Visual Basic step to that line for you so that you won't have to keep pressing F8 and Shift-F8.

1. From design mode, press F8.
2. Select Object: Form and then Proc: Resize.
3. Click anywhere on the *txtFile.Move*... line in the *Form_Resize()* event procedure.
4. Press Ctrl-F8. Visual Basic will step to the *txtFile.Move*... line for you.
5. If the line you select is in an event procedure, VB goes to run mode and waits for the event. Select mnuFileOpen in the Object: dropdown,

and click in the Proc: dropdown to see the *mnuFileOpen_Click()* event procedure in the code pane.

6. Click on any executable line in the *mnuFileOpen_Click()* event procedure, and press Ctrl-F8. VB will go to run mode.
7. From the *QuickEdit* menu, select File-Open. The program will break on the designated line.

F9 (Toggle Breakpoint)

When you're debugging a real program, you often need to stop at a line of code each time you run the program or each time that line is executed. It's not practical to use Ctrl-F8 every single time, and you might have multiple lines you want to stop at. If you want execution to stop repeatedly at a particular line of code, a *breakpoint* is in order. To add a breakpoint, click on the line of code at which you want to break and press F9 to toggle the breakpoint on. You can toggle the breakpoint off by clicking on the same line of code and pressing F9 again. You can have as many breakpoints as you like in your code. Whenever VB hits a breakpoint, it will switch to break mode, and the line of code you've marked will be boxed as the current line. Let's give it a try.

1. In design mode, select the *mnuFileOpen_Click()* procedure into the code pane.
2. Click on the first line of executable code (*If CheckFileDirty...*) and press F9 to place a breakpoint there.
3. Press F5 to go to run mode.
4. On the *QuickEdit* menu, select File-Open. VB will jump to break mode with the line of code you selected as the next line to be executed.

You can set or clear breakpoints at any time in all three modes. To clear all breakpoints, select Clear All Breakpoints from the VB Run menu, or press Ctrl-Shift-F9.

Ctrl-F9 (Set Next Statement)

You use Ctrl-F9 to set the "next" statement you want the program to execute to a different line of code in the currently executing procedure. Click on the line you want to execute next, and press Ctrl-F9. Any intervening code won't be executed. Use this command to skip over lines you don't want the program to execute or to repeat the execution of a line you've already executed. Although you can set any line of code in the current procedure as the next statement, you can't use the Ctrl-F9 command to move execution to a different procedure.

Shift-F9 (Instant Watch)

The Instant Watch command allows you to quickly view the contents of a variable in your code. To use this command, while you're in break mode, click on the variable whose contents you want to view and press Shift-F9. The Instant Watch window will pop up and show you the variable you've selected and its current value. Press Esc or click Cancel to return to your code, or click Add to add the variable to the Watch pane.

1. In design mode, place a breakpoint in the *SetCaption* support routine.
2. Press F5 to start the program.
3. In the *SetCaption* routine, click on the word *Caption*.
4. Press Shift-F9 to see the value of the Caption variable.
5. Press Esc or click Cancel to return to the code pane.

End

From the Run menu, you can select End to stop your program from running at any time. We don't recommend that you use Run-End, however, because Run-End short-circuits the normal shutdown process of the program. Some of the advanced examples later in the book will actually crash VB if you don't allow VB's normal shutdown process to be executed, so don't get in the habit of using this command.

Other Debugging Techniques

We've looked at all of the commands available in VB for stepping through code. However, we have only scratched the surface of actual VB debugging techniques. Debugging techniques to investigate on your own include using the call stack; using the Watch pane and the Immediate pane of the Debug window; changing variable values in the Immediate pane; evaluating watches; breaking code with watch expressions; and breaking on errors. These topics are beyond the scope of this chapter.

FYI

The Visual Basic Toolbar

Visual Basic provides a toolbar to make common commands more accessible. Now that we've looked at the keyboard and menu equivalents of each of the toolbar buttons, you are in a position to understand the action associated with each button. So let's look in the table below at what each button does. Notice that the availability of the various buttons depends on whether VB is in design, run, or break mode. (See Figure 3-3.)

Figure 3-3. *The Visual Basic toolbar in the three different modes.*

Button	Name	Use	Menu and Shortcuts	Available
	Form	Add a new form (.Frm) to the project.	Insert-Form	Design mode
	Module	Add a new module (.Bas) to the project.	Insert-Module	Design mode
	Open Project	Open a project.	File-Open **Ctrl-O**	Design mode
	Save Project	Save the current project.	File-Save Project	Design mode
	Lock Controls	Disable moving controls.	Edit-Lock Controls	Design mode; form active
	Menu Editor	Activate the menu editor.	Tools-Menu Editor **Ctrl-E**	Design mode; form active
	Properties	Activate the property sheet.	View-Properties **F4**	Design mode

(continued)

The Visual Basic Toolbar *continued*

Button	Name	Use	Menu and Shortcuts	Available
	Object Browser	Show the Object Browser dialog.	View-Object Browser **F2**	Design mode; break mode
	Project	Activate the project window.	View-Project **Ctrl-R**	All modes
	Run	Start the program in design mode; continue in break mode.	Run-Start **F5**	Design mode; break mode
	Break	Go to break mode from run mode.	**Ctrl-Break**	Run mode
	End	Return to design mode.	Run-End	Run mode; break mode
	Toggle Breakpoint	Add or remove a breakpoint.	Run-Toggle Breakpoint **F9**	All modes; code pane active
	Instant Watch	Watch the variable or expression under the cursor.	Tools-Instant Watch **Shift-F9**	Break mode
	Calls	Show the procedures called to reach the current procedure.	Tools-Calls **Ctrl-L**	Break mode
	Step Into	Execute a line of code; step in if a procedure.	Run-Step Into **F8**	Design mode; break mode
	Step Over	Execute a line of code; don't step into procedures.	Run-Step Over **Shift-F8**	Design mode; break mode

QuickEdit Enhancements

If you used the original version of *QuickEdit,* you were probably a bit frustrated by having to type the full path of the file into a simple text input box. And you might think that the amount of work necessary to upgrade such a basic approach to the standard Windows file open and file save dialogs would be significant. You'll be relieved to know that the upgrade is actually quite simple. In this section, we'll make *QuickEdit* a little friendlier.

CommonDialog File Dialogs

Visual Basic provides the CommonDialog custom control to make it easy to deploy standard color, font, file open, file save as, and printer dialogs in your programs. The CommonDialog control also makes it very easy for you to display a specific help topic from any Windows Help file.

To enhance *QuickEdit,* we'll use the CommonDialog control to handle opening and saving a file in our program. Our using the CommonDialog control will actually simplify the code, as you can see by comparing the original routine with the enhanced versions. (For easy comparison, see the code listing at the end of this chapter.)

Let's add a CommonDialog control to the *QuickEdit* form.

1. Activate the *QuickEdit* form by clicking the View Form button in the project Window.
2. Make sure the CommonDialog control is on the VB toolbox. (See Figure 3-4.) If it's not on the toolbox, select Custom Controls from the Tools menu and click on Microsoft Common Dialog Control.

Figure 3-4. *The CommonDialog control button on the VB toolbox.*

3. Place a CommonDialog control on the form. It doesn't matter where you put it—it will be invisible at run-time. This one control will allow us to use different kinds of standard dialogs in our program.
4. Select the control.
5. Using the property sheet, set the following properties for the control:

   Name = *ComDlg*
   CancelError = *True*
   DefaultExt = *.TXT*
   Filter = *Text (*.txt) | *.txt | All Files (*.*) | *.**

Now we're ready to use the CommonDialog control in our program.

The *mnuFileSaveAs_Click()* Event Procedure

```
Private Sub mnuFileSaveAs_Click()
Dim tmpFileName As String
    On Error Resume Next
    tmpFileName = m_strFileName
    With ComDlg
        .FileName = m_strFileName
        .Flags = cdlOFNPathMustExist Or cdlOFNOverwritePrompt Or _
                 cdlOFNNoReadOnlyReturn Or cdlOFNHideReadOnly
        .ShowSave
        If Err Then
            Exit Sub
```

(continued)

```
        Else
            m_strFileName = .FileName
            If SaveFile Then
                SetCaption
            Else
                m_strFileName = tmpFileName
            End If
        End If
    End With
End Sub
```

This version of *mnuFileSaveAs_Click()* is much simpler than our earlier version, and the results are a lot more attractive. We let the CommonDialog do all of the work. If the user cancels the dialog, an error is returned. The CommonDialog custom control also eliminates the possibility of the program's returning an invalid path or the name of a read only file, so the *SaveFile* routine has a much better chance of succeeding. Considering the simplified code and the more robust functionality, this version is a definite improvement over our earlier routine.

Cross-Reference See VBA Language Concepts: Library Constants, *With* Statement, Error Trapping

The *mnuFileOpen_Click()* Event Procedure

```
Private Sub mnuFileOpen_Click()
    If CheckFileDirty Then Exit Sub
    On Error Resume Next
    With ComDlg
        .FileName = ""
        .Flags = cdlOFNPathMustExist Or cdlOFNFileMustExist Or _
                 cdlOFNHideReadOnly
        .ShowOpen
        If Err Then
            Exit Sub
        ElseIf OpenFile(.FileName) Then
            SetCaption
        End If
    End With
End Sub
```

Although we don't save as much code with the new *mnuFileOpen_Click()* routine as we did with the new *mnuFileSaveAs_Click()*, we still have a much friendlier approach to opening a file because the user can point and click instead of typing in a path and file name. Once again, the Common Dialog assures us that the program will try to open an existing file, so the chances that *OpenFile* will fail are greatly reduced.

Simplified File-Save

Our old *mnuFileSave_Click()* event procedure seems pretty complicated when we consider that all we should really have to do is call the *SaveFile* support routine. The problem is that the user might select File-Save when there is no file in memory to save. Let's make this routine much simpler by disabling the File-Save menu item when there is no file in memory. This is actually pretty easy to do because VB fires an event when the top-level menu is selected, allowing us to enable or disable menu items. Here's the code—yes, this *is all* of the code.

```
Private Sub mnuFile_Click()
    'VB4 automatically coerces a non-zero length to
    'a Boolean True.
    mnuFileSave.Enabled = Len(m_strFileName)
End Sub
Private Sub mnuFileSave_Click()
    If m_fFileDirty Then SaveFile
End Sub
```

NOTE Normally, you bring up the code for a menu item by selecting that menu item at design-time. However, you won't bring up code if you select a top-level menu item that has menu items under it. You will have to use the Object: and Proc: dropdowns in the code pane if you want to view the code for *mnuFile_Click()*.

Full *QuickEdit* Code Listing

Here is all of the code for the final version of our *QuickEdit* program. The code is also located in the Chapter3\QuickEdit and Chapter3\QuickEdit2 (for the enhanced version) directories on the companion disc. This code listing shows comments and tips we left out of our earlier consideration of parts of the code. If a routine is specific to either the original or the CommonDialog version of *QuickEdit,* a comment before the procedure indicates which version of the program the routine belongs to.

frmQuickEdit CODE MODULE

```
Option Explicit

'These variables are used throughout this form's
'code to track the file name and whether the file
'has been changed.
Private m_fFileDirty As Boolean
Private m_strFileName As String

'This event procedure is called before the form is
'actually shown. Be sure everything looks right
'before the form actually becomes visible.
Private Sub Form_Load()
    If Len(Command$) Then OpenFile Command$
    SetCaption
End Sub

Private Sub Form_QueryUnload(Cancel As Integer, _
                            UnloadMode As Integer)
    'If file remains dirty, canceling this event by
    'setting Cancel to True will stop the unloading
    'of the form.
    Cancel = CheckFileDirty
End Sub

Private Sub Form_Resize()
    'ScaleHeight and ScaleWidth refer to the dimensions
    'of the client area of the window, meaning the area
    'inside the window's border, menu, and title bar.

    'This Move method call sets the textbox dimensions
    'to match the client area's dimensions.
    txtFile.Move 0, 0, ScaleWidth, ScaleHeight
End Sub

'Function returns True if the file is dirty and
'shouldn't be overwritten.
Private Function CheckFileDirty() As Boolean
    If m_fFileDirty Then
        'Use a message box to ask the user what to do next.
        Select Case MsgBox( "'" & m_strFileName & _
            "' is not saved.  Save now?", _
            vbYesNoCancel Or vbQuestion Or vbDefaultButton3)
            'This Case statement corresponds to the button
            'that was chosen in the message box. Note the
            'use of built-in vb constants instead of numbers.
            Case vbYes
```

```
                If Len(m_strFileName) Then
                    CheckFileDirty = Not SaveFile
                Else
                    mnuFileSaveAs_Click
                    CheckFileDirty = m_fFileDirty
                End If
            Case vbNo
                'Do nothing
            Case vbCancel
                CheckFileDirty = True
        End Select
    End If
    'If the execution of this function reaches this point
    'without explicitly setting CheckFileDirty, the return
    'value of the function will be False, which is the
    'default value for a Boolean variable.
End Function

'Use to save the current file.
Private Function SaveFile() As Boolean
Dim FNum As Integer
    'The next two calls may fail, so implement an error trap
    'to prevent the program from terminating prematurely.
    On Error GoTo SaveFileError
    'Always use FreeFile to get a file number.
    FNum = FreeFile
    'Open the file.
    Open m_strFileName For Output As FNum
    'Print the current text to the file.
    Print #FNum, txtFile.Text
    'Close the file to free the file for use by other
    'programs.
    Close FNum
    'Set the module-level flag and return, indicating a
    'successful Save.
    m_fFileDirty = False
    SaveFile = True
    'Leave the function to avoid running the error handler.
    Exit Function
SaveFileError:
    'Tell the user what went wrong.
    MsgBox Err.Description, vbExclamation
    SaveFile = False
End Function

'Open a file. This function is similar to SaveFile.
Private Function OpenFile(FileName As String) As Boolean
```

(continued)

```
Dim FNum As Integer
    On Error GoTo OpenFileError
    FNum = FreeFile
    'We are reading data in from the file, so open for Input.
    Open FileName For Input As FNum
    'Use the Input function to read the whole file into
    'the textbox with one statement. LOF indicates the
    'number of characters in an open file. Note: this line
    'will fire the txtFile_Change event, which sets the
    'm_fFileDirty flag, even though the file is not dirty!
    txtFile.Text = Input(LOF(FNum), #FNum)
    Close FNum
    'Clear the dirty flag.
    m_fFileDirty = False
    m_strFileName = FileName
    OpenFile = True
    Exit Function
OpenFileError:
    MsgBox Err.Description, vbExclamation
    OpenFile = False
    'Close all open files. This is a catchall just in
    'case the file is still open.
    Close
End Function

'Common Dialog Version
Private Sub mnuFile_Click()
    'This response to a menu click on the top-level
    'menu simplifies the mnuFileSave() event procedure.
    'The value returned from Len is automatically
    'coerced to a Boolean value (True or False) when
    'it's assigned to the Enabled property.
    mnuFileSave.Enabled = Len(m_strFileName)
End Sub

Private Sub mnuFileExit_Click()
    'This routine just duplicates the user action of
    'closing with the system menu. The user's choosing
    'File-Exit should result in the same effect as the
    'user's choosing Close on the system menu.
    Unload Me
End Sub

Private Sub mnuFileNew_Click()
    'If the current file is not dirty, then clear the
    'text and remove all evidence of the file.
    'Note: CheckFileDirty returns a Boolean value,
    'so it can be toggled with the Not operator. If a
```

```
    'non-Boolean value is used in a logical expression,
    'be sure to use the CBool() function on the first
    'element of the expression for correct results--
    'for example,'Not CBool(IntegerValue)'.
    If Not CheckFileDirty Then
        'txtFile implies txtFile.Text. Text is the
        'default value of a TextBox object, so txtFile
        'and txtFile.Text are equivalent.
        txtFile = vbNullString
        m_fFileDirty = False
        m_strFileName = vbNullString
        SetCaption
    End If
End Sub

'Original Version
Private Sub mnuFileOpen_Click()
Dim strNewFile As String
    'Find out if the current file information can be
    'overwritten.
    If CheckFileDirty Then Exit Sub
    'Get the new file name.
    strNewFile = InputBox$("Enter file path.")
    'InputBox returns "" if the user chooses the Cancel
    'button in the InputBox dialog.
    If Len(strNewFile) Then
        'Try to open the file.
        If OpenFile(strNewFile) Then
            SetCaption
        End If
    End If
End Sub

'Common Dialog Version
Private Sub mnuFileOpen_Click()
    If CheckFileDirty Then Exit Sub
    On Error Resume Next
    With ComDlg
        'Make sure the FileName has no old data.
        .FileName = ""
        'These flags do the following:
        '1) PathMustExist--return file path exists
        '2) FileMustExist--don't return bogus file
        '3) HideReadOnly--no ReadOnly check box on dialog
        .Flags = cdlOFNPathMustExist Or cdlOFNFileMustExist Or _
                cdlOFNHideReadOnly
        'CancelError property is True for ComDlg. Setting
```

(continued)

```
            'this property tells the ShowOpen method to throw an
            'error if no file was selected.
            .ShowOpen
            If Err Then
                Exit Sub
            'The full path is in .FileName. Use .FileTitle if you
            'want to get just the name of the file.
            ElseIf OpenFile(.FileName) Then
                SetCaption
            End If
        End With
    End Sub

    'Original Version
    Private Sub mnuFileSave_Click()
        If m_fFileDirty Then
            'Len(StringVariable) is much quicker than
            'StringVariable<>"" and returns the same information.
            'Any non-zero value evaluates to true in an If...Then
            'statement.
            If Len(m_strFileName) Then
                SaveFile
            Else
                'If we reach this code, then the user should
                'have chosen the Save As menu item instead of
                'Save, so emulate that user action by calling
                'the event procedure for File-Save As directly.
                mnuFileSaveAs_Click
            End If
        End If
    End Sub

    'Common Dialog Version
    Private Sub mnuFileSave_Click()
        'We don't need to check for a valid file name
        'because this menu is enabled only when the file
        'name is valid.
        If m_fFileDirty Then SaveFile
    End Sub

    'Original Version
    Private Sub mnuFileSaveAs_Click()
    Dim tmpFileName As String
        'SaveFile uses the module-level variable instead
        'of taking a parameter. If SaveFile fails, then
        'm_strFileName needs to be set to its previous value.
        'Therefore, we save the current value of m_strFileName
        'in order to reset m_strFileName if necessary.
```

```
    'Note: The use of a module-level variable makes the
    'SaveFile routine less versatile. A more general
    'SaveFile routine would take a FileName and possibly
    'a TextBox control to save in that FileName as
    'parameters. However, for this simple program,use
    'of the module-level variable for the FileName is
    'sufficient.

    tmpFileName = m_strFileName
Retry_mnuFileSaveAs:
    m_strFileName = InputBox$("Save File As...", , _
                              m_strFileName)
    If Len(m_strFileName) Then
        'Save File As always notifies the user if a file
        'of that name already exists. This block of code
        'will check for file existence and will reprompt
        'the user for a new file name if the first file
        'name is not acceptable.
        On Error Resume Next
        If Len(Dir$(m_strFileName)) Then
            If Err = 0 Then
                If vbNo = MsgBox("'" & m_strFileName & _
                                 "' already exists.  " & _
                                 "Replace existing file?", _
                                 vbYesNo Or vbDefaultButton2 Or _
                                 vbExclamation) Then
                    GoTo Retry_mnuFileSaveAs
                End If
            End If
        End If
        On Error GoTo 0
        'Let the support routines do all the work.
        If SaveFile Then
            SetCaption
        Else
            m_strFileName = tmpFileName
        End If
    Else
        m_strFileName = tmpFileName
    End If
End Sub

'Common Dialog Version
Private Sub mnuFileSaveAs_Click()
Dim tmpFileName As String
    On Error Resume Next
    tmpFileName = m_strFileName
```

(continued)

```
    With ComDlg
        'Give an initial value for the file name.
        .FileName = m_strFileName
        'These flags do the following:
        '1) PathMustExist--return file path exists
        '2) OverwritePrompt--prompt for file overwrite
        '3) NoReadOnlyReturn--file returned is writable
        '4) HideReadOnly--no ReadOnly check box on dialog
        .Flags = cdlOFNPathMustExist Or cdlOFNOverwritePrompt Or _
                 cdlOFNNoReadOnlyReturn Or cdlOFNHideReadOnly
        'CancelError property is True for ComDlg. Setting
        'this property tells the ShowSave method to throw
        'an error if no file was selected.
        .ShowSave
        If Err Then
            Exit Sub
        Else
            m_strFileName = .FileName
            'Check if file saved OK.
            If SaveFile Then
                SetCaption
            Else
                'FileSave failed: reset data.
                m_strFileName = tmpFileName
            End If
        End If
    End With
End Sub

Private Sub txtFile_Change()
    'Flag the file as dirty when any character is typed
    'in the textbox.
    m_fFileDirty = True
End Sub

Private Sub SetCaption()
    'If there is a file set, use the & concatenation
    'operator to combine its name with the title of the
    'application. The application title is set in the
    'Project Options dialog on the Tools menu.
    If Len(m_strFileName) Then
        Caption = App.Title & " - " & m_strFileName
    Else
        Caption = App.Title
    End If
End Sub
```

PART TWO

Objects and Visual Basic

IN THIS PART

From this point on, we'll assume a knowledge of Visual Basic and won't be reviewing fundamental VB elements as we go. In Part Two we'll look at the rich object-oriented features of Visual Basic.

So what's all the fuss over objects? We read about them on the boxes of all the hottest shrink-wrapped software, yet most people are still trying to figure out what they're good for. In Part Two, we'll find out why object-oriented programming is useful and how Visual Basic helps us program with objects.

Chapter 4 - Object Basics

Get some class, why don't you? In this chapter, we'll help you do just that. One of the new elements of Visual Basic 4 is the class. We'll define classes and learn how to use them in object oriented programming. We'll define properties and methods and learn what they're used for. Finally, we'll create a MailBox class.

Chapter 5 - Creating Objects

Classes are useless on their own. In Chapter 5, we'll learn how to breathe life into our classes by "instantiating" the classes we created in Chapter 4. We'll also investigate techniques for tuning performance, such as "hard typing." At the end of the chapter, we'll actually create an object from the class we created in Chapter 4. We know, we know—so much excitement in only one chapter.

Chapter 6 - Driving Other Objects with Visual Basic

We know you didn't buy this book just to learn how to roll your own objects. In this chapter, we'll use Visual Basic as a controller for OLE Automation–enabled applications. We'll turn the MailBox object from Chapter 4 into a stand-alone OLE Automation object and manipulate it with a separate VB program. We'll get into debugging VB-created OLE Automation servers, too. Finally, we'll explore one of the new features of VB4—creating dynamic link libraries (DLLs). And you thought you'd go to the movies tonight!

Chapter 7 - Using Insertable Objects and Container Controls

In this chapter, we'll use insertable objects and OLE container controls to enable the user of your application to control other visual OLE objects such as Microsoft Excel objects and Microsoft Word objects by means of in-place activation. We'll look at using menus and toolbars from other applications without ever leaving a Visual Basic form.

4

Object Basics

A lot of people are confused about what an object really is. In this chapter, we'll talk about objects and object-oriented programming (OOP) and about how Visual Basic helps you put the OOP paradigm to use more easily than traditional OOP languages do.

Our focus will be on the creation of efficient, useful, and reusable objects with Visual Basic.

OOP: The Wave of the Present

OOP has always promised the programmer:

- **Ease of use** by grouping related functionality in easily accessible objects instead of in separate and scattered procedures.
- **Improved efficiency** by enabling specialists in specific areas to concentrate on coding libraries of reusable objects that can be leveraged by other programmers.

Unfortunately, the software development industry hasn't consistently realized the benefits OOP seemed to promise. Traditional object-oriented programming languages, such as C++, usually impose a long, flat learning curve on the learner. And many potential OOP programmers continued to architect new procedural applications simply because learning enough to be able to design and implement an OOP application seemed too daunting a prospect and outweighed the potential benefits of OOP.

In a perfect world, an object can be used in a form in which only the specialist who implemented the object knows the specifics of the object's implementation. In the real world, the programmer using the object will frequently need to debug or modify the code that implements the object. If the programmer can't easily maintain the object code, use the object in a new project, or modify the object to fit the architecture of a new project, he or she probably has to invest as much development time as had already been invested in coding the object in the first place. An object is of value only if it can be easily maintained and adapted by someone other than the original programmer.

Compared to programs written in other OOP languages, Visual Basic programs are low maintenance programs because the code is easy to read and easy to debug. Visual Basic is also a "safe" language in that a small change in code is unlikely to cause a previously stable program to destabilize and start crashing.

Visual Basic 4 and OOP

Visual Basic 4 supports direct object creation and manipulation through the use of *class modules*. With a class module, you can easily define a type, or class, of object that can be created, destroyed, and renamed on the fly by your VB code. Once you have perfected your class implementation, you can expose the class for use by other programs. When your program exposes classes for use by other applications, it is known as an *object server*. Using Visual Basic 4.0 Professional Edition, you can create object servers in both DLL and EXE executable files. By referencing VB-created servers from outside your server application, you and other programmers can easily reuse many of the objects you've implemented for earlier programming projects.

The use of class modules to create objects brings the power and ease of use of the VB programming environment to OOP. Visual Basic takes care of the intricacies of low-level object implementation and lets you concentrate on what you want your objects to do.

Objects in Programming

In the normal, boring, non-OOP programming world, you call a procedure to perform a specific action. For example, the code for opening a file and putting each line of the file into a list box would look like this:

```
FileHandle = OpenFile("c:\windows\win.ini")
Do Until EOF(FileHandle)
    Line Input #FileHandle, strLine
    lstFileList.AddItem strLine
Loop
Close #FileHandle
```

Let's take a look at the same functionality as it would be written in object-speak. (If this code snippet is your first exposure to an object-oriented programming model, don't worry if the code doesn't make too much sense to you right now. You'll catch on later.) If you used a hypothetical File object instead of a procedural approach, the code to open a file and put each line of the file into a list box would look like this:

```
'Associate the File object with a real file.
MyFile.FileName = "c:\windows\win.ini"
'Tell the File object to open itself.
MyFile.Open
Do While MyFile.HasNextLine
    lstFileList.AddItem MyFile.NextLine
Loop
MyFile.Close
```

The focus of this code snippet is clearly on the MyFile object. The file location is specified by setting the FileName property of the MyFile object, and the object is instructed to take various actions on itself. Notice a significant difference between the first and second code snippets. In the first code fragment, the programmer tracks the file handle and the programmer closes the file. In the second code fragment, the MyFile object tracks the file handle, catches errors, and closes the file. You only need to use the words *MyFile.Open* to open a file or *MyFile.Close* to close a file.

Opening a file is rarely the goal of a program, but it is a frequently required task in most programs. Traditionally, the programmer must keep track of a file handle for each file that is open. A File object enables the programmer to concentrate on the task, such as filling a list, instead of worrying about how to keep track of file handles. In other words, OOP takes away a layer of complexity that is associated with procedurally structured I/O programming.

The code for a File object itself, once written, can also be used in other programs. By reusing the code you have already written, you can take advantage of the time that went into the creation of the file object code.

OOP gives you the capability of using multiple objects of the same class in your program. If the user needs to have two files open simultaneously, a traditional program would have to maintain two file handles and two file positions and clean up two different files. An object-oriented program would simply use two *instances* of a File class. The handles and positions would be maintained by the file objects themselves, which would allow for much more readable and maintainable code. Objects shield the programmers using the objects from the objects' internal implementations. Full containment, or hiding, of an object's internal implementation is known as *encapsulation.*

So What Is an Object?

Look around you. Depending on where you are, you might see a book, a computer, a car, a little kid, a stereo, a cloud, or leftovers from last night. These are all objects. They have properties that describe them, they have the ability to do things, and they have the ability to react to events that happen to them.

Objects and Classes

At this point, we need to make a careful distinction between the *definition* of a class and an *instance* of a class. A blueprint is a full definition of a particular kind of house. It contains the dimensions, material requirements, and structural information necessary to build that kind of house. However, a blueprint of a house is not a house. You can't live in it. The blueprint is useful only when it is handed over to a skilled contractor, who could build many houses of that kind from the same blueprint. Each of the houses would be structurally equivalent—the same class of house—but each house could have, say, a different color based on the preferences of the house buyer.

Let's tie this analogy to Visual Basic class modules. A class module is the blueprint of a particular class of object that you, the programmer, provide to VB. Once you have provided a class module, your program (the buyer) can request a new object of that class from VB (the contractor). Because you provide the complete specification for your class, the new object will have all of the properties, methods, and functionality you specified for the class. Your program (the buyer) is then free to modify the properties (house color, say) of the object.

This chapter will deal with creating class modules. We'll look at the process of creating an actual object from a class module definition of a class in Chapter 5.

Properties

The objects you see around you are all different. Each kind of object has a unique set of properties that define the class the object belongs to. For example, a car is distinguishable from a computer because of the different property sets associated with these objects. The properties for a car might include

WheelCount
BodyStyle
InteriorColor
ExteriorColor
MaxSpeed

while the properties for a computer might include

MonitorStyle
HardDriveSize
AvailableMemory
TypeOfMouse
CPU

You distinguish a particular instance of a class from other objects of the same class by setting the properties of each instance to specific values. When you change a car object's ExteriorColor property to red or your computer's CPU property to Pentium, you are setting a property of your object to a specific color or CPU value. When you make up the blueprint of your object—that is, when you write a class module—you need to choose your property set carefully.

The right properties

A class should have properties appropriate to that category, or class, of object. A File object would have no reason to have a Color property, for instance, because a File can't have a color, but Path and Attribute would be appropriate properties for a File object. Choosing appropriate and useful properties for a class is an important, although relatively simple, part of developing a class. Omitting unnecessary properties is just as important—and even easier to do.

The right values

An object created from a class can refuse to accept a given value for one of its properties. Providing a class of objects with this ability takes a little more work on the part of the programmer but enables objects of that class to protect themselves. When a program sets the FileName property of the File object we've been talking about, for instance, the object could check for the existence of the file name on the system before accepting the new value for the FileName property. If the new value for the FileName property isn't valid, the object could either silently reject the new value by refusing to change the property to the new value, or it could react by raising an error condition or displaying an error message. The choice is up to the programmer who defines the class. Error messages for objects should be explicit enough to tell the program using the object what went wrong, especially because another programmer may also use the object in the future for other programming projects.

To instruct your program to change a property value, use the syntax shown in Figure 4-1:

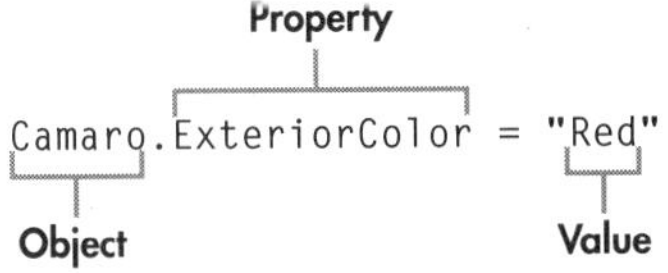

Figure 4-1. *Setting the value of one of an object's properties.*

The program phrase

```
Camaro.ExteriorColor = "Red"
```

means "Camaro, your exterior color is now red." The word on the left of the dot is the object. The word on the right of the dot is the property you want to set. And the word to the right of the equal sign (=) is the value the property is being set to.

Methods

As we stated earlier, objects do things. A car runs, a cloud floats, and a little child cries, among other things. In object-speak, these actions that an object performs are called *methods.*

Calling an object's methods

Your program can instruct an object to do something to itself by calling one of the object's methods. Methods are generally reflexive verbs, which means that the object both performs and receives the action. For example, a car object's methods might include *Start*, *Stop*, *SpeedUp*, *SlowDown*, *Steer*, and *Crash*. A driver, like a program, can tell a car to take any of these actions.

To have your program call a method, you use the syntax shown in Figure 4-2:

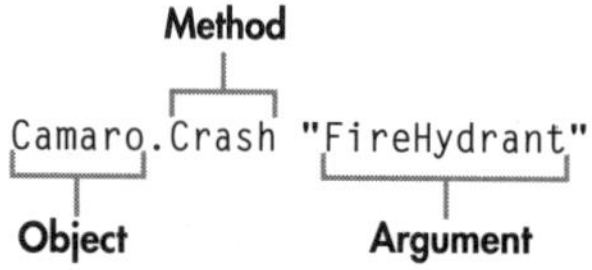

Figure 4-2. *Calling one of an object's methods.*

The program phrase

```
Camaro.Crash "FireHydrant"
```

means "Camaro, go crash into a fire hydrant." OK, let's get more realistic here.

The program phrase *MyFile.Open* we saw earlier (pages 78–79) means "MyFile, open yourself." Our file object would never be used to open another file because it knows only about its own existence and can act only on itself. The great benefit of this is that the MyFile object shields the programmer from having to deal with such details as file handles. Instead, the programmer simply calls a small number of MyFile object methods. For instance, the *Open*, *Close*, and *NextLine* methods are called in our earlier example.

Methods can return values

Just as a function returns a value, a method can return information about the action it was asked to perform. *MyFile.NextLine* not only moves the internal file position to the next line, but it also returns the current line. The returned value is then added directly to the list box. Here's the code again:

```
lstFileList.AddItem MyFile.NextLine
```

Translation: You're calling the *AddItem* method of a ListBox object (lstFileList). As an argument in that call to *AddItem*, you are passing in the return value of the *NextLine* method of the MyFile object. The current line of the MyFile file object is incremented at the same time by the *NextLine* method. Think for a second about everything that's happening in that one line of code before we move on.

The right methods

Following are examples of potential objects and a few correspondingly appropriate methods for them:

Object	Methods
File	*Open, Close, Copy, NextLine*
Record	*DeleteRow, AddField, DeleteField, InsertField*
List	*Append, Sort*
Cursor	*GoEnd, GoStart, Backward, Forward, Blink*
Monster	*Eat, Fight, Cower, Slobber*

Internal Information

Some of the variables and procedures in a class module don't need to be exposed to external procedures that use objects of that class. The implementation of an object will generally maintain some internal information and call some internal routines. The properties and methods exposed to other procedures, programs, and programmers by a complicated object rarely represent more than a fraction of the data and procedures the object needs to function correctly.

To understand this point, let's look at an example. We've already established that a car's properties might include WheelCount, ExteriorColor, and MaxSpeed and that a car's methods might include *Start, Stop,* and *Steer.*

However, there is also a great deal of internal information from which the programmer of the automobile object (the driver) is completely shielded. The driver's not having direct access to, an understanding of, or even an awareness of the following internal variables and procedures of an automobile doesn't detract from the usefulness of the automobile to the driver.

Internal variables: *Fuel_AirMixture, RPM, Temperature, OilPressure, Voltage, FiringOrder, FloatLevel,* and so on. Clearly, if a driver had to worry about all of the internal variables of an engine while driving at freeway speeds, a car object would be basically useless to him or her. The driver would rapidly invoke the *Crash* method.

Internal procedures: *PumpFuel, TurnShaft, BlowAir,* and so on. Like the internal variables, these internal procedures are invisible to the driver, and that doesn't detract from the driver's ability to drive the car.

In programming, a well-implemented object allows the programmer to easily use the object instead of having to worry about the internals of the object. On the freeway, a driver is free to admire the scenery (and watch the road) while driving instead of having to constantly adjust the engine temperature.

There's nothing wrong with understanding the internal implementation of objects with which we program, of course. However, *a full understanding of how an object is implemented is not required in order to make full use of the object.* Therein lies the power of reusable code as it's implemented in object-oriented programming.

Now that we have some understanding of what an object is and of why such creatures might be beneficial to the programming ecosystem, let's delve into some specifics of how an object is implemented using Visual Basic. Note that since the MailBox class module we describe below fully defines a MailBox class, you can proceed to the next chapter at this point to learn how to create a MailBox object instance. Not knowing the details of the internal implementation won't hamper your use of the MailBox class in the least. If you plan on implementing your own classes (which is what we'll be doing in most of the chapters in this book) instead of just using existing classes, proceed with this chapter.

Rolling Your Own Object

To learn how to implement an elementary object in Visual Basic, we'll define a very simple MailBox class in this chapter. We'll create instances of the MailBox class in later chapters. The MailBox class has two properties, HasMail and PostColor, that determine whether there is mail in the mailbox and the color of the post on which the mailbox sits.

The class also has two methods, *Draw* and *SetProperties*. *Draw* is used to render a picture of the mailbox, and *SetProperties* displays a dialog that can enable a user to set the HasMail and PostColor properties.

Picture This

Figure 4-3 shows two instances of the MailBox class. The first object has the default settings for a new object of the MailBox class: HasMail = *False* and PostColor = *0* (black). The second object's HasMail property is set to *True*, and its PostColor property is set to *7* (gray).

Figure 4-3. *Two instances of the MailBox class. One MailBox object (the default) doesn't have mail and has a black post. The other has mail and has a gray post.*

NOTE The legitimate values for the PostColor property are *0* through *15*. Assigning any other value to the PostColor property will cause an error.

MailBox Object: Step by Step

Let's get started with defining the MailBox class.

1. Open a new project in Visual Basic.
2. From the Insert menu, select Class Module. You'll get a new class module with a default name of Class1. (See Figure 4-4.)

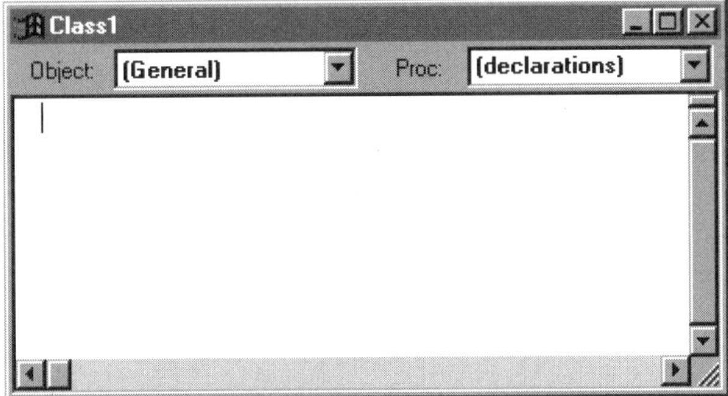

Figure 4-4. *A blank Visual Basic class module. This class module will eventually be molded into the definition of a MailBox class.*

3. Press F4 to activate the property sheet, and change the setting of the Name property to *MailBox*.

This is the beginning of our first class definition. We'll work with this class module until it defines a complete MailBox class. But before we can implement the MailBox class, we need to know how to expose properties and methods and how to shield the user of a MailBox object from the internal implementation of our class.

Private vs. Public

The programmer defining a class uses the keywords *Public* and *Private* to distinguish between the class's exposed properties and methods and the class's internal variables and procedures. If a variable or a procedure is declared *Private*, it's internal to the class module and can be set or called—accessed—only by procedures inside the class module.

You can change internal variables and procedures into properties and methods simply by declaring them with the *Public* keyword. You can still use them inside the class module, just as you can private variables and procedures, but they are also exposed to procedures outside the class module.

All sub, function, and property procedures in a Visual Basic class module default to public access. (We'll look at what a property procedure is in the section right after "Public Variables.") To designate a procedure as internal only, you must use the *Private* keyword. On the other hand, all module-level variables in a class module are private by default, so you must use the *Public* keyword to expose a module-level variable as a property of the class object. Public sub and function procedures become methods of the object. Public variables and property procedures become the properties of the object. Although the variables in a class module default to private access and procedures default to public access, you should still use the *Public* and *Private* keywords for clarity in your code or if you are unsure of the default in a particular coding situation.

Public Variables

The easiest way to implement a property in a class module is to declare a variable as *Public*. Once a variable has been defined with public access, it is exposed to all procedures both inside and outside the class module. The HasMail property of the MailBox object is defined in this way.

```
Public HasMail As Boolean
```

It's that simple to create an exposed property.

Although no validation code is associated with the HasMail property, VB does provide a certain level of built-in validation. It isn't possible to set HasMail to an invalid value because we defined the HasMail variable as a Boolean type, which means that HasMail can accept only values that can be coerced to *True* or *False*. Since VB won't allow a programmer to assign an improper value to a Boolean variable, a MailBox object can rely on HasMail's value at any time.

Although this simple, one-line way to expose a property works very well for the Boolean HasMail property, it has two disadvantages when you're working with properties in general: the problems of *validation* and *notification*. Let's explore as an example the validation and notification requirements of the fictional File object we described earlier in the chapter (see pages 78–79 again).

When a new value is assigned to a File object's FileName property, the File object shouldn't accept the value if the file doesn't exist on the system. The HasMail property of the MailBox object can rely on VB for value validation, but ensuring that a program using the File object can set the FileName property to only a legal value is a more complex requirement.

In addition to validating the new value of the FileName property, the File object should reset itself. If the File object already has a file open, then that file should be closed. The new file should be opened, and the file position should be reset to the top of the file. This is called *notification:* the File object is notified of the property value change, and its internal state is brought up to date.

Cross-Reference VBA Language Concepts: Boolean Comparison

Property Procedures

It should be clear by now that the one-line approach to defining a property doesn't provide the validation or notification required by many object properties. In order for an object to correctly handle the value assigned to one of its properties, it must be able to call a procedure to validate the value and/or take some action (notification). Since the PostColor property of the MailBox object, for example, will accept only values in the range *0* through *15*, the value assigned to the PostColor property must be validated to enforce that rule. Let's step through the code necessary to implement the PostColor property correctly as our first example of setting a validated property.

VB provides *Property Let* and *Property Get* procedures to validate a value assigned to a property before the new value will be stored in a private variable. The *Property Let* procedure is called when a value is assigned to a property:

```
<object>.<property> = <new value>
```

The *Property Get* procedure is called when the value is read out of the property:

```
<current value> = <object>.<property>
```

Property Let

You can use *Property Let* to create a procedure that acts like a public variable when it's set from outside the class module but that also contains the code necessary to validate values assigned to the variable. To use *Property Let,* you first create a private variable in the class module—one that can't be accessed from outside the class module. You then create a *Property Let* procedure that does the necessary validation. A programmer who wants to set the value of the private variable must do so by calling the *Property Let* procedure. Of course, the programmer setting the property doesn't need to know whether the property is a variable or a *Property Let* procedure that validates a variable. The external code for setting a property with a *Property Let* procedure looks just like the code for setting a public variable, but using a *Property Let* procedure with a private variable, instead of exposing a public variable directly, protects the programmer using the object from assigning an invalid value to the property.

Usually, a *Property Let* procedure raises an error if a new value isn't acceptable. The error result gives the programmer a chance to fix the problem instead of proceeding blindly with the false impression that all is well. If a *Property Let* procedure accepts the new value, the value is stored in a private variable.

Let's look at the code in the MailBox class module that validates the PostColor property. The goal of the validation code is to accept only the values *0* through *15* for the PostColor property.

First we create a private variable that will hold a MailBox object's color: m_PostColor. As in standard Visual Basic modules, the *m_* prefix signifies a module-level variable, a variable that's private to the module in which it is defined. (This prefix isn't used for public variables because it goes against standard naming conventions for exposed properties. An exposed property has the same name as the public variable or property procedure that defines it.)

```
Private m_PostColor As Integer
```

Next we create a *Property Let* procedure a programmer will use to update the m_PostColor variable. In this case, let's simply name the procedure *PostColor*.

```
Property Let PostColor(ColorIndex As Integer)
    Select Case ColorIndex
        'ColorIndex is acceptable.
        Case 0 To 15
            m_PostColor = ColorIndex
        'This ColorIndex is not allowed.
        Case Else
            Err.Raise 5, "MailBox Object: PostColor Property", _
                "PostColor must be from 0 through 15"
    End Select
End Property
```

You'll notice that the *PostColor* procedure has a ColorIndex argument. The value passed into the ColorIndex argument corresponds to the new value being assigned to the PostColor property. The following code snippet will try to set the PostColor property:

```
MyMailBox.PostColor = 16
```

The value on the right (*16*) will be passed to the *PostColor Property Let* procedure as the ColorIndex argument. In this case, the procedure will raise an error indicating that *16* is not an acceptable value.

When an error is raised while your code is running in the VB environment, the default behavior is to stop the program in the class module where the error occurs. If you would prefer to return the error to the procedure that called your object code, choose the Advanced tab of the Options dialog (select Tools-Options), and change the Error Trapping option to Break on Unhandled Errors. Now when the line

```
MyMailBox.PostColor = 16
```

calls the *PostColor Property Let* procedure, and that procedure raises an error, execution stops on the calling line instead of on the *Property Let*. (The error trapping options can also be set at run-time by means of the popup context menu of the code pane.)

Cross-Reference VBA Language Concepts: Rich Error Information, Error Trapping

Property Get

Once an object property has been set, a programmer using the object must also be able to access the property's current value, so the *Property Let* procedure has a companion procedure called *Property Get*. The *Property Get* procedure is generally much simpler than the *Property Let* procedure because the purpose of *Property Get* is simply to allow the programmer to retrieve a private variable's value.

Here's the *PostColor Property Get* procedure in our MailBox class for returning the value of the private variable m_PostColor:

```
Property Get PostColor() As Integer
    PostColor = m_PostColor
End Property
```

The following line of code would call the *PostColor Property Get* procedure:

```
colorOfPost = MyMailBox.PostColor
```

VB requires the arguments in the *Property Let/Property Get* pairs to correspond in type and position. The *Property Get* procedure always has one less parameter than the corresponding *Property Let* procedure, and the return type of the *Property Get* procedure must always be the same as the type of the last parameter of the *Property Let* procedure. Hence, the expression

```
Object.Property1 = Object.Property1
```

should never fail (assuming that both a *Property Let* and a *Property Get* have been implemented for Property1).

Although both *Property Let* and *Property Get* procedures are available, it is not necessary to implement both of them for every property. To define a read only property, implement just the *Property Get* and omit the *Property Let*, or use *Private Property Let*. Similarly, you can create a write only property by not defining a *Property Get* procedure.

Implementing Methods

Methods are even easier to implement than properties. To create a method that returns a value, create a public function in your class module. For a method with no return value, use a public sub. Remember that the return value from a function can be ignored, so if there is useful information to return, you can go ahead and implement a function without forcing all callers to look at the return value. As we noted before, the only difference between ordinary subs and functions and subs or functions that also act as methods is the *Public* keyword.

For an example of a method, let's look at the *SetProperties* method from the MailBox class. *SetProperties* doesn't return a value, so it's a sub. Even though the sub procedure defaults to public, we use the *Public* keyword explicitly to remind ourselves that *SetProperties* is a method.

```
Public Sub SetProperties()
Dim dlgForm As New MailBoxDialog
    Set dlgForm.MailBox = Me
    dlgForm.Show vbModal
End Sub
```

Cross-Reference You may not recognize some of the VBA keywords that show up in our *SetProperties* method. We'll take up the keywords *New*, *Set*, and *Me* in Chapter 5.

Built-In Class Events

Every class has two built-in event procedures you can choose to implement as you define your object classes. *Class_Initialize()* is called when an object of the class is created, and *Class_Terminate()* is called immediately before the object is destroyed.

To see outline code for a class's *Class_Initialize()* and *Class_Terminate()* event procedures, view the class module in the code pane, select Class from the Object: dropdown, and select either Initialize or Terminate from the Proc: dropdown.

The *Class_Initialize()* procedure is the best place to initialize internal variables. In our MailBox class, for instance, the PostColor property will receive a default value of *7* instead of *0* if you put

```
m_PostColor = 7
```

in the *Class_Initialize()* procedure.

Use the *Class_Terminate()* procedure to clean up before an object is destroyed. Generally, VB requires that the programmer do very little cleanup work. The memory used by internal and exposed variables is automatically freed when an object is destroyed. Not all cleanup is automatic, however. Any open file that was opened by and is owned by the object should be closed before the object is destroyed, and forms shown by the object should be unloaded at this point.

SUMMARY

- An object has properties and methods. Setting a property describes an object, whereas calling a method instructs the object to do something to itself.
- Public variables and property procedures define the properties of an object that can be set from outside a class module.
- The public subs and functions in a class module correspond to the methods of an object.
- You can hide the internal implementation of an object's methods and properties from the programmer who uses the object.

Referring to the creation and the destruction of an object makes it sound like a tangible entity. This chapter has skirted the issue of how an object is actually created. So far, all of our examples of using properties and methods have assumed that the object already exists. Now that we've covered some basic facts about implementing a class module, let's move on to breathing life into such a creature. In Chapter 5, we'll consider the birth, lifetime, and death of an object. You may want to pause here and imagine your object as it should be. Certainly, once you create it, it will begin to have a mind of its own...

5

Creating Objects

Microsoft Excel, Access, PowerPoint, and Word are all capable of exposing objects that can be manipulated by Visual Basic for Applications (VBA) code. Before we explore the Microsoft Office for Windows 95 objects in detail, however, we need to get a feel for what it takes to create and manipulate objects with VBA. By taking the time to get a good understanding of how to create and control an object in VBA, we'll have a much easier time creating and controlling Office 95 objects. The fundamentals of creating and manipulating objects with VBA are the same everywhere—regardless of whether the VBA "host" is VB4, Microsoft Excel, or Access—so in this chapter we'll concentrate on objects in general. In later chapters, we'll look at objects provided by particular applications.

NOTE Like the other Microsoft Office for Windows 95 products, Microsoft Access, which is included in the Professional Edition of Microsoft Office for Windows 95, exposes objects that can be manipulated by VBA code. And like Visual Basic 4 and Microsoft Excel, Access can act as a VBA "host." This book covers only the products included in the Standard Edition of Microsoft Office for Windows 95 and won't go into using Access as a VBA host.

Creating Instances from Classes

A class is of absolutely no use on its own. Although the class modules we learned to define in Chapter 4 give us the ability to create rich class descriptions, these class definitions are useless until we create instances of those classes. The process of creating an instance of a class is called (naturally enough) *instantiation,* and in this chapter, we'll deal with instantiating, or creating specific instances of, classes.

Think of that blueprint of a house we talked about in Chapter 4 as a House class. You can't live in the blueprint of the house. To get a House object to live in, you need to actually build a house. Once you've drafted the blueprint, you can hire a contractor to build one—or more than one—specific House instance. Fortunately, it's much easier to create an instance of a VB4 class than it is to build a house.

In this chapter, we'll use the MailBox class we defined in Chapter 4 to demonstrate declaring an object variable, creating an object, assigning an object to one or more object variables, and getting rid of the object when it's no longer needed. We've written a *Mailbox Object Sample* program, shown in Figure 5-1, that implements and uses MailBox objects, and we'll run this program occasionally to see what happens as we manipulate these objects. Although a partial code listing for the *Mailbox Object Sample* program appears at the end of the chapter, your understanding the principles we're making use of is more important than your being able to reproduce the program.

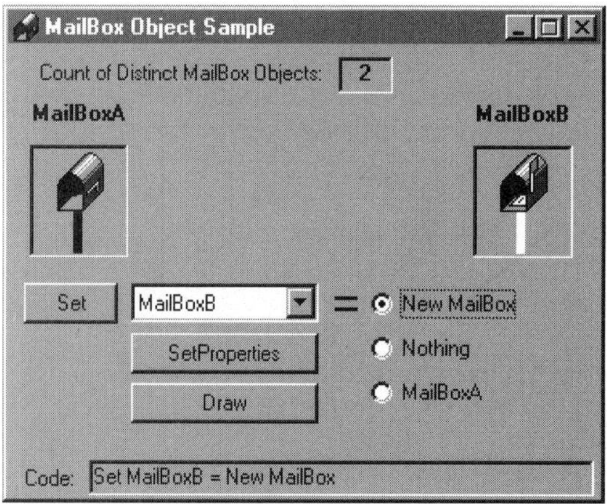

Figure 5-1. *The* MailBox Object Sample *program.*

Life Cycle of an Instance

Every object goes through various stages in its life cycle. As a programmer, you need to understand each of these stages in order to correctly control the objects you create.

Before we look at the *MailBox Object Sample* program, let's examine the stages in the life cycle of an object. First, we *declare* a variable. The variable we declare will represent the object in all stages of its life cycle and is known as an *object variable*. Declaring an object variable tells VBA of our intent to create an object somewhere in a procedure and gives us a way to refer to the object. Next, we actually *create* the instance somewhere in our code. After creating the instance, we can manipulate it using the object variable name we specified in the declaration statement. Finally, as soon as the object variable is set to nothing, the object is *destroyed* by VBA. Every object we use must go through this cycle of declaration, creation, use, and destruction.

Declaration

If we want to use an instance of a class in our program, we first tell VBA in a *type declaration statement* the class (type) of the object and the name of the object variable. As we do with a declaration for any other variable, we use the keywords *Dim*, *Public*, *Private*, and *Static* in the declaration of an object variable. As with the scope of other variables, the position of the object variable declaration in our module will determine whether our object variable has module-level or local scope.

Hard typing

Let's look at an example of an object variable declaration. To declare a module-level object variable of a hypothetical Vehicle class, we'd put this line at the top of our code module (the general declaration section):

```
Private MyVehicle As Vehicle
```

This line of code tells VBA we're going to use the variable MyVehicle to refer to an instance of the Vehicle class.

To create an instance of the MailBox class, the declaration line would be

```
Dim MailBoxA As MailBox
```

Once again, we're telling VBA we'll use the object variable MailBoxA somewhere in our program to refer to an instance of the MailBox class. (Remember that a module-level variable is private by default.) The use of *As Vehicle* and *As MailBox* in the declaration statements we've seen so far is known as *hard typing*. When we hard type an object variable to make it belong to a specific class, we tell VBA everything there is to know about the object before it is even created. VBA knows the properties and the methods exposed by the class and can let us know before the program runs whether we've used an object of the class correctly—that is, whether we've used a valid property or method of the object.

Other ways to declare object variables

By hard typing our object variables, we enable VBA to use our objects in the most efficient way possible at run-time, and we validate our use of the objects' properties and methods when the program is compiled. However, we don't have to hard type our object variables. VBA provides four other methods for declaring object variables that can be useful depending on the programming situation.

The first alternative for declaring an object variable looks like this:

```
Dim MailBoxA As Object
```

As Object tells VBA that the variable MailBoxA refers to is some kind of object—and that's all the information it provides. VBA doesn't know the type of the object that will be referred to by the MailBoxA variable. Because we haven't told VBA the class of our MailBoxA object variable, VBA can't warn us if we use a property or a method that doesn't belong to the object. We won't find out until run-time whether we're using a valid property or method of the object class.

The remaining three alternatives for declaring an object variable are essentially equivalent to one another:

```
Dim MailBoxA As Variant
```

is equivalent to

```
Dim MailBoxA
```

which is equivalent to

```
[No declaration]
```

Since Variant is the default type for VBA,

```
Dim MailBoxA
```

has exactly the same meaning as

```
Dim MailBoxA As Variant
```

You can also omit the declaration altogether if you want MailBoxA to be a Variant type, but only if you don't have *Option Explicit* set at the top of your module. The *Option Explicit* setting requires variables to be declared before they are used in code. It prevents subtle errors caused by the misspelling of variable names. Use it!

Declaring a variable as type Variant makes it harder for VBA to determine the actual type of the object referred to by your variable. A variable declared as Variant can contain an Integer, an object reference, a String, a String array, or any other VBA type. When you use a Variant variable to refer to an object, VBA can't assume at compile-time that the Variant variable will actually refer to an object at run-time. Consequently, VBA needs to check what type of data is contained in a Variant variable every time it encounters the variable at run-time. Once VBA determines that a variable declared as Variant contains an object reference, it uses the object reference the same way it uses an object reference contained in a variable declared *As Object*.

So we can declare an object variable five different ways:

```
Dim MailBoxA As MailBox       'As an object of the MailBox object class

Dim MailBoxA As Object        'As an object of some object class

Dim MailBoxA As Variant       'As a variable of some type

Dim MailBoxA                  'As a variable of some type

[No declaration]              'As an implicitly declared variable of
                              'some type
```

Although each of these declarations is syntactically correct VBA code, we're better off using the first, most explicit, kind of declaration. Let's look in depth at why hard typing our object variables is the best way to code in VBA.

Performance benefits of hard typing

When we set properties and call methods using our object variable, we are forcing VBA to communicate with our object at run-time. (Setting a property describes the running object, and calling a method instructs the object to take an action.)

If our object variable isn't hard typed, VBA must do a lot of extra communication with our running object in order to set one of its properties or call one of its methods. The extra communication goes on completely behind the scenes, but it requires a lot of extra effort on the part of VBA, which can hurt the performance of our program. To see an example of the extra effort VBA must go to, let's tap into the conversation between VBA and a Car object when a program wants to call the Car object's *Drive* method.

```
MyVehicle.Drive Destination:="Texas"
```

If MyVehicle is not a hard-typed variable, VBA must interrogate the object in the following sequence in order to enable a program to call the *Drive* method:

1. Object, do you have a property or a method called *Drive*? If you do, then return the identification number for *Drive*.
2. Object, I'm trying to call *Drive* as a method. I'm passing one argument called Destination. The Destination parameter is of the String type. Can you process this request?
3. Object, if you can process this request, then do so. The Destination argument has a value of "Texas". Tell me if the *Drive* method succeeds or fails.

If the object contained in the MyVehicle variable answers No to either of the first two questions, then the *Drive* method doesn't even get out of the garage. If VBA receives a positive response to both of the first two questions, then the *Drive* method will be called and will either succeed or fail. Even if the object is able to process the request and the *Drive* method succeeds, we have still forced VBA to engage in a lot of idle chatter instead of continuing with the execution of our program. The extra communication required to set a property or call a method of an object of unknown type takes up a lot of valuable time, especially if we're calling a lot of properties and methods. The overhead is even more significant when the object we're using is provided by another application, as we'll see in Chapter 6.

Setting properties and calling methods using an object variable that hasn't been hard typed can be compared to asking your mother-in-law if your spouse is able to kiss, asking permission to kiss your spouse (permission is granted only after a detailed description of the prospective kiss is submitted to the mother-in-law object), reporting back to the mother-in-law object after the kiss, and then repeating this process for every kiss.

If we hard type our object variables, VBA will be able to determine *at compile-time* whether we've asked our program to set a property or call a method that a running instance of our class won't be able to process correctly. Our code will fail to compile, and we'll never have to get a No answer from an instance at run-time. Since VBA determines at compile-time the validity of the call our program makes, VBA can get right down to business at run-time and make the call directly instead of having to first verify the validity of the call. As long as it knows that the object variable contains a valid object, VBA can communicate directly with the properties and methods of the object without having to constantly communicate with the object itself.

Going back to our kissing example: hard typing an object variable is equivalent to giving your spouse a [description deleted—the mother-in-law object doesn't need to know the details] kiss, without even asking the mother-in-law object—can you imagine? In this light, hard typing objects is a very romantic proposition indeed, especially if you plan on a lot of kisses. It's a good idea to get into the habit of hard typing now.

Let's summarize our understanding of hard typing variables:

- If we hard type a variable as belonging to a specific class, VBA is able to give us feedback at compile-time about whether we're setting a property or calling a method of the object correctly.
- When an object variable is hard typed, VBA can set a property or call a method of the object directly. If we choose not to hard type an object variable, VBA must interrogate the running object every time we set a property or call a method.

Object Creation

Passengers, fasten your seatbelts! You've been hearing about plans for an object trip for a couple of chapters, and now we're actually about to leave the ground.

A declaration of intent describing a future instance,

```
Dim MailBoxA As MailBox
```

will tell VBA that MailBoxA will refer only to an object of the MailBox class. However, until we assign an actual MailBox object to MailBoxA, the object variable will refer to nothing. When a program first starts, all object variables in the program refer to nothing.

Creating new objects

We can make the variable MailBoxA refer to a new MailBox instance by using the *Set* keyword to assign a new instance to the object variable. The new instance of the MailBox class is created by means of the *New* keyword as follows:

```
'Hard type the MailBoxA object variable.
Dim MailBoxA As MailBox
:
'Create an instance of the MailBox class.
Set MailBoxA = New MailBox
```

MailBoxA now refers to a new, running MailBox instance, which is much more useful than having MailBoxA refer to nothing.

Immediately after VBA creates a new instance of a VB class, the *Class_Initialize()* procedure is called—if we decided to add code to the initialize routine when we wrote the class module. The *Class_Initialize()* procedure should contain the code we want to execute to initialize the new instance of the class. For an example of a *Class_Initialize()* procedure, let's look at the *Class_Initialize()* code in the MailBox object class module:

```
Private Sub Class_Initialize()
    'Tell this application that an object has been created.
    gReferences.AddReference
End Sub
```

This routine tells the global gReferences object in the MailBox application that an instance of the MailBox class has just been created by calling the *AddReference* method of the global object.

The *Class_Initialize()* procedure is typically used to set default property values for an object. For example, if we'd like a newly created MailBox instance to have its HasMail property set to *True* and its PostColor property set to *15* (white), we'd modify *Class_Initialize()*:

```
Private Sub Class_Initialize()
    'Tell this application that an object has been created.
    gReferences.AddReference
    HasMail = True
    m_PostColor = 15
End Sub
```

If we don't specifically set default values at this point, all public and private module-level variables will default to *0* for numeric variables, *False* for Boolean variables, " " for strings, *Empty* for Variants, and *Nothing* for all object variables.

Notice something odd about the way we set the PostColor property? PostColor is implemented by means of a *Property Get/Let*, as described in Chapter 4. We don't want to execute the code in the *Property Let* procedure, so we assign the PostColor value directly to the private variable (m_PostColor) that holds the property value. We can do this because the procedure we're executing is contained in the MailBox class module.

Running the *MailBox Object Sample* application

Let's veer off now and take a look at the *MailBox Object Sample* application in action.

1. Copy the contents of the \Chapter4\MailBox directory from the companion CD to your hard drive.
2. Run the MailBx32.Exe program. This executable file was created from the MBoxObj.Vbp project located in the same directory. MailBx32.Exe both implements and uses the MailBox object. (In the next chapter, we'll make use of the MailBox object in a different program.)
3. Choose MailBoxA in the dropdown (or click the empty MailBoxA container).
4. Click the New MailBox option.
5. Click the Set button (or double-click the New MailBox option). You now see a MailBox object that has the default property values drawn in the MailBoxA container. The Count of Distinct Mailbox Objects has also increased from 0 to 1 (surprise!). The count of distinct objects was incremented by the *AddReference* method of the gReferences object, which was called by the *Class_Initialize()* event procedure of the MailBox class.
6. Click the SetProperties button, or double-click the MailBoxA container to get the MailBox Properties dialog. (See Figure 5-2.)

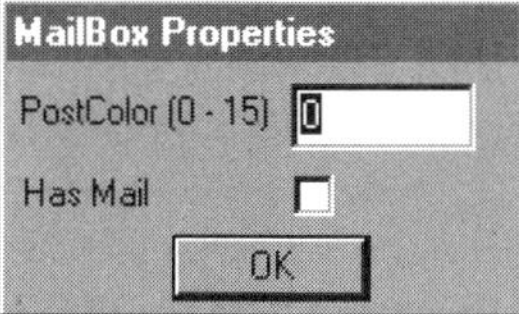

Figure 5-2. *The MailBox Properties dialog box.*

7. Set the PostColor to *11* and click the Has Mail option check box. Click OK. The MailBox Object Sample dialog should now look like the one shown in Figure 5-3.

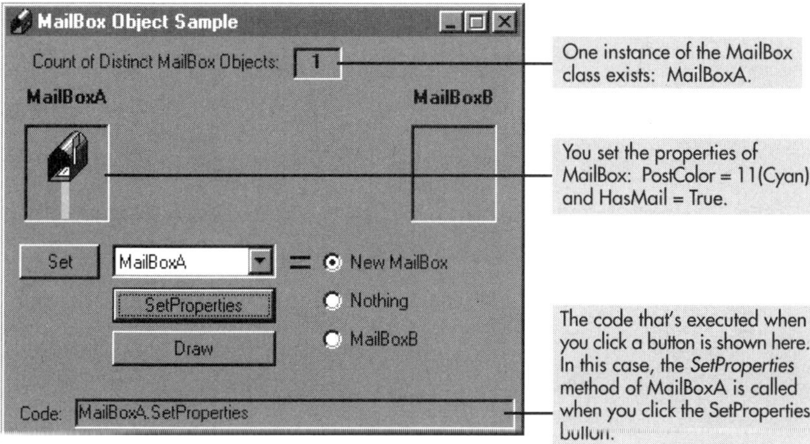

Figure 5-3. *MailBoxA: one instance of the MailBox class.*

You've had your first taste of creating and manipulating an object. You can close the *MailBox Object Sample* program for now if you like.

Implicit creation

We've explicitly created a MailBox object with the *New* keyword and assigned it to the MailBoxA variable using a *Set* statement. Using the *New* and *Set* keywords to assign a new object to an object variable is known as *explicit creation.* VBA also allows *implicit creation,* meaning that a *Set* statement is not required to assign a new object to an object variable. When implicit creation is specified, the object variable is automatically assigned a new instance the first time a property or method is called by means of the object variable. We specify implicit creation by using the *New* keyword in the object variable declaration statement. The following line of code is placed in the MBoxObj.Bas module to declare an implicitly created object variable with global scope:

```
Public gReferences As New References
```

When implicit creation is specified in this way, VBA will always check to see if an object is assigned to the gReferences object variable before calling a method or property by means of gReferences. This type of checking creates a small amount of overhead, but when you use implicit creation for an object variable, you will certainly never see the "Object variable not set" error message (VBA run-time error 91) because the object variable will never be used uninitialized.

When we use the *As New* syntax, we also lose some control over the object creation process because we don't explicitly tell VBA when to create the object. In fact, we can't even tell if an object has already been created because the phrase *obj Is Nothing* might actually create the object. (We'll take a look at using *Is Nothing* later in this chapter.)

So when should you rely on implicit creation? If you're not sure where an object variable will first be used in your program, implicit creation is very useful. For example, the *MailBox Object Sample* program has a References class that's used to display the current count of distinct objects. The program maintains one global instance of this class in the gReferences object variable. The *Class_Initialize()* procedure in the MailBox class calls the *AddReference* method of the gReferences variable, and the *Class_Terminate()* procedure calls the *ReleaseReference* method to keep the object count current. The Output-Label property of the class is set in the *Form_Load()* event procedure of the sample program's main form. So where should the References object referred to by the gReferences object variable be created?

Now we have a small dilemma. It is possible to have our program use the MailBox object without first loading the form—in fact, we'll have our program do this in the next chapter—so the MailBox object can't rely on the *Form_Load()* event procedure to create the References object referred to by the gReferences object variable. Therefore, sometimes gReferences does not refer to a running References object when the MailBox class's *Class_Initialize()* procedure calls the *AddReference* method, and sometimes it does. Since we can't determine where the References class needs to be instantiated, we use implicit creation. Implicit creation completely eliminates the need to initialize the gReferences variable with a *Set . . . = New* statement because the variable is self-instantiating.

Object Destruction

Just as an object is created by means of the *Set* and *New* keywords, an object can be destroyed at any time by means of the *Set* and *Nothing* keywords. The following line of code will destroy the object in MailBoxA:

```
Set MailBoxA = Nothing
```

Let's use the sample program to see what happens when an object is destroyed.

1. Start the MailBx32.Exe program again.
2. Click the Set button to create a new MailBox instance.
3. Click the Nothing option.
4. Click the Set button.

The object contained in the MailBoxA variable has now been destroyed. Just as the *Class_Initialize()* procedure is called right after an object is created, the *Class_Terminate()* procedure is called right before the object is destroyed. In the case of the MailBox class, the distinct object count is decremented in the *Class_Terminate()* procedure, just as it was incremented earlier in the *Class_Initialize()* procedure. Here's the *Class_Terminate()* procedure from the MailBox class module:

```
Private Sub Class_Terminate()
    'Tell this application that an object has been destroyed.
    gReferences.ReleaseReference
End Sub
```

Implicit destruction

When an object variable first comes into scope—when a program starts running, for instance—the variable always has a value of *Nothing*. You must either explicitly or implicitly assign a class instance to the object variable before you can call properties or methods on the variable. Conversely, when an object variable goes out of scope, an implicit *Set . . . = Nothing* is performed to destroy the object.

Multiple Object References

An object is assigned to a specific object variable when the object is first created. The object won't be destroyed until the object variable goes out of scope or is explicitly set to *Nothing*:

```
'Create a MailBox object.
Set MailBoxA = New MailBox
:
'Destroy the MailBox object.
Set MailBoxA = Nothing
```

To help you determine when an object will be destroyed, just remember this simple fact of object life: *for an object to remain in existence, it must be assigned to at least one object variable.* If any given object could be assigned to only one variable at a time, this rule would have only limited meaning. However, VBA allows an object to be assigned to several object variables at one time. In fact, once the same object is assigned to two object variables, there is no functional distinction between accessing the object through the second variable and accessing it through the first.

Let's look at an example. Suppose you have a Vehicle object assigned to the YourVehicle object variable. However, your family has only one car, so your vehicle is also driven by your 16-year-old son. Your family has a SonVehicle object variable to which the same Vehicle instance is assigned. Both the YourVehicle variable and the SonVehicle variable refer to a single Vehicle object with the following properties:

```
WheelCount = 4 Wheels
BodyStyle = 4-door, Sedan
InteriorColor = Brown Vinyl
ExteriorColor = Yellow
MaxSpeed = 60 MPH
```

Now let's say that your son takes a drive in SonVehicle:

```
SonVehicle.Drive
SonVehicle.Crash "Tree"
```

You'll be in for a surprise the next time you use YourVehicle because the BodyStyle property has changed to *4-door, Sedan with a BIG DENT.* You've probably noticed a control problem here caused by assigning an object to more than one object variable at the same time. The YourVehicle variable doesn't have complete control of the family's Vehicle instance because the same instance is assigned to the SonVehicle variable.

When an object is assigned to two variables, either variable can be used to set the properties or call the methods of the object. The code containing the other object variable has no knowledge of these settings or calls, so you might be in for a few surprises. (For a discussion of object variable identity, see the "Who am I?" section later in this chapter.) You can resolve this conflict by setting one of the object variables to *Nothing*:

```
Set SonVehicle = Nothing
```

This statement will leave YourVehicle as the only object variable to which the family's Vehicle instance is assigned. Having only one variable name to which the Vehicle instance is assigned will eliminate any surprises when you try to call the *Drive* method in the future. (You'll be implementing a SonBicycle object very soon.)

Assigning an object to variables

The *Set* statement is used to assign an object to an object variable, just as it was used to assign the newly created object to the initial variable. The same instance can be assigned to the variable MailBoxB, for example, as to the variable MailBoxA:

```
Set MailBoxB = MailBoxA
```

Assuming MailBoxA refers to a running MailBox instance, this statement causes the following to happen:

- If MailBoxB currently refers to a running instance, VBA does an implicit

  ```
  Set MailBoxB = Nothing
  ```

- VBA assigns the same MailBox instance to MailBoxB as to MailBoxA. MailBoxA and MailBoxB are then each said to have a *reference* to the same MailBox instance.

NOTE A *reference* is the assignment of a running object to an object variable. Given any object variable with a valid reference to an object, a new reference to the same object can be obtained with the *Set* statement. An instance *terminates* (vanishes) when its *reference count* reaches 0, meaning it is no longer assigned to any object variable.

Now that MailBoxA and MailBoxB refer to the same instance of the MailBox class, both the MailBoxA variable and the MailBoxB variable must be set to *Nothing* if the instance is to be destroyed. In other words, as long as at least one variable refers to the object, the object is not destroyed.

Let's look at our MailBox sample again.

1. Close and restart the MailBx32.Exe program.
2. Click the Set button to execute

   ```
   Set MailBoxA = New MailBox
   ```

3. Select MailBoxB from the dropdown. Click the Set button to execute

   ```
   Set MailBoxB = New MailBox
   ```

   The object count is now 2.
4. Click the SetProperties button, and select different properties for the instance assigned to MailBoxB. Click OK.
5. Change the selected option from New MailBox to MailBoxA. Click the Set button to execute

   ```
   Set MailBoxB = MailBoxA
   ```

Notice that the object count is now back to 1 and that MailBoxB now looks like MailBoxA. Since MailBoxB was the only variable that referred to the second MailBox instance, the implicit

```
Set MailBoxB = Nothing
```

destroyed the object that was assigned to MailBoxB.

6. Click the Nothing option and the Set button to execute

```
Set MailBoxB = Nothing
```

The object count remains 1.

7. Select MailBoxA from the dropdown. Click the Nothing option and the Set button to execute

```
Set MailBoxA = Nothing
```

The object count is now 0.

Notice that the object count remained at 1 when you set MailBoxB to *Nothing* in step 6. Remember that the object isn't destroyed until the last variable referring to it leaves scope or is set to *Nothing* (step 7). Play around with the *MailBox Object Sample* application to make sure you can control creating and destroying MailBox objects.

The ability to have multiple object variables refer to a single running object is a very powerful feature of VBA. For example, when you're using an object provided by the Microsoft Excel application, several different programs may each have an object variable that refers to the same Microsoft Excel Application object. It isn't necessary for each program to create a new instance. Similarly, when you assign an object to an object variable and then pass the object variable as an argument to a procedure, the argument name becomes a second variable referring to the same object. There is no need for the procedure to create a new object. As long as at least one variable with a reference to an object remains in scope and is not set to *Nothing*, the object won't be destroyed.

In VBA, an object has no inherent scope or lifetime and isn't tied to a specific object variable. Only the object variables themselves have scope associated with them. The destruction of an object is controlled indirectly by the scope of all object variables referring to that instance.

Who am I?

The object variables referring to an object know nothing about each other. And an object never knows the name of any of the object variables it is assigned to. Let's go back to our Vehicle class example. As far as you know, the Vehicle object in your driveway is controlled by the YourVehicle object variable. But from your son's perspective, it's controlled by the SonVehicle variable. The YourVehicle and SonVehicle object variables can coexist safely as long as you and your son are not trying to use the car at the same time! If you and your son try to use the car at the same time, coordination can be very difficult, if not extremely hazardous. For example, your son may try to drive away while you're putting gas in the car.

The Vehicle object meanwhile remains blissfully unaware that it has a split personality. From within the class module code, there's no way to determine the identity of the variables that hold references to an instance of the class. The instance knows only that at least one reference exists; otherwise, the *Class_Terminate()* event procedure would be executing and the instance would be on the brink of destruction.

Since different variables to which an object instance is assigned know nothing about each other, changing the properties of the instance from one variable can have unpredictable results on the other variable. If you have two variables referring to the same instance, and you change the instance's properties by referring to the instance by means of the first variable, the second variable doesn't know that changes have been made. Let's use the *MailBox Object Sample* program to understand this concept.

1. Close and restart the MailBx32.Exe program.
2. Click the Set button to execute

   ```
   Set MailBoxA = New MailBox
   ```

3. Select MailBoxB from the dropdown, and click the MailBoxA option. Click the Set button to execute

   ```
   Set MailBoxB = MailBoxA
   ```

4. Double-click the MailBoxB container as a shortcut to

   ```
   MailBoxB.SetProperties
   ```

5. Click the check box to change the HasMail property of MailBoxB. Then click OK.
6. The rendering of MailBoxB now looks different from the rendering of MailBoxA, but they still refer to the same instance. (The object count is 1.)
7. Choose MailBoxA in the dropdown, and click the Draw button to execute

   ```
   MailBoxA.Draw
   ```

   The object appearances are now synchronized.

What happened? In this case, we changed the HasMail property of our object by referring to the instance by means of the variable MailBoxB. As soon as we changed the HasMail property, our program knew to redraw the MailBoxB container on the form by calling the *Draw* method from MailBoxB. Since the variable MailBoxA knew nothing about the changes made by means of the variable MailBoxB, it had no reason to invoke the *Draw* method to update the container associated with the variable MailBoxA. The end result was a false impression of the state of the instance referred to by the variable MailBoxA. Let's look at a real world example:

- You get a reference to a Microsoft Excel Application object and load an add-in. (We'll look at Excel add-ins in Chapter 10.)
- Some other program with a reference to the same Microsoft Excel Application object decides to clean up Excel because too many workbooks are open. The add-in you loaded is unloaded by this other program.
- You get an error when you call a function in the add-in you'd loaded.

Since having several variables refer to the same object seems dangerous and difficult to coordinate, why would you want to use this feature at all? Because objects can be very large, and duplicating large objects is very expensive in terms of memory and program performance. If you want the MailBoxB object variable to refer to a MailBox object that has the same property values as the instance assigned to the MailBoxA object variable, you have two choices. The first is to assign a new MailBox instance to MailBoxB and copy the values for the HasMail and PostColor properties from the MailBoxA instance. The second is to assign the same instance to both variables. In general, you won't want to waste processor cycles and coding time by duplicating an existing object, so you'll choose the second option: you'll assign the same object to multiple variables. Since no data is actually copied when the instance is assigned to the second object variable, the cost of having multiple variables refer to a single object is much lower than the cost of having multiple duplicate objects. This powerful capability, which enables you to move very large objects with very little cost, is roughly equivalent to putting your whole office in your suitcase and flying across the country.

Am I you?

Although an object can't answer the question Who am I?, the object can reveal some information about its identity to the programmer. For example, because having several different variables refer to the same object can be very confusing, VBA provides the *Is* operator to check if two variables refer to the same instance:

```
If MyMailBox Is YourMailBox Then
    MsgBox "Get your own MailBox, please."
Else
    MsgBox "Thank You!"
End If
```

Are you there?

You can also check if the MyMailBox variable refers to an existing object by using the *Nothing* keyword with the *Is* keyword:

```
'If MyMailBox doesn't refer to a MailBox instance, create
'a new instance.

If MyMailBox Is Nothing Then Set MyMailBox = New MailBox
:
'Draw MyMailBox only if the MyMailBox variable refers to
'a running instance.
If Not MyMailBox Is Nothing Then MyMailBox.Draw MyContainer
```

What are you?

VBA also provides the *TypeOf* [object] *Is* [type] operator to determine the type of a generic object variable. Assuming you have both a MailBox object and a NewspaperTube object defined, you can check the type of one of your variables this way:

```
Dim obj As Object
Set obj = New MailBox
TypeOf obj Is MailBox        'Returns True
TypeOf obj Is NewspaperTube 'Returns False
```

You can also use the *TypeName* function to determine the type of an object variable:

```
If TypeName(obj) <> "MailBox" Then MsgBox "I'm not a MailBox"
If TypeName(MailBoxA) <> "MailBox" Then MsgBox "This can't happen"
```

TypeName can be very useful for debugging, but it's safer to use the *TypeOf...Is* operator in your code because then you enable the compiler to catch an unknown object type for you. If you use the *TypeName* function extensively, you're bound to make a mistake sometime, and the error will be difficult to track down. The following code will display the error message every time. (Look carefully at the spelling of "MailBox" in the code.)

```
If TypeName(MailBoxA) <> "MailBox" Then MsgBox "This can happen"
```

Avoid using hard-coded strings if you want easily maintained international applications. The *TypeOf. . . Is* operator is also much faster than *TypeName*.

NOTE The *TypeOf. . . Is* operator isn't available in Excel-VBA.

If your object variables are hard typed, you shouldn't have to rely on these What are you? programming methods to determine the type of an object variable because you have specified the type of the variable in your declaration statement. Using the *Is Nothing* syntax to check if the object variable contains an object is generally the only check you'll need to do on a hard-typed object variable.

Me

The *Me* keyword is an essential piece of the object puzzle because an object can't answer the question Who am I? All instances of a class share the code in the class module. *Me* refers to the instance that is currently executing the code.

The code that shows the SetProperties dialog uses the *Me* keyword to place a reference to the current instance—that is, to the MailBox object that is currently executing the code in the *SetProperties* method—into the MailBox property of the dialog:

```
Set dlgForm.MailBox = Me
```

The MailBox property of the object assigned to the dlgForm object variable now refers to the MailBox object whose *SetProperties* method was called.

Forms as classes

You may notice that the form used in the *MailBox Object Sample* program, MailBoxDialog, acts a lot like a class module. It should. All VB forms are classes and behave exactly as normal class modules do. Forms have *Class_Initialize()* and *Class_Terminate()* procedures, support public and private variables and functions, recognize the *Me* keyword, and support multiple instances. The public variables and functions of a form module define new properties and methods for the form. You can see the class-like behavior of forms by examining the *SetProperties* method of the MailBox object. It treats dlgForm just as it would any other object variable.

```
Public Sub SetProperties()
'Set up dlgForm to instantiate itself when first referenced.
Dim dlgForm As New MailBoxDialog
    'Set the MailBox property of the MailBoxDialog to this instance.
    Set dlgForm.MailBox = Me
    'Show the dialog.
    dlgForm.Show vbModal
End Sub
```

NOTE Calling *Unload* on a form object isn't sufficient to remove the object from memory. If the form has module-level (public or private) variables or static local variables, you must set the reference to the form to *Nothing* to destroy it completely. In *SetProperties*, the MailBox property of the MailBoxDialog still refers to an object in memory at the *End Sub* line. To see this, step through the code to the *End Sub* line, and execute

```
?dlgForm.MailBox Is Me
```

in the Debug window. You don't need an explicit *Set . . . = Nothing* in this case because VBA does this implicitly when the dlgForm variable goes out of scope.

Property Set/Get Procedures

VBA uses a different syntax to assign a value to a normal variable than it uses to assign an object to an object variable. You use an equal sign in the normal variable case. In the object case, you use an equal sign in conjunction with the *Set* keyword. VBA provides a *Property Let* procedure you can use to validate a value before assigning it to a normal property. To enable you to validate an object before assigning it to an object property in a class module, VBA provides a *Property Set* procedure.

In Chapter 4, we looked at *Property Let* and *Property Get* procedures, but we didn't consider a method for returning an object from a property procedure. We can return an object from a property procedure through *Property Set* and *Property Get* statements. The *Property Set/Get* procedure pair is similar to the *Property Let/Get* pair, but the *Set* keyword is used to assign the return value so that the *Property Get* procedure returns an object reference instead of an ordinary value. The MailBox class module could be enhanced with the following code to return neighboring MailBox objects:

```
Private m_NextMailBox As MailBox
:
Public Property Set NextMailBox(Neighbor As MailBox)
    Set m_NextMailBox = Neighbor
End Property
Public Property Get NextMailBox() As MailBox
    Set NextMailBox = m_NextMailBox
End Property
:
'Use of the NextMailBox property
Set CurrentMailBox.NextMailBox = MailBoxA       'Calls the Property Set
Debug.Print CurrentMailBox.NextMailBox.HasMail  'Calls the Property Get
```

As you can with an equivalent *Property Let/Get* procedure pair that doesn't validate a new value, you can implement the NextMailBox property by using

```
Public NextMailBox As MailBox
```

and omitting the property procedures. Here is a more useful *Property Get* procedure, one we could add to the MailBox class module. Note that the unqualified HasMail and PostColor properties in this code are implicitly qualified by the *Me* referring to the instance of the MailBox class that is currently executing the code:

```
Public Property Get Clone() As MailBox
Dim NewMailBox As New MailBox
    With NewMailBox
        .PostColor = PostColor
        .HasMail = HasMail
    End With
    Set Clone = NewMailBox
End Property
```

MailBox Object Sample Form Code

Here's the code for the main form, frmMailBox, from the *MailBox Object Sample* code. You'll find the full code for this program in the \Chapter4\MailBox directory on the CD that comes with this book.

frmMailBox Code Module

```
Option Explicit
Dim MailBoxes(1) As MailBox
Dim iCurrentBox As Integer
Private Sub cmbLeftSide_Click()
    iCurrentBox = cmbLeftSide.ListIndex
    optRightSide(2).Caption = cmbLeftSide.List((iCurrentBox + 1) Mod 2)
    cmdProperties.Enabled = Not MailBoxes(iCurrentBox) Is Nothing
    cmdDraw.Enabled = cmdProperties.Enabled
    cmdSet_GotFocus
End Sub

Private Sub cmbLeftSide_GotFocus()
    cmdSet_GotFocus
End Sub

Private Sub cmdDraw_Click()
    MailBoxes(iCurrentBox).Draw picContainer(iCurrentBox)
End Sub
```

```
Private Sub cmdDraw_GotFocus()
    lblCode = cmbLeftSide & ".Draw picContainer(" & _
              cmbLeftSide.ListIndex & ")"
End Sub

Private Sub cmdProperties_Click()
    With MailBoxes(iCurrentBox)
        .SetProperties
        .Draw picContainer(iCurrentBox)
    End With
End Sub

Private Sub cmdProperties_GotFocus()
    lblCode = cmbLeftSide & ".SetProperties"
End Sub

Private Sub cmdSet_Click()
    If optRightSide(0) Then
        Set MailBoxes(iCurrentBox) = New MailBox
    ElseIf optRightSide(1) Then
        Set MailBoxes(iCurrentBox) = Nothing
    Else
        Set MailBoxes(iCurrentBox) = MailBoxes((iCurrentBox + 1) Mod 2)
    End If
    cmdProperties.Enabled = Not MailBoxes(iCurrentBox) Is Nothing
    cmdDraw.Enabled = cmdProperties.Enabled
    picContainer(iCurrentBox).Refresh
End Sub

Private Sub cmdSet_GotFocus()
    lblCode = "Set " & cmbLeftSide & " = " & _
              optRightSide(CurrentOption).Caption
End Sub

Private Sub Form_Load()
    Set gReferences.OutputLabel = lblRefCount
    cmbLeftSide.ListIndex = 0
End Sub

Private Sub Form_QueryUnload(Cancel As Integer, UnloadMode As Integer)
Dim iExternalRefs As Integer
    'Get the total number of outstanding MailBox objects.
    iExternalRefs = gReferences.ReferenceCount
    'Adjust for those held by this application.
    If Not MailBoxes(0) Is Nothing Then
        iExternalRefs = iExternalRefs - 1
```

(continued)

```
            If Not MailBoxes(1) Is Nothing And _
               Not MailBoxes(1) Is MailBoxes(0) Then
                iExternalRefs = iExternalRefs - 1
            End If
        ElseIf Not MailBoxes(1) Is Nothing Then
            iExternalRefs = iExternalRefs - 1
        End If
        If iExternalRefs Then
            MsgBox "Can't close program. There are " & iExternalRefs & _
                " MailBox objects in use by other applications."
            Cancel = True
        End If
End Sub

Private Sub optRightSide_DblClick(Index As Integer)
    cmdSet_Click
End Sub

Private Sub optRightSide_GotFocus(Index As Integer)
    optRightSide(Index) = True
    cmdSet_GotFocus
End Sub

Private Sub picContainer_Click(Index As Integer)
    cmbLeftSide.ListIndex = Index
End Sub

Private Sub picContainer_DblClick(Index As Integer)
    If Not MailBoxes(Index) Is Nothing Then
        With MailBoxes(Index)
            .SetProperties
            .Draw picContainer(Index)
        End With
    End If
End Sub

Private Sub picContainer_Paint(Index As Integer)
    If Not MailBoxes(Index) Is Nothing Then _
        MailBoxes(Index).Draw picContainer(Index)
End Sub

Private Function CurrentOption() As Integer
Dim iSet As Integer
    Do Until optRightSide(iSet)
        iSet = iSet + 1
    Loop
    CurrentOption = iSet
End Function
```

SUMMARY

- The life cycle of an object includes its declaration, creation, assignment, and destruction.
- A class is of no use until an instance of the class has been created. The *New* keyword can be used with the *Set* statement to create an object. An *As New* declaration can also be used to instantiate an object the first time it is used.
- For performance reasons, it is much more efficient to hard type an object variable in a declaration than to use *As Object* syntax. Hard typing an object variable greatly reduces the overhead required for each call to the object.
- An object can be referred to by many variables. The object is destroyed only when all object variables that refer to it have been explicitly set to *Nothing* or have gone out of scope.
- The type of the object assigned to an object variable can be determined with the *TypeOf...Is* operator or the *TypeName* function.
- The *Me* keyword can be used in a class module to refer to the instance of the class that's currently executing—that is, to the instance whose method or property was called.
- Visual Basic forms are special cases of classes.
- An object can be used as a property of a class module by means of the *Property Set*/*Property Get* procedures.

6

Driving Other Objects with Visual Basic

With Visual Basic class modules, you can code classes that can be used as building blocks to help you construct powerful programs. The ability to use instances of the classes you've created is a powerful programming feature in and of itself, but using classes you've coded as part of your VB project is only the beginning of VB's object-rich feature set.

Adding Objects to Your VB Project

Intrinsic objects such as forms and controls are built into Visual Basic, but VB programs are not constrained to use only the objects provided by VB itself. When you add a class module to a project, you add to the collection of objects your VB program can create and manipulate. To understand this point, let's see what happens when the MailBox class module is added to a project. With the MailBox class module in a project, coding against a MailBox object is exactly the same as coding against a Form object, a Control object, or the Visual Basic for Applications Collection object. For each of these intrinsic classes, you can create a new instance, set properties, and call methods, and you can do those same things for the MailBox class. By adding a class module to a project, you extend the language features available to your project to include instances, properties, and methods of the class defined by your class module.

Furthermore, since you're human and you can type only so much code, limiting the set of objects available to your VB project to built-in class modules and to class modules you have written yourself would have been a shame. So there is no restriction that limits you to intrinsic classes or that forces you to personally code all of the classes available to your VB projects.

The set of objects available to procedures in a VB project isn't limited to the built-in VB objects and the objects you've defined in class modules for your project. Your programs can also use objects provided by other applications (Microsoft Excel and Microsoft Access, for instance) just as they'd use an object provided by VB. When a VB program creates an object whose class has been implemented by another application, the VB program is known as a *client* of the other application. The application that implements the object is referred to as an *object server.*

NOTE In the VB4 documentation, you'll see *object servers* referred to as *OLE servers* or *OLE Automation servers.*

The technology VB leverages to manipulate other applications' objects is *OLE Automation.* The ability to use objects provided by OLE Automation servers enables you to integrate control of these objects directly into your VBA code and thus extend the VBA language available to your project to encompass many more objects than the built-in VB and VBA objects and the objects created from the classes you've defined in your project. OLE Automation technology can save your fingers from typing hundreds of thousands of lines of code. These lines of code have not only been written already, but they've also been tested and used extensively by thousands of people. Of course, if you want to write a world class spreadsheet yourself instead of using Microsoft Excel, you're welcome to. Any takers out there? We didn't think so. Welcome to the ever-expanding world of OLE Automation!

Visual Basic's OLE and OLE Automation Capabilities

In order to reach a good understanding of OLE and of the OLE Automation capabilities of Visual Basic, we need to spend a little time exploring some basic OLE concepts.

OLE

OLE has long been viewed as the ability to place an object created in one application into a document that's being created in another application. For example, a user can place a Microsoft Word document in a Microsoft Excel spreadsheet and then, without leaving the Microsoft Excel program shell, use Word to edit the text by double-clicking on the image of the Word document object.

A document that includes objects from more than one application is known as a *compound document. Linking* and *embedding* are two different ways of associating the different objects in a compound document. If the Word document object contained in the Microsoft Excel spreadsheet is stored in a separate Word file, it's known as a *linked* object. The Excel spreadsheet—yes, it's an object too—keeps a pointer to the path and file name of the linked Word file. If the Word document object is stored in the same file as the Excel spreadsheet, it's known as an *embedded* object. Hence the original term Object Linking and Embedding.

NOTE Although OLE was originally an acronym for Object Linking and Embedding, it has come to mean much more. Since OLE was first developed, Microsoft has expanded the capabilities of OLE so that it now represents more than just the ability to create compound documents. Consequently, Microsoft has dropped the words that OLE used to represent (Object Linking and Embedding) and has turned OLE into a stand-alone name for its comprehensive object technology.

Starting with OLE 2, a user can seamlessly work on embedded objects using *in-place activation*. (Linked objects must be edited in the application that provides them.) With in-place activation, the user can use the menus and toolbars of the server application (Microsoft Word in our example) without leaving the shell of the client application (Microsoft Excel in our example). For a quick experience of in-place activation, try the following:

1. Start Microsoft Excel.
2. From Excel's Insert menu, select Object. You'll see a dialog that contains a list of the available kinds of objects.
3. From the list of available objects, select Microsoft Word Document.
4. From the Help menu, select About Microsoft Word.

No, that wasn't a typo! The About item on the Help menu points to Word, not Excel. If you look closely at your screen or at Figure 6-1 on the next page, you'll also notice that the toolbars and most other menus are now provided by Word, not Excel. However, the title bar on the application still says Microsoft Excel. Switching control of the Excel program shell from Excel to Word is an example of in-place activation. If you click outside the embedded Word document, on the spreadsheet that contains the activated object, you'll switch control back to Excel. Double-clicking in the Word document object will reactivate the Word document object and again give Word control of the Excel shell.

You, as the user, have activated a Word document embedded in a Microsoft Excel spreadsheet. We hope you had fun doing it, but we also know you didn't buy this book to figure out how users do in-place activation in Excel.

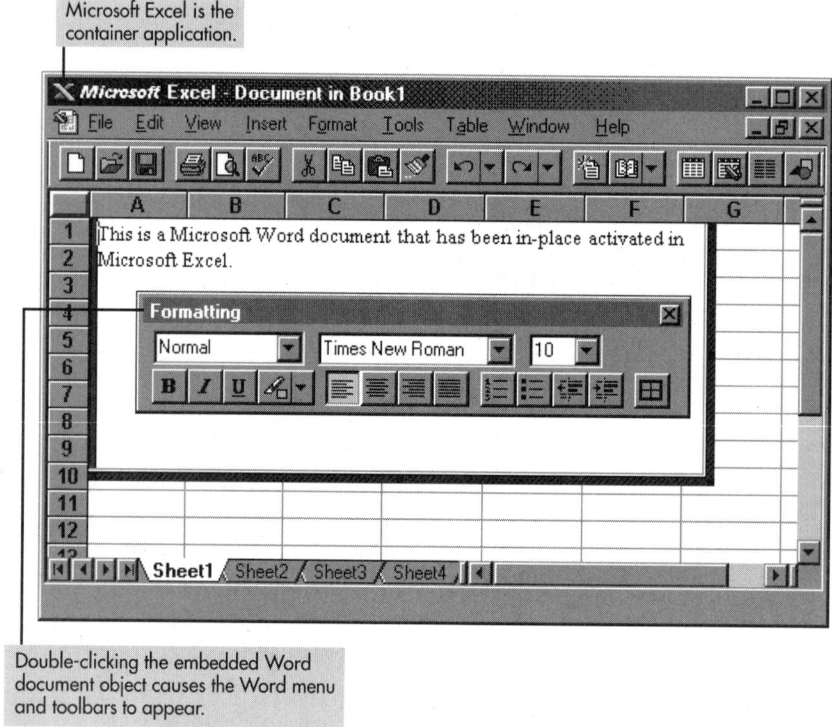

Figure 6-1. *A Word document active in a Microsoft Excel spreadsheet. The toolbars and menus belong to Word, not Microsoft Excel.*

OLE Automation

OLE Automation is the technology Visual Basic and Visual Basic for Applications (VB's language component) use to enable your project to control objects exposed by other applications. Using VBA code in Visual Basic, Microsoft Excel, Project, or Access, you can programmatically insert documents into a Microsoft Excel spreadsheet, drive custom Microsoft PowerPoint presentations, or insert contacts into Schedule+. In fact, almost anything a user can do in an Office for Windows 95 application can be automated with VBA code. Your customers get to sit back and watch as your code automatically takes care of repetitive tasks for them.

OK, so what parts of OLE and OLE Automation technology are implemented in VB? As a client, VBA code can programmatically create and manipulate objects provided by other applications. A VB form can also act as an in-place activation site for objects provided by other applications. When acting as an in-place activation site, the VB form can seamlessly integrate the menus and toolbars of the server application, just as we saw above when a Word document was activated in Microsoft Excel.

As an OLE Automation object server, a VB program can expose its objects, which can be used by other, client, applications through OLE Automation. However, VB forms can't be activated in-place by the client applications.

Using VBA Code to Manipulate Other Applications' Objects

In VB4, you can use VBA code to access external servers' objects through OLE Automation. But VB3 was able to manipulate external OLE Automation objects, so what's the big deal? The big deal is that a VB4 client project can contain a reference to an *object library* that fully describes the classes, methods, and properties exposed by an OLE Automation object server. You can hard type the object variables that refer to referenced objects, and VBA can verify your code at compile-time, just as it can verify code that creates objects of any other class. This ability of a VB project to use the definitions of external classes, methods, and properties combined in object libraries has been added to the Visual Basic product for release 4.0.

An OLE Automation object server provides a file called an object library that contains a full description of the classes exposed by the server. An object library can be a stand-alone file (.TLB for "Type Library"), or it can be contained in other files (.OLB, .EXE, or .DLL). If an object library is contained in an executable file (.EXE or .DLL), the executable will also be the server application that implements the objects described in the object library. (You can refer to an object library as a type library, too, but we'll mostly use the term object library in this book.)

Once you've reviewed the objects provided by the object servers on your system and decided which ones you'll need to write your program, you can enable the objects in your project by adding to your project a *reference* to the object library or libraries describing the classes. Before you can add a reference to its object library to your VB project, however, the object server must be correctly registered with the operating system. Once a reference to a library of objects has been established, a referenced object is treated just as an instance of one of your own classes or a built-in VB object class would be treated. You can add object library references to your project by means of the VB4 References dialog shown in Figure 6-2 on the next page. In the VB design environment, from the Tools menu, select References to reach this dialog. Go ahead and open the References dialog to see the object libraries that are already referenced by a new VB project.

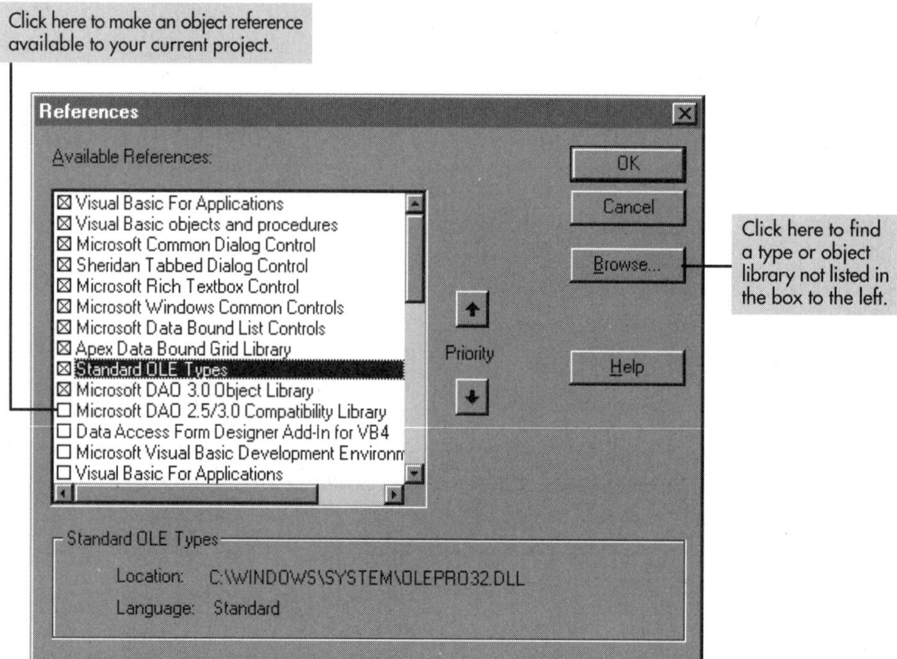

Figure 6-2. *The Visual Basic References dialog box.*

Default Library References

You'll notice right away that quite a number of object libraries are already checked in the References dialog. The first library listed will always be *Visual Basic For Applications*. Why is the VBA library considered an external reference? Most of VBA's run-time functionality is itself an extension of the core VBA language because it is implemented in a DLL that is an object server. The object library *Visual Basic For Applications* is contained in the file VEN2232.Olb, which describes the objects and other functions available in the VBA object server. The second object library in the list is *Visual Basic objects and procedures*, which describes the objects provided by the application hosting VBA—Visual Basic, Microsoft Excel, or Microsoft Access. In this case, the VBA host application is Visual Basic. Later on, when you open the VBA References dialog in Microsoft Excel, you'll see that the second object library referenced by default is *Microsoft Excel 5.0 Object Library* rather than *Visual Basic objects and procedures*.

Let's go over the other default library references. The *Microsoft Common Dialog Control, Sheridan Tabbed Dialog Control, Microsoft Rich Textbox Control, Microsoft Windows Common Controls, Microsoft Data Bound List Controls*, and *Apex Data Bound Grid Library* object libraries describe the custom controls VB puts on the toolbox when you open a new project. The *Standard OLE Types* library describes standard objects, such as Fonts and Pictures, commonly used by VB projects. The *Microsoft DAO 3.0 Object Library* enables your VB program to manipulate databases by means of Data Access Objects (DAO).

NOTE Default library references will vary depending on whether you have the Standard, Professional, or Enterprise edition of Visual Basic.

You can add a reference or remove your project's reference to an object library by clicking the library's check box in the left column of the Available References: list. VB won't let you remove the first two references in the list (*Visual Basic For Applications* and *Visual Basic objects and procedures*). And you won't be able to uncheck the custom control references here because the VB toolbox references them. If you won't be using data access in your project, you can remove the reference to the *Microsoft DAO 3.0 Object Library*.

NOTE If you want to change the references that are automatically added to a new Visual Basic project, open the Auto32ld.Vbp project file in the VB root directory and add or remove references and custom controls from that project. You can add or remove references to custom controls by means of the Tools-Custom Controls dialog. References to the controls in the References dialog will be removed automatically. After your object library and custom control references are set to your liking, select New Project from the File menu. Answer Yes in the dialog that asks whether you want to save the *Auto32ld* project. Any new project you open will now have the same object library and control references as the *Auto32ld* project you just saved.

Adding a Reference

The Visual Basic objects we've been using thus far in the book have been defined in an object library. In fact, the Form, TextBox, and CommandButton objects you manipulated in Chapter 3 were a part of the language only because your project contained a default reference to the *Visual Basic objects and procedures* object library. Let's go ahead and expand the number of objects you can use in your projects by adding a reference to another object library: the library describing the MailBox class we created in Chapter 4. Now we'll use the MailBox class in a VB project other than the *MailBox Object Sample* application in which we implemented the MailBox class. The MailBx32.Exe file created from the *MailBox Object Sample* project will act as the object server, and a project running in another instance of the VB design environment will act as the OLE Automation client.

1. Start VB or select New Project from the File menu to get a new project.
2. Select Tools-References to open the References dialog.
3. Check the *MailBox Object Sample* item in the Available References: list.
4. Click OK to close the References dialog.
5. On the form's property sheet, change the ScaleMode property of the form to *3 - Pixel* so that the MailBox object will be able to draw itself correctly on your form.
6. Insert the following code at the top of your form code module:

```
Dim MBox As New MailBox
Private Sub Form_Paint()
    MBox.Draw Me
End Sub
```

7. Press F5 to run the new project.

When you run the project, you'll see the *MailBox Object Sample* application we wrote in Chapter 5. The distinct object count on the *MailBox Object Sample* form will change to 1, and a default MailBox object (with a very long post) will draw itself in the upper left corner of the form in your current project. Now think about how much code you wrote. You got a lot of action for four lines of code. You now have full control of a MailBox object without having written any MailBox implementation code in your current VB project.

How does it feel to take advantage of previously written code? You've just leveraged the work we had already done in order to create a new MailBox object; but you never had to see our code to make full use of the MailBox object server. VBA makes it trivially easy to use objects implemented by other applications. In fact, once you have a reference to the correct object library, you can create and manipulate external objects with the same coding techniques you've learned for creating and manipulating built-in objects and objects created from VB class modules.

NOTE If you ran MailBx32.Exe while you were reading Chapter 5, its object library will be available because Visual Basic .Exe object servers are registered automatically the first time they're run. If the *MailBox Object Sample* object library isn't available in the Available References: list, the MailBx32.Exe file isn't installed or isn't registered on your machine. To install and register the *MailBox Object Sample* server on your machine, copy MailBx32.Exe to your hard drive and run it. You can also register it by typing the following command: *mailbx32 /regserver.*

If you want to remove MailBx32.Exe as an available reference, run *mailbx32 /unregserver* to remove all evidence of the application from your system registry. The /regserver and /unregserver command line arguments can be used with any VB-created .Exe server to register and unregister the object libraries provided by the server.

Using the Object Browser

Once you have a reference to an object library, you can use the VBA Object Browser, shown in Figure 6-3, to view the properties and methods of any class defined in the library. Select View-Object Browser (or press F2) to open the Object Browser. You can use the Object Browser to examine the classes available in each of the object libraries referenced by your project. In addition to viewing the properties and methods available for each class, you can see the arguments and return type of each method or the type of each property at the bottom of the Object Browser dialog. Click the question mark (?) button when it's enabled to get help on a class, property, or method.

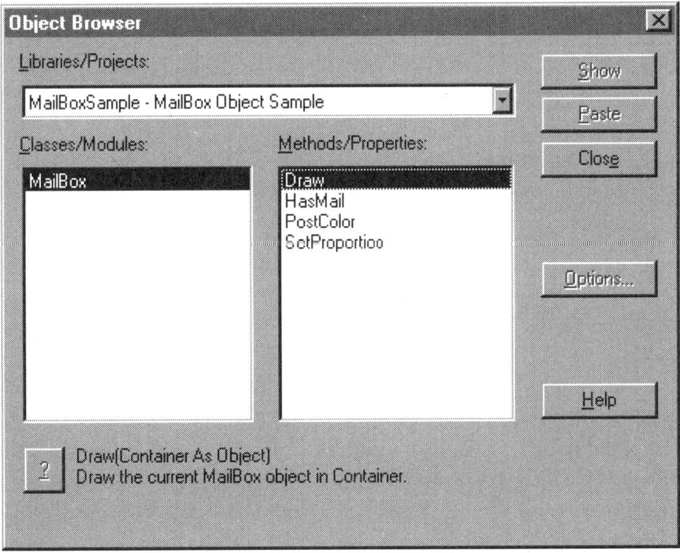

Figure 6-3. *The VBA Object Browser. The arguments and return types of a method or the type of a property is displayed below the list boxes, next to the question mark (?) button.*

NOTE For Visual Basic–created classes in the current project, only those properties that have been created by means of property procedures will show up in the Object Browser. Properties implemented by means of public variables won't appear. When another project references the finished object server, they will appear.

Generic Objects

Let's pretend for a moment that we want to use an object that isn't described in a registered object library. How can we create an instance of the class? How can we call the properties and methods of the object? VBA knows absolutely nothing about the object at compile-time, so the task of manipulating this generic object becomes much harder. (This scenario may sound familiar to anyone who has programmed external objects with VB3, which didn't read object libraries.) Let's go over the changes we'd need to make to our code to be able to create a MailBox object and call its *Draw* method without a reference to the *MailBox Object Sample* object library.

Here's the original code (line numbers are included for future reference):

```
Dim MBox As MailBox          '10
Private Sub Form_Load()
    Set MBox = New MailBox   '20
End Sub
Private Sub Form_Paint()
    MBox.Draw Me             '30
End Sub
```

Here's the code to create a MailBox object and call the *draw* method when the VB project doesn't have a reference to the object library that describes the MailBox object:

```
Dim MBox As Object                                    '10
Private Sub Form_Load()
    Set MBox = CreateObject("MailBoxSample.MailBox")  '20
End Sub
Private Sub Form_Paint()
    MBox.draw Me                                      '30
End Sub
```

Generic declaration: *As Object*

We use *As Object* instead of *As MailBox* in line 10 of the second code snippet because VBA doesn't know what a MailBox object is. *As MailBox* would fail to compile. The set of objects recognized by the VBA language in your project has not been extended via an object library reference to a MailBox class. It follows that the compiler won't recognize *New MailBox* either, so our normal means of creating an object isn't available for the MailBox class when its object library hasn't been referenced.

Generic instantiation: *CreateObject*

On line 20 of the second code snippet, in the *Form_Load()* event procedure, we create our MailBox object. If we waited until the *Form_Paint()* event procedure to create the MailBox object, we'd have to check *If MBox Is Nothing* every time the *Form_Paint* event was called instead of checking it only once in the *Form_Load()* event procedure.

Since the MailBox class is not described in a referenced object library, we can't use the *New* keyword to create a new object of that class. Instead, we use the *CreateObject* method in place of the *New* keyword to create a generic object. The parameter passed into the *CreateObject* function—"MailBoxSample.MailBox"—corresponds to a key the server application (MailBx32.Exe in this case) added to the system registry. We use the standard naming convention

<Server>.<ObjectType>

to uniquely identify the object in the system registry. Identifiers of this type are known as *Program Identifiers*, or *ProgIDs* for short. "Excel.Application" and "Excel.Sheet" are examples of ProgIDs. You can use a ProgID to specify the class of the object you want to create, even if your project doesn't have a reference to an object library that describes that class.

You can use *CreateObject* in place of the *New* keyword anytime, even when you have an object library reference for the class of the object you are creating, but the *New* keyword is the best way to create objects in VB4 because it requires less overhead at run-time than *CreateObject* does.

NOTE The *New* keyword isn't available in Excel VBA, so you must use the *CreateObject* method to create objects, even if an object library describing the class is referenced by your project.

Generic calls: late binding

Line 30 of the second code snippet, *MBox.draw Me*, looks almost exactly like the code it replaced, but the actual steps VBA takes to call the *Draw* method are much different. In Chapter 5, we recommended that you use hard typing in object variable declaration statements whenever possible. Well, in this case you can't hard type your object variable because the type is unknown at compile-time. Consequently, VBA must make a late-bound call to the *Draw* method. Remember, anytime you hard type an object variable, you enable VBA to access methods and properties directly instead of having to communicate with the (mother-in-law) object, which saves a lot of unnecessary overhead. A call to a method or property that doesn't require VBA to communicate with the object itself is said to be *early bound*. If VBA is unable to make an early-bound call, as with generic object variables, the call is *late bound*.

The other difference between the original code and the new code is the lower case *d* on the *Draw* method. When your project references the MailBox object library and you type in *mbox.draw me*, VBA changes the code to *MBox.Draw Me* automatically when you finish typing the line. The VBA code editor thus immediately indicates which names it can recognize as variables, classes, methods, properties, and constants. If you don't reference the MailBox object library, VB will change the same line of code to *MBox.draw Me*, instead of *MBox.Draw Me*. The only difference is the lower case *d* on the *draw* name. *MBox* is a recognized name because it is a variable you declared in your module. *Me* is a recognized VBA keyword. However, *draw* is an unknown name because your project doesn't reference an object library containing the *Draw* method. Having names go into the correct case when you commit a line of code gives you a visual indication of whether your code is correct. Automatic casing is just one more advantage of using object library references in your project.

NOTE If you entered the line *mbox.draw me* and VB changed it to *MBox.Draw Me* even though you didn't reference the MailBox object library, you have referenced another object library that contains a *Draw* method. To see this, open a new VB project. Open the Custom Controls dialog, and remove all checked controls. Now open the References dialog and remove all but the first two checked references. (VB won't allow you to remove either of the first two.) Try typing in the sample code again. The line with the *Draw* method will now read *MBox.draw Me.*

The *MailBox Client* Applet

A sample *MailBox Client* applet (MBoxCli.Vbp) is in the Chapter4\MailBox directory on the companion CD. We'll call it an applet rather than an application because it doesn't require very much code to work properly and because it doesn't do very much. It calls the properties and methods of the MailBox object, but you don't have to implement the class in this project. The user interface for *MailBox Client* is shown in Figure 6-4.

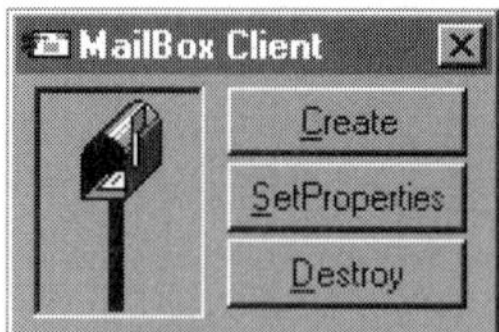

Figure 6-4. *The* MailBox Client *applet.*

Here is the code listing for the *MailBox Client* app. All of the references to the MailBox object and its methods and properties in this code will be compiled early bound because the project contains a reference to the *MailBox Object Sample* object library.

```
Option Explicit
Dim MBox As MailBox

Private Sub cmd_Click(Index As Integer)
    Select Case Index
        Case 0 'Create
            Set MBox = New MailBox
        Case 1 'SetProperties
            If MBox Is Nothing Then
                Beep
            Else
                MBox.SetProperties
            End If
        Case 2 'Destroy
            Set MBox = Nothing
    End Select
    'Repaint the image to show any changes.
    'The Refresh method fires a Paint event.
    picMailBox.Refresh
    'SetProperties activates the server window.
    'SetFocus reactivates the client window.
    SetFocus
End Sub

Private Sub picMailBox_DblClick()
    cmd_Click 1 'SetProperties
End Sub

Private Sub picMailBox_Paint()
    If Not MBox Is Nothing Then MBox.Draw picMailBox
End Sub
```

Run the program and check out how little coding you did to create a functional program!

The remainder of this chapter deals with creating object servers in Visual Basic. If you don't plan on creating your own servers, you can go on to the next chapter, which talks about using VB forms as in-place activation sites. We do recommend that you read on, though. A solid grasp of this material is essential for your understanding of some of the VB sample applications we'll look at later in the book. If you skip ahead, you'll probably find yourself coming back here later.

Creating Visual Basic Object Servers

As you've seen, creating class modules in Visual Basic is not difficult. Creating object servers in VB is just as simple as creating class modules. In fact, you only need to make a few mouse clicks in the property sheet to turn a VB class into an exposed object and your VB application into an object server.

When you design an application, you should consider carefully which class modules should be exposed to the outside world. You won't always expose every class you define. For example, the References class in the *MailBox Object Sample* app is used internally to display the distinct object count but would have no meaning to external applications. In fact, the true count of outstanding objects could potentially be corrupted if the class were exposed for external manipulation. The only class we expose in the *MailBox Object Sample* app is the MailBox class itself.

Exposing Classes

You set the availability and creatability of an object for use by external applications by setting the Public and Instancing properties of the class module. These two properties, along with the Name property, are on the property sheet when a class module is active in a code pane. You change these two properties to expose a class you have implemented for external use.

In most cases, when you expose a class for external use, you'll want to make the class both public and creatable. You make a class public by setting the Public property to *True* and creatable by setting the Instancing property to *1 - Creatable SingleUse* or *2 - Creatable MultiUse.*

Once you have set these properties, your class is exposed and can be used by other applications. That's all the work we had to do to make the MailBox object available for use by the *MailBox Client* app. So what do each of these properties do for the MailBox class or any other class?

When you set the Public property to *True* for at least one of the classes in your project, an object library is created and registered with the system when you go to run mode or when you create an executable file from your project. Having Public set to *True* for your class allows you (or another programmer) to hard type an object variable that refers to your object in a client application. In other words, the statement

```
Dim MBox As MailBox
```

will now be supported in the client application. However, setting the Public property alone isn't sufficient to allow users of your object to use the *New* keyword.

In order to support the statement

```
Set MBox = New MailBox
```

externally, you must also set the Instancing property. When you set Instancing to *Creatable SingleUse*, you specify that a new instance of your executable file will be started for each object created by a client application. Setting Instancing to *Creatable MultiUse* enables the client application to use a running object server, if one is available, instead of launching a new server to provide the object. For most cases, *MultiUse* is the recommended setting.

SingleUse is provided for cases in which many clients have to use instances of the same class, and either the methods they call take a long time to complete execution or they call many methods in a very short time. When you have multiple clients using instances of a class provided by a multiuse server and calling its properties and methods very frequently, there's a chance that the server won't be able to handle all of the requests at the same time and will delay one or more of the client requests. With a singleuse server, each client has an object that resides in its own instance of the object server, so no blocking occurs on 32-bit systems because each object server .EXE has its own thread of execution. The disadvantage, of course, is that a complete copy of the object server .EXE must be loaded into memory for each *SingleUse* object that's created.

When you make a class creatable as well as public, VB adds two extra keys and several subkeys to the system registry. One main key gives the physical location on disk of the server, and the other registers the ProgID value. The ProgID for a VB creatable class is the project name, a dot, and the name of the class. As we mentioned earlier, the program ID for the MailBox class is "MailBoxSample.MailBox".

You might be asking yourself at this point, Why would I ever want to have a public, noncreatable class? Well, suppose that you have a Palette object that contains a set of predefined colors and a Color object describing those colors. In this context, it makes no sense to have a Color object without a Palette object, so you would make Color noncreatable and Palette creatable and put a *GetColor* method in the Palette class, which would return a Color object, making it impossible for a client application to create a Color object without first creating a Palette object. Your code would look like this:

```
Dim MyPalette As Palette
Dim MyColor As Color
Set MyPalette = New Palette
'You can't do this line because Color is not creatable.
'Set MyColor = New Color
'Instead, you do this line.
Set MyColor = MyPalette.GetColor(5)
```

Having a noncreatable, public object is actually very common. Microsoft Excel, for instance, exposes 130 objects, only 3 of which are creatable.

Polite Object Servers: Staying Alive

What does staying alive have to do with an object server? Simple. If a server application has a visible user interface, a user can tell the server to shut down. In most cases, an app does what the user tells it to, but this is a special case. If client applications are using objects provided by the server app and the app shuts down when the user tells it to, the client will be left hanging. The client will get a run-time error the next time it calls a method on an object provided by the server because the server is no longer running. The server has the responsibility to keep track of the number of its objects owned by client applications and to refuse to shut down if one or more instances are outstanding.

Let's try this scenario with our *MailBox Client* application:

1. Run the *MailBox Client* application.
2. Click the Create button. The *MailBox Object Sample* server will start, and the distinct object count will increment to 1.
3. Try to close the server app by clicking the *Close* button.
4. You'll get the error message shown in Figure 6-5.

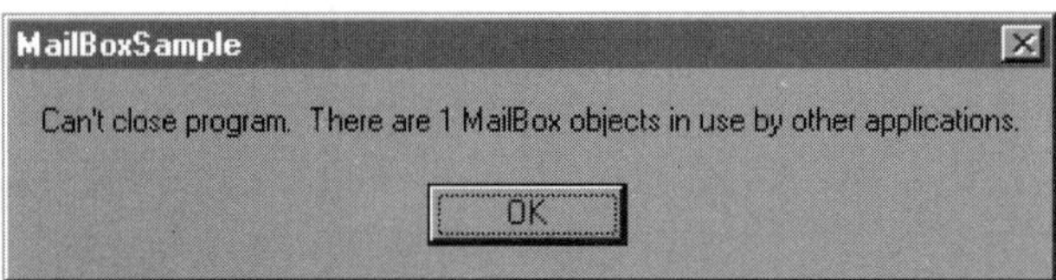

Figure 6-5. *The error message the* MailBox Object Sample *program displays if you try to close down the server application when one of its objects is in use by another application.*

5. Click OK to clear the message box.
6. Click Destroy on the MailBox Client dialog.
7. The *MailBox Object Sample* server closes automatically.

Here's the code that blocks the *MailBox Object Sample* server from unloading if a client still has a reference to its object:

```
Private Sub Form_QueryUnload(Cancel As Integer, UnloadMode As Integer)
Dim iExternalRefs As Integer
    'Get the total number of outstanding MailBox objects.
```

```
    iExternalRefs = gReferences.ReferenceCount
    'Adjust for those held by this application.
    .
    .
    .
    If iExternalRefs Then
        MsgBox "Can't close program. There are " & _
        iExternalRefs & _
        " MailBox objects in use by other applications."
        Cancel = True
    End If
End Sub
```

We use the *QueryUnload()* event procedure to block the server from unloading if any of its objects are still outstanding. You should use something similar to the References class implementation shown in the code listing at the end of Chapter 5 to keep track of outstanding references to all public classes.

Debugging an Object Server

In the course of any development process, you debug your code to find logic errors. Naturally, you'll need to do some debugging to find the logic errors in classes provided by your Visual Basic object servers. Fortunately, debugging a VB object server is just as easy as debugging any other VB app. Let's step through the process:

1. Load the MBoxObj.Vbp project into VB.
2. Press F5 to run the project.
3. Double-click the MailBox class (MAILBOX.CLS) in the VB project window to open the code pane with the MailBox class module.
4. Select the *SetProperties* subroutine from the Proc: dropdown.
5. Place a breakpoint at the top of the *SetProperties* subroutine.
6. Start a second instance of VB, and load the MBoxCli.Vbp project.
7. Press F5 to run the *MailBox Client* project.
8. Click the Create button on the *MailBox Client* dialog.
9. Click the SetProperties button.

Voilà! You hit the breakpoint you put on the *SetProperties* subroutine in your first instance of VB. At this point, you can proceed to step through your code, just as you do when you're debugging a stand-alone VB project. But although debugging a server is very similar to debugging a stand-alone project, a couple of tips will get you started off on the right foot and help you avoid pitfalls.

Start mode

We created a startup form for the *MailBox Object Sample* server, but many of your finished servers won't have a startup form. In fact, an object server might not have any visible user interface at all. An object server without a visible startup form will show *Sub Main* as the startup form on the Project tab of the Options dialog, and the *Sub Main* procedure will look like this:

```
Sub Main()
End Sub
```

Well, you can guess what happens when you press F5 to run this server—not much. VB starts the project and stops immediately after running *Sub Main*. We're stuck in a paradoxical situation: our server will stay alive only if there is an external reference to it, and we can't make it stay alive long enough to get an external reference to it. Fortunately, the VB designers were aware of this sticky situation and gave us an easy way out.

On the Project tab of the Options dialog, you'll find a StartMode setting. The default mode is Standalone, which exhibits the behavior you just saw. The alternative setting is OLE Server, which keeps your app running indefinitely, even after *Sub Main* has finished running. With the OLE Server start mode selected, you must stop the program's execution from the VB menu or toolbar or call the *End* statement in code to make the server stop running. You'll typically use OLE Server start mode only when you're debugging OLE servers.

Compile on demand

Two of the features new in Visual Basic 4 are *Compile On Demand* and *Background Compile*. These features can be activated in the Options dialog, Advanced tab. What does demand compilation do? Here's a brief example:

1. Load a new project into the VB design environment.
2. In the Options dialog, open the Advanced tab.
3. Make sure Compile On Demand and Background Compile are turned on.
4. Place a CommandButton control on your form.
5. Double-click the Command1 control to see the *Command1_Click()* event procedure.
6. Insert the word *BOGUS* into the procedure outline:

   ```
   Private Sub Command1_Click()
       BOGUS
   End Sub
   ```

7. Press F5 to run the project.
8. Click the command button.

You'll get a compilation error: "Sub or Function not defined." But something interesting has happened. You were in run mode, and now you're sitting at the beginning of the event procedure in break mode. However, you can't continue with your program until you fix the compile error.

Demand compilation means that VB compiles just enough of your code to start your program running, but no more. VB will fully compile a procedure the first time your program calls it. With demand compilation and background compilation both turned on, procedures that haven't yet been fully compiled will continue to compile as your program is running, even before such procedures have been called. If your program calls a procedure that won't compile, you'll have to fix the compile error so that the program can continue to run. If you can't fix the compile error, you'll have to return VB to design mode and try again.

If you're debugging an OLE Server in the VB design environment, you should make sure you have Compile On Demand turned off. Why is this? Remember that some edits can't be made in break mode. If your client calls a method that has a compilation error that can't be fixed in break mode, you'll try to make a change in your code that isn't supported in break mode, and VB will prompt you to return to design mode. VB will also warn you that your project is in use by another application and that you're about to make a rude shutdown. Your client app will also get an error because the server it was relying on is no longer available. This whole scenario is very messy, and you can avoid it by turning off demand compilation. There is also a Start With Full Compile item on the Run menu (Ctrl-F5) that you can use instead of the Start menu item to force a full compilation of your code before any code is executed.

SingleUse vs. MultiUse

Trying to debug an exposed object that has its Instancing property set to *Creatable SingleUse* can be very frustrating. After your client creates an instance of your singleuse class, any attempt to create another instance will result in a run-time error—even if the first instance is destroyed! This is because SingleUse means that only one instance can be created during the life of the object server and because the VB development environment can't run two instances of the object server project. You must stop the project and run it again each time you want to debug your object server.

One solution to this dilemma is to make your creatable classes multiuse (*Instancing = 2*) instead of singleuse. When you actually create an executable file for your project, switch Instancing back to *SingleUse*.

Compatible Servers: The Server Identity Crisis

In order to support OLE Automation, Visual Basic places a series of several Globally Unique Identifiers (GUIDs) in the system registry to tell external applications about the objects exposed by an object server. A GUID looks like

{13198123-998D-11CE-AB5B-D41203C10000}. You can use the *RegEdit* program provided with Windows to view the system registry. When VB goes to run mode, GUIDs are generated as follows: a GUID for the object library itself, a GUID for each public class, and an additional GUID for each public class that is also creatable. VB stores these GUIDs in the registry. When VB switches back to design mode, the GUIDs created for your exposed objects are removed from the registry. New GUIDs are generated and registered each time you switch an object server project from design mode to run mode.

All of this GUID switching can create a severe identity crisis. Here's why. You'll usually want to debug your server in run mode. As we've seen, to debug the server, you need to call it from a client running in another instance of VB. The client project has a reference to the server project. If you switch both the client and the server from run mode to design mode and restart the server, you'll be unable to restart the client because the identifiers (the GUIDs) for the object library you have referenced will have been removed from the registry and regenerated. The GUIDs referenced by your client application will no longer be valid. In order to get valid references back into the client, you need to manually reestablish them through the References dialog. This means opening the References dialog twice—once to remove the MISSING reference and once to add the new reference. You'll soon find this process tedious and annoying.

Compatible servers come to the rescue. In the Options dialog, on the Project tab, you'll find a Compatible OLE Server: option. ServerB is said to be compatible with ServerA if ServerB exposes all of the classes, properties, and methods ServerA does and if ServerB registers its objects and object library with the same GUIDs ServerA uses. ServerB is free to expand its set of exposed classes as well as to add new properties and methods to the objects exposed by ServerA.

How do compatible servers help with a server's identity crisis? When the compatible server option is set, no new GUIDs are generated when the server switches from design to run mode. VB simply modifies the registry settings to point clients to the running VB project. When your project switches back to design mode, the registry is modified again to point to the compatible server instead of the running VB project.

You've already seen the compatible server option in use without even knowing it. You were able to run the *MailBox Client* applet with MailBx32.Exe acting as the server, and you were able to run the same client with the *MailBox Object Sample* project running as an object server in VB. You switched the object from running in an executable to running in the design environment and back again without having to touch the References dialog in the client project. All of this was possible because we listed MailBx32.Exe as the compatible server for the *MailBox Object Sample* server project for you.

Creating a minimal compatible server

When you sit down at your computer to begin implementing a VB object server, you should have a pretty good idea of the objects you want to expose to other applications. Take the time to figure out the methods, properties, and arguments that will be required to make your exposed objects fully functional. Note, however, that you're rarely going to get it right the first time. You'll probably find that attempts to fully specify an object before implementation of the object has begun will fall short of the mark. Chances are, you'll fail to foresee some subtlety that will later force you to revise your original specification and change the exposed objects you're implementing. If you set the compatible server option and then end up having to delete properties, delete methods, or change arguments, you'll get frequent warnings from VB that the current change you're making to your class will make your server incompatible with the compatible OLE server. For example, changing an argument from an Integer to a Long will generate a warning that you're making your server incompatible.

To overcome this eventuality, make an executable file from a project that has no properties or methods in any of its public classes and use this executable as the compatible server for your project. Let's walk through the steps to make a minimal compatible server for a project called *MyServer* that exposes one class called MyClass:

1. Open a new project in VB.
2. In the Options dialog, on the Project tab, change the project name to *MyServer*.
3. On the same tab, change the Application Description: field to *My Awesome Server*. This description will appear in the References dialog of a client application. Click the OK button to close the Options dialog.
4. From the Insert menu, select Class Module.
5. On the Property Sheet, change the Name property to *MyClass*, and set Public to *True* and Instancing to *2 - Creatable MultiUse*.
6. From the File menu, select Make EXE File.
7. Enter *BaseExe.Exe* as the file name. Click OK to close the Make EXE File dialog.
8. Reopen the Options dialog to the Project tab.
9. Click the ellipsis button (. . .) to the right of the Compatible OLE Server: field to open a file dialog.
10. In the file dialog, select BaseExe.Exe as the compatible server. Click the Open button to exit the file dialog.

11. Click OK to close the Options dialog.
12. Hang on to the project for use in the next section.

What just happened? In steps 1 through 7 you created a simple executable called BaseExe.Exe (ServerA). Then you created a new version of the project (ServerB) that you want to be compatible with the first. Remember that, by definition, a server can remain compatible as long as you only add properties and methods to a class without changing the existing properties, methods, and arguments for the classes that must remain compatible. Now you can go ahead and code the rest of the MyClass class without having to worry about compatibility. Later on in your development cycle when the properties, methods, and arguments of the MyClass class have stabilized, you'll want to delete BaseExe.Exe and list MyServer.Exe as the compatible server.

Object Browser Information

While moving around in the Object Browser, you may have noticed descriptive information about objects that goes beyond the names and arguments of the objects' methods and properties. At the bottom of the Object Browser dialog, below the argument list, is a brief description of the object. There is also a question mark (?) button you can use to view a help topic about the currently selected object, method, or property. You can put similar information in the object library of your VB object server to help you remember how to use your objects and to help other people learn to use them.

Let's set the description and help information for a method. We'll continue with the project we created in the previous section.

1. Add the following subroutine to the MyClass class module:

   ```
   Sub MyMethod()
   End Sub
   ```

2. Press F2 to view the Object Browser.
3. From the Libraries/Projects: dropdown, select MyServer = My Awesome Server.
4. From the Classes/Modules: list, select MyClass.
5. In the Methods/Properties: list, select MyMethod [Sub]. (See Figure 6-6.)

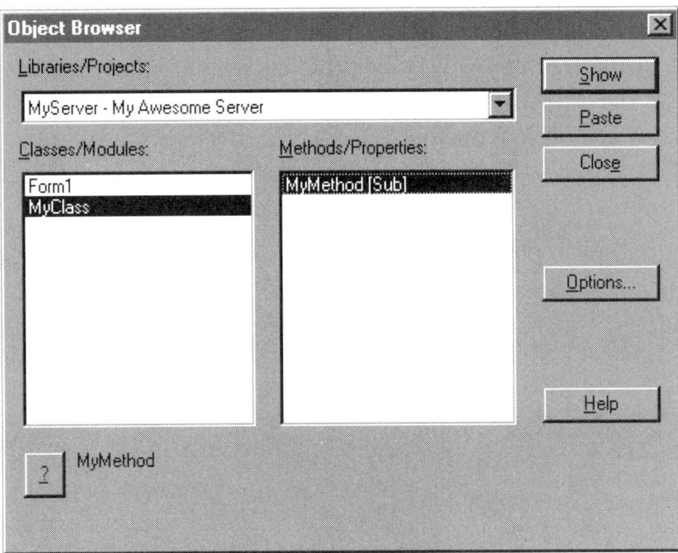

Figure 6-6. *The methods and properties of the* MyClass *class of the* MyServer *project, as shown in the Object Browser.*

6. Now click the Options button.
7. In the Member Options dialog, set the Description: and Help Context ID: for the *MyMethod* method. (See Figure 6-7.) Click OK to return to the Object Browser. Notice that the description you just entered is now visible at the bottom of the dialog.

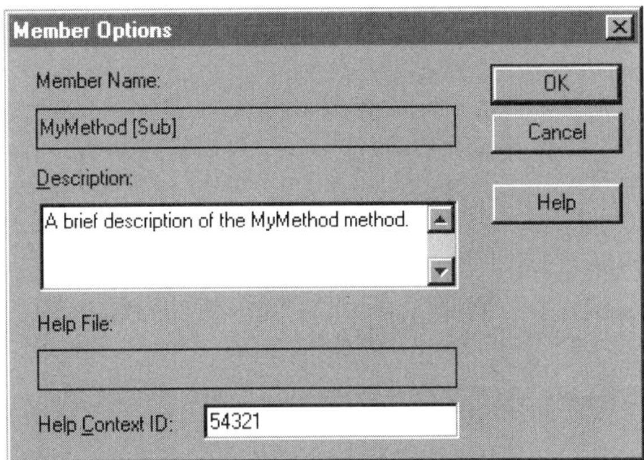

Figure 6-7. *The Member Options dialog box of the Object Browser.*

NOTE You can enter the name of the help file for a project on the Project tab of the Options dialog. This will enable the question mark (?) button on the Object Browser when the project is selected and will put the file name in the read only Help File: field of the Member Options dialog.

Object Servers in DLLs

As you develop Visual Basic object servers, you'll find that many of the classes you expose are used only by external applications. Little or no user interface is required for many classes because many classes essentially become components of the external applications using them. A good example of a component object server is DAO3032.Dll, which implements the data access objects. The .Dll extension on this file tells us a lot about it. It's a DLL (dynamic link library, or application extension), not an EXE (executable file). You can't start DAO3032.Dll as you can an executable file.

DAO is a true component. It can be loaded and used only to support a running application. The operating system, in conjunction with the calling application, loads and unloads the DLL, so the end user never has to know that a DLL was loaded. DAO is also an example of an *in-process server* (DLL) because it runs as part of the same process as the application that's using it. Microsoft Excel and our sample *MailBox Object Sample* server are examples of *cross-process* (EXE) *servers*.

NOTE In the VB4 documentation, EXE servers are called *out-of-process servers*.

A cross-process server, because it is an EXE, can be launched directly by the end user. You can use VB to make both in-process and cross-process servers.

Advantages and Limitations of In-Process Servers

There is one huge advantage in using a DLL as a server: speed. Calling a server implemented in another process requires a huge amount of overhead. In fact, calling a method of an object implemented in a cross-process server usually takes more time than actually running the method! An analogous scenario would be getting up and walking across the room to change the channel on the television (gasp!). Actually changing the channel takes much less time than getting to the television and back to the couch and potato chips. Consider a DLL server to be a remote control: you can instantly set the channel property of the television without burning any calories.

Besides the initial cost of loading the DLL, almost no overhead is required to manipulate the objects exposed by a DLL object server. You can use more of your precious CPU cycles for running the methods of your objects instead of for calling the methods. The overhead of calling into a DLL is about the same as the overhead for calling a procedure in the same project.

But let's look at some of the limitations of objects that are implemented in DLL servers:

- All forms must be shown modally. By definition, a modal window must be closed before you can continue with your application. A modal window is generally known as a dialog. The File-Open and File-Save dialogs we used in Chapter 3 with the *QuickEdit* program are good examples of modal windows. See the *SetProperties* method of the *MailBox Object Sample* program for an example of showing a modal form.
- You must implement *Sub Main*. A startup form is never modal, so a DLL can't have a startup form. However, since you must start somewhere, *Sub Main* is required. *Sub Main* will be called before the first object is created after the DLL is first loaded. For smooth integration with calling applications, keep code in *Sub Main* to a bare minimum. Showing a form, creating objects, or making data access calls in *Sub Main* is a bad idea.
- Creatable objects must be multiuse. A singleuse server has no meaning in a DLL since a process can't load the same DLL twice.
- The *End* statement won't compile if you try to use it in a DLL. A well-behaved DLL shouldn't terminate the application that loaded it.
- DLL servers don't support interoperability, which means that you can't call an object implemented in a 32-bit DLL from a 16-bit application. OLE supports full interoperability for cross-process servers.
- VB4 can't make 16-bit DLLs. This shouldn't be a big concern for us, but it is important information for anyone who needs 16-bit apps. You can still put your 16-bit object server in an EXE. In 16-bit, you'll still get all of the advantages of having an object server, but your object server won't be able to run in-process, so you'll lose the speed advantages you gain in using DLL servers in 32-bit operating systems.
- An untrapped run-time error in a *Class_Initialize()* or *Class_Terminate()* procedure will crash your DLL and the calling application, so be careful.

NOTE The list above just scratches the surface. For a complete list of the restrictions associated with objects implemented in DLL servers, search VB's online help for Programming Restrictions for In-Process OLE Servers.

Making an In-Process (DLL) Server

If your project can comply with the limitations we've just surveyed, you can make a DLL server. From the File menu, choose Make OLE DLL File, enter the name of your DLL, and click OK. That's all. Note that you can make a DLL server compatible with either a DLL or an EXE. If you create both DLL and EXE servers that implement the same object classes and both servers are currently registered with the system, VBA will use the in-process server by default when it creates a new object unless the EXE server is already running.

Debugging a DLL Server

Executable files you create with VB4, whether they're DLLs or EXEs, can't be debugged directly. You must use the VB development environment in run mode to debug your projects. In order to debug a project as though it were a DLL, check Use OLE DLL Restrictions in the Options dialog, Advanced tab. When your project is running with DLL restrictions, attempting to use any of the restricted functionality listed above will cause a compile-time or run-time error.

You won't see the performance benefits of DLL servers until you actually make a DLL. Any server running in the design environment, whether it is simulating an EXE or a DLL, runs cross-process.

Using an In-Process *MailBox* Server

The MailBox directory contains a MailBx32.Dll executable file and the MBox-Dll.Vbp project that was used to create it. Let's use the DLL server:

1. Open the *MailBox Client* project, MBoxCli.Vbp.
2. From the Tools menu, select References to open the References dialog.
3. Remove the reference to *MailBox Object Sample*.
4. Add a reference to *MailBox Object, DLL Server*. If the entry doesn't appear, use the Browse button on the References dialog to open a file dialog. Locate MailBx32.Dll, select it, and click OK. The server's object library will now appear in the References dialog.
5. Click OK to close the References dialog.
6. Run the *MailBox Client* project. Use all the buttons.

To help you keep things straight, here are the main differences between using a DLL server and an EXE server:

- A DLL doesn't have the main form you saw in the *MailBox Object Sample*.
- If you use a DLL, the object is more responsive. The object is created more quickly, and it redraws more quickly than if you use a cross-process server.
- If you use a DLL, an end user can't close down the server, so you don't have to worry about external reference counts.

Performance Comparison

The MBoxPerf.Vbp project is included in the MailBox directory to give you a better feel for the performance differences between DLL and EXE servers. Performance is measured both hard typed and late bound for the in-process and cross-process versions of the MailBox server. You'll want to adjust the number of iterations to match the speed of your machine before clicking any of the buttons. The number of iterations you see in Figure 6-8 was performed on a fast 90-MHz Pentium machine, so adjust accordingly.

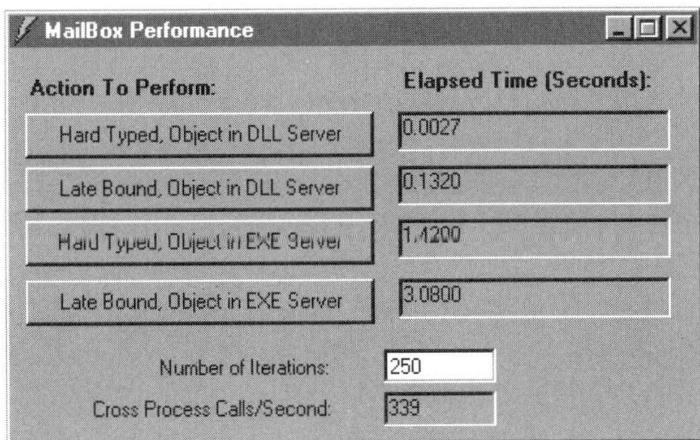

Figure 6-8. *The* MailBox Performance *app with some typical results.*

Here is the code listing for the *MBoxPerf* performance application. Note that this app actually runs 100 times the specified number of iterations for a hard-typed DLL server object and 10 times the specified number of iterations in the late-bound DLL case. The extra iterations are required in order to get an accurate time measurement. This code is a good example of a typical performance benchmark application.

MBoxPerf Code

```
Option Explicit
'VBA.Timer is accurate to 1/10 of a second; GetTickCount is
'accurate to 1/1000 of a second.
Private Declare Function GetTickCount Lib _
    "kernel32" () As Long
'Win16 declares on companion CD
Dim iIterations As Long
Dim m_DllMailBox As MailBoxDll.MailBox
Dim m_ExeMailBox As MailBoxSample.MailBox

Private Sub cmdGo_Click(Index As Integer)
Dim DllEarly As MailBoxDll.MailBox
Dim DllLate As Object
Dim ExeEarly As MailBoxSample.MailBox
Dim ExeLate As Object
Dim KeepTime As Long
Dim i&
    lblTime(Index).Caption = ""
    lblTime(Index).Refresh
    Select Case Index
        Case 0
            Set DllEarly = m_DllMailBox
            KeepTime = GetTickCount
            For i& = 1 To iIterations * 10
                DllEarly.PostColor = DllEarly.PostColor
            Next i&
            KeepTime = (GetTickCount - KeepTime) / 10
        Case 1
            Set DllLate = m_DllMailBox
            KeepTime = GetTickCount
            For i& = 1 To iIterations
                DllLate.PostColor = DllLate.PostColor
            Next i&
            KeepTime = (GetTickCount - KeepTime)
        Case 2
            Set ExeEarly = m_ExeMailBox
            KeepTime = GetTickCount
            For i& = 1 To iIterations
                ExeEarly.PostColor = ExeEarly.PostColor
            Next i&
            KeepTime = GetTickCount - KeepTime
        Case 3
            Set ExeLate = m_ExeMailBox
            KeepTime = GetTickCount
            For i& = 1 To iIterations
```

```
                ExeLate.PostColor = ExeLate.PostColor
            Next i&
            KeepTime = GetTickCount - KeepTime
    End Select
    lblTime(Index).Caption = Format$(KeepTime = 1000, "0.0000")
End Sub

Private Sub Form_Activate()
    'The MailBox EXE server stole the focus.
    'Reactivate our application.
    SetFocus
End Sub

Private Sub Form_Load()
    'Set the initial value of iIterations.
    txtIterations_Change
    'Instantiate a DLL server and an EXE.
    Set m_DllMailBox = New MailBoxDll.MailBox
    Set m_ExeMailBox = New MailBoxSample.MailBox
End Sub

Private Sub lblTime_Change(Index As Integer)
    'Try to calculate cross-process calls per second
    'when the late-bound fields change. Each iteration
    'is calling the PostColor property twice. A late-bound
    'call makes two cross-process calls, so multiply iIterations
    'by a factor of 4.
    Select Case Index
        Case 1, 3
            If Len(lblTime(1)) Then
                If Len(lblTime(3)) Then
                    lblXProcPerSecond = _
                        CInt(iIterations * 4 / (lblTime(3) -lblTime(1)))
                    Exit Sub
                End If
            End If
            lblXProcPerSecond = ""
    End Select
End Sub

Private Sub txtIterations_Change()
    On Error Resume Next
    iIterations = txtIterations.Text
    'Beep if the text can't be coerced to a numeric value.
    If Err Then Beep
End Sub
```

One final lesson we can learn from this *MailBox* performance app is how to deal with duplicate class names in the same project. Both the EXE and the DLL *MailBox* servers expose MailBox classes. If you don't specify which MailBox class you want to use, VBA will resolve the MailBox class to the object library that appears nearest the top of the references list. The priority buttons on the References dialog allow you to adjust the relative priority of referenced object libraries.

If you need to refer to a class with a duplicate name defined in an object library that doesn't have the highest priority, you must qualify the declaration of the object variable with the name of the object library. Since it wasn't worth remembering the order in which we had added the references to our two *MailBox* servers, in the performance app we qualified all references to the MailBox object name with the name of the object library containing it. If an object name can be resolved by two different referenced object libraries, you may want to qualify the object name with the library name to clarify your code.

```
Dim m_DllMailBox As MailBoxDll.MailBox
Dim m_ExeMailBox As MailBoxSample.MailBox
:
Set m_DllMailBox = New MailBoxDll.MailBox
Set m_ExeMailBox = New MailBoxSample.MailBox
```

Qualifying an object reference with an object library name will be a frequent requirement when your VB application controls more than one Office application because most of the Office applications expose a class called Application.

SUMMARY

- The set of classes available for use in the Visual Basic for Applications language can be extended in any given Visual Basic project to include external objects exposed by object libraries. Even VB objects such as buttons and forms are recognized by VBA because the VB project maintains a reference to an object library describing the basic VB objects.

- Once you have used the References dialog to add a reference to an external object library to your project, you can view the properties and methods of the classes implemented in the referenced object library by means of the Object Browser. You can also manipulate a library object in VBA code in the same way you would any internally implemented object, but you don't need to see the code that implements the object you're using.

- You can create and manipulate external objects in a late-bound fashion if you don't have an object library for the implemented objects. However, the flexibility of generic objects comes at a price. You incur a severe performance penalty when you use generic, late-bound object variables instead of using an object library.

- A VB application can expose any of its class modules as an externally available class by setting the Public property on the class module. An object can be created from a class by means of the *New* keyword if the Instancing property of the class is set to *Creatable SingleUse* or *Creatable MultiUse*.

- A server that also exposes a user interface must keep careful track of the objects it has created for external applications. A server that has outstanding objects owned by other applications should refuse to shut down until all of the external objects have been destroyed.

- A VB object server can be debugged just as a normal VB application can be—with breakpoints and other standard debugging techniques. A compatible server should be used to simplify repeated debugging sessions.

- VB is capable of creating both in-process (DLL) and cross-process (EXE) OLE servers. In-process servers should be used when speed is crucial and the exposed objects don't require features that aren't supported by DLL servers.

We know enough about the world of OLE Automation objects now to be able to explore and manipulate the extensive object libraries exposed by Office for Windows 95 applications. In Chapter 7, we'll use a VB form as an in-place activation site. And starting with Chapter 8, we'll manipulate objects exposed by the Office for Windows 95 applications and enable those applications to manipulate objects exposed in VB object servers.

7

Using Insertable Objects and Container Controls

So far we've been focusing on the object-oriented aspects of Visual Basic as a stand-alone product. In the rest of the book we'll look at how to use VB with the various OLE Automation objects of Microsoft Office for Windows 95. Before we do that, though, let's take a chapter to get acquainted with some objects that will save you a lot of time and give you a simple way to enable your VB applications to integrate with other applications that support OLE: insertable objects and OLE container controls.

Both insertable objects and OLE container controls show up in your VB toolbox. Insertable objects are made available when you install any application that is an in-place activation server on your machine, although you still need to add the specific objects to your toolbox if you want to use them. The OLE container is a standard control that comes with VB. If you want an object to appear on a VB application's form and you want immediate functionality—you want the user to be able to double-click on an object to in-place activate it, for example—consider using an insertable object or an OLE container control.

Using Insertable Objects

An insertable object allows you to make use of the powerful user interface features of other applications such as Microsoft Excel within your own Visual Basic programs. Once you've put an insertable object such as a Microsoft Word document or a Microsoft PowerPoint slide on a VB form, a user can in-place activate the embedded object—usually by double-clicking—and manipulate the object with all the functionality of the application that supplied the insertable object—sometimes called the *native application.*

Take a look at the VB form shown in Figure 7-1.

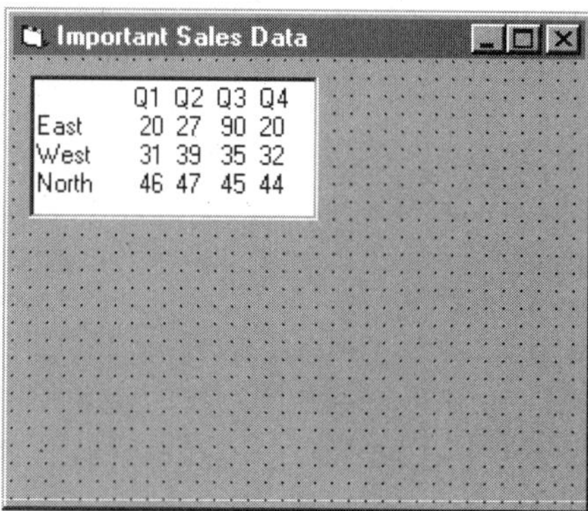

Figure 7-1. *A Visual Basic form containing basic data.*

This form contains basic data that could benefit from being spruced up with a graph. And let's say you wanted the user to be able to change the type of graph, the colors, the data series, and so on. You'd have to write a ton of code to pull it off. Enter insertable objects. Stick a Microsoft Graph insertable object into the form. When a user runs your VB application, she'll be able to activate the graph object and make any changes to the graph that she could make if she were running Microsoft Graph itself. See Figure 7-2 for an example of how the new running application might look. And you could achieve this miracle without writing any code!

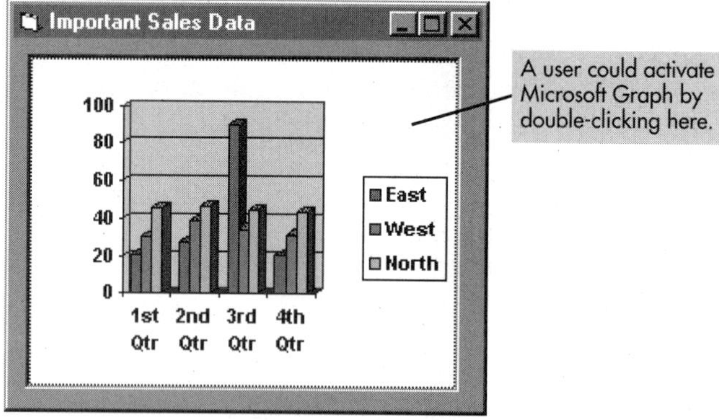

Figure 7-2. *A Visual Basic form containing a Microsoft Graph insertable object.*

Generally, you'd want to use insertable objects to make use of features unique to a certain application, features you wouldn't want to replicate yourself in your VB applications. Suppose you wanted a VB form that contained a bitmap. That would be easy enough to achieve with a VB Image control or a VB PictureBox control. But what if you wanted the user to be able to edit the picture? You wouldn't want to write the code that would enable the user to paint with different colors and brushes and to use the other functions that already exist in an application such as Paintbrush. Why reinvent Paintbrush?

Using an insertable object is a quick way to introduce another application's capabilities into your VB application form so that a user can manipulate, say, a Microsoft Excel spreadsheet, a Word document, or a PowerPoint slide or presentation on your form. If you know at design-time what type of OLE object is going to be used by your program, you can make good use of an insertable object. Let's look at setting up insertable objects at design-time.

Adding an Insertable Object at Design-Time

You use the Visual Basic Custom Controls dialog to add insertable objects to your VB toolbox just as you do to add VB controls. Let's add a WordPad insertable object to your VB toolbox so that you can use a WordPad document in a VB application.

1. From the VB Tools menu, select Custom Controls. You'll see a dialog box like the one shown in Figure 7-3.

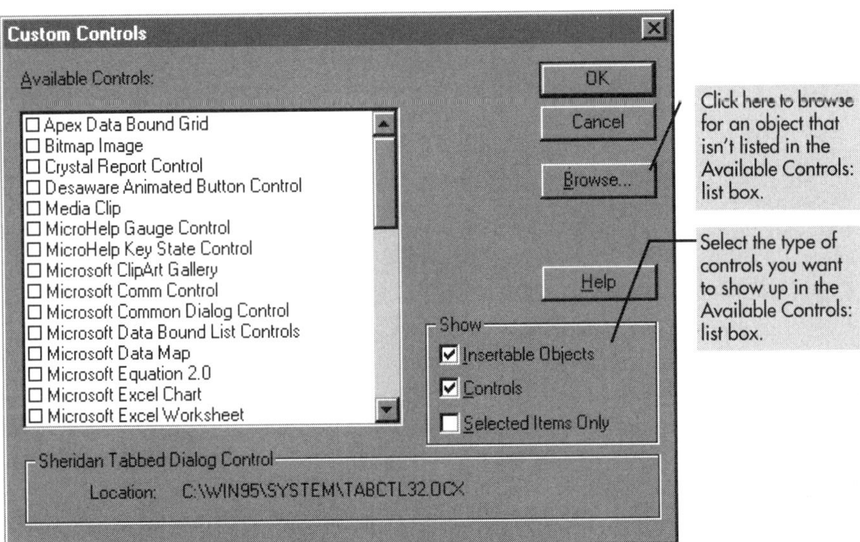

Figure 7-3. *The Visual Basic Custom Controls dialog box.*

You use this dialog to determine which insertable objects (and/or controls) are available on your toolbar.

2. Make sure the Insertable Objects check box inside the Show frame is selected. If it isn't, click to select it.
3. Select WordPad Document under the available controls.
4. Click OK, and notice that a button for the WordPad Document insertable object shows up in your toolbox. See Figure 7-4.

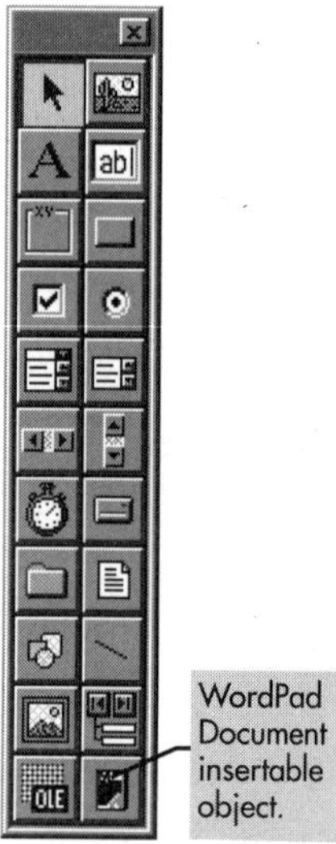

Figure 7-4. *The Visual Basic toolbox containing a button for a WordPad Document insertable object.*

5. Click the WordPad Document insertable object button, and insert a WordPad document into your VB form.
6. Type some words into the document—include some formatted text by using the menu options that appear on the form—and then press Esc.
7. Click on the form outside the text area, and press F5 to run your program.

   Your form will come up, and the text you typed in, including its formatting, will be displayed on the form. If you double-click on the text, the WordPad application will come up, and you'll be able to edit the text. If you had created a menu on your VB form, the form would have a position set aside for a menu bar so WordPad would have been in-place activated, that is, opened as part of the VB form rather than coming up as a separate application.

NOTE A form must have a menu in order for an insertable object to in-place activate, and the form's NegotiateMenus property must be set to *True*. See page 170 for a discussion of toolbars and menus.

8. Make some changes. If the document was in-place activated, press Esc when you have completed your changes. If the WordPad application was activated, close WordPad to return to your VB form.

   Your changes will be saved in the embedded document.

Manipulating an Insertable Object at Run-Time

An insertable object has only four events—and four corresponding event procedures—associated with it: *DragDrop*, *DragOver*, *GotFocus*, and *LostFocus*. Each of these events works just as it does with other Visual Basic custom controls. Aside from responding to these four events, the program can't control an insertable object at run-time unless the object's native application supports OLE Automation.

Using OLE Automation with insertable objects

Some of the Microsoft applications that provide insertable objects support OLE Automation. You can use a Visual Basic project to programmatically manipulate the data in these objects that come from other applications through the VB custom control Object property. For example, you'd use the following statement to set the title of a PowerPoint slide insertable object from within a VB program at run-time. (See Chapter 13 for information on automating PowerPoint.)

```
'olePPSlide is the PowerPoint slide insertable object.
'You address the Object property of the insertable
'object just as you would address a separate instance
'of the real thing (a PowerPoint slide).
olePPSlide.object.Objects.Title.Text = "This is the new title."
```

Unfortunately, you can't programmatically activate an insertable object, so, while the change to the slide title will actually take place, the insertable object itself won't reflect the change unless the user manually activates the object while running the VB program by double-clicking on the object. Then the change to the title will show up on the slide object in your VB program. Programmatic changes that the user can't immediately see aren't all that useful.

NOTE Not all insertable objects support OLE Automation.

Insertable objects are put to best use if you know what application you want to take up real estate on your form and if you want to just turn over control of that part of your form to the user at run-time. If you want to take advantage of the capabilities OLE Automation offers, you're better off using an OLE container control instead of an insertable object because you can programmatically activate the object so that the user can see any programmatic changes you make at run-time.

Using OLE Container Controls

An OLE container control is similar to an insertable object in that it appears on a Visual Basic form, is an object native to another application, and can be in-place activated by the user at run-time. There are some big differences, though. Here's a list of the principal differences between an OLE container control and an insertable object:

- You can change the class of the object contained in an OLE container control—tantamount to changing the object's native application—at design-time or at run-time. For example, you can switch a container control from being a PowerPoint slide to being a Word document.
- Each OLE object class can support its own set of verbs, and OLE container controls support their classes' verbs. OLE container control verbs include open in-place, open application in a separate window, hide the application that created the object, and other application-specific commands.
- OLE container controls can be programmatically activated, saved, retrieved, and deactivated at run-time, and the VB application will reflect those commands on-screen without needing intervention from the user.
- OLE container controls can be either embedded or linked, unlike insertable objects, which can only be embedded. (We'll talk about linking in this section.)

Creating a Container Control Object at Design-Time

If you know what application class you initially want an OLE container control to belong to you can assign the control an OLE object at design-time, by either embedding the object information in the control or linking the control to a separate file.

Creating an embedded container control object at design-time

An embedded container control object, like an embedded insertable object, resides in your application and contains its own set of data. You can create a new embedded object for a container control, or you can import an object from an existing file. But if you embed an object in your Visual Basic form and make changes, the changes will exist only in the object on your form, even if you initially imported the file from somewhere else. The changes won't show up in the original file.

A new object Let's try embedding a new WordPad object into a container control on a VB form. (If you're running Windows NT 3.51, you don't have WordPad. Substitute a Microsoft Excel spreadsheet for the WordPad document in this exercise.)

1. Place an OLE container from the VB toolbox on your VB form. You'll immediately see the Insert Object dialog shown in Figure 7-5. You'll use the dialog to initialize the OLE container control with a new object.

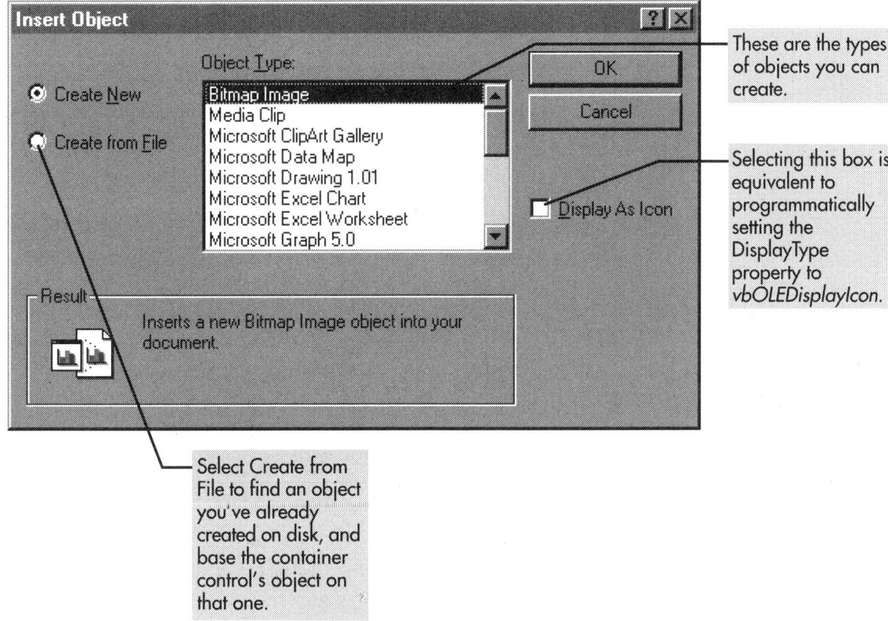

Figure 7-5. *The Visual Basic Insert Object dialog box with Create New selected.*

2. Select Create New.
3. In the Object Type: list, find and click on WordPad Document, and then click OK.

   With Create New selected, you'll be able to create a completely new WordPad document instance in this control. If Create from File were selected, you'd be able to import, or copy, the contents of an already existing object into your container control.

4. Type some text into your new WordPad document. Your form should look something like the one shown in Figure 7-6 on the next page.

Figure 7-6. *A new WordPad document in an OLE container control.*

Create the document you'd like to see when your VB form loads. You can edit the document right there on your form!

5. When you're finished, click somewhere else on the form or press the Esc key. Your object is no longer active.
6. If you want to use the actual WordPad program to edit your object, right-click on the object and, from the popup menu, select Open. There you go: WordPad actually loads, and you can use WordPad to edit your object to look exactly the way you want it to when a user loads your program. When you're finished editing your object, close WordPad and you'll see your changes on the form.
7. Press F5 to run your program and see what a user of your program would see. The program comes up, and the user sees a WordPad document embedded in your program screen.
8. Double-click on the WordPad object. As the user, you can now edit and resave the document. As the programmer, you've achieved the functionality of WordPad without having to write the code!

NOTE WordPad came up when the user double-clicked on the document object because the OLE container control's AutoActivate property is set to *Double-Click* by default. We'll look at this property later in the chapter.

FYI

Embedding from the Windows 95 Explorer

Now let's try something else just for fun.

1. Go to the Windows 95 Explorer, and locate any Office file—*.Doc, *.Xls, or *.Ppt. Right-click on the file name, and select Copy from the popup menu.
2. Go back to VB in design mode, right-click on your OLE container, and then select Paste from the popup menu.

Cool, huh? Visual Basic is integrated with the Windows 95 Explorer so that the file you copied has been embedded in your OLE container control.

An object created from an existing file You've created a new WordPad object and stored it in an OLE container control. But what if you already have a document that you want to embed in your VB form—say, a Microsoft Word file? To base the embedded container control object on an already existing file, follow these steps:

1. Repeat step 1 of the preceding section.
2. In the Insert Object dialog, select Create from File instead of Create New. (See Figure 7-7.)

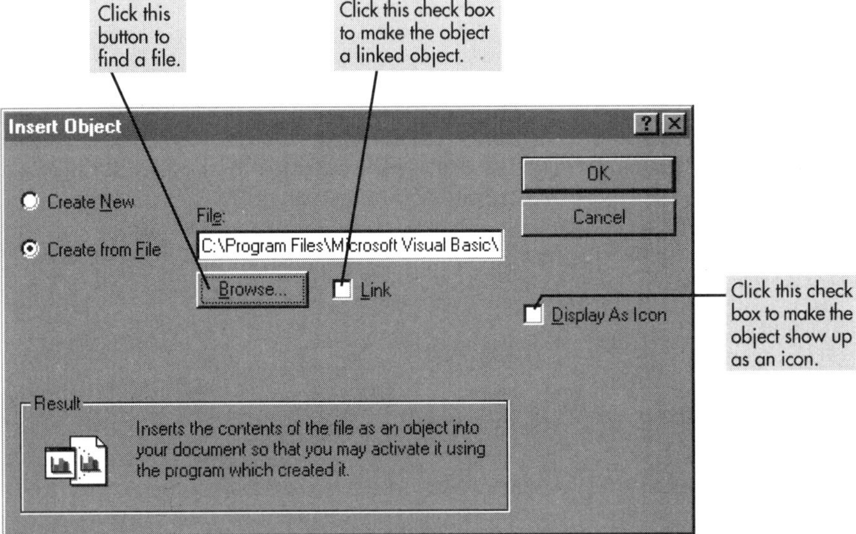

Figure 7-7. *The Visual Basic Insert Object dialog box with Create from File selected.*

3. Now click the Browse button and select a Microsoft WordPad file from which to embed your object—Xyz.Doc, say. A copy of Xyz.Doc will now be embedded in your OLE container control. Subsequent changes in the original version of Xyz.Doc won't flow through to the object embedded in your form, and changes you make to the Xyz.Doc embedded in your container control won't flow back to the original version of Xyz.Doc.

Linking an object to a container control at design-time

Let's say that you wanted to use a document that was out on the network in one of your VB program's container controls and that you wanted any changes to the document on the network to flow through to the document in your Visual Basic form. Suppose also that you'd like to be able to make changes to that file directly from the container control in your VB program and have those changes be reflected in the original file out on the network. By clicking the Link check box in the Insert Object dialog (see Figure 7-7 on the previous page), you can link the object instead of embedding it, which means that changes to the original file will be reflected in your object and vice versa. OK, let's try it.

1. Right-click on the old OLE container control in your VB form, and select Insert Object from the popup menu. The object you assign to the container control now will replace the current one. In this case, we're going to replace an embedded copy of Xyz.Doc with a link to the original version of Xyz.Doc.
2. Select Create from File.
3. Click the Browse button, and find the Xyz.Doc file that we used in the previous exercise.
4. Select Xyz.Doc, and click Insert.
5. Select the Link check box and click OK. Click Yes when you're prompted to delete the existing embedded object. The Xyz.Doc object is now linked to the container control rather than embedded in it.
6. From the Windows 95 Start menu, select Run, type in *WordPad*, and then click OK.

NOTE If WordPad doesn't come up, it probably isn't installed on your system. Install Accessories from the Windows 95 Installation CD.

7. Find your original copy of Xyz.Doc, make some changes, save it, and exit WordPad.

8. Press F5 to run your program, and double-click on the Xyz.Doc document on your form. Notice that the linked document on your form changes to reflect the changes you made to the original document and that WordPad comes up along with the linked file.
9. Make changes to the file in WordPad, save the file, and exit. The changes are now saved in Xyz.Doc and are reflected in your VB application.
10. Exit your VB application.

Creating a Container Control Object at Run-Time

If you don't know initially what object you want an OLE container control to contain, that's OK. You can assign an OLE object to the container control at run-time by using the control's methods and properties in your code. In past versions of Visual Basic you'd assign a value to the Action property to initiate an action on the OLE container control. The Action property is still supported in VB4, but VB4 comes with more sophisticated ways to manipulate an OLE container control.

The following two tables list the OLE container control properties and methods we'll look at in this chapter and their VB Help descriptions. Check VB Help for a more thorough list and treatment.

IMPORTANT OLE CONTAINER CONTROL PROPERTIES

Property	*Description*
AppIsRunning	Returns or sets a value that indicates whether the application that created the object in the OLE container control is running. Not available at design-time.
AutoActivate	Returns or sets a value that enables the user to activate an object by double-clicking the OLE container control or by moving the focus to the OLE container control.
Class	Identifies the type of the object contained by the OLE container control.
DataField	Specifies the field name used to retrieve the value of a control from a database.
DataSource	Specifies the Data control used to bind data to the OLE container control. Not available at run-time.
DisplayType	Indicates whether an object displays its contents or an icon.
Object	Indicates that the properties and methods provided by the active class are being called rather than the properties and methods with the same names that are provided by VB. A run-time, read-only property.
ObjectVerbFlags	Returns the menu state for each verb in the ObjectVerbs array.
ObjectVerbs	Returns the list of verbs an object supports.

(continued)

IMPORTANT OLE CONTAINER CONTROL PROPERTIES *continued*

Property	***Description***
ObjectVerbsCount	Returns the number of verbs supported by an object.
OLEDropAllowed	Returns or sets a value that determines whether an OLE container control can be a drop target for drag-and-drop.
OLEType	Determines whether the object in the OLE container control is embedded in or linked to the control.
OLETypeAllowed	Determines the type of object you can create (Linked, Embedded, or Either).
PasteOK	Returns a value telling you whether the contents of the clipboard can be pasted into the control.
SizeMode	Determines how an object's icon or data image is displayed in the OLE container control.
SourceDoc	When you're creating a linked object, determines which source file to link. When you're creating an embedded object, determines the file to use as a template.
SourceItem	Specifies data within a file to link (linked objects only).

IMPORTANT OLE CONTAINER CONTROL METHODS

Method	***Description***
CreateEmbed	Creates an embedded object.
CreateLink	Creates a linked object.
DoVerb	Executes the specified (or default) verb on the object.
FetchVerbs	Updates the list of verbs an object supports.
InsertObjDlg	Displays the Insert Object dialog box, which allows the user to select at run-time the type of object (linked or embedded) that will be inserted into the OLE container control.
PasteSpecialDlg	Brings up the Paste Special dialog box, which allows the user at run-time to paste an object from the system clipboard to the container control.
ReadFromFile	Loads an object from a data file created by means of the *SaveToFile* method.
SaveToFile	Saves an object to a data file.
Update	Retrieves current data from a source document and displays it in the container control.

Creating an embedded container control object at run-time

You can use the *CreateEmbed* method to create an embedded object programmatically at run-time. *CreateEmbed* has two arguments: sourcedoc, which is the file from which the object should be created, and class, which is the kind of object you are embedding.

NOTE The class argument is needed only if you want to create an empty embedded object, leaving out the sourcedoc argument.

The following code creates an embedded object from an existing file:

```
OLE1.CreateEmbed "C:\ObjProg\Chapter7\Income Statement.Xls"
```

This code creates an empty embedded Excel object:

```
OLE1.CreateEmbed "", "Excel.Sheet"
```

Creating a linked container control object at run-time

You can use the *CreateLink* method to link an object to a container control at run-time. *CreateLink* takes one required argument, sourcedoc, which is the file from which the object should be created, and an optional argument, sourceitem, which specifies the data within a source file that you want to be linked to the container control. This code links a Microsoft Excel document to a container control at run-time:

```
OLE1.CreateLink "C:\ObjProg\Chapter7\Income Statement.Xls"
```

This code links a section of a Microsoft Excel document to a container control at run-time:

```
OLE1.CreateLink _
  "C:\ObjProg\Chapter7\Income Statement.Xls", "R5C2:R11C9"
```

This code links an Excel range designated by the name *GrossMargin* to a container control at run-time:

```
OLE1.CreateLink _
   "C:\ObjProg\Chapter7\Income Statement.Xls", "GrossMargin"
```

Once you've linked an object to a container control at run-time, the object acts just as it would if you had linked it at design-time: a user can activate it, make changes, and so forth.

Letting the User Specify Container Control Objects at Run-Time

To enable the user to create container control objects at run-time, have your Visual Basic program display the Insert Object dialog. (Refer back to Figure 7-5.) The *InsertObjDlg* method brings up the Insert Object dialog, which presents the list of available objects. Just as you, the programmer, did in the earlier examples, now the user decides whether the objects he or she chooses from the list will be embedded or linked.

Here's how the code might look:

```
Private Sub Command1_Click ()
   With OLE1
        'Display Insert Object dialog box.
        .InsertObjDlg
        'Check for success.
        If .OLEType = vbOLENone Then
            Msgbox "Object Insert Failed"
        End If
    End With
End Sub
```

Once you call the *InsertObjDlg* method, the user makes choices in the dialog and clicks OK to finish creation of the object.

NOTE You can programmatically set the type of object allowed—linked or embedded or either—with the OLETypeAllowed property. Once the object is created, you can determine whether the OLE container control contains a linked object, an embedded object, or no object using the OLEType property.

Verbs

OK, so we have an OLE container control with an object in it. What do we do now? Each object has its own set of verbs—things it can do—and the *DoVerb* method enables you to programmatically use any verb that an object supports.

You use *FetchVerbs*, ObjectVerbs, and ObjectVerbsCount to find out what verbs an object supports. The *FetchVerbs* method returns the verbs attached to a certain object. ObjectVerbs is a zero-based string array attached to the control object that will contain the returned list of verbs. And ObjectVerbsCount tells you how many verbs are in the ObjectVerbs array.

This code uses the three elements to determine what verbs an object (in this case, a Microsoft Excel spreadsheet) supports:

```
Dim Counter As Integer
  With OLE1
        .CreateEmbed "", "Excel.Sheet"
        'Update the list of available verbs.
        .FetchVerbs
```

```
        'The first element (0) in ObjectVerbs signifies
        'the default verb but also duplicates another
        'verb in the list. So we start cycling with 1
        'because the verb with that index is the first
        'unique verb in the list. We end with
        'ObjectVerbsCount - 1 because ObjectVerbsCount
        'includes the duplicate verb.
        For Counter = 1 To .ObjectVerbsCount - 1
            MsgBox .ObjectVerbs(Counter)
        Next Counter
    End With
```

The standard set of verbs any object should support include *vbOLEPrimary*, *vbOLEShow*, *vbOLEOpen*, *vbOLEHide*, *vbOLEUIActivate*, *vbOLEInPlaceActivate*, and *vbOLEDiscardUndoState*. Depending on how the object is implemented, these verbs may or may not show up in the ObjectVerbs array. Check Visual Basic Help for more information. The two verbs you'll probably use most often are *vbOLEShow* and *vbOLEOpen*. *vbOLEShow* activates an object for editing. If the application that created the object supports in-place activation, the object is activated within the OLE container control. *vbOLEOpen* opens the object in a separate application window.

Let's look at an example of using the *DoVerb* method with the *vbOLEInPlaceActivate* verb. The following code creates an empty embedded object and then activates the application that created it by means of the *DoVerb* method.

```
OLE1.CreateEmbed "", "Excel.Sheet"
OLE1.DoVerb vbOLEInPlaceActivate
```

OLE Container Control Properties

The new OLE container control that comes with Visual Basic 4 contains several properties that make programming the container control at run-time much easier then ever before. We'll review a few of those properties in this section.

The AutoActivate property

The AutoActivate property is attached to an OLE container control that determines the conditions under which an OLE source application is activated. AutoActivate can be set to the values listed in the table on the next page.

THE AutoActivate PROPERTY VALUES

Value	*Constant*	*Description*
0 - Manual	vbOLEActivateManual	The control's object must be activated through code. Use the *DoVerb* method.
1 - Focus	vbOLEActivateGetFocus	The application that provides the object is activated when the user single-clicks the control.
2 - Double-Click	vbOLEActivateDoubleclick	(The default) The application that provides the object is activated when the user double-clicks the control.
3 - Automatic	vbOLEActivateAuto	The application that provides the object is activated according to the object's normal method of activation—either when the control receives focus or when the user double-clicks the control.

The SizeMode property

SizeMode determines how a control is sized and/or displayed on your form. Its possible values and descriptions from VB Help are shown in the table below.

THE SizeMode PROPERTY VALUES

Value	*Constant*	*Description*
0 - Clip	vbOLESizeClip	(The default) The object is displayed in the control in its actual size. If the object is larger than the container control, its image is clipped by the control's borders.
1 - Stretch	vbOLESizeStretch	The object's image adjusts its proportions so that it can fill the control.
2 - Autosize	vbOLESizeAutoSize	The control adjusts its size so that it can display the entire object. This value is a good one to use because you don't have to worry about sizing.
3 - Zoom	vbOLESizeZoom	The object adjusts to fill the control as much as possible while still maintaining its original proportions. This value is a better one to use than Stretch because the object doesn't get as distorted.

The OLEDropAllowed property

OLEDropAllowed adds a lot of flexibility to the OLE container control at run-time. If you set this property to *True* (at either design-time or run-time), a user can drag data from an OLE application and drop the information into the OLE container control at run-time. The control will automatically accept the drag-and-drop operation from applications that support OLE drag and drop.

The AppIsRunning property

You can tell if the application that created the object in your OLE container control is running with the AppIsRunning property. You can also use this property to start and stop the application.

To check if the application is running, you'd use code like the following:

```
If OLE1.AppIsRunning Then MsgBox "Yup, it's running!"
```

To stop the application, you'd use code like this:

```
OLE1.AppIsRunning = False
```

The PasteOK property

The PasteOK property tells you if the current information in the clipboard can be pasted into the container control. Here's an example:

```
'If container control will accept contents
'of clipboard, then paste them into the control.
With OLE1
    If .PasteOK Then .Paste
End With
```

OLE Container Control Methods

The following sections discuss the OLE container control methods.

The *Update* method

If an object is linked to the container control, the object isn't automatically aware of changes that are made to the sourcedoc. To programmatically update the linked object, use the *Update* method, as in the following line:

```
OLE1.Update
```

The *SaveToFile* and *ReadFromFile* methods

When the user closes a form or exits an application, any changes the user made to any embedded objects are lost. You can use the *SaveToFile* method to save updated data from an object to a file.

NOTE The file won't be saved in the native format of the object's class (WordPad format, for example, or Microsoft Excel), so you won't be able to just double-click on the file in Windows Explorer to edit it. You'll have to use the *ReadFromFile* method to load it again.

For linked objects, changes the user makes to the object are stored in the sourcedoc, so you don't need to use the *SaveToFile* method.

Let's write a program to open a file and save it as an object in a container.

1. Put an OLE container control, containing a Microsoft Excel Worksheet, on a new Visual Basic form.
2. Enter some data in one of the worksheet cells.
3. Add a button to the form.
4. Rename the button cmdSaveOLEObject, and change the caption to Save OLE Object.
5. In the *cmdSaveOLEObject_Click()* event procedure, type the following code:

```
Private Sub cmdSaveOLEObject_Click ()
Dim FileNum as Integer
    'Get file number.
    FileNum = FreeFile
    'Open Blah.Ole.
    Open "C:\ObjProg\Chapter7\Blah.Ole" For Binary As #FileNum
    'Save Blah.Ole.
    OLE1.SaveToFile FileNum
    'Close Blah.Ole.
    Close FileNum
End Sub
```

6. Press F5 to run your program, and click the Save OLE Object button. C:\ObjProg\Chapter7\Blah.Ole is now saved with the data from your container control.

You can reload the object into your OLE container control using the *ReadFromFile* method. Let's modify the program we just wrote to read the file back into the container control:

1. Return to design mode, and create a new button on your form. Call it cmdLoadOLEObject, and change the caption to Load OLE Object.

2. Create the following *cmdLoadOLEObject_Click()* event procedure:

```
Private Sub cmdLoadOLEObject_Click ()
Dim FileNum as Integer
    'Get file number.
    FileNum = FreeFile
    'Open Blah.Ole.
    Open "C:\ObjProg\Chapter7\Blah.Ole" For Binary As #FileNum
    'Read Blah.Ole.
    OLE1.ReadFromFile FileNum
    'Close Blah.Ole.
    Close FileNum
End Sub
```

3. Press F5 to run your program.
4. Double-click on the container control, and insert data into some of the cells. Press Esc when you're done.
5. Click Load OLE Object. Your changes are replaced with the original worksheet you saved in your container control.

The *Updated* Event

How do you know when you need to save the contents of an OLE container control? The control has an *Updated* event and corresponding event procedure. You might use the *Updated()* event procedure to set a "dirty" flag as we did in the *QuickEdit* program in Chapter 2 to indicate that the contents of the container have been changed. Reset the flag when you save the contents of the object. To avoid locking up your program, be sure not to change the object in the *Updated()* event procedure; just set a dirty flag as shown in the following example:

```
Private Sub OLE1_Updated(Code As Integer)
    intDirtyFlag = True
End Sub
Private Sub Form_QueryUnload(Cancel As Integer, UnloadMode As Integer)
    If intDirtyFlag Then SaveOLEFileSub
End Sub
```

The *PasteSpecialDlg* method

You display the Paste Special dialog at run-time to enable the user to paste either an embedded or a linked object from the clipboard. You can use the OLETypeAllowed property to determine or set the type of object creation (linked, embedded, or either) a control supports. If the PasteOK property setting is *True*, Visual Basic will paste the object into the container control.

Here's the code:

```
With OLE1
    If .PasteOK Then .PasteSpecialDlg
End With
```

Binding an OLE Container Control to a Database

Visual Basic data controls let you write no-code database applications. Starting with Visual Basic 4, you can link an OLE container control directly to the Data control. This is easy to do! Let's look at a quick example:

1. Put a data control from the VB toolbox shown in Figure 7-8 on a fresh VB form.

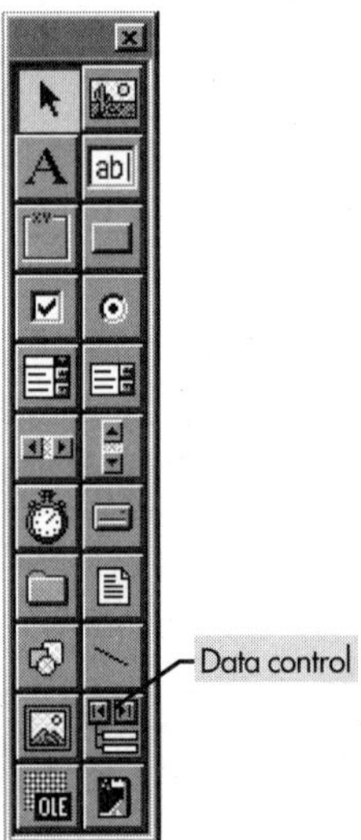

Figure 7-8. *The Data control on the Visual Basic toolbox.*

2. Rename the data control datNorthwind.
3. Set the data control's DatabaseName property by clicking the *ellipsis* (. . .) button and browsing to find the Northwind.Mdb database in the \Chapter7 directory on the companion CD.
4. Set the data control's RecordSource property by clicking the down-arrow button to see the options—the tables in the database. Select the Employees table.

5. Put an OLE container control on your form. Cancel the Insert Object dialog when it appears. Your form should look like the one shown in Figure 7-9.

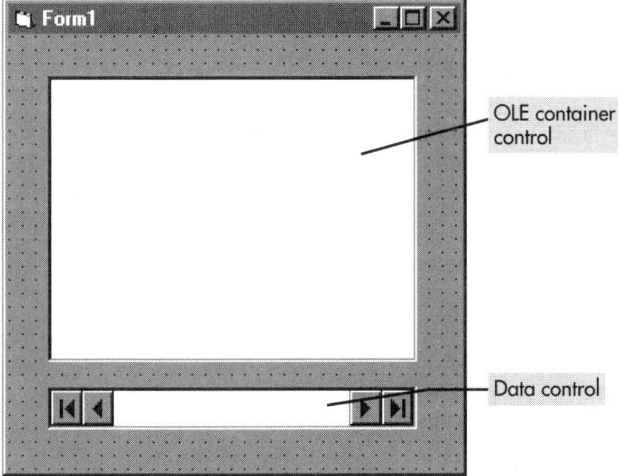

Figure 7-9. *A Visual Basic form with an OLE container control and a data control.*

6. Set the container control's SizeMode property by clicking the down-arrow button and selecting 2 - AutoSize.

NOTE When an OLE container control's SizeMode property is set to *2 - AutoSize,* the control is automatically sized to accommodate the display size of the object contained in the control. If the display size of the object changes, the control automatically resizes itself.

7. Set the container control's DataSource property by clicking the down-arrow button to see the one option, which is the only data control you've put on the form: datNorthwind.

8. Set the container control's DataField property by clicking the down-arrow button to see the fields in the Employees table. Select Photo.

9. Press F5 to run the program. You should be able to click the arrows to move back and forth between the employee pictures. Find one you want to, er, edit, and double-click on the picture. It will come up in Paintbrush, ready for you to edit. After you add a mustache and exit Paintbrush, your changes will be saved in the database. Voilà. Pretty easy to save and retrieve OLE objects to a database, eh?

Toolbars and Menus

Toolbars and menus are a snap to build for a single Visual Basic form. But because you're focusing on objects instead of stand-alone applications, you have to be concerned with integrating your VB form toolbars and menus with the toolbars and menus from other objects and applications.

Things get a little tricky when you start having to negotiate toolbars and menus among forms, insertable objects, OLE container controls, and so on. You become the traffic cop. It may sound a little tough, but it's not really all that hard. See the VB Help file if you need information about creating toolbars and menus. In this section, we'll look at some of the issues you'll run into while playing traffic cop to toolbars and menus from multiple applications.

MDI Applications

You'll have to engage in some toolbar wizardry if you deal with multiple document interface (MDI) applications. If you don't know what an MDI application is, take a look at Figure 7-10. You'll notice that there are actually two forms: one looks like a container form—that's the MDI parent form—and one looks like it's inside the container form—that's the child form.

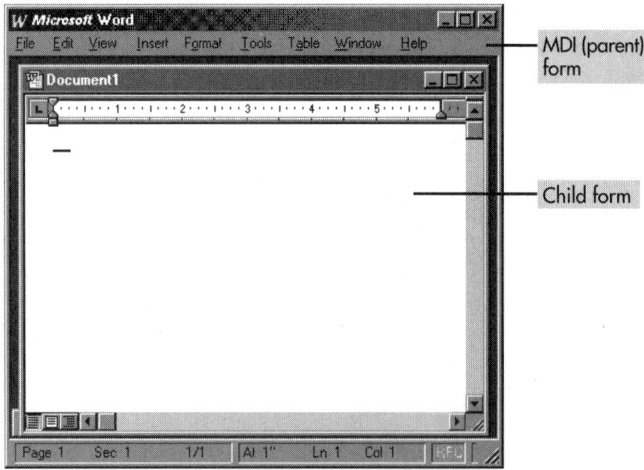

Figure 7-10. *A Microsoft Word screen showing the parent and child forms characteristic of an MDI application.*

To create an MDI application, you first create an MDI form and then create one or more child forms.

1. Create a new VB project. From the Visual Basic Insert menu, select MDI Form. Name it frmParent.

NOTE An application can have only one MDI form.

2. If your project doesn't already contain another form, create one and call it frmChild.
3. Set the new form's MDIChild property to *True*.

MDI applications and toolbars

The steps you just took to create an MDI parent form and a child form allow you to enable your program to negotiate toolbars among applications. Let's see how it's done:

1. Put an OLE container control on the child form, and turn it into a Microsoft Excel worksheet.
2. Press F5 to run the program, and double-click on the worksheet. You'll see the Microsoft Excel toolbars show up on the MDI form.

NOTE This worked because the NegotiateToolbars property of the MDI form is set to *True* by default.

MDI applications and menus

Menus in MDI applications are a little deceptive. An MDI form can have its own menus, but the menus of its child forms will show up on the MDI form instead, replacing the MDI form's menus. Let's see how this works:

1. On frmParent, create a menu with the caption ParentFile and the name mnuParent.
2. Press F5 to run the application. The menu comes up just as you expect it would.
3. On frmChild, create a menu with the caption ChildFile and the name mnuChild. Press F5 again, and you'll notice that the child form's menu has replaced the menu on the MDI form.
4. Close the child form, and the parent form's menu will reappear.

Put any menu items that have to do with the child form on the child form itself. Put any menu items that have to do with the overall application or that you want to appear only if no child forms are open on the MDI form.

Menus, insertable objects, and OLE container controls

What about menus for other applications? When you put an insertable object or a container control on a form and a user activates it, you'd expect the object to be in-place activated and that the user would see the object's native menus rather than the Visual Basic form's menus, right? Let's try it:

1. Create a new VB project, and put a WordPad insertable object on the form. Notice that the WordPad menus appear on your form.
2. Put some text in the WordPad object, and format the text just for fun. Then press the Esc key.
3. Now press F5 to run the program.
4. Double-click on the text.

Notice anything strange? When you actually run the program and double-click to edit the text, the insertable object doesn't in-place activate. Rather, WordPad comes up as a separate application. For the insertable object to in-place activate, you need to create at least one menu item on your VB form:

1. Quit the application to return to design mode.
2. Put a menu item on your VB form. Name it whatever you want, but deselect the Visible box in the Menu Editor dialog so that the menu is hidden.
3. Now press F5.
4. Double-click on the text.

This time, the object in-place activates, and the WordPad menus show up on your form. What's the moral? You need to have at least one menu on your VB form—even if it isn't visible—in order to support full in-place activation of an insertable object. This is true for OLE container controls, too.

NOTE If you set the NegotiateMenus property on the form to *False*, an insertable object or a container control will not in-place activate, even if you have a menu on your VB form.

You can create whatever menus you want for a form, but if you create a form menu item with the same name as the name of a menu item on the insertable object or container control object, then when the object is in-place activated, the menu items you created with the same name will be replaced by the menu items of the object. You can remedy this by invoking the menu editor to set the NegotiatePosition: option for each menu item on your form to *1 - Left*, *2 - Middle*, or *3 - Right*. The setting indicates where you want that version of the menu item to go if a menu item of an object you have to menu negotiate with has the same name as a menu item of the form. A form's menu item set to the default NegotiatePosition, *0 - None*, won't be visible when an object is in-place activated.

One interesting exception in all of this is the File menu. You'll notice that when you in-place activate an object, the File menu doesn't show up. You'll want to create your own File menu with a NegotiatePosition property of *1 - Left*.

A Sample Application

Let's take a look at a sample application that demonstrates some of the principles we've just been looking at. Just copy this sample—in the \Chapter7\OLE Controls Sample directory—from the companion CD to your hard disk so that you won't have to re-create it.

Basically, we'll create a form that enables your Visual Basic program to retrieve OLE objects from and save OLE objects to a Microsoft Access database. (You don't need to have Access installed on your machine to run this sample.) We'll use two controls—the OLE container control and the data control—and a little bit of code to make this happen. You'll also be able to set a variety of the properties of the container control programmatically, on the fly.

Let's get started.

1. Bring up the VB project *OLE Control Sample.*
2. View the frmChild form, and set the focus on the form's data control.
3. Change the DatabaseName property of the form's data control to point to objects.mdb by pressing the *ellipsis* (. . .) button and browsing in the Chapter7\OLE Controls Sample directory that you copied from the companion CD to your hard disk. This database contains several embedded OLE objects.
4. Press F5 to run the program. The application should look like the screen shown in Figure 7-11 on the next page.

The globe is a Microsoft Excel map. If you click on the *next record* arrow (the right-pointing arrow) of the data control at the bottom of the screen, you'll see the next record in the database: a Microsoft Excel worksheet. If you keep going, you'll see other OLE objects: a WordArt object, a ClipArt object, an Access calendar control, a bitmap, and so on. For now, go back to the first record in the database, the Microsoft Excel map of the world. The OLE container control is the same size it was at design-time. Notice that the Size Mode: setting is vbOLESizeStretch, which means that the object is being "sized" to fit the control.

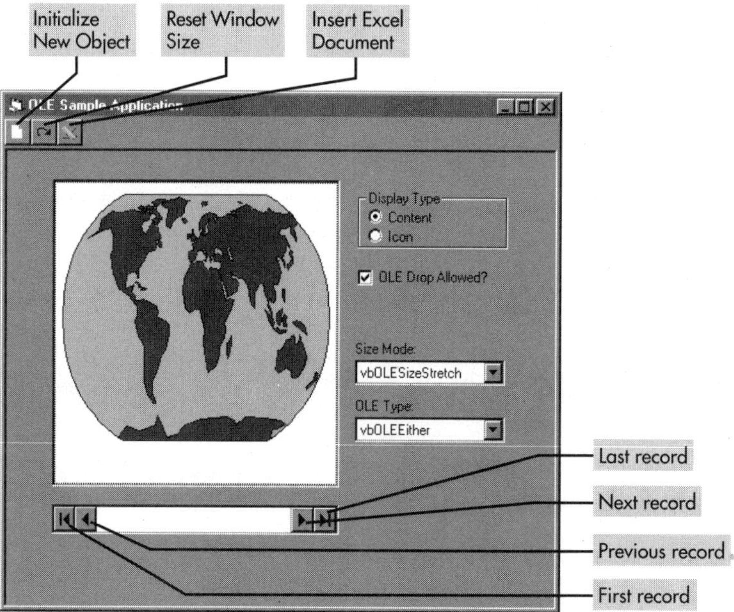

Figure 7-11. *The OLE Sample Application interface, featuring a container control and a data control as well as miscellaneous controls to change settings.*

Now let's play a little.

1. Change the Size Mode: setting to vbOLESizeAutoSize. Now the control has adjusted its size to the original size of the object it contains. If you returned the Size Mode: setting to vbOLESizeStretch, the object would stay the same size because currently the control and the object are the same size.
2. Click the Reset Window Size button on the application's toolbar to return the container control to its original size.

Now let's try zooming.

1. From the Size Mode: dropdown, select vbOLESizeZoom. This time, the object is resized to fit the control, but it keeps its original proportions. (Notice the line at the bottom of the container control showing that the object wasn't vertically stretched to fit the control.) For now, return to the vbOLESizeAutoSize setting.
2. Bring up Microsoft Word or Microsoft Excel, and open a document or create a new document. Now drag and drop a selection of that document into the OLE container control. The object should move over without a hitch.

3. Now uncheck the OLE Drop Allowed check box.
4. Try dragging and dropping again. The operation should fail.
5. Click the *last record* button on the data control to see the last record. To create a new record, click the *next record* button. You should see the Insert Object dialog. You could insert any object here, but for now just press Esc.
6. Click the Insert Excel Document button on the application's toolbar. We've slapped a little OLE Automation code in there to show that you can automate objects that are in the OLE container control.
7. In the Display Type frame, select Icon. Notice that the OLE container control doesn't change to an icon immediately. Only objects you create from this time forward will be represented by icons. Try clicking the Initialize New Object button on the application's toolbar and inserting an object into the container control. It will show up as an icon.
8. Finally, from the OLE Type: dropdown, select vbOLELinked.
9. Now click the Initialize New Object button. You'll notice that you won't be able to create an embedded object. You're given the option only to create a linked object.

Play around with this application a little, and then dive into the code to understand why each of the elements of the application does what it does. If you get an error, you should be able to figure out why you got the error by looking at the code.

MDIForm1 Form

```
Private Sub Toolbar1_ButtonClick(ByVal Button As Button)
    With frmChild.OLEObject
        Select Case Button.Key
            'If the user clicks the NewObject button, use
            'the InsertObjDlg method to create a new OLE
            'class instance in the oleObject button.
            Case "NewObject"
                .InsertObjDlg

            'If the user clicks the ResizeWindow button,
            'coerce the window into 3855 by 3735. The user
            'will need to use this button if he or she has
            'previously set SizeMode to vbOLESizeAutoSize,
            'the window has been resized, and the user wants
            'to return the window to its original size.
```

(continued)

```
            Case "ResizeWindow"
                .Height = 3855
                .Width = 3735

            'If the user clicks the InsertExcelDoc button,
            'insert an Excel spreadsheet and input the
            'following data.
            Case "InsertExcelDoc"
                .CreateEmbed "", "Excel.Sheet"
                With .object
                    .Range("B1:E1").Value = Array("Q1", "Q2", "Q3", "Q4")
                    .Range("A2:E4").Value = Array( _
                                    Array("West", 400, 450, 500, 550), _
                                    Array("Central", 450, 500, 550, 600), _
                                    Array("East", 500, 550, 600, 650))
                    .Range("F2:F4").FormulaR1C1 = "=SUM(RC[-4]:RC[-1])"
                    .Range("B5:E5").FormulaR1C1 = "=SUM(R[-3]C:R[-1]C)"
                End With
        End Select
    End With
End Sub
```

frmChild Form

```
Private Sub cboSize_Click()
    'When the user changes the value of the SizeMode
    'combo box, set the .SizeMode property of
    'OLEObject to the appropriate value.
    OLEObject.SizeMode = cboSize.ListIndex
End Sub

Private Sub cboType_Click()
    'When the user changes the value of the OLE
    'Type combo box, set the .OLETypeAllowed
    'property of oleObject to the
    'appropriate value.
    OLEObject.OLETypeAllowed = cboType.ListIndex
End Sub

Private Sub chkDropAllowed_Click()
    'The OLEDropAllowed property tells the program
    'whether to allow a user to drag and drop (or
    'Paste Special) from another application.
    OLEObject.OLEDropAllowed = chkDropAllowed.Value
End Sub
```

```
Private Sub datOLE_Reposition()
    'If the user has navigated to the end of the
    'database and created a new record, dbEditAdd
    'will be True.

    'If dbEditAdd is True, then use the InsertObjDlg
    'method to create a new object to go into the
    'new record.
    If datOLE.EditMode = dbEditAdd Then
        OLEObject.InsertObjDlg
    End If
End Sub

Private Sub Form_Load()
    'Set OLEDropAllowed option to True.
    chkDropAllowed.Value = vbChecked
    'Set DisplayType "Content" option to True.
    optDisplay(0).Value = True
    'Set OLE Type combo box to vbOLEEither.
    cboType.ListIndex = vbOLEEither
    'Set SizeMode combo box to vbOLESizeStretch.
    cboSize.ListIndex = vbOLESizeStretch
End Sub

Private Sub optDisplay_Click(Index As Integer)
    'This procedure sets the DisplayType property.

    'vbOLEDisplayContent causes the program to display
    'the actual information contained in the object,
    'whereas vbOLEDisplayIcon causes the program to
    'display an icon that represents the object instead.
    'This change applies to newly created objects only.

    'Set DisplayType to 0 (Content) or 1 (Icon) depending
    'on which option the user clicks.
    OLEObject.DisplayType = Index
End Sub
```

SUMMARY

- Insertable objects are application-specific, pseudo-controls created by Visual Basic that enable the user of your program to in-place activate an object owned by another application, the "native application."
- You can use OLE Automation with insertable objects, but you can't programmatically activate the insertable objects, which makes programmatically controlling insertable objects a little difficult. Full control of an insertable object is best left to the user.
- OLE container controls are like insertable objects, except that they are not locked into containing objects from specific applications. You can change the class of the object contained in an OLE container control at design-time or run-time, and the user can change the class of the object at run-time.
- Objects in an OLE container control can be programmatically activated, saved, loaded, and deactivated at run-time. Programmatic changes to the control are reflected on the screen.
- Objects in an OLE container control can be either embedded or linked, unlike insertable objects, which can be embedded only.
- If the object in an OLE container control supports OLE Automation, you can make programmatic changes to objects on your forms.
- You use the *InsertObjDlg* function to allow the user to choose what type of object an OLE container control becomes at run-time.
- OLE container control properties such as AppIsRunning, OLEDropAllowed, SizeMode, and AutoActivate let you programmatically determine how the object in the control is presented.
- You can use the OLE container control's *ReadFromFile* and *SaveToFile* methods to save an object's data directly to a binary file.
- You can bind an OLE container control to the Visual Basic Data control and thus reduce the amount of code it takes to save OLE objects to a relational database.
- If you want a user to be able to in-place activate an insertable object on a form, you must have a menu—even a hidden one—on the form.
- To support toolbars for an in-place active object, you must use an MDI application.

PART THREE

Microsoft Excel and Visual Basic Object Interactions

IN THIS PART

Just when you thought you were getting up to speed with Visual Basic's built-in and custom objects, we're about to throw more objects into the picture—a lot more. Microsoft Excel, the spreadsheet program of the Microsoft Office application suite, is also an object server that can be controlled by Visual Basic programs. Microsoft Excel is also a VBA language host, so it can control its own objects as well as the custom objects you create in Visual Basic. In this part of the book, we'll deal with questions such as "If I can control Microsoft Excel from Visual Basic, why and when should I write VBA code in Excel?" and "How can I take advantage of Visual Basic custom objects and forms in my Microsoft Excel workbook applications?"

Chapter 8 - Microsoft Excel Object Basics

There's no way we can fully cover all the complexities of the objects exposed by Microsoft Excel, but we can give you a serious jump start. We'll look at the top-level objects in Microsoft Excel and at concepts that apply to the full set of Excel's objects. You'll learn how to create macros using VBA code in Excel and how to call those macros from both Microsoft Excel itself and Visual Basic programs.

Chapter 9 - Performance-Tuning Excel-VBA

Once you get started writing VBA code in either Visual Basic or Microsoft Excel, it's really easy to get those fingers flying and type in a lot of code. Unfortunately, it's just as easy to write VBA code that's reaaaaaaaaaally slow, especially when you're trying to manipulate cross-process OLE Automation objects—say, controlling Microsoft Excel from a Visual Basic program. This chapter will help you rein in runaway code so that you can take full advantage of those precious CPU cycles. The topics we take up in this chapter focus on Microsoft Excel objects, but the concepts are applicable to all Visual Basic programs.

Chapter 10 - Finishing a Custom Workbook

A bunch of code isn't a finished product. To be useful, the functionality represented by your code must be easily accessible to the end user of your product. A custom solution in Microsoft Excel isn't finished until you've provided a user interface for running your code from a menu or a toolbar. In this chapter, we'll also work with Excel add-ins—the user doesn't even have to see your custom workbook.

Chapter 11 - Using Visual Basic Objects in Microsoft Excel

Visual Basic lets you create custom objects. In particular, Visual Basic helps you make really cool forms. To finish up our discussion of Microsoft Excel and Visual Basic, we'll create a form in Visual Basic designed to run seamlessly with Microsoft Excel. With this example, you'll see how to use powerful Visual Basic features such as drag and drop and data binding—and how to launch these features from a toolbar button inside Microsoft Excel. As in Chapter 10, we're focusing on integrating custom Visual Basic solutions with Microsoft Excel, but the concepts are equally applicable to creating Visual Basic solutions that don't require Microsoft Excel.

8

Microsoft Excel Object Basics

Microsoft Excel exposes an almost intimidating number of objects—130 public classes, to be exact. Three of these classes are creatable—that is, they can be instantiated with *New* and *CreateObject*. For your programming pleasure, Excel also provides a very long list of constants (773 at last count) to help you manipulate Excel's objects in VBA code. By adding a reference to *Microsoft Excel Object Library* to your Visual Basic project, you can hard type any of the classes in Excel's object model and use all of Excel's predefined constants. (The term *object model* refers to the relationships among different classes available in an object library.)

Our goal in this section of the book won't be to perform an in-depth analysis of each of the 130 objects exposed by Excel. To accomplish that goal, we'd need to greatly "Excelerate" our pace and resign ourselves to a book several hundred pages longer. Several books do take a more exhaustive approach to manipulating Excel's object model. We recommend *Developing Microsoft Excel 95 Solutions with Visual Basic for Applications*, 2d Ed., by Eric Wells (Microsoft Press, 1995). We'll concentrate instead on the Excel objects that are fundamental to all programming tasks that make use of Excel.

In this chapter we'll examine Excel as a VBA host. Our efforts to explore the object model will concentrate on the top-level objects in Excel—Application, Workbook, Window, Worksheet, and Range. We'll discuss manipulating instances of these classes in Excel-VBA macros and externally in Visual Basic 4. Our code will be designed to be portable between Excel-VBA and VB4-VBA.

Excel-VBA Basics

In this book, we're considering Visual Basic for Applications to be the language component of Visual Basic. The distinction between VBA and VB can get fuzzy at times because the two components are so tightly integrated in the Visual Basic product. If we were dealing with VBA code in VB4 only, the distinction between the language (VBA) and the host (VB) would be pointless. However, Microsoft Excel, Microsoft Access, and Microsoft Project also host the VBA language. A VBA host is any application that can contain VBA code.

The VBA version integrated into Excel has most of the language features supported in the VB version of VBA. The version of VBA we call Excel-VBA is version 1.0, and VB4-VBA is version 2.0. Naturally, some of the VB features we've used so far in version 2.0 of VBA aren't in version 1.0. We'll note the missing language features as we go along. The main difference between Excel-VBA and VB4-VBA, however, is the method used to actually run the code. VB launches a program using a startup form or *Sub Main.* VBA code is then executed in response to events fired by the user's interaction with forms and controls. Excel-VBA code is executed in a much different fashion. To understand the difference, we need to back up and look at the kinds of VBA routines Excel supports. VBA routines in Excel fall into four categories: macros, event handlers, user-defined functions, and support routines. (How's that last item for a catchall category?) We'll look at an example of each routine type.

Before we look at the macro type of routine, let's start Excel and open a code pane so that we'll know where to type in our VBA code for any kind of routine in Excel.

1. Start Microsoft Excel. You'll see a default workbook called *Book1.*
2. From the Insert menu, select Macro, and then select Module from the Macro submenu.
3. Type in the following code. Here's a first difference between the VB and the Excel hosts: you'll have to type in your own *End Sub* statement.

```
Sub SayHello()
    MsgBox "Hello!"
End Sub
```

4. Click anywhere in the *SayHello* procedure. See Figure 8-1.
5. Press F5 to run *SayHello.* Click OK to clear the message box to allow the macro to terminate.

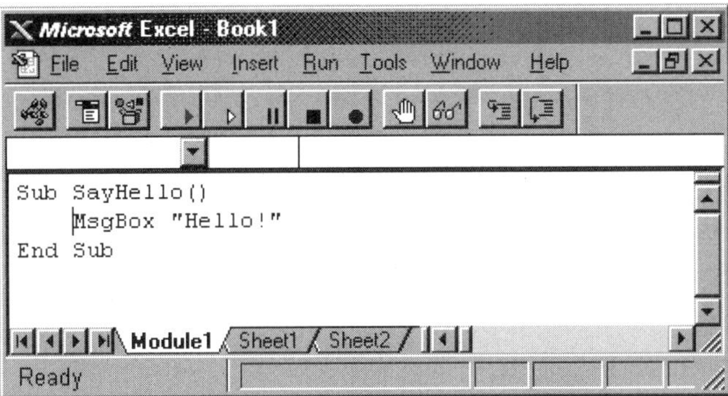

Figure 8-1. *A VBA macro module in a Microsoft Excel workbook.*

NOTE The code for all of the procedures in this chapter is on the companion disc in \Chapter8\Chapter8.Xls. Until we tell you differently, look for the procedures on the Miscellaneous tab of the Chapter8.Xls workbook.

Macros

A macro is any procedure that takes no arguments and returns no value—that is, any VBA Sub procedure with an empty argument list qualifies as a macro. You can run a macro at any time just by calling its name. Any information the macro needs in order to run is provided by the context in which you run it rather than by arguments. The Macro dialog available by means of the Microsoft Excel Tools menu shows a list of all available macros from all open workbooks and loaded add-ins—we'll get to add-ins in Chapter 10. A procedure declared with the *Private* keyword can't be used as a macro. If you designate a procedure as private in Excel-VBA, you can call the procedure from VBA code in the same module, but you can't call it as a macro from the same workbook and you can't call it at all from another module or workbook. Here's another example of a simple macro:

```
Sub ActiveCellRed()
    With ActiveCell
        .BorderAround Weight:=xlThick, ColorIndex:=3
        With .Font
            .Bold = True
            .ColorIndex = 3
        End With
    End With
End Sub
```

The *ActiveCellRed* macro makes the active cell of the current worksheet red. You'll get a run-time error if you run this macro when a worksheet isn't active.

ActiveCellRed is a typical Microsoft Excel macro. You should use it only within the context you've designed it for. If you use it in the wrong context, the macro will be useless and cause an error. Let's run the *ActiveCellRed* macro.

1. Using the tabs on the Excel workbook containing the *ActiveCellRed* macro, select a worksheet.
2. Click on the cell you want to turn red.
3. Select Tools-Macro to open the Macro dialog.
4. Select *ActiveCellRed*, and press Enter, or double-click the macro name in the list box. See Figure 8-2.

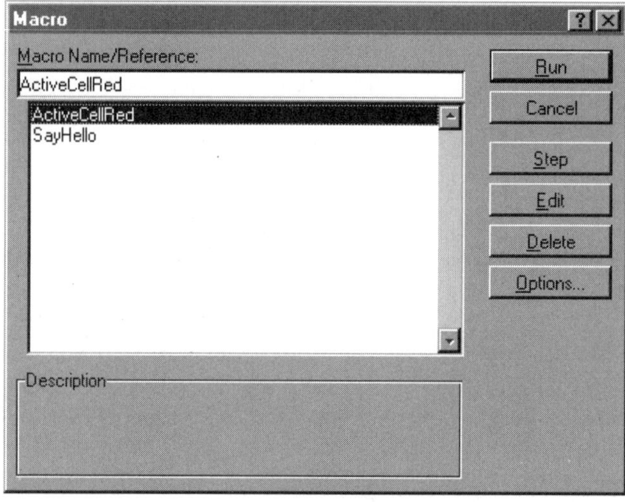

Figure 8-2. *The Macro dialog box with the* ActiveCellRed *macro ready to run.*

When you click on a different cell, you'll see a red border around the cell that was selected when you ran the macro.

Event Handling Macros

You can also use macros to handle events. Event handlers in Microsoft Excel are macros that run when the user generates a specific event. Microsoft Excel supports events in a much more limited and different way than Visual Basic. Unlike a VB event procedure whose name is predefined by VB, the macro that runs when an Excel object fires an event is determined when the name of the macro is assigned to a property of the object that raised the event. Another difference between events in Excel and events in VB is that certain Excel objects, called *drawing objects*, can have only one type of event per object. A Button object, for example, has an OnAction property that points to the name of a macro that is the one event for that object. Let's add a Button object to our worksheet to call our *ActiveCellRed* macro.

1. Activate *Sheet1* in a workbook that contains the *ActiveCellRed* macro.
2. Right-click on any toolbar to get a context menu with a list of toolbars.
3. In the context menu, select the Drawing toolbar.
4. Drop a Button object onto the worksheet. Adding an object to a worksheet is similar to adding a control to a VB form. On the Drawing toolbar, click the Create Button object button to get a crosshair mouse cursor. Click and drag a rectangle onto the worksheet, and release the mouse button to get a new Button drawing object. See Figure 8-3.

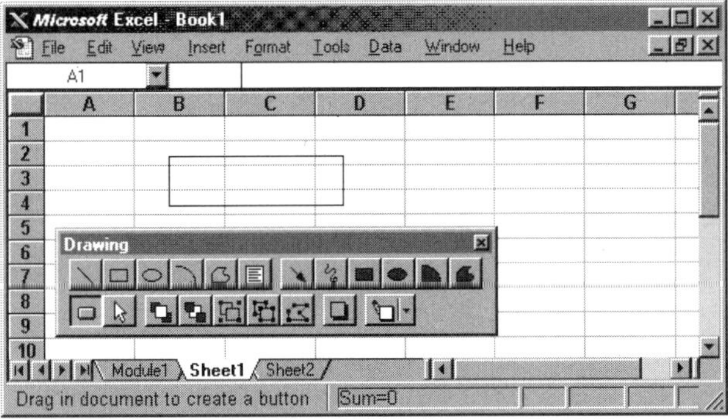

Figure 8-3. *The Drawing toolbar with a Button object selected and the rectangle in which the button will appear when the mouse is released.*

5. You'll immediately see the Assign Macro dialog. From the list of available macros, select *ActiveCellRed.* See Figure 8-4 on the next page.
6. Select a cell, and click the new button to turn the cell red.

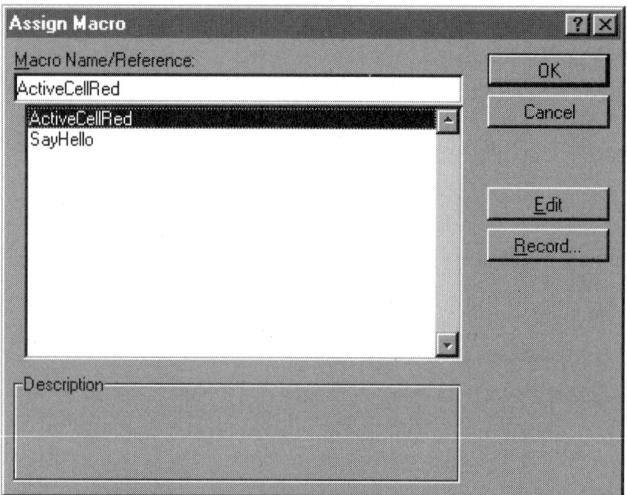

Figure 8-4. *The Assign Macro dialog box.*

To give you an idea of the kinds of events provided by Excel's objects, here are all of the names of Excel's event handler properties and methods: OnAction, OnCalculate, OnData, OnDoubleClick, OnEntry, *OnKey*, *OnRepeat*, OnSave, OnSheetActivate, OnSheetDeactivate, *OnTime*, *OnUndo*, OnWindow, and finally *SetLinkOnData*. You can use Excel-VBA Help for information about the events associated with these properties and methods. The OnAction property is the most common and is available on 44 Excel objects.

NOTE Once you have assigned a macro to a button, the macro will run when you click the button. To select a drawing object for editing (as opposed to calling the *OnAction* macro), use Ctrl-Click, or click the Drawing Selection toolbar button on the Drawing toolbar and then click the button you assigned the macro to. You can assign a macro at any time using Assign Macro from the shortcut menu, displayed by right-clicking on the object.

User-Defined Functions

A *user-defined function* (UDF) is a routine you define and add to the set of worksheet functions already provided by Microsoft Excel. The *DaysLeftInYear* function shown below is an example of a user-defined function.

```
Function DaysLeftInYear(DateInYear As Date) As Integer
    DaysLeftInYear = DateSerial(Year(DateInYear), 12, 31) _
                     - DateInYear
End Function
```

A user-defined function, like any other worksheet function, is called whenever Excel recalculates a worksheet that uses the function, so you need to be careful to limit the amount of code in your UDFs in order to optimize recalculation speed for your worksheet.

Because of the optimized nature of Microsoft Excel's recalculation loop, certain operations will cause run-time errors if they're used in UDFs. For example, you can't show a Microsoft Excel dialog from a UDF, add or remove workbooks or worksheets (or anything else that might modify the calculation dependencies) from a UDF, or change the appearance of a cell during execution of a UDF.

Since UDFs are designed to be used transparently as worksheet functions, Excel allows you to set the description and the function category so that your functions will look just the way Excel's built-in functions do. Let's do this for the *DaysLeftInYear* function and then call the function by means of a formula in a cell.

1. Type the *DaysLeftInYear* function listed above into a module sheet.
2. Press F2 to open the Object Browser. Find the *DaysLeftInYear* function. See Figure 8-5.

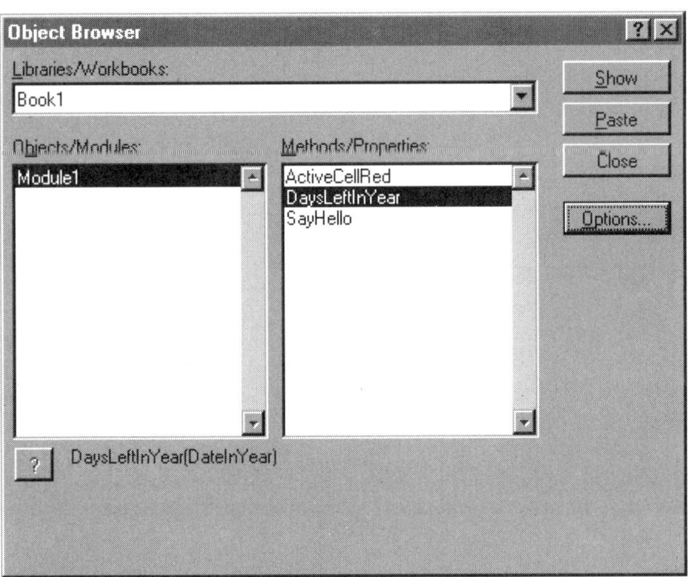

Figure 8-5. *The Excel-VBA Object Browser showing the* DaysLeftInYear *user-defined function.*

3. Click the Options button.

4. Set the Description: field in the Macro Options dialog to *Days left before the end of the year.*
5. Set the Function Category: field to *Date & Time.* See Figure 8-6.

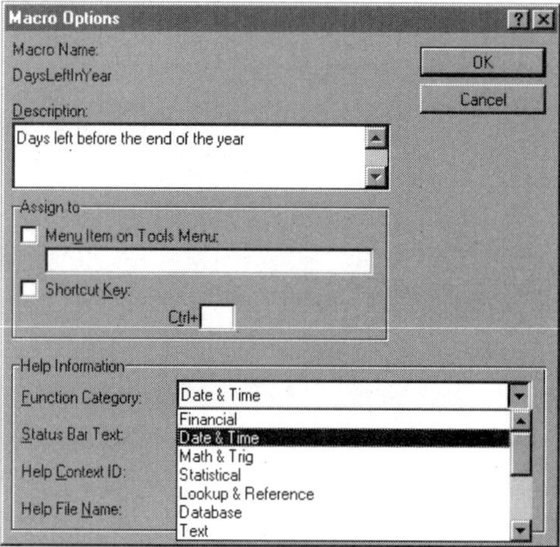

Figure 8-6. *The Macro Options dialog box.*

6. Close the Macro Options dialog and then the Object Browser dialog.
7. Activate the worksheet by clicking the tab Sheet1.
8. Activate the formula bar by clicking in the rightmost field directly above the worksheet. See Figure 8-7.

Figure 8-7. *The formula bar after you have activated it.*

9. Click the *fx* button to start Microsoft Excel's Function Wizard.
10. Select *DaysLeftInYear* in the Date & Time category. Click the Next > button in the Function Wizard. See Figure 8-8.
11. Enter *NOW()* for the DateInYear argument, and press Enter twice to finish. See Figure 8-9.

You might have noticed that the description you entered in the Object Browser Macro Options dialog showed up at the bottom of the first page of the Function Wizard (Figure 8-8). Once you've provided the implementation and description of your user-defined function, you're able to call your function and see its description just as you would for a built-in Excel worksheet function.

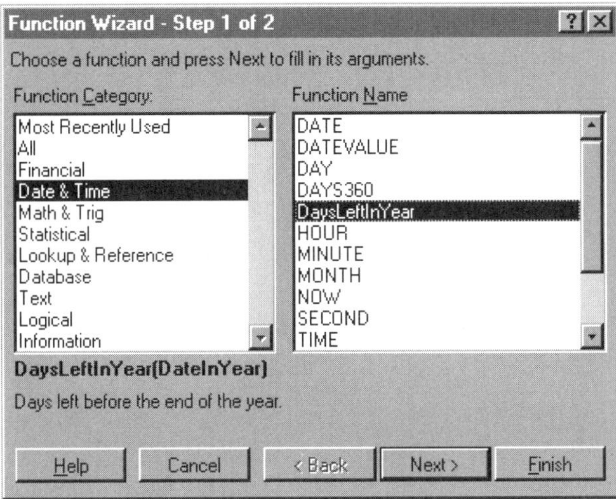

Figure 8-8. *The first page of Microsoft Excel's Function Wizard with the user-defined function* DaysLeftInYear *selected.*

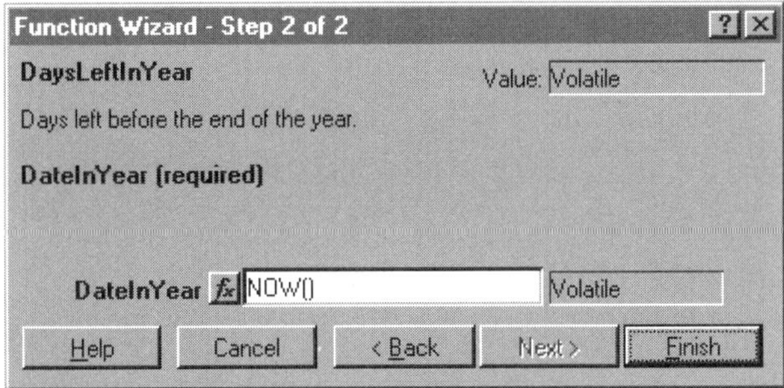

Figure 8-9. *Entering argument values for the* DaysLeftInYear *function.*

Support Routines

Any Microsoft Excel procedure that doesn't fit nicely into the macro, event handler, or user-defined function niche is considered a support routine. As in the case of support routines in VB, a support routine in Excel can't be called directly from the host. The support routine must be called from a macro or a user-defined function that in turn has been called by Excel.

A support routine is generally defined to be called by a macro or a user-defined function in the same workbook as the support routine. When it doesn't make sense for a routine to be called by an external workbook—and it usually doesn't—you should make the routine private. However, a private sub or function can't be called by procedures in other modules in the same workbook or as an event-handler. Excel-VBA has a per-module option to designate that you want other modules in only the same workbook to have the privilege of using routines in your module. Typing

```
Option Private Module
```

at the top of the module sheet makes all procedures in that Excel-VBA module available to all of the modules in the same workbook but not to modules in other workbooks.

Once you have declared an entire module private, you can call macros in that private module from the Macro dialog if the workbook containing the macro is active, or you can call macros as event handlers for objects in the containing workbook. However, a function in a private module can't be used as a user-defined worksheet function. Macros in a private module don't appear in the macro list of the Macro or Assign Macro dialog, so you have to type in the name of such a macro yourself when you want to run it.

Debugging

If you've gotten used to debugging in VB4-VBA, you'll be disappointed by the debugging options available in Excel-VBA. Excel-VBA allows you to set breakpoints, add watches, and use the Immediate pane. However, you can't make any edits in break mode or set the next statement as you can in VB4-VBA. If you've programmed XLM macros—XLM was the only macro language in Microsoft Excel up through version 4—VBA macro debugging will seem like a big step forward, but Excel-VBA debugging functionality is very weak when compared to the debugging capabilities of VB4-VBA.

On a more positive note, though, you can easily take advantage of the Debug window in Microsoft Excel to test your code before you integrate it with other modules. Unlike the Debug window in Microsoft Excel 5, the Debug window in Microsoft Excel 7 isn't modal, so you can manipulate sheets, workbooks, and other elements of your Excel workspace when the Debug window is open. Let's call the macro and the user-defined function we've written from the Debug window:

1. Activate the VBA module containing the *SayHello* and *DaysLeftInYear* procedures.
2. Press Ctrl-G to open the Debug window.
3. In the upper pane of the Debug window, with the Immediate tab active, type *SayHello*, and then press Enter. You've just run the *SayHello* macro.
4. Type *?DaysLeftInYear(Now)*, and press Enter to run the function.

5. Type *for each sheet in sheets: ?sheet.name: next* and press Enter to get a list of sheet names in the active workbook. See Figure 8-10.

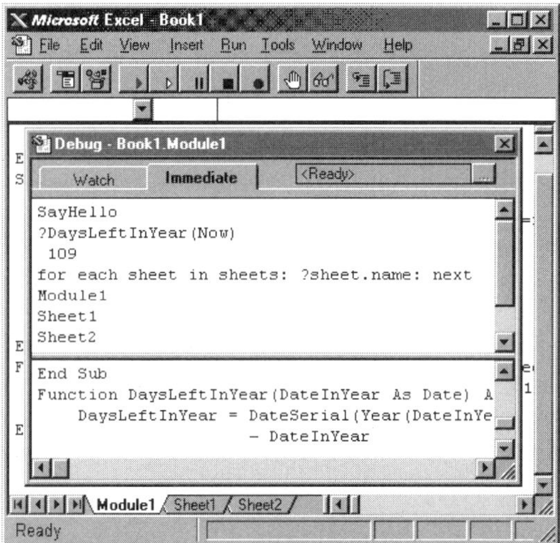

Figure 8-10. *The Excel-VBA Debug window with the* DaysLeftInYear *function.*

In the Debug window, you can run any macro or function you like at any time. You can also call any other code snippet you like (as demonstrated in step 5) as long as you can write it on one line. Use a colon (:) between multiple statements on one line, as shown in step 5 above. The question mark (?) is shorthand for the Print command. To print in the Debug window from a procedure, use the *Debug.Print* command.

Top-Level Objects

Looking at Microsoft Excel on screen, as in Figure 8-11 on the next page, you can visually identify numerous components that have counterparts in the set of exposed programmable Excel objects. Excel itself is the *Application object.* As you might expect, the Application object contains other objects that are available only when the Application object is running. Given this natural dependency among objects, we can call the Application object a *parent object.* A *child object* is any object that can be returned by a property or a method of its parent object. Therefore, the Toolbar object is a child of the Application object since *Application.Toolbars("Standard")* returns the Standard Toolbar object. In other words, the return value of the *Toolbars* method of the Application object is a Toolbar object.

Most of the children of the Application object are themselves parent objects. A Workbook object is the parent of Worksheet, Chart, Module, DialogSheet, and Window objects. Just as a parent object can have many children, a single type of object can have several potential parent objects. For example, a Window object can be a child of either an Application or a Workbook object, and a Drawing object can be a child of a Worksheet, a DialogSheet, or a Chart object. Excel objects are related to each other in a hierarchy, with the Application object at the top. The parent-child relationships among objects in an object library form a *hierarchical object model.* Much of the time you spend learning to program Excel (and other applications' object models) will focus on learning to navigate the object model. Navigating an object model means moving through the object hierarchy from a given object to that object's child or parent objects. See the Microsoft Excel object model in Appendix C. Use the Object Navigator tool on the companion CD (described in Appendix B) to help you generate hierarchical code expressions.

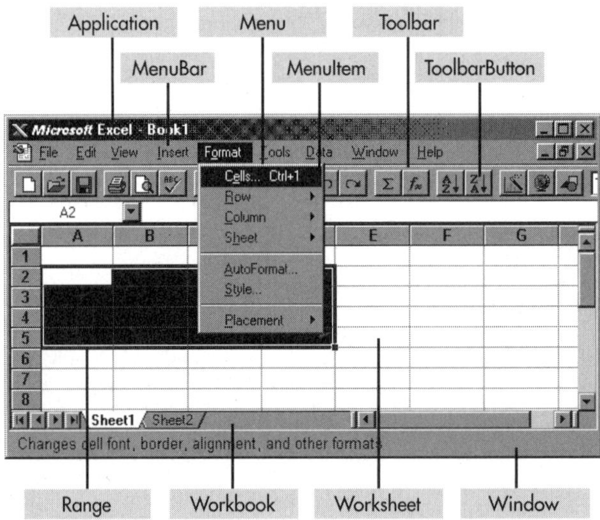

Figure 8-11. *Graphical counterparts to some of Excel's objects.*

Most of Excel's objects come in *collections.* A collection is a group of objects that are of the same type or that are related to each other in some other way. You can get a specific object from a collection by specifying either the name of the object or the numeric index of the object. The name of the object, or *key,* is unique for each object in the collection. Excel collections are one-based, so an index of *1* (not *0*) specifies the first object in any collection. Calling a method or setting a property on a collection applies the action to every object in the collection. Let's look at the Workbooks collection. We'll use *Close* as an example of calling a method on specific objects in a collection.

```
Workbooks.Item("Report.Xls").Close    'Close Report.Xls, using the
                                      'Item property.
Workbooks(1).Close                    'Close the first workbook, Item
                                      'implied.
Workbooks("Report.Xls").Close         'Close Report.Xls, Item implied.
Workbooks![Report.Xls].Close          'Close Report.Xls, bang(!)
                                      'notation.
Workbooks.Close                       'Close all workbooks.
```

Cross-Reference VBA Language Concepts: Option Base, Collections: Collection Lookup

Application Object

The Application object sits at the top of the object model. The most important job of the Application object is to provide access to collections of child objects. You can jump to the Application object from any other object in Excel's object model by means of the Application property, which is available for every object in Excel (including the Application object).

The Application object also provides access to many of Excel's worksheet functions—*Npv*, *Match*, *Min*, and so on. This access to worksheet functions enables you to use a worksheet function directly in VBA code without having to put it in the formula of a cell. Let's look at some of the properties and methods of the Application object. (On the CD that comes with the book, Application object code snippets and procedures are on the For Application tab of Chapter8.Xls.)

Application object code snippets

Here are several common tasks that make use of properties and methods of the Application object.

```
'Turn off warning dialogs to eliminate user interaction.
Application.DisplayAlerts = False

'Don't allow Excel to repaint the screen.
Application.ScreenUpdating = False

'Show the status bar, set the text in the status bar,
'and return control of the status bar to Excel when done.
Application.DisplayStatusBar = True
Application.StatusBar = "Retrieving Data..."
:
:
Application.StatusBar = False
```

(continued)

```
'Display different text in Excel's title bar.
Application.Caption = "Invoice Entry"

'See if you're running on a 32-bit operating system.
If Instr(Application.OperatingSystem, "32-bit") Then ...

'Maximize Excel's main window.
Application.WindowState = xlMaximized
```

DoFullScreen, HideFullScreen, and *UndoFullScreen*

Here is some code that enables you to use the Application object to make Excel cover the whole screen. FullScreen mode hides the Excel title bar, all docked toolbars, and the status bar. This code turns the status bar back on. An *OnTime* event handling macro is used to clear the Full Screen toolbar, which automatically appears when the DisplayFullScreen property is set to *True*.

```
Sub DoFullScreen()
Dim XLApp As Application
    Set XLApp = Application
    With XLApp
        .ScreenUpdating = False
        .DisplayFullScreen = True
        .DisplayStatusBar = True
        .ScreenUpdating = True
        'DisplayFullScreen always shows the Full Screen toolbar.
        'Hide the Full Screen toolbar immediately after this macro
        'finishes running.
        .OnTime Now, "HideFullScreenToolbar"
    End With
End Sub

Sub HideFullScreenToolbar()
    Application.Toolbars("Full Screen").Visible = False
End Sub

Sub UndoFullScreen()
    Application.DisplayFullScreen = False
End Sub
```

Workbook Object

A Workbook object corresponds to an actual Excel file (.Xls file extension). The Workbook object is used as a parent object to enable navigation from the name of an Excel file to the Worksheet, Window, Chart, and Module objects contained in the file. Since it represents a file, the Workbook object has file management methods (*Save, SaveAs, SaveCopyAs, Close*) and properties for the name and path of a file (Name, Path, FullName). Saving files is very important, so let's spend some time using the Workbook object to close and save the current Excel file. (On the CD that comes with the book, Workbook object code procedures are on the For Workbook tab of Chapter8.Xls.)

CloseWorkbookNoSave

Here is some code to close the current workbook without worrying, for the moment, about saving it.

```
Sub CloseWorkbookNoSave()
    ActiveWorkbook.Close SaveChanges:=False
End Sub
```

CloseWorkbookSave

This code closes the current workbook and always saves it. If the workbook hasn't been saved before, the code gets a name for the workbook from the user. *CloseWorkbookSave* will return *True* on a successful save.

```
Function CloseWorkbookSave() As Boolean
Dim wbkToClose As Workbook
Dim SaveAsName As Variant
    'Any write to the disk may fail; be prepared.
    On Error Resume Next
    Set wbkToClose = ActiveWorkbook
    With wbkToClose
        'Check if workbook has been previously saved.
        If Len(.Path) = 0 Then
            SaveAsName = .Application.GetSaveAsFilename( _
                         InitialFilename:=.Name)
            'Check if return value is False (dialog was canceled).
            If VarType(SaveAsName) = vbBoolean Then Exit Function
            .Close SaveChanges:=True, Filename:=SaveAsName
        Else
            .Close SaveChanges:=True
        End If
    End With
    If Err Then
        MsgBox Error$()
    Else
        CloseWorkbookSave = True
    End If
End Function
```

CloseWorkbookPrompt

The following code closes the current workbook and has Excel prompt the user to save a dirty file or get a name for an unsaved file. If the workbook is still in the Workbooks collection after the *Close* method is called, then the workbook wasn't closed. *CloseWorkbookPrompt* returns *True* if the workbook is closed successfully.

```
Function CloseWorkbookPrompt() As Boolean
Dim wbkToClose As Workbook
Dim strName As String
    Set wbkToClose = ActiveWorkbook
    With wbkToClose
        strName = .Name
        'Be prepared for a write failure to the disk.
        On Error Resume Next
        .Close
    End With
    If Err Then
        MsgBox Error$()
    Else
        'If strName is still a workbook, then Close failed.
        Workbooks strName
        If Err Then CloseWorkbookPrompt = True
    End If
End Function
```

If you scan the Workbook properties and methods in the Object Browser, you'll notice that you have *Save* and *Close* methods but no *New* or *Open* method. Since a not-yet-created or an unopened workbook is not an object, the *Add* and *Open* methods are provided in the Workbooks collection, instead of the Workbook object, so that a new Workbook instance can be created. The *Add* and *Open* methods correspond to the File-New and File-Open menu items. These methods create or open and then activate a Workbook object.

Window Object

A Window object corresponds to a window that displays a sheet—usually a worksheet. A workbook can have more than one open window, or sheet, associated with it. Multiple windows per workbook allow the user to view multiple sheets in a single workbook or multiple views of the same sheet simultaneously. To get a new window by means of Excel's menus, the user selects New Window from the Window menu. The *TileWindowsInActiveWorkbook* macro arranges all windows in the active workbook. (On the companion CD, the Window object code procedures are on the For Window tab of Chapter8.Xls.)

TileWindowsInActiveWorkbook

This macro restores and tiles all visible windows in the current workbook, including windows that are currently minimized.

```
Sub TileWindowsInActiveWorkbook()
Dim winIterator As Window
Dim XLApp As Application
    Set XLApp = Application
    With XLApp
        'Turn updating off to avoid flashing.
        .ScreenUpdating = False
        'Make sure visible windows aren't minimized.
        For Each winIterator In .ActiveWorkbook.Windows
            If winIterator.Visible Then _
               winIterator.WindowState = xlNormal
        Next
        'Let the Arrange method do all the work.
        .Windows.Arrange ArrangeStyle:=xlTiled, _
                         ActiveWorkbook:=True
        'Redraw the screen.
        .ScreenUpdating = True
    End With
End Sub
```

The Window object also provides a set of properties that enable you to modify the display of a worksheet window. You might think at first that Display-Gridlines should be a property of Worksheet since worksheets have gridlines, but what would happen if a worksheet were visible in two different windows and you wanted gridlines in one window but not in the other? Since a single worksheet can be visible in multiple windows, DisplayGridlines is a property of Window, not of Worksheet. The Window object has many Display properties. The *DisplayOn[Off]InActiveWindow* macro applies each of these properties to the active window. The ApplyDisplayMacrosHere worksheet in Chapter8.Xls is provided as a target for these two macros, so activate this sheet before you call either macro. See Figure 8-12 on the next page.

NOTE If you can't find an object, a method, or a property when you expect it in the object model, try using the Object Navigator tool (on the companion CD and described in Appendix B) to locate it and link it to its parent and child objects.

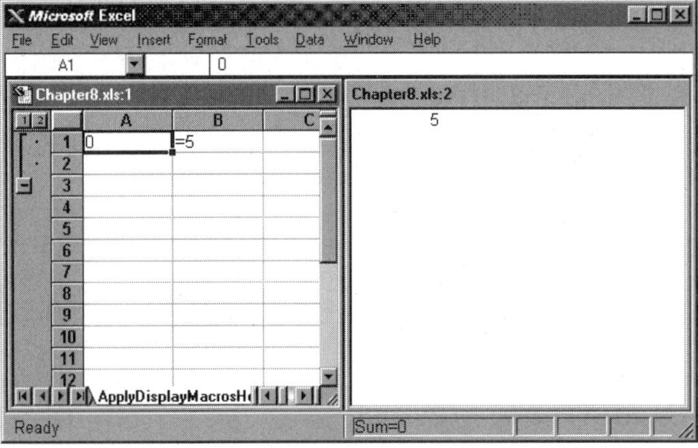

Figure 8-12. *The results of the* DisplayOnInActiveWindow *macro on the left and the* DisplayOffInActiveWindow *macro on the right.*

DisplayOn[Off]InActiveWindow

This code sets each of the Display properties of a Window object to *True[False]*.

```
Sub DisplayOnInActiveWindow()
    SetActiveWindowDisplay True
End Sub
Sub DisplayOffInActiveWindow()
    SetActiveWindowDisplay False
End Sub
Sub SetActiveWindowDisplay(OnOff As Boolean)
Dim winActive As Window
    Set winActive = ActiveWindow
    With winActive
        .DisplayFormulas = OnOff
        .DisplayGridlines = OnOff
        .DisplayHorizontalScrollBar = OnOff
        .DisplayVerticalScrollBar = OnOff
        .DisplayOutline = OnOff
        .DisplayHeadings = OnOff
        .DisplayWorkbookTabs = OnOff
        .DisplayZeros = OnOff
    End With
End Sub
```

QUERY **Q:** If DisplayGridlines is a property of Window, not Worksheet, how do I turn off gridlines in the ActiveSheet?

A: Use the following code.

```
ActiveSheet.Parent.Windows(1).DisplayGridlines = False
```

Sheet Objects

A workbook in Excel can contain five different kinds of sheets. The most common of the sheet objects is the Worksheet, which is the gridlined spreadsheet with which your end user will spend the most time. A sheet in a workbook can be activated with a mouse click on the sheet tab at the bottom of an Excel workbook. To activate a specific sheet from VBA code, use the Sheets collection from the Workbook object to get a sheet object and the *Activate* method to activate it. (The Worksheet object code snippets and procedures are on the For Worksheet tab of Chapter8.Xls.)

Worksheet object code snippets

This code shows how to activate a specific sheet object from the Sheets collection in a Workbook object and assign the sheet object to an object variable.

```
Dim WB As Workbook
Dim WS As Worksheet
:
'Activate the sheet corresponding to the first tab.
WB.Sheets(1).Activate

'Get the "Invoice Data" worksheet.
Set WS = WB.Sheets("Invoice Data")

'Same as previous line, with different syntax. The []
'brackets are required with the bang(!) syntax only
'if there is a special character, such as a space, a
'period (.), or a hyphen (-), in the name of the sheet.
Set WS = WB.Sheets![Invoice Data]
```

Although we'll concentrate our efforts on manipulating Worksheet-type sheet objects, being familiar with the other types of sheet objects is also important, so let's look at a brief description of each of the sheet object types.

Worksheet

A Worksheet is Excel's data repository in which all numeric data and formulas are kept and all calculations are made. An end user will spend more time looking at a Worksheet than at any other kind of object in Excel. Select Insert-Worksheet from Excel's menu to get a new Worksheet object.

Chart

A Chart is a graphical representation of data contained in a worksheet. To insert a Chart-type sheet into a Workbook, select As New Sheet from the Chart submenu of the Insert menu. You can also insert a Chart into a worksheet without using a new sheet, in which case the chart is known as a ChartObject.

Module

A Module is a sheet that contains VBA code. All of the VBA macros you write in Excel will be contained in Module sheets. To get a new Module-type sheet, select Module from the Macro submenu of the Insert menu.

DialogSheet

A DialogSheet is used to create a modal dialog in Excel. You define an Excel dialog in much the same way you define a VB form, but each drawing object available for Excel dialogs has only one event associated with it. We won't do much with DialogSheet objects in this book because we think it's much easier to make dialogs with Visual Basic forms than with Excel DialogSheets, and this is a VB book. Select Dialog from the Macro submenu of the Insert menu to get a new DialogSheet object.

Excel4MacroSheet

VBA was introduced as the Excel macro language in Microsoft Excel 5. Users of Excel versions before 5 relied on the XLM macro language for creating customized Excel applications. An XLM macro is written on a special worksheet called a *macrosheet.* XLM is still supported, and a macrosheet is now called an Excel4MacroSheet. Select MS Excel 4.0 Macro from the Macro submenu of the Insert menu to get a new Excel4MacroSheet.

In addition to the Sheets collection, which contains all sheets in a workbook, a Workbook object also contains Worksheets, Charts, DialogSheets, Modules, and Excel4MacroSheets collections that group the sheet objects by type. All of the sheet-type object collections have similar methods. Here are examples of some of the methods common to all of the sheet-type object collections.

Worksheet object code snippets

This code adds, moves, and copies a worksheet.

```
Dim WB As Workbook
Dim WB2 As Workbook
Dim WS As Worksheet
:
:
'Add and activate a new worksheet.
WB.Worksheets.Add

'Add a worksheet after the first sheet in the workbook.
'Excel can't add after the last sheet, so use the Move
'method to reliably position a new sheet on the last tab.
'Note that the Add method returns the new Worksheet object,
'so the Move method can be applied directly to the return
'value of the Add method without your needing to use a
'temporary Worksheet object variable.
```

```
With WB
    With .Sheets
        Set WS = .Item(.Count)
    End With
    .Worksheets.Add.Move After:=WS
End With

'Move a sheet to another workbook.
WB.Sheets(1).Move Before:=WB2.Sheets(1)

'Copy all worksheets from one workbook to another.
WB.Worksheets.Copy Before:=WB2.Sheets(1)
```

Range Object

A Range object is a cell in a worksheet or a rectangular block of cells, a discontinuous block of cells, a row of cells, several columns of cells, all cells in a worksheet, or any combination of those groupings. In other words, any grouping of cells that can be selected by the mouse in Excel can be a Range object.

If you want to write any program in Excel, you'll need a good understanding of the Range object because all data in Excel is stored in cells and is accessed programmatically by means of a Range object. Because it's so complex, the Range object is frequently a serious stumbling block for the beginning, or even intermediate, Excel-VBA programmer. Because the Range object is so fundamental to a majority of macros written in Excel, we'll spend some extra time investigating the not-so-obvious subtleties of this object.

To get a Range object, you call the *Cells* and *Range* methods from a Worksheet object. The *Cells* and *Range* methods take two arguments each, and each method returns a Range object. It's the means of specifying the Range object to return that's different between the two methods. In the following code snippets, assume that WS is an object variable containing a reference to a Worksheet object.

Cells method, arguments RowIndex and ColumnIndex

- **Syntax 1:** RowIndex and ColumnIndex are set to correspond by number to a row and a column in the worksheet.

  ```
  Debug.Print WS.Cells(1, 1).Address
  Output: $A$1
  Debug.Print WS.Cells(3, 5).Address
  Output: $E$3
  ```

- **Syntax 2:** ColumnIndex is omitted. RowIndex is the number of the cell on the worksheet, counted in row-major order—that is, Excel counts cells left to right until it runs out of columns and then moves to the next row. We'll look at this syntax again in the section "Counting cells, rows, and columns" a little later in this chapter.

```
Debug.Print WS.Cells(1).Address
Output: $A$1
Debug.Print WS.Cells(2).Address
Output: $B$1
Debug.Print WS.Cells(257).Address 'First row plus one cell
Output: $A$2
```

Range method, arguments Cell1 and Cell2

- **Syntax 1:** Cell1 and Cell2 are single-cell range objects returned by the *Cells* method that form the corners of the rectangular region returned by the *Range* method. Cell2 can be omitted if it is the same as Cell1.

```
With WS
    Debug.Print .Range(.Cells(1, 1), .Cells(2, 2)).Address
End With
Output: $A$1:$B$2
```

- **Syntax 2:** Same as Syntax 1 except that Cell1 and Cell2 are set to the addresses of the corner Range objects instead of to the Range objects themselves.

```
Debug.Print WS.Range("A1", "B2").Address
Output: $A$1:$B$2
```

- **Syntax 3:** A single address of a rectangular region.

```
Debug.Print WS.Range("A1:B2").Address
Output: $A$1:$B$2
```

FYI

Cell Addresses in Microsoft Excel

If you aren't familiar with cell addresses in Microsoft Excel, you might want to play with the *ShowCurrentAddress* macro on the Miscellaneous module sheet in Chapter8.Xls. To call this macro, activate a worksheet, and from the Tools menu, select Current Address. You'll see a message box that shows you the address of the selected range on the active worksheet. The address is shown in both A1 and RC address styles.

Here are some tips on selecting ranges. To select complex ranges, hold down the Ctrl key and select multiple ranges with the mouse. To select an entire row or column, click the row or column header. To select all cells in the worksheet, click the blank column header in the upper left corner of the worksheet.

The methods *Cells* and *Range* can also be called as methods of the Application and Range objects. *Application.Cells* and *Application.Range* are equivalent to *ActiveSheet.Cells* and *ActiveSheet.Range. RangeObject.Range* is a much trickier case that deserves some attention. Here's what you *shouldn't* do when you call the *Range* method from a Range object. (Our goal is to return range $C$3:$D$4.)

```
Set RangeObj = WS.Cells(3, 3)
With RangeObj
    Debug.Print .Range(.Cells(1, 1), .Cells(2, 2)).Address
End With
```

Here's our result:

```
Output: $E$5:$F$6
```

What happened? Calling the *Range* method with the Range object (RangeObj) causes the *Range* method to offset by 3 rows and 3 columns to return cell $C$3. This is the base offset for calculating the address of the new Range. The address is calculated using the *Cells* method. We've already used RangeObj once with the *Range* method to get the starting offset of $C$3. Now we use RangeObj again with the *Cells* method (remembering that the period [.] in front of the call to the *Cells* method means that the RangeObj object in the *With* statement is called from the *Cells* method). The result is that RangeObj causes an offset of another 3 rows and another 3 columns when the *Cells* method is called, this time moving us from the base offset of $C$3 to $E$5 (column C counting as offset 1, column D as offset 2, and column E as offset 3). What this means is that instead of saying, "Give me a 2 by 2 block of cells offset 3 rows and 3 columns from cell $A$1," we said, "Give me a 2 by 2 block of cells offset 3 rows and 3 columns from cell $C$3." To force the base offset back to $A$1, call the *Range* method from the worksheet that is the parent of the starting Range object, not from the starting Range object itself. Let's try again.

```
Set RangeObj = WS.Cells(3, 3)
With RangeObj
    Debug.Print .Parent.Range(.Cells(1, 1), .Cells(2, 2)).Address
End With
```

Here's our result:

```
Output: $C$3:$D$4
```

Complex ranges

Our code snippets to this point have dealt with contiguous rectangular Range objects only. However, a Range object can also represent several noncontiguous rectangles at a time. Each distinct rectangle in a Range object is called an *area.* The *Areas* method of the Range object is used to retrieve each individual rectangular region. A set of these regions, or areas, makes up an Areas collection.

If *RangeObj.Areas.Count* is greater than *1*, then RangeObj is said to be a complex range. Each area is itself a Range object, so the *Cells* method can be called to get all the cells in each area of a complex range. Refer to Figure 8-13 to see a graphic example of a complex Range object. Here's a macro to return the total number of cells in any Range object. (On the companion CD, Range object procedures are on the For Range tab of Chapter8.Xls.)

```
Function CellCount(R As Range) As Long
Dim area As Range
Dim TotalCells As Long
    For Each area In R.Areas
        TotalCells = TotalCells + area.Cells.Count
    Next
    CellCount = TotalCells
End Function
```

QUERY **Q:** The *CellCount* function isn't always accurate. Why not?

A: Two separate areas can overlap, in which case, some cells might be counted twice.

The *RangeDiff* function in Chapter8.Xls, RangeDiff module, is a complicated example of manipulating the Range object. *RangeDiff* takes two complex Range objects as arguments and returns a Range object containing all cells in the first range that are not in the second. If you haven't had your fill of the Range object by the end of this section, *RangeDiff* should satisfy you.

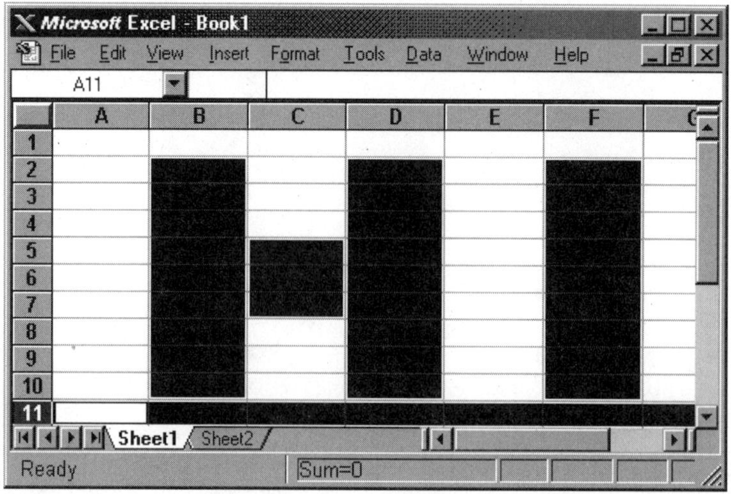

Figure 8-13. *A complex Range object that includes five areas.*

Counting cells, rows, and columns

Microsoft Excel treats Rows and Columns as special types of Range objects. The *Rows* and *Columns* methods of the Range object enable you to manipulate a Range by rows and columns instead of by individual cells as you would with the *Cells* method. You can apply the *Cells* method to a Range object returned by the *Rows* or *Columns* method to get the cells in a row or column. The Count property provides an easy way of examining the number of range objects returned by the *Cells*, *Rows*, and *Columns* methods.

```
Set RangeObj = WS.Range("A1:B2")
Debug.Print RangeObj.Cells.Count
Output: 4
Debug.Print RangeObj.Rows.Count
Output: 2
Debug.Print RangeObj.Columns.Cells.Count
Output: 4
Debug.Print RangeObj.EntireRow.Count
Output: 2
Debug.Print RangeObj.EntireRow.Cells.Count    'Excel has 256 cells
                                              'in a row.
Output: 512
```

Generally when you use a single argument to call the *Cells* method, the cell counting is done in row-major order—left to right until columns run out and then on to the next row. However, if you apply the *Columns* method to a Range object, the *Cells* method will count in column-major order—that is, top to bottom until rows run out and then on to the next column.

```
Set RangeObj = WS.Range("A1:B2")
Debug.Print RangeObj.Cells(2).Address           'Default is row-major.
Output: $B$1
Debug.Print RangeObj.Rows.Cells(2).Address
Output: $B$1
Debug.Print RangeObj.Columns.Cells(3).Address   'Count down the
                                                'column first.
Output: $B$1
Debug.Print RangeObj.Columns.Cells(5).Address   'Index larger than
                                                'Cells.Count.
Output: $C$1
```

The last line of code demonstrates using the *Cells* method to return a cell outside the region bounded by the original Range object. The *Cells* method will continue its counting pattern (in our example, moving down two rows, over one column, and back up to the first row) until it reaches the edges of the worksheet (16,384 rows by 256 columns).

If a Range object is complex, the *Cells* method will *not* jump to the first cell of the second area when the RowIndex argument reaches the size of the first area. In fact, the *Cells* method keeps right on going with the counting pattern established for the first area. The *NthCell* function shown here can be used in place of the *Cells* method for getting a numbered cell from a complex Range object.

```
Function NthCell(ByVal N As Long, R As Range) As Range
Dim area As Range
Dim pos As Long, oldpos As Long
    For Each area In R.Areas
        pos = pos + area.Count
        If pos >= N Then Exit For
        oldpos = pos
    Next
    Set NthCell = area(N - oldpos)
End Function
```

Range object example: Extracting values from an autofiltered column

The NWindProductsTable worksheet in the Chapter8.Xls workbook contains all of the data from the Products table of the Northwind Traders sample database. The data has been filtered on the UnitPrice column to show the 10 most expensive items. The *ArrayFromFilteredColumn* function (shown on the For Range module sheet of Chapter8.Xls) is used to put the values from a given filtered column into an array of values.

ArrayFromFilteredColumn takes StartCell, ColumnNumber, and Values() arguments. On return, Values() contains the values from the unfiltered cells in the ColumnNumber column of the table containing StartCell. We return the size of the Values() array in the name of the function. We'll use the following methods of the Range object to pull the values from the filtered column:

CurrentRegion Expand a Range object to include all adjacent cells. The range expansion stops when the edge of the spreadsheet or a row or a column full of blank cells is reached.

Columns Return the ColumnNumber column from the current region.

```
'Using the CurrentRegion and Columns methods
Set SearchRange = StartCell.CurrentRegion.Columns(ColumnNumber)
```

Offset Shift a Range object by a specified number of rows and columns. We shift the column containing our data down one row so that we won't include the row header in the returned value.

Resize Leave the upper left corner of the Range object unchanged, but change the number of rows and columns. In our example we'll leave the number of the columns the same, but since the *Offset* method shifted our row beyond the end of the table, we need to shrink the height of the Range object by one row.

SpecialCells Return all cells in a Range object that match a given criterion. For this method, the criterion is xlVisible, meaning all visible cells.

```
'Using Offset, Resize, and SpecialCells methods
With SearchRange
:
    Set SearchRange = .Offset(1, 0). _
                      Resize(.Cells.Count - 1, 1). _
                      SpecialCells(xlVisible)
:
End With
```

ArrayFromFilteredColumn Using the Range object methods we've just seen, get values for all visible cells in the ColumnNumber column of the region containing StartCell. Put these values in Values(), and return the number of values found.

```
Function ArrayFromFilteredColumn(StartCell As Range, _
                                 ColumnNumber As Integer, _
                                 Values() As Variant) As Integer
Dim area As Range
Dim cell As Range
Dim SearchRange As Range
Dim iCurrentCell As Integer
    Set SearchRange = StartCell. _
                      CurrentRegion.Columns(ColumnNumber)
    With SearchRange
        On Error Resume Next
        Set SearchRange = .Offset(1, 0). _
                          Resize(.Cells.Count - 1, 1). _
                          SpecialCells(xlVisible)
        If Err Then Erase Values: Exit Function
        On Error GoTo 0
    End With
    ReDim Values(CellCount(SearchRange)) 'Option Base 1 is set.
    With SearchRange
        For Each area In SearchRange
            For Each cell In area
                iCurrentCell = iCurrentCell + 1
                Values(iCurrentCell) = cell.Value
            Next
        Next
    End With
    ArrayFromFilteredColumn = iCurrentCell
End Function
```

(continued)

```
'A macro to call ArrayFromFilteredColumn
Sub DoFilteredColumnFour()
Dim i%
Dim Values() As Variant
    For i% = 1 To ArrayFromFilteredColumn( _
                    Sheets!NWindProductsTable.Cells(1), 4, Values)
        Debug.Print Values(i%)
    Next
End Sub
```

Creating Microsoft Excel Objects from Visual Basic

Now that you're familiar with the top-level objects in Microsoft Excel, we can proceed with creating Microsoft Excel objects from a Visual Basic project. Three classes in Excel are both public and creatable: Application, Worksheet, and Chart.

It might seem that our earlier experience with creating and destroying objects would apply here. Creating objects provided by the Excel object server should be no different than creating objects provided by any other server. We should just be able to add a reference to the Excel object library to our project and use *New* or *CreateObject* to create an object that will be destroyed when we set the last object variable that refers to the object to *Nothing*. Unfortunately, it isn't that easy with Excel objects.

GetObject and Application Objects

We need to examine two new object concepts before we can understand the creation and destruction of Excel's objects. The first concept is embodied in the *GetObject* function, which can get a reference to a running object on the system or get a reference to an object that has been saved in a file. The second concept, application objects, has to do with VBA's ability to set properties and call methods directly—without qualifying the property or the method with a dot (.).

The versatile *GetObject*

The *GetObject* VBA function is a companion to the *CreateObject* function. The *GetObject* function uses a ProgID (Excel.Application) as *CreateObject* does, but *GetObject* is much more versatile. With *GetObject*, you can get a running instance of an object, open an object that has been saved in a file, or simply duplicate the functionality of *CreateObject*. The *GetObject* function takes two arguments, PathName and Class. The PathName argument is omitted or is an empty string (" ") or is the path of a file. The Class argument is a ProgID, or it is omitted. You must specify PathName or Class (or both)—you can't omit both.

Getting a running object To get a reference to a running instance of an object, leave the PathName argument blank and set the Class argument to a ProgID. If an object that matches the ProgID is running, then *GetObject* will return a reference to the running instance. If an instance isn't running, you'll get a run-time error.

```
Dim XLApp As Excel.Application
    'Get a running Excel instance (or an error).
    Set XLApp = GetObject(, "Excel.Application")
```

Opening a specific file If the PathName argument is specified, *GetObject* will open the file with a specified object type.

```
Dim XLSheet As Excel.Worksheet
    'Get a reference to a saved workbook.
    Set XLSheet = GetObject("Chapter8.Xls", "Excel.Sheet")
```

If the file extension of your file (.Xls) is registered with the system, the Class parameter can be omitted, so the following two lines are equivalent:

```
Set XLSheet = GetObject("Chapter8.Xls", "Excel.Sheet")
```

and

```
Set XLSheet = GetObject("Chapter8.Xls")
```

Creating a new instance If the PathName argument is an empty string, *GetObject* works just as *CreateObject* does.

```
Dim XLApp As Excel.Application
    'Start a new Excel instance.
    Set XLApp = GetObject("", "Excel.Application")
```

Microsoft Excel Application objects

In Excel, the following line of code is valid:

```
Application.Caption = "Invoice Entry"
```

Application isn't part of the core VBA language, but it isn't called as a method of an object either. So how can VBA call the *Application* method? Fasten your seat belts for this intriguing revelation. The Application object is not the highest-level object in Excel's object model! There is a higher-level object in Excel's model called _Global, with a creator name of _ExcelApplication. (See the "Creator Names for Creatable Objects" sidebar on page 213.) The _ExcelApplication creator name is flagged in a referenced object library as an Application object.

When it finds an Application object in a referenced object library, VBA provides an implicit object variable declaration for the object. Although you can't see the following line, VBA generates code similar to this line in your project for every Application object in every referenced object library in your project:

```
Public [_ExcelApplication] As New [_ExcelApplication]
```

When you access a property or a method of the _ExcelApplication object, VBA provides an implicit _ExcelApplication instance for you. And you've probably figured out by now that the _ExcelApplication object has an *Application* method. The _ExcelApplication object also has *ActiveSheet*, *ActiveChart*, *Cells*, *Range*, and many other methods. When you write

```
Application.Caption = "Invoice Entry"
```

VBA sees

```
[_ExcelApplication].Application.Caption = "Invoice Entry"
```

When an OLE object is marked as an Application object, the object server that implements the class will usually register its creator class with the system in order to support *GetObject*. When a running VBA project first uses an Application object, VBA tries a *GetObject* to see if the object class is registered with the system. A new instance is created only if the object class isn't registered. Excel, however, doesn't register _ExcelApplication, so the following code will start a new instance of Excel the first time it is called in a project.

```
Dim XLApp As Excel.Application
    Set XLApp = Excel.Application
    'VBA sees this line as
    'Set XLApp = [_ExcelApplication].Application.
```

If _ExcelApplication were registered with the system, a running instance of Excel would be used as the object server instead of a new instance of Excel. Although the implicit *GetObject* fails for Excel, remember the Application object syntax for other Application objects exposed by Office for Windows 95 applications, which correctly register their application objects. We rely on this syntax for manipulating Microsoft PowerPoint objects in Chapter 13, for instance. But don't use the Application object syntax to get a running instance of Excel. For Excel, you will have to use the *GetObject* function to find a running instance of the Application object instead of relying on the implicit Application object variable provided by VBA.

FYI

Creator Names for Creatable Objects

When an OLE class is both public and creatable, two names are associated with an object of that class. One name, the *creator name*, is used to create the object, and the other, the *actual name*, is the name associated with the class (Application, Worksheet, and so on). The creator name and the actual name can be used interchangeably in VBA code, with one exception: after the *New* keyword, you can use the creator name but not the actual name. Since the creator name can be used universally, ActualName is marked as hidden in an object library so that you won't see two names for the same class in the Object Browser. In most VBA code, the distinction between the creator name and the actual name is completely transparent.

For a VB-created public, creatable class, the creator name is the name you give the class in the property sheet, and the actual name is the creator name with an underscore (_) preceding it; so we'd have, for example, Class1 and _Class1. The *TypeName* function in VB4 will strip the leading underscore from an actual name, so the two names are indistinguishable in VB4. However, the leading underscore won't be stripped from the actual name in Excel-VBA. In the case of Excel's top-level object, _Global is the actual name and _ExcelApplication is the creator name. To see both names in action, try this code in the Immediate pane of Excel's Debug window:

```
?TypeName([_ExcelApplication])
```

Here's our result:

```
_Global
```

Creating Excel's Application Object

When you write VBA macros in Microsoft Excel, you always have an Application object at your beck and call. You don't have to do anything special to create it, and you generally don't have to do anything to destroy it. Creation and destruction of the Application object occur when the user starts and exits Excel. When you are writing a program in Visual Basic that uses Excel's objects, your program is responsible for opening and closing Excel. It turns out that opening Excel for use as an object server is just like opening any other server application, but closing Excel is more complicated. Since Excel is such a large program, starting multiple instances of Excel would rapidly eat memory on your system, so a smart program that uses Excel will use an existing instance of Excel whenever possible in order to save memory.

Setting an object variable that contains an Application object to *Nothing* isn't sufficient to close Excel. In other words, the following code will still leave a running copy of Excel on your system. (A reference to Excel's object library is assumed.)

```
Dim XLApp As Excel.Application
Set XLApp = CreateObject("Excel.Application")
XLApp.Visible = True
Set XLApp = Nothing
```

To close an instance of Excel, you need to call the *Quit* method. The *Quit* method corresponds to the File-Exit menu item on Excel's menu. When a user tries to close Excel, Excel will prompt the user to save any spreadsheets that haven't been saved. When you use the *Quit* method, the same thing will happen. If you have a workbook that hasn't been saved, calling the *Quit* method will cause Excel to put up a dialog box asking the user to save the file. Your program won't continue past the *Quit* method until the user responds to Excel's dialog.

```
:
XLApp.Quit
Set XLApp = Nothing
```

The dangers of the *Quit* method

Microsoft Excel is both a stand-alone program and an OLE object server. This means that an end user can have a workbook open in Excel and then start up another program that uses an Excel Worksheet object. Consider the following sequence of events:

1. The user opens a workbook in Excel.
2. The user starts another program.
3. The other program opens a workbook in Excel.
4. The user ends the second program.
5. The second program closes all open workbooks and quits Excel.
6. The user tries to go back to working in Excel, but Excel is gone!

In Chapter 6, we looked at the idea of a polite object server. An object server should never close down if an object created by the server is still in use by the user or by another application. Blindly calling the *Quit* method causes Excel to be a rude object server. When you call the *Quit* method, Excel will shut down and might abandon objects it has created for other client programs. In "A wrapper class for the Application object," below, we'll address the two main problems associated with the *Quit* method:

- The *Quit* method may require end user feedback in order to complete execution. If all workbooks aren't closed, the user may be forced to respond to Excel message boxes.
- By blindly using the *Quit* method, you can force Excel to be a rude object server. In order to be a polite server, Excel shouldn't shut down if a user or another application is using an Excel workbook.

Using *New* with the Application object

You don't have to use *CreateObject* to instantiate Excel's Application object. Although you can't use the *New* keyword with the Application object directly, you can use the *New* keyword with the hidden _ExcelApplication object. The *NewExcelApplication* function shown here uses implicit instantiation to create an _ExcelApplication object and then calls the Application property to get a reference to the newly created Application object.

```
Function NewExcelApplication() As Excel.Application
Dim XL As New [_ExcelApplication]
    Set NewExcelApplication = XL.Application
End Function
```

A wrapper class for the Application object

The ExcelLaunch class shown below takes care of the details of using *GetObject* to find a running instance of Excel and correctly using the *Quit* method. The *Class_Initialize()* procedure attempts a *GetObject* to find a running instance of Excel.Application. If the *GetObject* call fails, implicit instantiation is used to create a new object. The number of open workbooks is used as a key to determine whether or not *Quit* should be called. *Quit* is called only if no workbooks are open, so the code that uses the ExcelLaunch class to provide an Excel.Application should always close all workbooks before the Application object is destroyed. As the following code snippet demonstrates, using the ExcelLaunch class reduces the amount of code you need to write in other modules to launch Microsoft Excel.

```
Dim XLLaunch As New ExcelLaunch
Dim XLApp As Excel.Application
:
:
Set XLApp = XLLaunch.XLApplication
```

Here's the code listing for the ExcelLaunch class. You'll find this code on the companion CD in XLLaunch.Cls in the Chapter8 directory. You need a reference to Excel's object library to use this class in your own project.

```
Option Explicit
Private m_XLApp As Excel.Application
Private m_fWeLaunchedIt As Boolean
Private m_LaunchError As Long

'If CloseExcelIfEmpty is set when an instance of
'this class is destroyed, then Excel will always
'be terminated if there are no open workbooks.
'Otherwise, we terminate Excel only if we launched it.
Public CloseExcelIfEmpty As Boolean

Public Property Get XLApplication() As Excel.Application
    'See if an error was raised as Excel was launched.
    If m_LaunchError Then Err.Raise m_LaunchError
    'Return the Application object.
    Set XLApplication = m_XLApp
End Property

Private Sub Class_Initialize()
Dim NewExcel As New [_ExcelApplication]
    'Default to always closing an empty Excel.
    CloseExcelIfEmpty = True

    'Class_Initialize is considered an event. Errors
    'can't be returned from events, and an untrapped
    'run-time error is fatal. Just keep any error value
    'and raise the error when the XLApplication Property
    'Get procedure is called.
    On Error Resume Next
    Set m_XLApp = GetObject(, "Excel.Application")
    If Err = 0 Then
        m_fWeLaunchedIt = False
        Exit Sub
    End If
    Err.Clear
    Set m_XLApp = NewExcel.Application
    If Err Then
        m_LaunchError = Err
        Err.Clear
    Else
        m_fWeLaunchedIt = True
    End If
End Sub

Private Sub Class_Terminate()
    On Error Resume Next
    'If there are no open workbooks, then go ahead
    'and shut down Excel.
```

```
    If m_XLApp.Workbooks.Count = 0 Then
        'Quit Excel if this class first launched it
        'or if the CloseExcelIfEmpty flag is set.
        If m_fWeLaunchedIt Or CloseExcelIfEmpty Then m_XLApp.Quit
    End If
End Sub
```

Unfortunately, we can't make any guarantees that the ExcelLaunch class is completely robust. It's possible for a client application to be using Excel without having a workbook open. For example, an add-in file opened as a workbook won't be reflected in *Workbooks.Count*. (See Chapter 10 for a discussion of add-ins.) The only way to guarantee politeness with Excel is never to call the *Quit* method.

Creating Excel's Worksheet Object

The three public, creatable classes that Excel exposes (Application, Worksheet, and Chart) can be instantiated with *CreateObject*. Since Worksheet and Chart objects are created and destroyed in the same way, we'll concentrate on creating a Worksheet object. Everything we say about creating a Worksheet object in this section can also be applied to creating a Chart object. Here's how we create a Worksheet object.

```
Dim WS As Excel.Worksheet
Set WS = CreateObject("Excel.Sheet")
```

We now have a Worksheet object running on the system. A Worksheet is not a top-level object, so it can't run on its own. The parent of a Worksheet object is a Workbook object, and the parent of a Workbook object is the Application object, so an instance of both the Workbook class and the Application class will be created along with the Worksheet object to provide the necessary framework for the Worksheet object. Without these two levels of parent objects, the Worksheet object can't be created.

NOTE Excel's object library does support the *New* keyword to create Worksheet and Chart objects, but in a nonobvious fashion. The creator name for a Worksheet is _ExcelSheet, and _ExcelChart is the creator name for the Chart object. (See the "Creator Names for Creatable Objects" sidebar back on page 213.)

If an instance of Excel is already running on the system, creating a new Worksheet object will add a Workbook object (with the caption Object) that contains a single Worksheet object (called Sheet1) to the running instance of Excel, so you don't have to worry about launching a new instance of Excel when you create a Worksheet object. Creating a Worksheet object has one big advantage over creating an Application object and adding a Worksheet object to it. As long as the Application object's Visible property is *False* when you destroy a Worksheet object you've created instead of adding a Worksheet object to the Application object, the Application object will be destroyed as well. There's no need to call the *Quit* method. Here are sample routines to create and destroy a Worksheet object.

```
'Use the creator name for easy instantiation.
Dim WS As New [_ExcelSheet]
Sub OpenSheet()
    WS.Application.Visible = True
End Sub
Sub CloseSheet()
    If WS Is Nothing Then Exit Sub
    With WS.Application
        If .Workbooks.Count = 1 Then .Visible = False
    End With
    'This will close Excel along with the worksheet.
    Set WS = Nothing
End Sub
```

Cross-Reference See VBA Language Concepts: Qualified Object Types: Using Square Brackets

When a Worksheet object is created, it will always be visible. If you don't want the Worksheet object to be visible, hide the Window object that contains the Worksheet object.

```
WS.Parent.Windows(1).Visible = False
```

Hiding the Window object that shows the Worksheet object is generally a good idea if you need to execute a lot of code to make the worksheet presentable to the user. Temporarily hide the Window object that contains the worksheet, and then show the Window object again when its worksheet is fully formatted and ready for display. When you use *GetObject* to open an existing workbook from a file instead of creating a new Worksheet object, the open window will always be hidden.

SUMMARY

- Like Visual Basic, Microsoft Excel is a host application for the Visual Basic for Applications language. Apart from the language enhancements added to VBA 2.0, Excel-VBA is fully compatible with VB4-VBA. VBA code written against any set of objects can be used by projects in either application as long as the object library describing the objects is referenced. Therefore, code written in Excel can be pasted directly into a VB project with little modification, and vice versa.
- The Debug window in Microsoft Excel can be used to directly run any VBA procedure—and even simple code snippets. You can't edit VBA code in Excel while it is running.
- Excel calls VBA code in a much different fashion than Visual Basic does. Excel calls subroutines with no argument as macros, which are called from the Macro dialog or as events on drawing objects. User-defined functions can be called from a formula in a worksheet, just as the built-in worksheet functions can be called. Any procedure can be called from other VBA code.
- Excel provides a huge object model, containing 130 public classes, that can be used to control almost every part of Excel from VBA code. The object model is hierarchical, with the Application object at the top of the hierarchy. Individual child objects below the parent Application object are referenced as items in collections.
- The Application object is used to control Excel's workspace. Properties and methods such as StatusBar, *DisplayFullScreen*, WindowState, *DisplayAlerts*, and ScreenUpdating are used to control the appearance of Excel's working environment. Methods like *Workbooks*, *Windows*, *Toolbars*, and *Menubars* are used to return collections of child objects.
- The Workbook object is used primarily as a parent to the various Sheets collections and as the object that's saved to disk. The Workbook object has *Save*, *SaveAs*, *SaveCopyAs*, *Close*, and other disk- and file-related methods. A new Workbook object is created by a call to the *Add* method of the Workbooks collection.
- All workbooks and sheets are displayed in Window objects. A workbook can have multiple windows, so display settings such as gridlines, column headers, and workbook tabs are controlled through the Window object.
- Sheet-type objects, which include Worksheet, Chart, Module, and DialogSheet objects, can be easily added and deleted from a workbook.

You can also move sheet objects to different positions in the same workbook or move or copy sheets to a different workbook.

- The Range object is probably the most often used and most complicated object in Excel. The *Cells* and *Range* methods of a Worksheet object are used to get a Range object. A Range object that contains multiple areas is known as a complex range. Applying the *Cells*, *Columns*, and *Rows* methods to a Range object can modify how a specific cell is indexed in a Range object.
- Excel objects can be used by a Visual Basic program. Application, Worksheet, and Chart objects can be created directly by means of the *CreateObject* function or the *New* keyword. Other objects are referenced and created using methods of the creatable objects.
- The *GetObject* function can be used to find a running instance of one of Excel's three public, creatable objects. Using *GetObject*, you can also open a chart or a worksheet that has been saved on disk as an .Xls file.
- Although it's easy to create Excel's Application object from VB, closing down cleanly and in a polite way is very difficult. Arbitrary use of the *Quit* method can leave an end user of your program answering Excel dialogs or can leave another client of Excel stranded with orphaned Excel objects. Although some checks can be made to ensure safe shutdown of Excel, it's impossible to be 100 percent robust as a polite server and still use the *Quit* method.

Now that we've seen the basics of using Excel-VBA and creating Excel objects in Visual Basic, it's time to move on to more advanced topics. With the information in this chapter, you can drive Excel objects from Visual Basic projects. The next three chapters go further. We'll get into coordinating code running in Excel with code running in Visual Basic to achieve optimal integration between Microsoft Excel and Visual Basic programs. You'll be much happier with your Excel/VB programs when you know how to coordinate the two applications, instead of simply driving one app from the other. In Chapter 9 we'll look at performance issues for Excel-VBA, and we'll look at fine-tuning the use of Excel objects in Visual Basic projects.

9

Performance-Tuning Excel-VBA

If you're using Visual Basic for Applications in Microsoft Excel for the first time, within a few hours you'll be able to write Excel macros that automate simple tasks—such as applying a special format to the currently selected cells. With a few more days of determined effort, you'll be able to write relatively complicated programs in Excel, programs that go well beyond combining several point-and-click operations into a single action. At that point, you'll be on the road to fully automating Excel, even to the point at which an end user will see nothing that looks like the normal Microsoft Excel interface in your program!

Along about that time, however, you might notice that your program is really slow. To make matters worse, you might not have any idea why. The point of this chapter, primarily, is to help you avoid the frustration of finishing a project only to find that you need to rewrite a lot of its code to improve its performance. The secondary objective of this chapter is to help you improve existing Excel-VBA projects that don't satisfy performance requirements.

Selection-Centric vs. Object-Centric Macros

There are two ways to make Microsoft Excel perform almost any action. The first way, of course, is to use the mouse and the keyboard. The second way is to use a macro. The easiest way to program a macro in Excel is to use Excel's macro recorder, which translates user input into VBA code. This method creates a macro that simulates the mouse and keyboard actions through commands using the object model. A macro can activate a sheet, select a range, and enter a formula—just as if you were doing it by hand. Since we haven't really worked with Excel's macro recorder yet, let's look at a simple example of how it works.

1. Start Microsoft Excel. You'll see a default workbook with no data in it.
2. From the Record Macro submenu on the Tools menu, select Record New Macro.
3. You'll see a dialog asking you for the name of the macro. Click OK to accept the default name (*Macro1*). The Stop Recording toolbar will appear. (See Figure 9-1.) The single button on the Stop Recording toolbar looks just like the End button on the VB toolbar.

Figure 9-1. *The Stop Recording toolbar with its single button.*

4. Use the tabs at the bottom of the workbook window to select Sheet2.
5. Click in Cell A1.
6. Type *10* and press Enter.
7. Click the Stop Macro button on the Stop Recording toolbar.
8. Using the workbook tabs, switch to Module1 to see the macro you've just recorded:

```
Sub Macro1()
    Sheets("Sheet2").Select
    Range("A1").Select
    ActiveCell.FormulaR1C1 = "10"
    Range("A2").Select
End Sub
```

Each action you performed while the macro recorder was running produced at least one line of code. If you run *Macro1*, it will duplicate the exact actions you performed in steps 4 through 6. Sheet2 will be selected, and then the first cell. The value *10* will be entered into the first cell, and a new cell will be selected.

Every step in *Macro1* will be visibly apparent to anyone who uses the macro. If your goal is to set the first cell on Sheet2 to *10*, you probably don't want to see all of the user actions required to set the value. You'd probably prefer to set the value directly. Let's write a new macro to set the value of Sheet2!A1 (Sheet2, cell A1) in the most direct way possible:

```
Sub Macro1Plus()
    Sheets("Sheet2").Cells(1).Value = 10
End Sub
```

Macro1Plus is much shorter and much more direct than *Macro1*. The main difference between the results of these two macros is that running *Macro1Plus* doesn't change the current selection and has no visible effects on Excel's workspace. If you have a range in Sheet1 selected when you run *Macro1Plus*, the same range will still be selected and Sheet1 will still be active after the macro has finished running. When you run *Macro1* with a range in Sheet1 selected, however, your current selection will become Sheet2!A2. (If you manually return to Sheet1, your original range will still be highlighted).

Almost all of the actions available through Excel's object model can be performed without a change of the current selection in Excel. And there are many reasons to avoid writing macros that change the current selection. Here are a few:

- Any time you change the current selection, Excel must repaint at least part of the screen. And repainting the screen is one of the most time-consuming operations any program for Windows, Excel included, will perform.
- A macro that relies on the current selection usually takes much longer than a macro that manipulates an object directly.
- An end user is unlikely to use your macro more than once if calling the macro creates extra work for him or her. Changing the current selection back to a previous selection after a macro has run might require the user to perform a lot of extra work.

The code generated by the macro recorder is *selection-centric*. Selection-centric code relies on setting and changing the current selection to perform any action. Methods and properties such as *Select*, Selection, ActiveCell, *SelectedSheets*, and ActiveWindow are used extensively in selection-centric macros to establish the selected cell, range, sheet, or active window.

An *object-centric* macro manipulates objects directly instead of first selecting them. The macro can modify any cell in any open worksheet in Excel directly—without the need for *Select*, Selection, ActiveCell, and the other procedures and properties used in selection-centric macros. Since you can't rely on Excel's macro recorder to write such selection-independent code, writing object-centric macros requires more work on your part. But the end result will be well worth the work you'll invest. Object-centric macros are faster, smaller, and friendlier to the end user than selection-centric macros.

Doing the Job Once

One of the easiest performance mistakes you can make when writing VBA code is to force Excel to duplicate work it has already completed. A request to Excel for the ActiveSheet, for the Selection, or for a reference to a specific cell takes time, and there isn't any reason to make Excel do the same work more than once. In the following code snippet, the ActiveWorkbook property and the *WorkSheets* and *Cells* methods are all called twice:

```
ActiveWorkbook.WorkSheets(1).Cells(3, 5).Value = 10
ActiveWorkbook.WorkSheets(1).Cells(3, 5).Font.Bold = True
```

Compare this code with the rewritten version shown below. This time, we eliminate duplicate calls by keeping a reference (Range1) to the object we're modifying:

```
Dim Range1 As Range
Set Range1 = ActiveWorkbook.Worksheets(1).Cells(3, 5)
With Range1
    .Value = 10
    .Font.Bold = True
End With
```

Forcing Early Binding in Excel

Unless you're very careful, you can end up making almost every call into Excel's object model late bound. (See Chapter 6 for a description of early and late binding.) The root of this problem lies in the design of Excel's object library. Every property in Excel's object library is typed as Variant, and every method that returns a value also returns a variant. Since the property and method-return types are variants, VBA can't early-bind to them, so late-bound calls are required. As we saw in Chapter 6, an early-bound setting of a property or call to a method requires a hard-typed object variable or return type.

NOTE In Excel-VBA (VBA 1.0) you can't make recursive early-bound calls. Therefore, in the expression *Obj.Prop.Method*, *Obj.Prop* is an early-bound call, but *.Method* is late bound even when *Obj.Prop* returns a hard-typed object. In VB4 (VBA 2.0), you can chain as many early-bound calls as you like. Since Excel's object model always returns variants, this is a moot point for Excel's objects, but it is something you should know when you're optimizing calls from Excel to Visual Basic object servers.

In Chapter 8, we noted that _ExcelApplication, not Application, was the top-level object in Excel's object model. In order to force early binding, you need to remember that unqualified calls to Excel's object actually bind to _ExcelApplication. Therefore, the following line of code:

```
Debug.Print Application.Caption
```

is actually interpreted as

```
Debug.Print [_ExcelApplication].Application.Caption
```

The Application property early-binds to _ExcelApplication, but the Application property, just like all Excel methods, returns a reference variant, so the Caption property will be late bound to the object! Since the overhead for late-bound calls is approximately twice the overhead for early-bound calls, you should eliminate late-bound code whenever you can. The switch from late-bound calls to the Application object to early-bound calls to the Application object is actually quite simple: you just need to create an object variable of type Application and make calls to the Application object from the object variable instead of from the Application property. Here's an example of doing just that:

```
Dim XLApp As Application
Set XLApp = Application
Debug.Print XLApp.Caption
```

To see the reduction in overhead you can achieve by acting on this performance tip, run the following *ApplicationLeftTest* macro from the companion CD's Chapter9\Chapter9.Xls Excel workbook. (This macro will take significantly longer to run if you launch it from the Immediate pane of the Debug window, so be sure to use the Tools-Macro menu or F5 to start the macro.) There's almost no cost associated with reading the Left property of the Application object, so we can accurately measure the overhead required to call the Application property. You should find that when you're using an Application-type object variable instead of the Application property your code runs more than twice as fast, as shown in the dialog in Figure 9-2 on the next page. (Your results may differ from those shown in Figure 9-2 depending on the speed of your PC and on what other software you're running.)

```
Sub ApplicationLeftTest()
Dim XLApp As Application
Dim KeepTime As Double
Dim Time1 As Double, Time2 As Double
Dim tmpInt As Integer, iCount As Integer

    'Get timings using Application property directly.
    KeepTime = Timer
    For iCount = 1 To 10000
        tmpInt = Application.Left
    Next iCount
    Time1 = Timer - KeepTime
```

(continued)

```
    'Get timings using an Application object variable.
    Set XLApp = Application
    KeepTime = Timer
    For iCount = 1 To 10000
        tmpInt = XLApp.Left
    Next iCount
    Time2 = Timer - KeepTime

    'Display the results.
    MsgBox "Application.Left: " & _
           Format$(Time1, "0.00") & Chr$(13) & _
           "XLApp.Left:       " & _
           Format$(Time2, "0.00") & Chr$(13) & _
           "Performance:      " & _
           Format$(Time1 / Time2, "00%")
End Sub
```

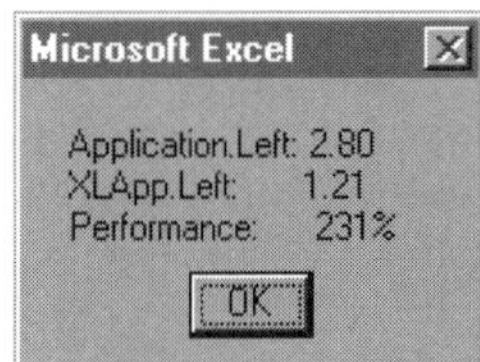

Figure 9-2. *The results from the* ApplicationLeftTest *performance macro.*

You will have to write a very long macro if you're going to notice a significant performance increase as a result of using this performance tip. Both early and late binding are very fast when you're manipulating Microsoft Excel from a VBA macro. However, there is some performance difference between early and late binding, and every little bit helps. You'll see the real performance difference between the two when you control Microsoft Excel from inside a Visual Basic program. Since such cross-process OLE Automation has a high overhead, cutting the overhead in half is a major performance win. Code written with efficiency (as well as reusability) in mind should always access properties and methods from a hard-typed object variable instead of late-binding to the variants returned by Excel's unqualified methods and properties (Application, Selection, ActiveCell, ActiveWindow, and so on).

NOTE Excel can't early-bind calls from the Application object to the exposed worksheet functions (*Average*, *Sum*, and so on) because the worksheet functions are listed without arguments in the object library. If, from within an Excel macro, you try to call a worksheet function from an Application-type variable, you will get a "Wrong number of arguments" compile-time error:

```
Dim App1 As Application
Set App1 = Application
x = App1.Sum(1, 2)    'Returns an error at compile-time
```

If you need to use a lot of worksheet functions, you can still minimize the use of the Application property by calling the functions from an Object-type variable that references the Application object:

```
Dim App2 As Object
Set App2 = Application
x = App2.Sum(1, 2)    'x is now equal to 3 (1 + 2).
```

The "Count the Dots" Principle

To set a property or call a method of an object, you use a dot (.). The dot syntax should be very familiar to you by now. Although a dot takes up very little space in code, it can be costly in execution time. The "count the dots" principle is simple: the more dots you have in your code, the more slowly your code will run.

"Your code will run more slowly" is a pretty vague statement. To make this observation more measurable, let's look at what's required to call a method of an object. The work required to successfully call a method can be broken into two pieces. The first part is the work actually done by the method. The second is the overhead required to call the method.

The work done by a method itself—part 1 of the cost of calling a method—is hard to speed up. There's no way to optimize the code of a method in a shipped OLE server, so you just have to live with the method's performance. However, you can limit your use of slow methods. For example, given a hypothetical Polygon object, you would call the *Render* method (a method that draws an image to a destination object) only after all points had been added to the polygon, not after each individual point was added.

Even though you have very little control over the performance of the methods and properties you use when you're driving an OLE Automation object server with VBA code, you do have complete control over how you call an object. This is where the count the dots principle comes in. Minimizing the number of dots in your program is the single most important performance booster for VBA procedures that make extensive use of objects. By counting the dots in your code, you can easily determine the amount of overhead that controlling your objects will demand.

Late-Bound Dots

As we saw in Chapters 5 and 6, at least twice as much overhead is required to call a method using an object variable declared *As Object* instead of a hard-typed variable. So when you're counting those dots, count 2 for every late-bound dot and 1 for every early-bound dot to get the most accurate estimate of your overhead.

Cross-Process Dots

Dot counting is especially important when you're controlling objects created by cross-process servers—controlling Microsoft Excel objects from a Visual Basic program, for instance. The performance application *MBoxPerf.Vbp* at the end of Chapter 6 demonstrated the huge performance difference between in-process and cross-process servers. *MBoxPerf.Vbp* also indicated the number of cross-process calls a machine can make every second. Refer back to Chapter 6 if you need to measure performance on your work machine or target systems. Just to give you a frame of reference: the Pentium-90 machine on which this chapter is based processes 320 dots per second.

Counting Hidden Dots

Not all dots in your VBA code are visible. If you use application objects or default properties in your program, it will contain hidden dots.

Application object dots

Earlier in this chapter and in Chapter 8, we noted that the top-level object in Excel's object model is _ExcelApplication, so

```
ActiveCell.Value = 10
```

is seen by VBA as

```
[_ExcelApplication].ActiveCell.Value = 10
```

In this case, you can see only one dot in the code, but VBA actually has to deal with two dots. The first dot is for the call to ActiveCell, and the second dot is for setting the Value property of the returned Range object.

Default value dots

You can also assign a value to a Range object without using the Value property:

```
ActiveCell = 10
```

In this case, the Value property is implied. This simple line of code actually contains two dots, although you can't see them. The first is the dot VBA must handle in order to call ActiveCell. The second is the implied dot VBA handles in order to set the Value property. And since ActiveCell returns a variant, this second dot is late bound, for which we count 2, so the dot counting total for assigning *10* to ActiveCell is 3.

Dot Counting Examples

In the code examples that follow, let's count the number of dots VBA must handle as it executes the code. In each code example, the same methods are called and the same properties are accessed, but the dot count ranges from 4 through 10. Be sure you can find and correctly count all of the hidden and visible dots before you move on. Remember: a late-bound dot counts 2, not 1; Selection is a property of the _ExcelApplication object; and these examples assume that a Range object is selected.

Legend:

```
= △ early hidden
= □ early visible
= ○ late
```

Example 1

```
△Selection⊙Font⊙Bold = True
△Selection⊙Font⊙Italic = True
```

Answer: 10 (2 early hidden, 0 early visible, 4 late)

Example 2

```
With △Selection⊙Font
  ⊙Bold = True
  ⊙Italic = True
End with
```

Answer: 7 (1 early hidden, 0 early visible, 3 late)

Example 3

```
Dim Range1 As Range
Set Range1 =△Selection
Range1⊡Font⊙Bold = True
Range1⊡Font⊙Italic = True
```

Answer: 7 (1 early hidden, 2 early visible, 2 late)

Example 4

```
Dim Range1 As Range
Set Range1 =△Selection
With Range1⊡Font
  ⊙Bold = True
  ⊙Italic = True
End With
```

Answer: 6 (1 early hidden, 1 early visible, 2 late)

Example 5

```
Dim Font1 As Font
Set Font1 =△Selection⊙Font
With Font1
  ⊡Bold = True
  ⊡Italic = True
End With
```

Answer: 5 (1 early hidden, 2 early visible, 1 late)

(continued)

Legend:
= △ early hidden
= □ early visible
= ○ late

Example 6

```
Dim Range1 As Range
Dim Font1 As Font
Set Range1 =△Selection
Set Font1 = Range1□Font
Font1□Bold = True
Font1□Italic = True
```

Answer: 4 (1 early hidden, 3 early visible, 0 late)

Example 7

```
Dim Range1 As Range
Dim Font1 As Font
Set Range1 =△Selection
Set Font1 = Range1□Font
With Font1
  □Bold = True
  □Italic = True
End With
```

Answer: 4 (1 early hidden, 3 early visible, 0 late)

Containing only two simple lines of code, Example 1 (with 10 dots to be processed) is clearly the easiest to write. Examples 6 and 7 (4 dots) are more complicated but much more efficient. From a VBA performance perspective, declaring an object variable to hold an object reference is very cheap. From a programmer's perspective, new variables mean a few more lines of code. Now that you know how to reduce overhead in your code, you can decide for yourself how much overhead you want to go to the trouble of cutting. Just remember that you have to type in the code only once but your users have to run the code's procedures many times.

Conversing Between Visual Basic and Microsoft Excel

The most straightforward way for an application written in Visual Basic to control Microsoft Excel objects is to have the VB program reference Excel's object library and directly manipulate the Excel object model. If there is a complicated task to do, however, a low number of cross-process dots per second on a given hardware platform can make even the most optimized code painfully sluggish. A macro that runs in seconds in an Excel module sheet can take minutes to run cross-process from VB. Even if you heed this warning and master the count the dots principle, you might still be surprised the first time you control Excel from a VB program at how slow cross-process object model manipulations really are.

Before you decide that controlling Microsoft Excel from a Visual Basic program is just too slow, note that it is possible for the two applications to communicate with each other with better than acceptable speed. If a VB program or an Excel macro uses an object provided by a cross-process server, every call to the object must cross the *process boundary*. Crossing the process boundary is also known as making a *context switch*. The fewer times your program makes a context switch, the faster your program will run. In the next few pages, we'll look at techniques for executing multiple commands with a single context switch. By batching commands, you can reduce the number of context switches in your program down to the point at which the cross-process performance hit will be negligible.

Calling Excel Macros From VB

Since Microsoft Excel can run VBA code, you can put any VBA code that controls Excel's object model and is dot intensive into an Excel macro. If you load the workbook that contains your macro into Excel, you can call the macro directly from a VB program using the *Run* method of the Excel Application object. Since a few steps are involved in doing this correctly, let's walk through a small example of calling an Excel macro from a VB program.

1. Start Microsoft Excel.
2. Insert a module into the default workbook. (From Excel's Insert menu, select Macro and then Module.)
3. Add the following macro to the module:

```
Sub CloseThisWorkbook()
    ThisWorkbook.Close SaveChanges:=False
End Sub
```

4. Save the workbook as C:\ObjProg\Chapter9\CTW.Xls.
5. Close Microsoft Excel.
6. Start Visual Basic.
7. Add a reference to Excel's object library to the default project.
8. Add a CommandButton control to Form1.
9. Double-click on the Command1 control and insert code so that the *Command1_Click()* event procedure looks like this:

```
Private Sub Command1_Click()
Dim WS As Excel.Worksheet
Dim XLApp As Excel.Application
    Set WS = GetObject("C:\ObjProg\Chapter9\CTW.Xls")
    WS.Parent.Windows(1).Visible = True
    Set XLApp = WS.Application
    With XLApp
        .Visible = True
        .Run "CTW.Xls!CloseThisWorkbook"
        If .Workbooks.Count = 0 Then .Quit
    End With
End Sub
```

NOTE You can't use the *GetObject* function to open a workbook that doesn't contain at least one worksheet. Therefore, even if your workbook contains only macros, you'll need to keep an empty worksheet in the workbook if you want to use *GetObject* to open the workbook.

10. Press F8-step (not F5-start) to begin running the program, and click the Command1 control. You'll break at the top of the *Command1_Click()* event procedure.
11. Press F8 repeatedly to step through the event procedure.

Notice that the CTW workbook is closed by the Excel *CloseThisWorkbook* macro in the workbook, not by a call to the *Close* method in VB's *Command1_Click()* event procedure. The technique used to call the single-line *CloseThisWorkbook* macro can be applied to calling macros of any length. By moving chunks of dot-infested, Excel-specific code across the process boundary from VB to Excel, you can significantly reduce the number of cross-process dots in your program and dramatically increase performance with minimal effort.

To call an Excel macro from Visual Basic with the Excel *Run* method, you must qualify the name of the macro you want to run with the name of the workbook. In the preceding example, we used *CTW.Xls!CloseThisWorkbook*. This syntax isn't always sufficient to specify which Excel macro you want your VB program to run. If the macro name isn't unique in the workbook—it is legal to put a macro with the same name into two different modules in the same workbook—you must include the name of the module that contains the macro. Our sample macro name in such a case would change to *CTW.Xls!'[Module1].CloseThisWorkbook'*. The square brackets are required when a module name has a space, and a dot always goes between the module name and the macro name. The single quotation marks are also required when a module name is specified.

Excel's *Application.Run* method can also be used both to call a procedure in Excel that takes parameters and to pass back the return value of a function. The parameters to a sub or a function are passed as additional arguments to the *Run* method. For example, if we were to change the *CloseThisWorkbook* macro to take a SaveChanges argument, we would adjust our code as follows:

```
'In Microsoft Excel
Sub CloseThisWorkbook(SaveChanges As Boolean)
    ThisWorkbook.Close SaveChanges:=SaveChanges
End Sub

'In Visual Basic
.Run "CTW.Xls!CloseThisWorkbook", False
```

You can pass as many arguments as you want to the Excel *Run* method (as many as 30, which is a figure well beyond rational coding behavior). However, you'll be disappointed if you try to pass variables by reference using the *Run* method. All arguments to the *Run* method are passed by value, which means that changes made to a variable passed as a parameter to the *Run* method won't be reflected in the passed-in variable after the *Run* method returns. The only way to return information from the *Run* method is to call a function with a return value or, in rare cases, to intentionally raise an error on the Excel side of the process boundary. If you call a function using the *Run* method, the *Run* method will return the value returned by the function.

Using Visual Basic Class Instances in Microsoft Excel Macros

To call a Microsoft Excel macro from Visual Basic, you use the Excel *Run* method. But how can you execute a procedure in a VB program from Excel? VB doesn't have a *Run* method. Fortunately, VB's OLE server capabilities let you define custom objects with methods that can be called from Excel macros. Consider a method of your VB custom object to be a customized version of the Excel *Run* method. Although parameters can't be passed by reference to Excel's *Run* method, parameters can be passed by reference to your VB custom method, so changes made to a variable passed by reference to a VB method by an Excel macro persist after the method terminates.

As we saw in Chapter 6, Visual Basic can create either in-process (DLL) or cross-process (EXE) OLE object servers. The overhead required to use objects created by a VB DLL server in Excel macros is no greater than the overhead required for using native Excel objects in Excel macros. If you choose to use EXE servers rather than in-process DLL servers, any call you make from an Excel macro to the VB-created object is subject to the same performance overhead as calls to an Excel object from VB. For best results, design your cross-process object servers to reduce the number of boundary-jumping dots. Here's a quick example. Given a hypothetical StatusWindow class that displays a VB form, let's look at two approaches to creating the window—this code would be in an Excel module:

```
Dim StatusWindow As StatusWindow
Sub StartStatus1()
    Set StatusWindow = CreateObject("FormServer.StatusWindow")
    With StatusWindow
        .Left = 0
        .Top = 0
        .Width = 200
        .Height = 100
        .Visible = True
    End With
End Sub
```

and

```
Sub StartStatus2()
    Set StatusWindow = CreateObject("FormServer.StatusWindow")
    StatusWindow.Show Left:=0, Top:=0, Width:=200, Height:=100
End Sub
```

Both *StartStatus1* and *StartStatus2* are written for optimal dot efficiency. There is no late binding and no duplicated code in either. The difference between the two routines is that *StartStatus2* uses a single dot to do the same work that *StartStatus1* does with five dots. If the StatusWindow class didn't have a *Show* method, *StartStatus1* would be the only alternative. From this short example, it should be clear that fast communications across the process boundary require not only tight client-side coding, but object servers designed to reduce the calls needed to control their exposed objects.

In our example, the hypothetical VB StatusWindow class was instantiated in an Excel module. This is the only way to use a VB class instance in Excel because there is no way to pass an instance from VB to Excel. This is a limitation of the Excel *Run* method. If you pass an object variable as an argument to the *Run* method, Excel will pass the default value of the class passed to your macro instead of a reference to the object itself. If the class doesn't have a default value, the *Run* method fails. Since you can't specify a default value for a VB class, passing a VB object to the *Run* method will always generate a run-time error. We'll explore some techniques for getting around this limitation of the *Run* method in the "*XLCallBack* Sample" section of Chapter 11.

FYI

Miscellaneous Gotchas: Surprises in Working with Microsoft Excel and Visual Basic

There are a few cases in which working with VB and Excel created surprises for the authors. We've decided to take the fun of finding these hidden treasures of programming frustration away from you. Of course, you're not obliged to read this sidebar.

Qualified Class Names

If there exists, or if you have created, a public and creatable class in a VB project that you want to reference in an Excel macro, you can qualify the name of the class with the name of the referenced object library that contains that class, but you'll need to use a leading underscore on the class name.

With most references you qualify, you can simply use the name of the object library, like this:

```
Dim Obj As LibName.Class
(Dim Obj As Excel.Application)
```

However, with a public and creatable VB class the syntax above would return an error message, "Object library feature not supported." If you ever get this message on a *Dim* statement, try using this syntax:

```
Dim Obj As LibName.[_Class]
(Dim Obj As VBProject.[_VBClass])
```

This limitation applies not only to objects created from VB classes. The Microsoft Access Application object will result in the same error and will require the same workaround. However, just adding a leading underscore doesn't provide the correct name for all objects. If you still get an error after adding the underscore and square brackets, *Dim* the variable *As Object*, assign an instance of the class to your variable, and use TypeName to get the name you need to put after the library name in your *Dim* statement. If the name you get back has a leading underscore, put square brackets around it. For example:

```
Dim TestObject As Object 'SomeLib.Object
Set TestObject = CreateObject("SomeLib.Object")
MsgBox "Dim the variable with this name: " & TypeName(TestObject)
```

Cross-Reference VBA Language Concepts: Qualified Identifiers: Square Brackets

DisplayAlerts and ScreenUpdating

DisplayAlerts and ScreenUpdating are two properties of the Excel Application object. The statement,

```
Application.DisplayAlerts = False
```

suppresses all Excel dialogs, eliminating the need for user input. And

```
Application.ScreenUpdating = False
```

prevents Excel from refreshing the screen, eliminating screen flash. Both of these properties are used frequently in Excel macros. However, when called cross-process, neither of these properties has any affect. To use DisplayAlerts and ScreenUpdating, you need to make sure the calls to set them are made on the Excel side of the process boundary. You can do this either by using the Excel *Run* method from VB or by putting the Visual Basic code that controls Excel into an in-process (DLL) OLE server. The classes provided by the in-process server must be created in an Excel macro, not by a VB program—unless the VB program is another DLL loaded by Excel.

Variant Array Bounds

An array in a variant passed from VB to Excel will always get passed to Excel with a lower bound of *1*—even if the lower bound of the array in VB was *0* or some other value. The data in the variant array hasn't changed—just the upper and lower bounds.

Cross-Reference VBA Language Concepts: Arrays in Variants

External Types in Public Classes

Within a VB public class module, you can define a property or method to have a return value with an external type—that is, a type defined in a referenced object library. For example, a Recordset type object is an external type because the Recordset class is defined in the Microsoft *DAO 2.5/3.0 Compatibility Library* object library, not in a VB project's class module.

A problem occurs if an Excel project contains a reference to an object library for a server running in the VB design environment, in which case any attempt to early-bind to a property or method in the referenced object library that returns an external type will fail at compile-time. The workaround is to temporarily change the return type from a hard type (*As Recordset*) to a generic object type (*As Object*). If the server the Excel project is referencing is running in an EXE or a DLL instead of in the VB environment, the code will compile cleanly in either case, so the return type should be switched back to the hard-typed reference. (Refer back to Chapter 4 for more information on defining properties and methods in class modules.)

Assigning Arrays to Multi-Cell Ranges

A common task in Microsoft Excel is to assign an array of elements to a range of cells. The most obvious way to do that is to step through the array and cells one value and one cell at a time and assign a value from the array to each cell in the range. While this will work, it is also painfully slow, which is why we're taking this subject up in the performance chapter. There is a much better way to move an array of values into a range of cells. The array can be assigned to a multi-cell, rectangular range with a single statement. The only requirement is that the range object in question have the same dimensions as the array. Here's an example. (*AssignArrayToRange* is on the companion CD in Module1 of Chapter9\Chapter9.Xls.)

```
Sub AssignArrayToRange(ByRef Data As Variant, StartCell As Range)
Dim ParentSheet As Worksheet
Dim WorkRange As Range
    If IsArray(Data) Then
        'Force early binding to the Worksheet object.
        Set ParentSheet = StartCell.Parent
        With ParentSheet
            'Create a range with the same dimensions as the
            'Data array's dimensions.
            Set WorkRange = _
                .Range(StartCell, _
                       .Cells(StartCell.Row + _
                       UBound(Data, 1) - LBound(Data, 1), _
                       StartCell.Column + _
                       UBound(Data, 2) - LBound(Data, 2)))
            'Assign the whole array with a single statement.
            WorkRange.Value = Data
        End With
    Else
        'Data is a single value. Just assign it to StartCell.
        StartCell.Value = Data
    End If
End Sub
```

The dot count for *AssignArrayToRange* is 6 no matter how big the array is. If we were to assign values to individual cells, the dot count would depend on the size of the array and the code would be unacceptably slow for a large array.

SUMMARY

- Writing powerful macros isn't enough to make your customized Excel programs accessible to an end user. To be truly useful, the code in your workbook must offer good performance.
- Although you can create Excel macros to simulate user input with the mouse and the keyboard, directly manipulating objects instead of relying on the current selection produces much more efficient VBA code. Object-centric programming produces faster, shorter, and more user-friendly code than a selection-centric approach.
- Many methods in Excel's object model return object references. By keeping a reference to a returned object in a hard-typed object variable, you can avoid forcing Excel to repeatedly call methods that return the same object reference. Doing the job once minimizes the work Excel needs to do to run your VBA macros.

- Unqualified properties and methods in Excel, such as Application, ActiveSheet, ActiveWorkbook, and Selection, don't return hard-typed object references, so calling methods directly from such properties and methods produces late-bound code. To force early binding with Excel's objects, assign an object reference to a hard-typed object variable and call methods and access properties using the object variable instead of the late-bound, unqualified method.

- Dots in VBA translate into property and method calls. By minimizing the number of dots in your code, you also minimize the number of calls required by OLE Automation. Since every call produces overhead, reducing the number of dots also reduces the overhead required to manipulate OLE Automation objects. A late-bound dot carries twice as much overhead as an early-bound dot.

- Since Visual Basic executables and custom Excel workbook solutions must run cross-process to interact with each other, controlling VB-created objects from Excel or controlling Excel-created objects from VB can be very slow. If you have an extensive piece of code that makes multiple calls to Excel's object model, your chunk of code will run fastest if it's put on the Excel side of the process boundary. By putting the code into an Excel macro and using the Excel *Application.Run* method to call the macro from VB, you can make multiple calls from VB into Excel's object model with a single cross-process call.

Performance tuning alone isn't sufficient to make a finished custom workbook project. In the next chapter, we'll look at adding customized menus and toolbars to a workbook as well as at creating auto-run macros to initialize a workbook. We'll also take an extensive look at Microsoft Excel add-ins, which are often the end result of a custom Excel application. A properly designed add-in can be integrated seamlessly into Excel, giving end users the menus and toolbars they need to run your macros—without their ever having to see the macro code or even the workbook that's doing all the work.

10

Finishing a Custom Workbook

The Microsoft Excel Macro dialog is extremely useful for debugging and running Visual Basic for Applications macros. However, forcing an end user to open the Macro dialog to run a macro is very poor programming practice. Imagine documentation for your custom solution that reads,

> After opening the workbook, please select Tools-Macros, select the *Custom1!Setup* macro, and run it. Do this each time you open the workbook. To analyze your most recent data, use the Macro dialog box to run the *Custom1!FullAnalysis* macro.

A scenario like this one suggests that while you've done a lot of work to make your program powerful and efficient, your workbook isn't user friendly. Your solution lacks the few final details that will make it useful for someone besides yourself!

There are two significant omissions in the custom solution we've just hypothesized. The first missing element is some form of auto-initialization. When your workbook is opened, it should initialize itself without needing any help from your user. The second missing element is a standard Windows user interface for calling your custom macros. Sending your user to the Excel Macro dialog doesn't count as providing him or her with a standard Windows user interface. By creating menu items and toolbars that correspond to macros you've put into your workbook, you can guarantee that the user will never have to resort to the Macro dialog in order to use your program.

Auto Macros

You'll frequently want to have some VBA code run immediately after a workbook is opened. For example, you may want to show a splash screen or a copyright notice or just make sure that a toolbar will be visible. Similarly, when a custom workbook is closed, you'll frequently need to clean up the workbook. To initialize a workbook, simply put a macro called *Auto_Open* containing all of your initialization code into your workbook. And put all of your cleanup code into an *Auto_Close* macro. Excel will run these macros for you when a user opens and closes the workbook.

Examples of both an *Auto_Open* macro and an *Auto_Close* macro are shown below. The *Auto_Open* macro makes sure an attached toolbar is always visible. (See "Attaching Custom Toolbars to a Workbook," later in this chapter.) The *Auto_Close* macro marks the workbook as saved if it's read only so that the user won't be prompted to save a read only workbook file.

```
Sub Auto_Open()
    Toolbars("MyToolbar").Visible = True
End Sub

Sub Auto_Close()
Dim WB As Workbook
Dim WBPath As String
    Set WB = ThisWorkbook
    With WB
        WBPath = .Path
        'Run this only if the workbook has already been saved.
        If Len(WBPath) Then
            If Right$(WBPath, 1) <> "\" Then WBPath = WBPath & "\"
            'If the file is read only, then stop Excel from
            'prompting the user to save it.
            If GetAttr(WBPath & .Name) And vbReadOnly Then
                .Saved = True
            End If
        End If
    End With
End Sub
```

NOTE To prevent an *Auto_Open* macro from executing—during debugging, say—hold down the Shift key while opening the workbook.

RunAutoMacros: Auto Macros from VBA

Auto_Open and *Auto_Close* will be called only if the user opens the workbook from one of Microsoft Excel's menus. If you use VBA code to open or close a workbook that contains an *Auto_Open* or an *Auto_Close* macro, Excel won't run the macro for you. However, the *RunAutoMacros* method of the Excel Workbook object lets you call the auto macros yourself.

```
Dim WB As Workbook
Set WB = Workbooks.Open("MySheets.Xls")
WB.RunAutoMacros xlAutoOpen
```

This code runs *Auto_Open* in MySheets.Xls and is almost equivalent to

```
Dim WB As Workbook
Set WB = Workbooks.Open("MySheets.Xls")
Application.Run WB.Name & "!Auto_Open"
```

There are two vital differences between these code snippets, though. One difference is that the first code snippet will run *Auto_Open* if it exists in the workbook and do nothing if the workbook doesn't contain an *AutoOpen* macro while the second code snippet will fail with a run-time error if there's no *Auto_Open* in the workbook. The second difference is that if the workbook isn't activated, executing *RunAutoMacros* will activate it, whereas the *Run* method in the second code snippet won't activate the workbook. If you call *RunAutoMacros* immediately after opening a workbook, as we did in our first code snippet, you won't see the side-effect of activating the workbook because the *Open* method always activates the newly opened workbook.

Customizing Menus

Microsoft Excel has numerous menu bars. In fact, a different set of menus is displayed depending on which type of sheet is currently active. The four built-in Excel menu bars are Worksheet, Chart, No Documents Open, and Visual Basic Module. In addition, three shortcut menu bars define all of the context menus. To allow the user to easily run your macros, you might want to modify these built-in menu bars. You can add menus to a built-in menu bar or add menu items to a built-in menu. If this isn't sufficient for the needs of your program, Excel also lets you create custom menu bars with their own menus and menu items. Let's take a look both at modifying built-in menu bars using the Excel Menu Editor and at creating custom menu bars in VBA code. Note that you can modify the built-in menu bars from VBA but that you can't create or modify custom menu bars with the Excel Menu Editor.

Using the Microsoft Excel Menu Editor to Modify Menu Bars

With the Microsoft Excel Menu Editor, you can easily add or remove menu items from any of the menus on Excel's built-in menu bars. Since there are four built-in menu bars, you will need to add the same new menu item to all four menu bars if you want your custom macro to be accessible through a menu option no matter which type of sheet a user has active.

As an example, let's replace the File-Save menu item with a macro that creates a logged history of when files were saved by the user. Since the No Documents Open menu bar doesn't have a Save item in its File menu, we need to modify only the Worksheet, Chart, and Visual Basic Module File menus. (You'll find the *FileSaveLogged* macro on the companion CD in Chapter10\Chapter10.Xls.)

1. Open a new workbook, insert a module sheet, and add the following macro:

```
Sub FileSaveLogged()
Dim WB As Workbook
Dim iFNum As Integer
    Set WB = ActiveWorkbook
    With WB
        'Checking for a path is the easiest way to tell
        'if a workbook has been saved before.
        If Len(.Path) Then
            .Save
        Else
            .SaveAs
        End If
        iFNum = FreeFile()
        Open "C:\ObjProg\Chapter10\XLSaved.Log" _
            For Append As iFNum
        'Log the name of the workbook and the date and
        'time it was saved.
        Print #iFNum, .Name, Now
        Close iFNum
    End With
End Sub
```

2. Press F2 to open the Object Browser.
3. Select the *FileSaveLogged* macro and click the Options button.
4. Set the shortcut key to *Ctrl-S* and the status bar text to *Saves Document.* These are the shortcut key and status bar settings for the File-Save menu item we need to duplicate in order to replace the existing File-Save functionality with *FileSaveLogged.*
5. Click OK to close the Options dialog, and then close the Object Browser.
6. With your module sheet active, from the Tools menu select Menu Editor.
7. In the Menu Bars: dropdown, select Worksheet.
8. In the Menus: list, select &File.

9. In the Menu Items: list, select &Save.
10. Click the Delete button to remove the built-in menu item.
11. Click the Insert button to insert your own menu item.
12. Set the Caption: field to &Save.
13. Set the Macro: field to *FileSaveLogged*, which will be in the dropdown. Your Menu Editor dialog should look like the one shown in Figure 10-1.

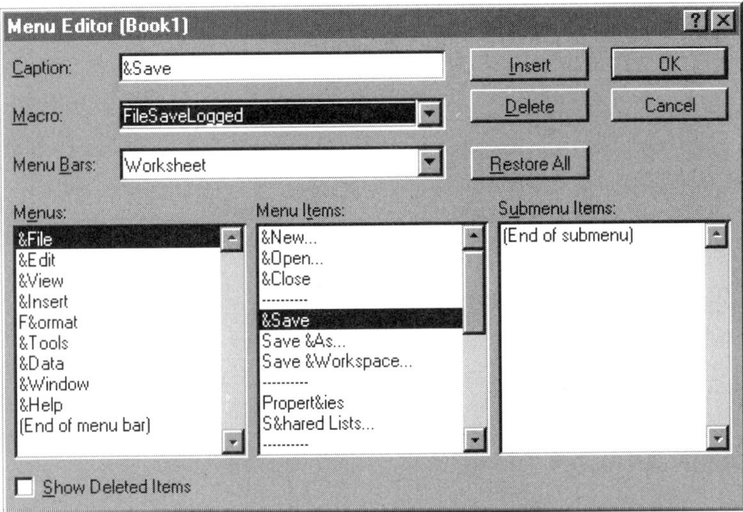

Figure 10-1. *The Menu Editor dialog box showing the File-Save menu item about to be inserted with the* FileSaveLogged *macro assigned to the menu item.*

14. Repeat steps 8 through 13 for the Chart and Visual Basic Module menu bars.
15. Click OK to close the Menu Editor dialog.

Now, as long as your workbook is open, the *FileSaveLogged* macro will be called whenever a user selects File-Save.

By replacing or adding menu items and menus to the built-in menu bars, you seamlessly integrate custom functionality with Excel's built-in functionality. You can also delete menu items, or even whole menus, to prevent users from performing certain actions. For example, if you delete the Insert menu, anyone using Excel while your workbook is open can't add a module sheet to the workbook.

Creating Custom Menu Bars in Code

Since Microsoft Excel is a multiple workbook environment, each open workbook should be independent of other open workbooks. Arbitrarily imposing the menu requirements of your custom workbook on all workbooks just wouldn't be very neighborly. If your workbook requires highly customized menus, you should create your own menu bars instead of modifying Microsoft Excel's. Unlike built-in menu bars, custom menu bars aren't automatically associated with sheets in a workbook, so you can't use the Microsoft Excel Menu Editor to create custom menu bars. If you want to use a custom menu bar in your workbook, you'll have to build it with VBA code. The procedure to build a custom menu bar is generally called from an *Auto_Open* macro.

The easiest example of building a custom menu bar is creating one with no menus on it. For simplicity's sake, we'll look at this easiest case first. When an empty menu bar is active, no menus are visible. The following macro procedure will add the EmptyBar menu bar to the MenuBars collection and add and activate an empty menu bar in the workbook.

```
Sub ShowEmptyMenuBar()
    MenuBars.Add("EmptyBar").Activate
End Sub
```

Before you actually run this macro, you need to prepare a way to get back your built-in Excel menu bar. The obvious answer is to just write a procedure that will delete the EmptyBar menu bar—something like this code:

```
MenuBars("EmptyBar").Delete
```

But the obvious answer won't work. Attempting to delete the active menu bar fails silently. The default built-in menu bar doesn't get activated, and you don't get a run-time error. Before you can delete a custom menu bar, you need to deactivate it by activating the built-in menu bar that belongs to the type of worksheet currently active. Only one of the four standard menu bars can be activated at any given time, so the easiest way to activate the correct built-in menu bar—the one the empty menu bar has replaced—is to try to activate all four built-in menu bars as follows:

```
Sub ActivateBuiltInMenuBar()
Dim MBars As MenuBars
    On Error Resume Next
    Set MBars = MenuBars
    'Try to activate each built-in menu bar.
    'Only one of the following statements will succeed.
    With MBars
        .Item(xlWorksheet).Activate
        .Item(xlChart).Activate
        .Item(xlModule).Activate
```

```
        .Item(xlNoDocuments).Activate
    End With
    Err = 0
End Sub
```

Now that we have deactivated the EmptyBar menu bar by activating a built-in menu bar, we can delete the empty menu bar from the MenuBars collection. The *DestroyEmptyMenuBar* macro will undo the no-menus state created by the *ShowEmptyMenuBar* macro:

```
Sub DestroyEmptyMenuBar()
    ActivateBuiltInMenuBar
    On Error Resume Next
    MenuBars("EmptyBar").Delete
End Sub
```

A Custom Menu Bar Example

Now that you know how to add and delete a custom menu bar, let's look at a small-scale example that actually contains a menu, a menu item, and the menu item's submenu. The submenu also contains one menu item. We'll call this custom menu bar PrivateMenuBar. Refer to Figure 10-2 to see the menu structure. PrivateMenuBar should be active only when the workbook that contains it is active, and the default menus should be restored when the workbook is deactivated. The workbook will also be self-initializing with an *Auto_Open* macro, and it will clean up the MenuBars collection with an *Auto_Close* macro when the user closes it.

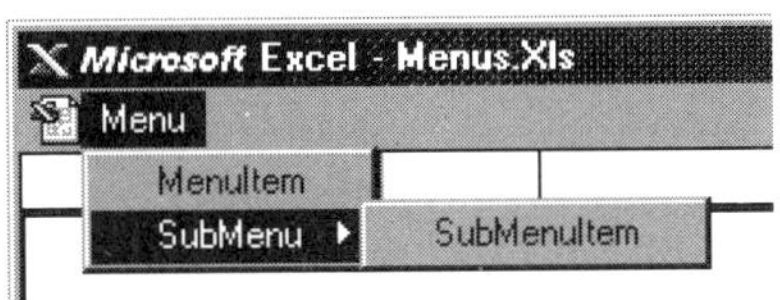

Figure 10-2. *The PrivateMenuBar menu structure.*

Creating menu structures in VBA

Creating a menu bar is only the first step in building a set of menu items. In Excel, the MenuBar object is the parent of the Menus collection. Each Menu object is in turn the parent of a MenuItems collection. A MenuItems collection contains both MenuItem objects and Menu objects. See Figure 10-3 on the next page. To add a MenuItem object to the MenuItems collection, use the *Add* method. To add a Menu object (for a submenu) to the MenuItems collection, use the *AddMenu* method. The *RebuildMenuBar* and the *DeleteMenuBar* macros build and destroy the PrivateMenuBar menu structure. (The full sample code for this section is included on the companion CD in Chapter10\Menus.Xls.)

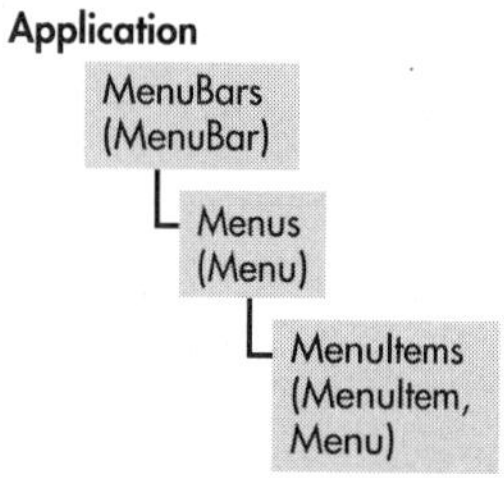

Application
- MenuBars (MenuBar)
  - Menus (Menu)
    - MenuItems (MenuItem, Menu)

Figure 10-3. *The object model for the MenuBars collection.*

```
Sub RebuildMenuBar()
    'Make sure PrivateMenuBar isn't already there.
    DeleteMenuBar
    'Add the MenuBar.
    With MenuBars.Add("PrivateMenuBar")
        'Add a Menu and get the MenuItems collection.
        With .Menus.Add("Menu").MenuItems
            'Add a MenuItem.
            .Add Caption:="MenuItem", _
                OnAction:="'MenuMacro ""MenuItem""'"
            'Add a SubMenu with a MenuItem.
            .AddMenu("SubMenu").MenuItems.Add _
                Caption:="SubMenuItem", _
                OnAction:="'MenuMacro ""SubMenuItem""'"
        End With
    End With
End Sub

Sub DeleteMenuBar()
    'You can't delete an active menu bar.
    'Restore the built-in menus.
    ActivateBuiltInMenuBar
    On Error Resume Next
    MenuBars("PrivateMenuBar").Delete
End Sub
```

Assigning the same macro to multiple menu items

The OnAction argument of the *MenuItems.Add* method sets the name of the event macro that will run when the user selects the menu item. In *RebuildMenuBar*, we set the menu items to call the *MenuMacro* macro.

```
Sub MenuMacro(WhichMenu As String)
    MsgBox WhichMenu
End Sub
```

You might notice that *MenuMacro* doesn't look like a standard macro because it takes an argument. Well, we weren't telling the whole truth in Chapter 8 when we said that a macro is limited to subroutines with no arguments. You can use a macro with arguments as an event handling macro by putting literal values (*1, 2.5, "Hello"*) as arguments into your macro expression and enclosing the whole expression in single quotation marks. In *RebuildMenuBar*, we used the following string as an event handler:

```
"'MenuMacro ""SubMenuItem""'"
```

If you were to assign the same macro to the OnAction property of a drawing object, you would type *'MenuMacro "SubMenuItem"'* in the Macro Name/Reference: field of the Assign Macro dialog. The extra quotation marks in the example above are not needed in this case because we are typing into a field in a dialog rather than assigning a value. For dynamically created menu items, either you need to use this technique to call one *OnAction* macro from multiple menu items or you need to create one macro for each menu item. Calling only one macro that contains a *Select Case* statement to determine which menu item called the macro is by far the easiest solution.

Initializing and activating a private menu bar

Now that we have the code to build a dynamic custom menu bar and the macro to call when a menu item is chosen, we need procedures to call the macros to create and delete the custom menu bar. We'll use *Auto_Open* to create PrivateMenuBar and *Auto_Close* to destroy it. But creating the menu bar isn't sufficient to show it. We need to finish initializing the workbook by setting event handlers for our workbook for the *OnSheetActivate* and *OnSheetDeactivate* events.

```
Sub Auto_Open()
    RebuildMenuBar
    With ThisWorkbook
        .OnSheetActivate = "DoActivate"
        .OnSheetDeactivate = "DoDeactivate"
    End With
End Sub

Sub Auto_Close()
    DeleteMenuBar
End Sub
```

All we have to do now is activate PrivateMenuBar when our workbook is activated and deactivate the menu bar when the workbook is deactivated. However, the OnSheetActivate and OnSheetDeactivate properties, as their names imply, fire their events on activation and deactivation of sheets, not workbooks. When you switch sheets in the same workbook, you'll trigger both a deactivate and an activate event. We need to be sure that we won't switch to the built-in menu bar and then back to PrivateMenuBar when we're only switching sheets in the same workbook. The *DoActivate* and *DoDeactivate* macros shown below handle workbook activation correctly. *DoActivate* ensures that the custom menu bar remains active while the workbook is active. And *DoDeactivate* reactivates the built-in menu bar when another workbook is activated before this workbook is closed.

```
Sub DoActivate()
    'Activate does nothing to the menu bar if the
    'menu bar is already active.
    MenuBars("PrivateMenuBar").Activate
End Sub

Sub DoDeactivate()
    'Shows the built-in menu bar--but only if this
    'workbook is no longer the active one.
    If ThisWorkbook.Name <> ActiveWorkbook.Name Then
        ActivateBuiltInMenuBar
    End If
End Sub
```

Your workbook is now ready to run. You can run *Auto_Open* by hand to initialize the menu states, or you can just save the workbook and reopen it. Excel will run the macro for you, and you'll have a custom menu bar when your new workbook is active.

Attaching Custom Toolbars to a Workbook

We're going to skip the issue of creating custom toolbars in Microsoft Excel and jump straight to attaching custom toolbars to a workbook. For help with creating a custom toolbar, select Answer Wizard from Microsoft Excel's Help menu and search on "add new toolbar." Creating toolbars dynamically in VBA is very similar to creating menu bars, but toolbars are more complicated and the object model manipulations required are beyond the scope of this book. We've included a sample program on the companion CD in Extras\ToolBar.Xls to help you manipulate Toolbar and ToolbarButton objects.

To attach a custom toolbar to a workbook, select Attach Toolbars from the Tools menu on the VBA menu bar. You'll see a list of all the custom toolbars that can be attached to the workbook as well as a list of previously attached toolbars. Adding and deleting toolbars with the Attach Toolbars dialog, shown in Figure 10-4, is straightforward. To attach toolbars to the workbook, select the toolbars in the Custom Toolbars: list and click the Copy >> button to move them to the Toolbars in Workbook: list. To delete a previously attached toolbar from the workbook, select the toolbar from the Toolbars in Workbook: list and click the Delete button. (The button in the middle of the dialog toggles between the Copy >> button and the Delete button, depending on which list is currently active.)

There is no way to view or edit a previously attached toolbar. To edit a toolbar, you need to delete it, create a new toolbar, and attach that one.

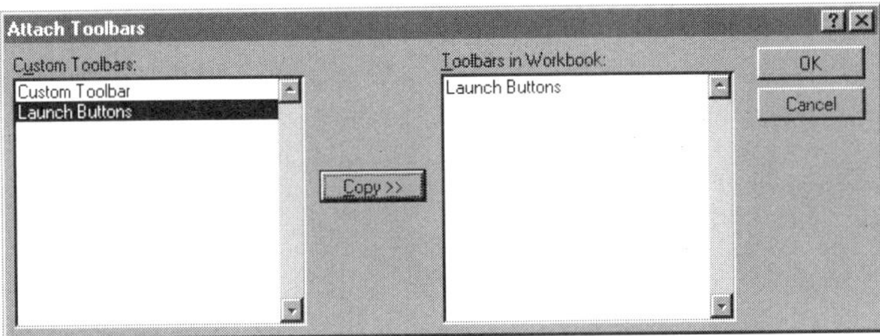

Figure 10-4. *The Attach Toolbars dialog box.*

NOTE To simplify modification of ToolbarButton properties on a custom toolbar, use the ToolbarButton Customizer add-in (ToolBar.Xla) found in the Extras directory on the companion disc. This add-in lets you set the status bar text, tip text, and macro associated with a Toolbar-Button, as well as edit the button face. (See "Microsoft Excel Add-Ins" on the next page.)

When a workbook with attached toolbars is loaded, Microsoft Excel checks for existing toolbars in the environment with the same names as the attached toolbars' names in the workbook. If matching toolbar names are found, nothing is done. If matching toolbar names aren't found, the attached toolbars are added to the custom toolbars in Excel. The position of each toolbar (docked position, floating position, and so on) will be saved along with the attached toolbar itself. As a general rule, you should drag your custom toolbars to an undocked position near the upper left corner of Excel's client area. Putting a newly loaded toolbar in this position makes it very clear to an end user that a toolbar has been added to the environment.

Setting Workbook Properties

All Microsoft Office documents, including Excel workbooks, can contain summary information that lets other programs get information about your file without actually opening it. For example, you can include Title, Author, and Comments properties in your workbook. And Microsoft Office File-Open dialogs can open files with properties that match certain criteria. For example, you can open all files that contain the word *financial* in the Comments: field of the summary information. In Microsoft Excel, you open a workbook Properties dialog, like the one shown in Figure 10-5 on the next page, by selecting File-Properties.

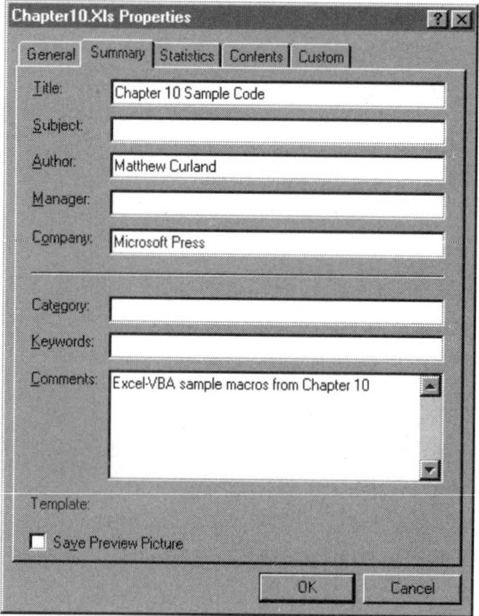

Figure 10-5. *The Summary tab of a Microsoft Excel workbook Properties dialog box.*

Microsoft Excel Add-Ins

End users must be able to easily load and run your program. Users don't care what your code looks like, and since VBA code is frequently proprietary, you don't want to show it to them anyway. We've already looked at adding finishing touches such as menus, toolbars, and automatic initialization routines to a workbook. Before you let your performance-tuned-about-to-be-distributed-program-with-lots-of-menus out the door, you'll usually want to turn it into an *add-in*.

What is an add-in? Understood in its general sense, an add-in is an extension to a program that provides new functionality to or modifies existing behavior in the host program. An add-in should integrate seamlessly with its host program, meaning that the end user should see no distinction between add-in functionality and native functionality when using the host program with the add-in loaded.

A Microsoft Excel add-in is a special type of workbook. The default file extension for an add-in is .Xla instead of .Xls. An add-in can add menu items, toolbar buttons, and user-defined functions to Excel's environment, but so can a normal workbook. So what makes an add-in unique?

When you start Microsoft Excel as a stand-alone application, add-ins are loaded for you. You don't need to explicitly open a file as you do with a workbook. However, for performance reasons, when Microsoft Excel is launched as an OLE Automation server, no add-ins are loaded. If your client program requires an add-in to be loaded, you can load and install it programmatically.

Add-ins can be *demand-loaded*, which means that the add-in is partially loaded when Microsoft Excel first starts but not fully loaded until a *demand* is made on the add-in. An add-in in a partially loaded state has associated menu items and toolbar buttons loaded and puts user-defined functions into the Function Wizard, but the add-in isn't fully loaded until one of its procedures is actually called. An add-in that's installed and available for use but not yet fully loaded is said to have been *fast-loaded*. (*Fast-loaded, demand-loaded,* and *partially loaded* are terms we can use interchangeably when we talk about add-ins.)

Excel keeps track of add-ins for you with the add-in manager. By using the add-in manager, which is available programmatically through the AddIns object, you can easily install and uninstall add-ins in the Microsoft Excel environment.

You can call procedures in add-ins with the Microsoft Excel *Run* method without qualifying the procedure name as you do when you call a workbook procedure. For example:

```
'Procedure in a workbook
Application.Run "MyXLS.XLS!MyMacro"
'Procedure in an add-in
Application.Run "MyMacro"
```

Once an add-in has been created, it can't be resaved. To change the add-in, you must re-create it.

If you put your code in an add-in, you don't have to worry about whether the add-in has been saved when you close it. Although worksheets in an add-in can't be viewed, an add-in can contain worksheets. You may find that you use a scratch sheet in an add-in, for instance, to programmatically perform calculations and store data. If you use a scratch sheet in an add-in, it will always contain the same data when the add-in is first loaded that it did when you created the add-in. The user will never be prompted to save the scratch-sheet data, and the data will be thrown away when the add-in is closed.

VBA code in an add-in is secure. There is no way for the code you write in an add-in to be listed back by other parties. (Unless someone figures out how to read VBA binary format.)

Overall, add-ins are fast and powerful. They enable you to load macros without making a workbook visible to the end user of your customized Excel interface. The code in an add-in is always fully compiled, so there's never a lag between calling a macro and having the macro run. Modules in a workbook may also be fully compiled, but full compilation isn't guaranteed. If a macro is modified but not run before the workbook containing the macro is saved, one of two things must happen to force the macro to compile before it can be run: this or any other macro in the same module must be run, or the workbook must be turned into an add-in.

Creating an Add-In

Once you've finished debugging your custom macros in your workbook, you'll usually want to turn the workbook into an add-in. Actually creating the add-in from the workbook is easy. Let's walk through the steps:

1. Activate a module in your workbook to get the VBA menu bar.
2. From the Tools menu on the VBA menu bar, select Make Add-In.
3. Enter or select a name for your add-in, and click the Save button.

Once you've created the add-in, there's no way to modify the add-in file itself. You can, however, modify the workbook you used to create the add-in and overwrite the first add-in file. If you've created the add-in but haven't saved the workbook, Excel will warn you that the workbook is the editable version of the add-in and should be saved.

Now that you've mastered the final step in creating an add-in, let's go back and pick up some techniques for making good add-ins. Since you can't debug code in an add-in, it's to your advantage to get the code right before you actually create the add-in.

Beware of the active state

Worksheets in an add-in are never active, and the add-in workbook itself is never active. If you aren't careful about qualifying your objects correctly, you'll find that the VBA code in your workbook runs well but that the add-in you created from the workbook doesn't work. Let's look at the following code as an example:

```
Sub ShowDialog()
    DialogSheets("SampleDialog").Show
End Sub
```

For testing purposes, *ShowDialog* works great. However, an unqualified call to the *DialogSheets* method defaults to *ActiveWorkbook.DialogSheets.* The result is that when you've finished testing and creating an add-in, *ShowDialog* won't work unless your active workbook happens to have a DialogSheet called SampleDialog in the Sheets collection. To refer to a sheet in the Sheets collection in the add-in workbook, you need to qualify your object with the ThisWorkbook property as follows:

```
Sub ShowDialog()
    ThisWorkbook.DialogSheets("SampleDialog").Show
End Sub
```

Failing to account for the active state is the source of the vast majority of bugs that show up in the add-in version of a workbook but not in the workbook itself. You can avoid this problem by relying on the object-centric programming model we suggested in Chapter 9. With object-centric programming, your programs will rarely rely on the current selection or the active state; consequently, your transition from workbook to add-in will be totally painless.

Creating a demand-loaded add-in

Demand-loading is one performance benefit of using add-ins. However, add-ins don't support demand-loading by default. To enable an add-in to demand-load instead of fully load when Microsoft Excel is started, you need to set two names in the add-in workbook: "__ReadOnly" and "__DemandLoad" (two leading underscore characters before each word). Let's practice adding these names to a workbook:

1. Start Microsoft Excel.
2. Insert a module into the default worksheet (Insert-Macro-Module).
3. Open the Debug window (Ctrl-G or View-Debug on the VBA menu).
4. Activate the Immediate pane in the upper half of the Debug window.
5. Run the following two lines of code in the Immediate pane by typing in each line of code and pressing Enter:

   ```
   Names.Add "__ReadOnly", True, False
   Names.Add "__DemandLoad", True, False
   ```

   The add-in created from your workbook will now be fast-loaded when Microsoft Excel is launched if the add-in is active in the add-in manager. Because the third argument to the *Add* method is Visible and you've set Visible to *False,* the two names you just defined are hidden. They won't appear in any lists of defined names available in the Excel environment. You can view or delete hidden names only by using the Names collection in VBA code.

6. To see an example of using Names to view and then delete the "__ReadOnly" name, type the following in the Debug window:

   ```
   ?Names("__ReadOnly")            'Check the value of the
                                   '__ReadOnly name.
   Names("__ReadOnly").Delete      'Delete the __ReadOnly name
                                   'from the workbook.
   ```

7. Close the Debug window.

Loading an Add-In

To use the macros in an add-in, your program must load the add-in into Microsoft Excel. There are six possible states for an add-in, including four possible loaded states:

1. The add-in is just an .Xla file. Excel has no knowledge of the file, and the file isn't open.
2. The add-in is in the AddIns collection and appears in the Add-Ins dialog—that is, it's registered with Excel—but the add-in isn't installed.
3. The add-in is partially loaded. The menus and toolbars are displayed in Excel as if the add-in were fully loaded, but no code has been loaded or executed.
4. The add-in is fully loaded.
5. The add-in is loaded as a normal workbook.
6. The add-in is loaded through the VBA References dialog.

State 1—turning a workbook into an .Xla file

If a workbook contains support routines for other workbooks, you might want to turn it into an add-in. Turning a workbook into an add-in has two big advantages. First, if your code is in a workbook, an end user can close the workbook from Excel's menus and thus disable the workbook's support routines and cause unexpected run-time errors. An add-in opened as a workbook isn't visible to the end user and will be protected from such user actions. The second advantage is that you don't have to show your add-in in the add-in manager in order to use it, whereas the macros in a workbook are always visible and can be accessed directly by the user. If you have a big project that consists of several add-ins, you'll probably want only one of the add-ins to show up in the Add-In Manager dialog.

We've already seen how to create an .Xla in the "Creating an Add-In" section earlier in this chapter, so let's move on to state 2.

State 2—registering an add-in with Excel

Once an add-in has been registered with Excel, it's easy to load the add-in through simple manipulation of the AddIns collection and the associated AddIn objects. However, getting a new add-in into the AddIns collection is not a trivial endeavor, especially when a Visual Basic project is controlling Excel as an object server. Let's look at two approaches to registering an add-in file with Excel.

FYI

Deleting an Add-In

There's no way programmatically or through Microsoft Excel's menus to remove an add-in once it has been registered. If you want to remove an add-in, you need to use the system registry. First, make sure that the add-in is not checked in the add-in manager, and then use the RegEdit utility that ships with Windows 95 to delete values from the following key in the system registry (in Windows NT, use RegEdt32 instead of RegEdit):

```
HKEY_CURRENT_USER\Software\Microsoft\Excel\7.0\Add-in Manager
```

Through Microsoft Excel's menus An add-in registered by means of the Add-Ins dialog is always fully loaded.

From the Microsoft Excel Tools menu, select Add-Ins to open the Add-Ins dialog. See Figure 10-6. If you've just created an add-in you'd like to add to the list in the Add-Ins dialog, click the Browse button in the Add-Ins dialog and find your new .Xla file in the Browse dialog. Click OK in the Browse dialog to see the new entry in the Add-Ins dialog. The title of your new add-in, which you set earlier in the Excel Properties dialog shown back in Figure 10-5 on page 250, is now in the Add-Ins Available: list with a check mark beside it. Click OK in the Add-Ins dialog to load the new add-in.

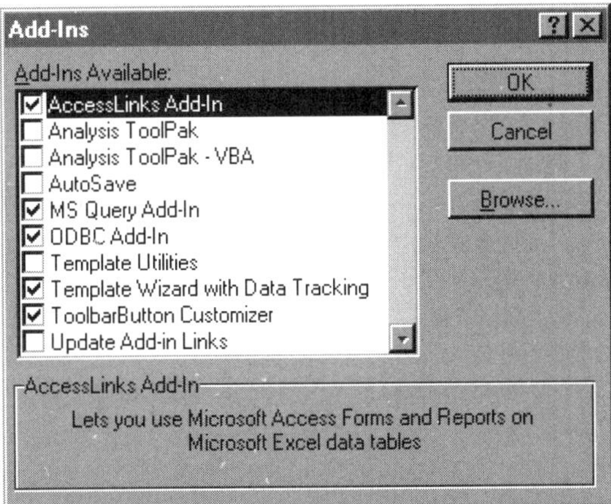

Figure 10-6. *The Add-Ins dialog box.*

NOTE The add-in title, which appears in the Add-Ins dialog's Add-Ins Available: list, corresponds to the Title: field of the Summary tab on the Microsoft Excel Properties dialog (File-Properties). The description at the bottom of the Add-Ins dialog corresponds to the Comments: field of the same tab. Be sure to set these properties for a workbook before creating an add-in from it. Refer to "Setting Workbook Properties," earlier in this chapter.

Through code Even though we've observed that registering an add-in is a major undertaking, registering an add-in through VBA code is actually fairly simple if we use an Excel macro. Given a path for the add-in file, a single line of code will place the add-in in the AddIns collection. If the add-in is already registered with Excel, adding it again has no effect and doesn't generate an error.

```
AddIns.Add MyAddinPath$
```

The difficulty arises when you run the equivalent line of code from the Visual Basic side of the process boundary, in which case it will fail if VB launched the instance of Excel the VB program is using. To work around this problem, you might write a VBA macro to run on the Excel side of the process boundary, code to call the macro that actually loads the add-in. This kind of situation is a great opportunity to exploit the dynamic creation of Excel macros from a VB project. You'll find the following function, *LoadAddIn*, along with the *NewTempFile* support function it calls, on the companion CD in Chapter10\AddInHlp.Bas.

```
Public Function LoadAddIn(XLApp As Excel.Application, _
                          XLAFileName As String) As String
Dim WB As Excel.Workbook
Dim strTempFile As String, iFNum As Integer
    On Error GoTo CleanUp

    'Create a temporary file with the VBA code in it.
    strTempFile = NewTempFile("tmp")
    iFNum = FreeFile
    Open strTempFile For Output As iFNum
    Print #iFNum, "Function AddAddIn(FName As String) " & _
                  "As String" & vbCrLf & _
                  "AddAddIn = AddIns.Add(FName).Title" & vbCrLf & _
                  "End Function"
    Close #iFNum
    iFNum = 0

    'Create a new workbook.
    Set WB = XLApp.Workbooks.Add
    With WB
```

```
        'Load the VBA code from strTempFile into a module
        'of the workbook.
        .Modules.Add.InsertFile strTempFile
        'Run the function. The function loads the add-in
        'XLAFileName into the Excel application.
        LoadAddIn = XLApp.Run(.Name & "!AddAddIn", XLAFileName)
    End With
CleanUp:
    If iFNum Then Close #iFNum
    If Len(strTempFile) Then Kill strTempFile
    If Not WB Is Nothing Then WB.Close SaveChanges:=False
End Function
```

State 3—partially loading an add-in

It's difficult to tell whether an add-in is fully or only partially loaded. In fact, the Installed property of the AddIn object returns *True* for both fully and partially loaded add-ins. In order for its macros to run, an add-in must be fully loaded. A partially loaded add-in becomes fully loaded when a macro in the add-in is called directly via an Excel menu or a ToolbarButton object. That allows all of the macros in the add-in to run. But when a procedure is called via the Excel *Run* method, a partially loaded add-in doesn't become fully loaded, so its macros won't run. Therefore, when you're coding against add-ins that might be partially loaded, you can't assume that the first call to the *Run* method will work correctly. Here's a code snippet that traps this error and makes the appropriate adjustments:

```
Dim XLApp As Excel.Application
Dim AddIn As Excel.AddIn
:
:
On Error Resume Next
XLApp.Run "AMacro"
If Err Then
    'Turn error trapping off. If this fails again,
    'then let the procedure error out.
    On Error Goto 0
    AddIn.Installed = False
    AddIn.Installed = True
    XLApp.Run "AMacro"
Else
    On Error Goto 0
End If
```

If you think this is an excessive amount of code just to call a macro, you're right. Demand-loaded add-ins are a great feature for fast Microsoft Excel startup time, but an add-in in a partially loaded state can wreak havoc on code that requires a fully loaded add-in. The best solution is to reserve the demand-load feature for add-ins containing procedures that are called only from menus and toolbars and as user-defined worksheet functions. For add-ins that contain code executed exclusively from other VBA routines, either install the add-in when it's first used (Installed = *True*) and uninstall it when you no longer need it (Installed = *False*), or load the add-in as a normal workbook (state 5) or through the VBA References dialog (state 6).

NOTE The *Auto_Open* macro is never run when a workbook is demand-loaded. If initialization must be run in a demand-loaded add-in, make sure you've initialized the workbook correctly before actually running your macros.

State 4—fully loading an add-in

The *Add* method of the AddIns collection demonstrated in our *LoadAddIn* function gets us only to state 2—the add-in is registered with Excel. And as we mentioned earlier, you can't execute a macro in a partially loaded add-in using the Microsoft Excel *Run* method, so in order to use macros in the add-in with the Excel *Run* method, we must move the add-in to state 4—the add-in is fully loaded. Two steps are involved in the move from state 2 to state 4: (1) get an AddIn object from the AddIns collection, and (2) set the Installed property of the AddIn object to *True*. The key used to get the AddIn object from the AddIns collection is the title of the add-in, which (conveniently) is returned by our *LoadAddIn* function. Let's use the *RunMacroInAddIn* routine to load and install a hypothetical add-in called Test.Xla, and then let's run the *TestMe* macro in the add-in. For simplicity, we'll create a new instance of Excel. (*RunMacroInAddIn* is included on the companion CD in Chapter10\AddInHlp.Bas along with LoadAddIn.)

```
'Use sub just to call RunMacroInAddIn.
Sub RunTest()
    RunMacroInAddIn "C:\ObjProg\Chapter10\Test.Xla", "TestMe"
End Sub
Sub RunMacroInAddIn(AddInPath As String, MacroName As String)
Dim XL As New [_ExcelApplication]
Dim XLApp As Excel.Application
Dim AddIn As Excel.AddIn
    On Error GoTo CleanUp
    Set XLApp = XL.Application
    'Load the add-in into a workbook and get an AddIn object.
    Set AddIn = XLApp.AddIns(LoadAddIn(XLApp, AddInPath))
    'Install the add-in.
    AddIn.Installed = True
    'Use the Run method to call the macro.
```

```
    XLApp.Run MacroName
    'Uninstall the add-in so that it won't load the next
    'time Excel starts.
    AddIn.Installed = False
CleanUp:
    If Not XLApp Is Nothing Then XLApp.Quit
    With Err
        'If something happened, raise the error again.
        If .Number Then .Raise .Number
    End With
End Sub
```

State 5—loading an add-in as a workbook

As we've noted, an add-in is just a special kind of workbook. In fact, if you want to use an add-in as a code repository and don't need the add-in manager to load your add-in for you when Excel starts, you can skip the add-in manager altogether and just treat an add-in as if it were a workbook. If you open an add-in as a workbook, all of the procedures in your add-in can be called by the Excel *Run* method without its having to specify a workbook name, which is just like calling a procedure in an add-in that has been loaded through the Add-Ins dialog. The following code opens an add-in workbook and runs its *TestMe* macro.

```
Dim XLApp As Excel.Application
Dim WB As Excel.Workbook
:
Set WB = XLApp.Workbooks.Open("C:\ObjProg\Chapter10\Test.Xla")
XLApp.Run "TestMe"
WB.Close
```

When an add-in is loaded as a workbook, it acts as a very private workbook—you have to know exactly where to look to find it. An add-in opened as a workbook doesn't show up in the Workbooks collection as a normal workbook does. *Workbooks.Count* doesn't change when an add-in is opened as a workbook. The only way to get an object variable to refer to an add-in workbook is directly from the return value of the *Workbooks.Open* method, as in the preceding code snippet, or by the name of the workbook, as in the following code snippet:

```
Dim XLApp As Excel.Application
:
XLApp.Workbooks.Open "C:\ObjProg\Chapter10\Test.Xla"
XLApp.Run "TestMe"
XLApp.Workbooks("Test.Xla").Close
```

State 6—loading an add-in as a reference

Until now, you've seen a macro in an add-in executed only via the Excel *Run* method. And all the code you've seen that registers, installs, and loads add-ins (except *AddIns.Add*) runs equally well on both sides of the Microsoft Excel–Visual Basic process boundary. The final state in which to use an add-in is limited to Excel workbooks. You can't use an add-in in this state from a Visual Basic-VBA project. To use macros from an add-in or from a normal workbook in another workbook, just add a reference to the add-in or workbook to the other workbook. Suppose, for example, that you had a Text.Xla file on your disk. From any other Excel workbook, you would do the following to call the Text.Xla *TestMe* macro:

1. Insert a new module sheet into the workbook if it doesn't already have one, or activate an existing module.
2. From the Microsoft Excel menu bar, select Tools-References to open the References dialog.
3. Click Browse, and find Text.Xla.
4. Click OK twice to close the Browse and References dialogs.
5. Add the following line of code to a subroutine or function in your module to call the *TestMe* macro:

   ```
   TestMe
   ```

   No, we didn't forget anything. That's all the code. If you really want the code to be longer, or if you also have a *TestMe* macro in your own workbook, you can qualify *TestMe* with the add-in name as follows:

   ```
   [Text.Xla].TestMe
   ```

The References method of accessing code in add-ins and external workbooks has the advantage of easier coding and better performance because you don't have to use the *Run* method to execute your code. But there is one severe disadvantage to using a referenced add-in or workbook. The path of a referenced add-in or workbook is compiled into the referencing workbook. This can cause problems when applications are installed on different machines, where the file locations could be different.

If you use the add-in manager to load your add-in, the path of your add-in is kept for you by Excel. If you load an add-in as a workbook, you can prompt the user to find the add-in file if it's missing and continue with the program. But if an add-in references another workbook or add-in and the referenced file can't be found, there's nothing you can do except physically move a copy of the missing file to the expected location—and there's no way of programmatically determining either the name or the path of the missing file.

Another disadvantage to using a reference to an add-in or a workbook is that you can't load and unload the add-in or workbook. As long as the referencing workbook is open, so is the referenced add-in or workbook. Large VBA programs often have dependencies on several different workbooks and add-ins. If you have a big project, you may not want to keep all dependent workbooks open all the time. When you want control over the size and the number of the workbooks you have loaded at any given time, you can break a large add-in into several smaller add-ins. The add-in that contains your toolbars and menus can be fast-loaded and designed to dynamically load and unload the supporting add-ins or workbooks.

We've seen three main methods for loading an add-in—through the AddIns collection, as a workbook, and as a referenced workbook. But we haven't developed an absolute bias in favor of any of the three. There isn't a best method for using add-ins. All of the methods we've seen for loading, unloading, and calling into add-ins have advantages and disadvantages, and you need to decide what best fits the needs of your current project. Many projects will use a combination of all three methods. Here are some rough recommendations.

If the primary use for the add-in is to provide custom menus and toolbars to enhance Excel's working environment, you should use the add-in manager and create a demand-loaded add-in.

If your add-in is a code repository, open the add-in as a workbook.

For optimal speed, but with additional setup costs, load the add-in as a referenced workbook in your project.

SUMMARY

- Performance alone isn't enough to create a finished custom workbook solution. Self-initialization code, menus, and toolbars are all required to make a workbook useful to an end user.
- *Auto_Open* and *Auto_Close* macros are called by Excel when a workbook is opened using Excel's menus or toolbars. If a workbook is opened or closed using VBA code, the *RunAutoMacros* method must be used explicitly to force Excel to call *Auto_Open* or *Auto_Close.*
- There are two ways to customize Excel's menus. The first is to use the menu editor to add menus or menu items to built-in Excel menu bars and menus. The second is to dynamically create custom menu bars, menus, and menu items using VBA code. To be a good Excel neighbor, limit your use of customized menu bars to times when the custom workbook is active.

- An Excel add-in is a specialized type of workbook that is usually the end result of a custom workbook project. Add-ins are the best mechanism for customizing Excel's environment because the end user can't unhide or unload an add-in as he or she can a custom workbook. Code in an add-in can't be viewed or edited.
- VBA code in add-ins should rely on the object-centric programming model to avoid bugs that appear in the add-in but not in the workbook from which the add-in was created.
- An add-in can be loaded via the add-in manager, as a workbook, or as a reference. The technique you use to load your add-in depends on how the add-in will be used.

It's time to move away from general Excel programming and customization concepts and into specific examples. In Chapter 11, we'll use Visual Basic objects and forms from both in-process and cross-process servers in Excel-VBA code. We'll put the object creation and manipulation techniques we've learned up to this point to use while demonstrating tight integration of Excel and VB objects into a single custom programming solution.

11

Using Visual Basic Objects in Microsoft Excel

It's time to get serious about programming Visual Basic objects. Chapter 11 is focused much differently than the chapters you've seen up to this point. We're going to be working for tight integration of Microsoft Excel with Visual Basic objects using two in-process and two cross-process Visual Basic object servers. We won't focus on every line of code. Instead, we'll look at the architecture required for good Excel and VB integration. We'll concentrate on applying the programming techniques we saw in Chapter 9 to optimize performance in a custom solution that spans process boundaries.

Along the way, we'll consider a few tidbits on programming that we'll call "support topics." In this chapter, a support topic will be information that isn't central to the architecture of the sample but is used to create the finished product. Drag and drop operations, for example, aren't central to communication between Excel and VB, but drag and drop is used in our *DataForm* sample. Drag and drop will be covered as a support topic.

This chapter is mostly code listings. Spend some time looking at the code and reading the comments. And run the samples. You'll have a much easier time understanding the samples if you actually run them. All of the completed samples are on the companion CD in the Chapter11 directory.

Before we take up our first sample, we need to get up to speed on establishing parent-child relationships between objects. After the section of the chapter on "The Parent Object Dilemma," we'll look at the following samples:

- ***ExcelTimer*** An in-process VB object server that provides a periodic timer for Excel.
- ***DataForm*** A VB form used to manipulate data from a database and return the selected data to an Excel spreadsheet.

- ***In-process DataForm*** The in-process version of the *DataForm* sample.
- ***XLCallBack*** An example of running an Excel macro in the background while continuing to interact with a VB form.

The Parent Object Dilemma

In the course of programming objects, you'll frequently find that you want two interdependent object references to be controlled by a single object reference. For example, a Visual Basic Form object can't be made public. To use a VB form from a cross-process application, you have to define a public class that creates and destroys the form. We call an instance of the public class a *parent object* and the form a *child object*. We'll design a class module, which we'll call FormAParent, to be the parent of a form called FormA. To walk through this demonstration in Visual Basic, create a new project with a form named FormA, a class module named FormAParent, and a regular module named Module1. Set the startup form to *Sub Main* using the Project tab of the Options dialog. Enter the following code in the FormAParent class module:

```
Private m_FormA As FormA
Private Sub Class_Initialize()
    Set m_FormA = New FormA
End Sub
Private Sub Class_Terminate()
    Unload m_FormA
End Sub
Public Sub Show()
    m_FormA.Show
End Sub
```

Enter the following code in Module1:

```
Sub Main()
Dim FormAController As New FormAParent
    FormAController.Show
End Sub
```

The code in Module1 loads and shows an instance of FormA using the FormAParent class. Press F5 to run Module1. The form will appear only briefly because it will get unloaded when the *Sub Main* procedure terminates and the FormAController object variable goes out of scope.

Parent Objects: The Problem

The code shown above is only a minimal example. It isn't practical for a real application. For an application to be useful, there needs to be two-way communication between the parent object and the child object. So far, FormAParent can call methods and set properties on FormA, but not vice versa. If FormA is to call methods and set properties of FormAParent, FormA must include an object variable that contains a reference to FormA's parent object.

An additional requirement for making a useful application is that the parent object be able to control the destruction of the child. When the child object is a form, destruction of the child includes unloading the form, so we have to block an end user from clicking the *close* button on the title bar to unload the form.

To meet these stringent parent-child requirements, let's add some code to the *Form_QueryUnload()* event procedure in FormA and add an *OnHide* method to FormAParent that can be called by FormA in *Form_QueryUnload()*. Enter this code in the code module of FormA:

```
Option Explicit
Public Parent As FormAParent
Private Sub Form_QueryUnload(Cancel As Integer, _
                             UnloadMode As Integer)
    'The form should unload only if Unload is called in code.
    'If Unload hasn't been called, just hide the form and
    'notify the parent object.
    If UnloadMode <> vbFormCode Then
        Me.Hide
        Parent.OnHide
        Cancel = True
    End If
End Sub
```

Enter the additional code (the *OnHide* method has been added and the *Class-_Initialize()* event procedure has been modified) to make your FormAParent class module look like the following:

```
Private m_FormA As FormA
Private Sub Class_Initialize()
    Set m_FormA = New FormA
    'Give m_FormA a reference to this class so
    'that the form can call the OnHide method.
    Set m_FormA.Parent = Me
End Sub
Private Sub Class_Terminate()
    Unload m_FormA
End Sub
Public Sub Show()
    m_FormA.Show
End Sub
Public Sub OnHide()
    'Called when the user unloads the form
End Sub
```

Having made these changes, go ahead and rerun the program. You'll probably expect the form to appear and immediately disappear just as it did before. But the form stays on the screen! Clicking the *close* button on the form hides the form as expected, but the program still doesn't end. The VB toolbar indicates that the program is still running. To stop the program, you have to click the End button on the Visual Basic toolbar. What happened?

If an object is to be destroyed, all references to the object must be released. Let's look carefully at the references to the FormAParent object when the *End Sub* line of *Sub Main* is about to be executed. The first reference to the FormA-Parent object is held by the FormAController object variable declared in *Sub Main* in Module1. A second reference to FormAParent is held by the Parent object variable declared in FormA. When the *End Sub* line of *Sub Main* is executed, the FormAController variable will be released, but the Parent variable doesn't get released until the FormA object is destroyed, which doesn't happen until FormAParent is destroyed. Since FormA and FormAParent are holding references to each other, the two objects are preventing each other from being destroyed.

Since we're requiring effective communication between parent and child objects, parent and child need to contain references to each other. In other words, the longevity problem we've just seen isn't going to go away: we need to explore ways around it. The easiest way to fix this problem is to add a *Quit* method to the FormAParent class. Any code with a reference to a FormAParent instance would have to call the *Quit* method before releasing the object variable. Of course, a *Quit* method would leave us with a server just as difficult to terminate cleanly as Microsoft Excel. (Refer back to Chapter 8, "Creating Excel's Application Object," for more information on the difficulties of terminating Excel from VB.) Since we want an external application to be able to destroy our objects with a simple *Set. . . = Nothing* statement, a *Quit* method isn't a viable alternative.

Parent Objects: A Solution

If an object is to start self-destructing, it must think that there aren't any outstanding references to it. (Remember that setting an object variable to *Nothing* only releases a reference to an object. When the object thinks there aren't any more references, it self-destructs.) The solution to our object longevity problem lies in convincing the parent object that there is really only one reference to the parent object instead of two. To convince the parent object to self-destruct at the appropriate time, we have to undo one of the safety features of the Visual Basic for Applications language.

VBA is designed to be a safe programming language, which means that there is no way to crash a program that uses only native VBA keywords and functions. One safety feature of the language is the automatic reference counting that occurs when the *Set* statement is used. The *Set* statement assigns a reference to a running object to an object variable and increases the internal reference count of the running object. Since an object can't be destroyed until the last reference to it has been removed, incrementing the internal reference count guarantees that an object variable will never point to an object that has already been destroyed—which would crash the program. However, while an external object variable contains a reference to the parent object (the running object), the parent object will stay alive regardless of whether the child object contains a reference to the parent. In other words, if we can give a reference to the parent to the child object *without incrementing the parent object's internal reference count,* the external object will keep the parent alive for as long as the parent is in use. The child can use the parent object without artificially keeping the parent object from terminating, and the problem will be solved. Refer to Figure 11-1.

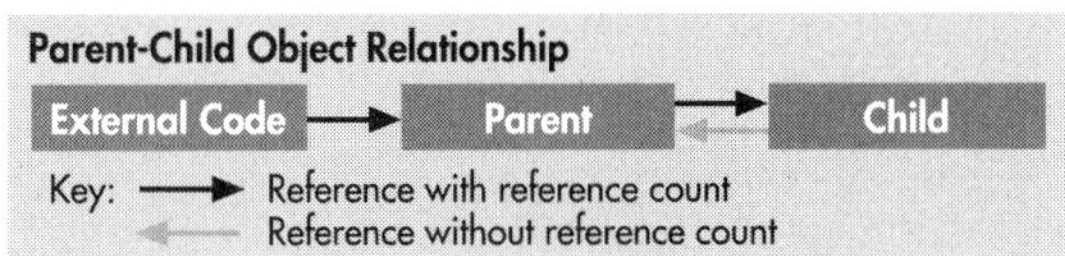

Figure 11-1. *The references scenario for a two-way parent-child relationship.*

Of course, since VBA is a safe language and it would be possible to crash if you started playing with reference counting yourself, VBA doesn't provide any way to change the reference count. To change the reference count, you must use an external API call. We've provided code for you in the ChildObj.Bas file on the companion CD in the Chapter11\DataForm directory to change the reference count of an object. By adding this file to your project, you can use our *SetChildObject* and *ReleaseChildObject* subroutines, which take care of the parent-child reference counting problem. Select Add File from the VB File menu to add ChildObj.Bas to your project. Now let's modify the *Class_Initialize()* and *Class_Terminate()* event procedures of FormAParent to see how to use the *SetChildObject* and *ReleaseChildObject* procedures. Notice that the *Set m_FormA.Parent=Me* in the *Class_Initialize()* procedure has been replaced with *SetChildObject Child:=m_FormA, Parent:=Me.* If you make the following modifications, the program will once again terminate cleanly.

Edit your project to match the following code in the FormAParent class module. (*Class_Initialize()* and *Class_Terminate()* have been modified.)

```
Private m_FormA As FormA
Private Sub Class_Initialize()
    Set m_FormA = New FormA
    'Give m_FormA.Parent a reference to this instance
    'without increasing the reference count.
    SetChildObject Child:=m_FormA, Parent:=Me
```

(continued)

```
End Sub
Private Sub Class_Terminate()
    Unload m_FormA
    'Set m_FormA.Parent to Nothing without changing
    'the reference count.
    ReleaseChildObject m_FormA
End Sub
Public Sub Show()
    m_FormA.Show
End Sub
Public Sub OnHide()
    'Called when the user unloads the form
End Sub
```

With the final version of the FormAParent class module, you can run the program and the form will appear and disappear just as it's supposed to. (You can find the finished version of this demonstration code on the companion CD in the Chapter11\ParentChildDemo directory. Open ParentChildDemo.Vbp.)

Now that you've seen the ChildObject routines in use, let's go over the steps for using them. **First Warning:** If you don't follow the directions, your program will die a horrible death—that is, it will crash. **Second Warning:** If you use the End button on the VB toolbar, *ReleaseChildObject* will never be called and your program will die a horrible death—and crash the entire Visual Basic design environment as well. To see the second kind of crash in action, save your project and put a breakpoint on the *End Sub* line of *Sub Main* in Module1 in our earlier example. Run to the breakpoint, and click the End button. Restart VB and repeat this exercise to remind yourself not to click the End button if you're overriding VB's internal reference counting.

Now we can follow the steps below to use the *SetChildObject* and *ReleaseChildObject* routines in the ChildObj.Bas file:

1. The parent class must have a module-level private object variable of the type of the child class (or *As Object*). The object variable must *not* be declared with the *New* keyword. In our example, in the FormAParent parent class, we accomplish this with the line

   ```
   Private m_FormA As FormA
   ```

2. The parent object should create a new instance of the child object in the *Class_Initialize()* procedure and assign a reference to the m_FormA object variable described in step 1:

   ```
   Set m_FormA = New FormA
   ```

3. After the FormA child is created and before the *Class_Initialize()* procedure finishes running, the parent class needs to call the *SetChildObject* procedure with two parameters, the child object variable and *Me*:

```
SetChildObject m_FormA, Me
```

4. In the *Class_Terminate()* procedure in the parent class, we need to call the *ReleaseChildObject* procedure with one parameter, the child object variable:

```
ReleaseChildObject m_FormA
```

5. The child object class must contain a public variable or a public Property Set/Get procedure pair of the type of the parent class (or *As Object*). This variable or property must be called *Parent*. Be sure not to use the *New* keyword in the variable declaration. In our example we accomplish this in the FormA code module with the line

```
Public Parent As FormAParent
```

6. Never use *Set. . . = Nothing* with the Parent property. Always use *ReleaseChildObject [ChildObjectVariable]* in the parent class or *ReleaseChildObject Me* in the child class. In general, you can avoid this issue by just relying on the *Class_Initialize()* and *Class_Terminate()* event procedures as we showed in steps 3 and 4.

This seems like a lot of steps, but you can actually do everything in nine lines of code:

```
'The ParentObject class module
Private m_MyChild As ChildObject
Private Sub Class_Initalize()
    Set m_MyChild = New ChildObject
    SetChildObject m_MyChild, Me
End Sub
Private Sub Class_Terminate()
    ReleaseChildObject m_MyChild
End Sub

'The ChildObject class module
Public Parent As ParentObject
```

Now that we know how to establish a parent-child object relationship between two objects in a way that will be transparent to an external object variable that references the parent object, we can proceed with creating Visual Basic servers that allow us to use VB forms from inside Microsoft Excel, other Visual Basic programs, or any other VBA host.

Child object support routines

Here's all of the code for the ChildObj.Bas support file. As long as you follow the steps above, you don't really need to know what's happening internally, but you might be curious.

```
'Use the CopyMemory API to copy object references
'without a Set statement.
#If Win32 Then
Declare Sub CopyMemory Lib "kernel32" Alias "RtlMoveMemory" _
            (pDest As Any, pSource As Any, ByVal ByteLen As Long)
#Else
Declare Sub CopyMemory Lib "kernel" Alias "hmemcpy" _
            (pDest As Any, pSource As Any, ByVal ByteLen As Long)
#End If

Public Sub SetChildObject(Child As Object, Parent As Object)
    'Set the Parent property of the child object.
    Set Child.Parent = Parent
    'Decrement the reference count of the Parent object.
    'The Parent object reference count was incremented
    'in the Set statement, so the net change in the
    'reference count for this procedure is zero.
    ReleaseReference Parent
End Sub

Public Sub ReleaseChildObject(Child As Object)
    If Not Child Is Nothing Then
        With Child
            'Increment the reference count so that
            'Set ... = Nothing can decrement it.
            'End up with a net change of zero.
            AddReference .Parent
            Set .Parent = Nothing
        End With
    End If
End Sub

'C++ equivalent of AddReference
'void AddReference(IDispatch FAR* pObj)
'{
'    IDispatch FAR* pTmpObj = pObj;
'    if (pTmpObj)
'        pTmpObj->AddRef();
'    pTmpObj = NULL;
'}
Private Sub AddReference(AnyObject As Object)
Dim tmpObj As Object
    Set tmpObj = AnyObject
```

```
    CopyMemory tmpObj, 0&, 4
End Sub

'C++ equivalent of ReleaseReference
'void ReleaseReference(IDispatch FAR* pObj)
'{
'    IDispatch FAR* pTmpObj = pObj;
'    if (pTmpObj) {
'      pTmpObj->Release();
'      pTmpObj = NULL;
'    }
'}
Private Sub ReleaseReference(AnyObject As Object)
Dim tmpObj As Object
    CopyMemory tmpObj, AnyObject, 4
    Set tmpObj = Nothing
End Sub
```

Parent objects extra: other parent-child issues

The case of the parent dilemma we've just solved is a simple one—controlling a Visual Basic form through a VB class instance owned by an external application. In this case, a reference to the child object is never passed outside the tightly controlled parent-child structure. However, you may also want to establish similar parent-child relationships in cases in which a reference to the child object is held by an object variable in code outside the framework of the parent-child structure. (This advanced section isn't required reading for understanding the examples in the rest of this chapter. You can skip to the "*ExcelTimer* Sample Application" section at this point without loss of continuity.)

The problem with passing a reference to the child object to a variable outside the safe confines of the parent object is that the Parent property of the child object can be set to *Nothing* or to another instance of the ParentObject class. As in real life, unexpectedly switching parents or losing a parent in your VB application can have devastating effects on a child. Apart from issuing forceful warnings to the programmers using your objects that the Parent property shouldn't be modified, there's no robust way to have your code protect the Parent property and still function correctly.

The most robust solution is to actually create two versions of the child object, one for internal use and the other for external consumption. The externally visible child object maintains a reference to both the internal child object and the parent object. By keeping a reference to the parent object, the external child object remains valid until the external child is destroyed. The external object referencing the external child is also referencing the parent, but if the external child did not keep a reference to the parent itself, releasing the external reference to the parent would orphan the child. As an orphan, the external child object would remain alive but would no longer be fully functional. Refer to Figure 11-2 for a diagram of this more complicated parent-internal child-external child structure.

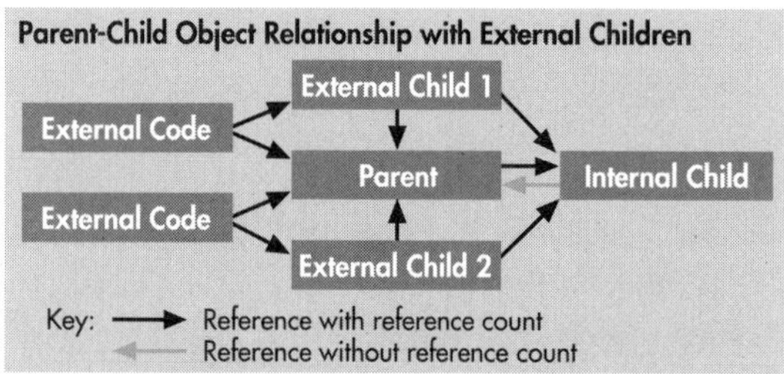

Figure 11-2. *A parent-child relationship with external references to external child objects.*

Here's the code to set up a parent-child relationship with an external child object.

```
'*******************************************************************
'Code for hypothetical InternalChildObject
Public Parent As ParentObject
Sub Method()
    'Do something.
End Sub
'All of the code for the real internal child object
'goes here.

'*******************************************************************
'Code for hypothetical external ChildObject
Private m_Parent As ParentObject
Private m_InternalChild As InternalChildObject

'The InternalChild argument must be declared As Object
'to make this class public because the InternalChildObject
'class should never be public and hard-typed object arguments
'in public sub, function, and property procedures must be
'typed as public classes.
Public Sub Initialize(InternalChild As Object)
    'Make sure Initialize doesn't do anything after the
    'first call.
    If m_InternalChild Is Nothing Then
        Set m_InternalChild = InternalChild
        'The external child needs to keep an extra reference
        'to the parent object to ensure that the child isn't
        'orphaned if the external reference to the parent is
        'released before the external reference to an instance
        'of the external class.
```

```
        Set m_Parent = InternalChild.Parent
    Else
        'The Initialize method is exposed to the external
        'program. Raise an error if the external program
        'tries to call this method.
        Err.Raise Number:=5, _
                  Description:="Object already initialized."
    End If
End Sub

Public Property Get Parent() As ParentObject
    Set Parent = m_Parent
End Property

'For all other public methods and properties, just call the
'internal child object.
Public Sub Method()
    m_InternalChild.Method
End Sub

'*******************************************************************
'Code for the hypothetical ParentObject
Private m_InternalChild As InternalChildObject
Private Sub Class_Initialize()
    'Create the internal child to do all the work.
    Set m_InternalChild = New InternalChildObject
    'Give the internal child a noncounted reference
    'to the parent (Me).
    SetChildObject Child:=m_InternalChild, Parent:=Me
End Sub
Private Sub Class_Terminate()
    'Safely release the noncounted reference.
    ReleaseChildObject m_InternalChild
End Sub
Public Property Get Child() As ChildObject
Dim NewExternalChild As New ChildObject
    'Each time an external program requests a reference
    'to the child object, create an external child object.
    'Initialize the child object with a reference to the
    'internal child object, which does all the work.
    NewExternalChild.Initialize m_InternalChild
    'Return a reference to the new external child.
    Set Child = NewExternalChild
End Property
```

Using both the ChildObject and the InternalChildObject classes, you can solve the problem of exposing the volatile Parent property. (The Parent property is volatile because if you, or someone using your objects, uses Parent the wrong way, the program will crash.) However, an extra cost is involved because you create a new instance of the external child class every time the Child property is called. Creating a new object for each call to the Child property also means that external code can't use the *Is* operator to compare two external child objects that refer to the same InternalChildObject instance, as shown in the failure of this code:

```
Dim TheObject As ParentObject
:
:
If Not TheObject.Child Is TheObject.Child Then
    MsgBox "You'll execute this line every time."
End If
```

The workaround for this situation is to give every instance of the internal child a unique ID property. By adding a Property Get to the external child that returns the ID number, you can compare two instances of the external child.

NOTE The IntegerStack class used in the *XLCallBack* sample later in this chapter can be used to provide a unique integer ID to each instance of an internal child class.

Remember: Establishing a parent-child relationship requires careful programming practices. Be careful in particular about using the End button on VB's toolbar. If you click the button before all parent objects have been destroyed, you'll crash. (If an application is started in the design environment with the StartMode option on the Project tab of the Options dialog set to OLE Server, you'll need to click the End button to get back to design mode. Just don't click it before the last object has been released.) By using the *SetChildObject* and *ReleaseChildObject* procedures, you're bypassing VB's built-in reference counting safety features. If you follow the practices outlined here, you won't have any problems. If you don't, you'll repeatedly die a horrible death. Be smart: always save your project before going to run mode.

The *ExcelTimer* Sample Application

Let's start with the easiest of our four sample applications: using a Visual Basic DLL to provide a periodic timer in Microsoft Excel. Excel provides the *OnTime* method on the Application object to run a macro at a specified time, but *OnTime* isn't a true periodic timer. A macro specified in *OnTime* will be called only once. To make the macro run repeatedly, *OnTime* must be called repeatedly. The macro called by the *OnTime* method also fails to run in some cases until well after its specified starting time. For example, if an Excel dialog is open, *OnTime* won't run until the user closes the dialog.

VB's timer control is designed to run much differently than the *OnTime* method in Excel. When a timer control is enabled, it fires an event procedure every Interval milliseconds, no matter what else is happening. Interval is a property of the timer control. The *ExcelTimer* sample DLL calls an Excel macro whenever the *Timer* event is fired by a timer control. The end result is that you can use a true periodic timer in Excel.

ExcelTimer Architecture

The *ExcelTimer* project has three different components: in Microsoft Excel, a module that creates an ExcelTimer object and provides a macro to run when the *Timer* event fires; in Visual Basic, an ExcelTimer class module that's used to set properties of the timer and call the Excel macro; and the frmExcelTimer form, where the timer control is located. The ExcelTimer class is a parent of the frmExcelTimer form.

The basic architecture is very simple: Excel creates an ExcelTimer class and specifies a macro to be run when the timer is fired. When the *Timer* event fires on the control, the *Timer_Timer()* event procedure calls the *OnTime* method in the ExcelTimer class, which calls the macro specified by Excel. Figure 11-3 illustrates the *ExcelTimer* architecture.

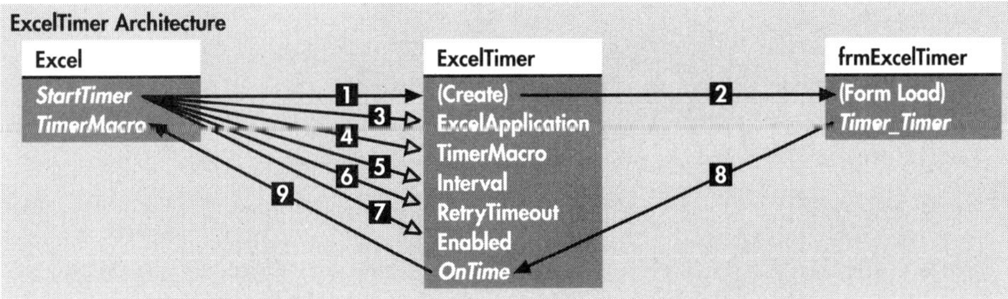

Figure 11-3. *Calls among objects in the* ExcelTimer *sample.*

In the figure, open-head arrows indicate setting or reading a property, and solid-head arrows show a call to a method. We don't have to worry about the number of calls among objects because *ExcelTimer* runs in-process. (The *ExcelTimer* project can be found on the companion CD in the Chapter11\ExcelTimer directory. Open ExcelTimer.Vbp.)

The frmExcelTimer form

The frmExcelTimer form isn't meant to be displayed. It's just used as a place to hold a timer control. We've named the timer control Timer and set the Enabled property to *False* at design time to stop the timer from firing until it's explicitly enabled by Excel. The code for frmExcelTimer, shown on the next page, is minimal.

```
'The standard Parent property
Public Parent As ExcelTimer

Private Sub Timer_Timer()
    'Let the parent object do all the work.
    Parent.OnTime
End Sub
```

The ExcelTimer class

The ExcelTimer class has five public properties (ExcelApplication, TimerMacro, Interval, RetryTimeout, and Enabled) and one public method (*OnTime*). Let's go over the code for each property and method and describe how each piece of the ExcelTimer class is used.

ExcelApplication property (read only) The property that needs to be set in Excel before the timer is enabled. The *Timer* event needs an Excel.Application object in order to call the *Run* method to call a macro in Excel.

```
'XLApp is declared As Object to avoid an early-binding
'bug in Excel, but the m_XLApp object variable is
'hard typed, so we maintain early binding internally.
Public Property Set ExcelApplication(XLApp As Object)
    Set m_XLApp = XLApp
End Property
```

TimerMacro property The name of the macro to run when the *Timer* event fires. The macro name should be prefixed with the name of the workbook, as in, for example:

```
XLTimer.TimerMacro = ThisWorkbook.Name & "!TimerMacro"

'The TimerMacro property procedures
Public Property Let TimerMacro(NewMacro As String)
    m_TimerMacro = NewMacro
End Property
Public Property Get TimerMacro() As String
    TimerMacro = m_TimerMacro
End Property
```

Interval property The property that sets the periodicity of the timer in seconds. The conversion to milliseconds for the Interval property on the timer control is done in the Property Let procedure:

```
Public Property Let Interval(Seconds As Single)
    'The timer control's Interval property is in
    'milliseconds. Convert from seconds from input
    'argument.
```

```
    m_TimerForm.Timer.Interval = Seconds * 1000
End Property
Public Property Get Interval() As Single
    'The timer control's Interval property is in
    'milliseconds. Convert to seconds for return value.
    Interval = m_TimerForm.Timer.Interval / 1000
End Property
```

Enabled property The property that establishes whether or not the timer is enabled.

```
Public Property Let Enabled(State As Boolean)
    m_TimerForm.Timer.Enabled = State
End Property
Public Property Get Enabled() As Boolean
    Enabled = m_TimerForm.Timer.Enabled
End Property
```

RetryTimeout property The property that sets the number of seconds to keep trying to run *TimerMacro*. There's a chance that Excel might be busy when *TimerMacro* is run. Excel could be in the middle of a large calculation, for example. If RetryTimeout is *0*, only one attempt is made to call *TimerMacro*.

```
Public Property Let RetryTimeout(Seconds As Single)
Dim TestMaxInterval As Long
    'Try to raise an overflow error here before
    'm_RetryTimeout is set to avoid an overflow in
    'the OnTime method.
    TestMaxInterval = Seconds * 1000
    m_RetryTimeout = Seconds
End Property
Public Property Get RetryTimeout() As Single
    RetryTimeout = m_RetryTimeout
End Property
```

***OnTime* method** The method in which all the work is done. *OnTime* serves as a bridge between the *Timer_Timer()* event procedure on the frmExcelTimer form and *TimerMacro* in Excel.

```
Public Sub OnTime()
Dim StartTicks As Long
Dim MaxInterval As Long
    'Excel might be busy when the Timer event fires.
    'If RetryTimeout is set, then keep trying to call
    'TimerMacro.
    If RetryTimeout Then
```

(continued)

```
        'Convert m_RetryTimeout from seconds to milliseconds.
        MaxInterval = m_RetryTimeout * 1000
        StartTicks = GetTickCount
    End If

    'Turn on error trapping in case the Run method fails.
    On Error Resume Next
    Do
        'Run the macro in Excel.
        m_XLApp.Run TimerMacro
        'If an error occurs, try again if we're within the
        'interval specified by the RetryTimeout property.
        If MaxInterval > 0 And Err Then
            If StartTicks + MaxInterval < GetTickCount Then Exit Do
            'Clear the error object.
            Err.Clear
            'Use DoEvents to try to let Excel finish.
            DoEvents
        Else
            Exit Do
        End If
    Loop
    With Err
        'This method is called by an event procedure.
        'Returning an error from this procedure would
        'raise an untrapped error in the Timer_Timer() event
        'procedure. An untrapped run-time error in an
        'event procedure in a VB DLL is fatal to both the
        'DLL and the client application. Clear the error
        'object before returning.
        If .Number Then .Clear
    End With
End Sub
```

The rest Here's the rest of the code for the ExcelTimer class.

```
'VBA's timer function resets itself to 0 at midnight,
'which could cause the OnTime macro to wait for almost
'24 hours if we were to rely on Timer! The GetTickCount
'API returns the number of milliseconds since Windows
'started running and turns over at most once every
'49 days, so GetTickCount is more reliable for calculating
'expired time because there is a much smaller chance that
'the tick count will roll over while we're using it.
#If Win32 Then
Private Declare Function GetTickCount Lib "kernel32" () As Long
#Else
Private Declare Function GetTickCount Lib "User" () As Long
```

```
#End If

Private m_XLApp As Excel.Application
Private m_TimerMacro As String
Private m_RetryTimeout As Single
Private m_TimerForm As frmExcelTimer

Private Sub Class_Initialize()
    'Create the hidden child form. A new form is
    'created for each timer used by Excel.
    Set m_TimerForm = New frmExcelTimer
    'Establish the parent-child relationship.
    SetChildObject Child:=m_TimerForm, Parent:=Me
End Sub

Private Sub Class_Terminate()
    'Unload the form. Correctly unloading and
    'destroying the form is absolutely essential
    'to safely shutting down the DLL and Excel.
    'As a parent object, this object must completely
    'destroy its internal child object.
    Unload m_TimerForm
    'Clean up the parent-child relationship.
    ReleaseChildObject m_TimerForm
End Sub
```

Using ExcelTimer

The *ExcelTimer* project produces an in-process OLE server ready for use in Excel. Let's walk through a minimal example of using the ExcelTimer class.

1. Open a new workbook in Excel and insert a module sheet.
2. From the VBA menu bar, select Tools-References, and add a reference to Enable Timer events in Excel. If this option isn't visible in the Available References: list, click Browse and locate ExcelTimer.Dll.
3. Add the following code to the module sheet you've inserted in the Excel workbook:

```
Private XLTimer As ExcelTimer
Sub StartTimer()
    If XLTimer Is Nothing Then
        Set XLTimer = CreateObject("Timers.ExcelTimer")
        With XLTimer
            Set .ExcelApplication = Application
            .TimerMacro = ThisWorkbook.Name & "!TimerMacro"
            .Interval = 3 'Call every 3 seconds.
```

(continued)

```
                .RetryTimeout = 2 'Try for 2 seconds.
            End With
        End If
        XLTimer.Enabled = True
    End Sub

    Sub StopTimer()
        If Not XLTimer Is Nothing Then
            XLTimer.Enabled = False
        End If
    End Sub

    Sub TimerMacro()
        Beep 'Do something useful here.
    End Sub
```

4. Run the *StartTimer* macro.
5. When the beep gets annoying, run the *StopTimer* macro.

NOTE If you try to run the *StartTimer* macro and get a User Defined Error on the *CreateObject* method, run Regsvr32.Exe against ExcelTimer.Dll. (Regsvr32.Exe is included on the Visual Basic 4 CD.) This will register the DLL in your system. Try running *StartTimer* again.

The *ExcelTimer* sample is very straightforward but illustrates techniques we'll be using in the more complicated *DataForm* sample coming up next. In *ExcelTimer*, we used a class module to control a VB form, established a parent-child relationship between a class and a form, and called an Excel macro in response to an event. We'll use these same basic techniques for communicating between Excel and VB in the *DataForm* sample.

The *DataForm* Sample Application

The *DataForm* sample application is an example of using a Visual Basic form in a custom Microsoft Excel solution. Because every program should have a particular task, let's state the purpose of this sample program up front. The goal of the *DataForm* sample is to extract selected data from a bibliographical database about the titles available from a specific publisher and put the data into an Excel spreadsheet. We'll use data from the bibliographical database (Biblio.Mdb) that ships with VB. Figure 11-4 shows the *DataForm* sample. The window on top (DataForm Sample) is a VB form. The Show DataForm toolbar button shown to the left is used to start the DataForm.Exe object server and show the form.

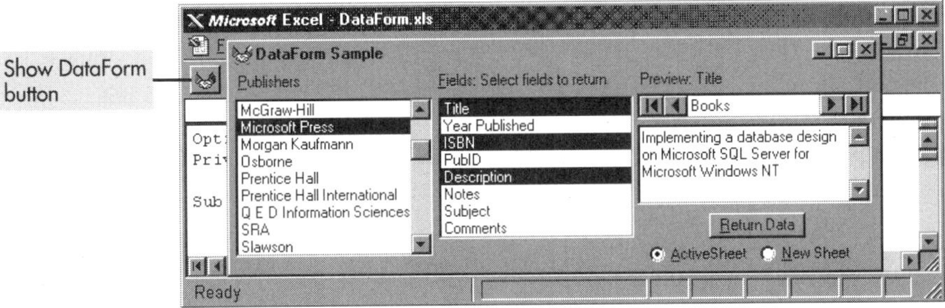

Figure 11-4. *The running* DataForm *sample application.*

You can tell that the DataForm Sample form isn't the active window because its title bar isn't highlighted. Although Excel is active, the form is displayed on top of Excel. The ability to activate Excel, which implies deactivating the form, means that the form is modeless. In Windows, a modeless window that always appears on top of another window is called a *floating window.* The DLL version of the *DataForm* sample, which we'll look at later in the chapter, is a modal form. In fact, the only reason we implemented *DataForm* as a cross-process (EXE) server instead of in a DLL was to enable a modeless floating window.

Before you jump into the *DataForm* architecture, take some time to play with the sample application itself. Since *DataForm* is a server, you'll need to register it with the system as follows:

1. Copy DataForm.Exe and DataForm.Xla from the Chapter11\DataForm directory on the companion CD to your local hard drive.
2. In Windows Explorer, double-click on DataForm.Exe. You'll see this on-screen message:

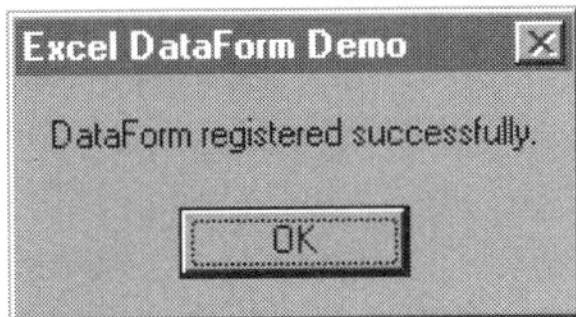

3. Start Excel.
4. From the Tools menu, select Add-Ins.
5. Click the Browse button to get a file dialog. Open DataForm.Xla.
6. Make sure the DataForm Sample Add-In item is selected.
7. Close the dialog.

A new toolbar will appear with the Show DataForm button shown in Figure 11-4 on page 281. Click the button to show the DataForm. (If a file dialog appears, looking for Biblio.Mdb, locate the file in the Microsoft Visual Basic directory and click OK to bring up the *DataForm* application.) When the DataForm Sample form first appears, the Return Data button will be disabled. To enable the Return Data button, you need to select fields to return to Excel in the Fields: list box. If the Return Data button still isn't enabled, select a different publisher—not all publishers have books listed in this database. Once the Return Data button is enabled, go ahead and click it to return data to Excel. If you choose to return data to the active sheet by clicking the ActiveSheet option button, *DataForm* will overwrite existing data, so be careful. While you're playing with the sample, try closing and reopening the form. Also notice what happens when you minimize the form or when you minimize Excel while the form is being displayed. After you've returned data to Excel a few times and are comfortable with the functionality of the *DataForm* sample, you're ready to proceed.

DataForm Architecture

The main focus in the *DataForm* sample's architecture is to minimize the number of cross-process calls. When you look at Figure 11-5, your first reaction will probably be shock at the number of calls that are made to complete a relatively simple operation. (In the figure, an open-head arrow indicates setting or reading a property and a solid-head arrow represents a call to a method.) Although the number of calls makes the architecture look complicated, the number of cross-process calls (anything coming from or pointing to Microsoft Excel) is kept to a minimum. And when you look at the code, you'll see that the number of cross-process calls between Microsoft Excel and the Visual Basic object really is minimal. By making one cross-process call to run a single Excel macro responsible for all manipulation of objects implemented by Excel, we avoid making costly cross-process calls each time we set the value of a cell or change a format on our destination worksheet.

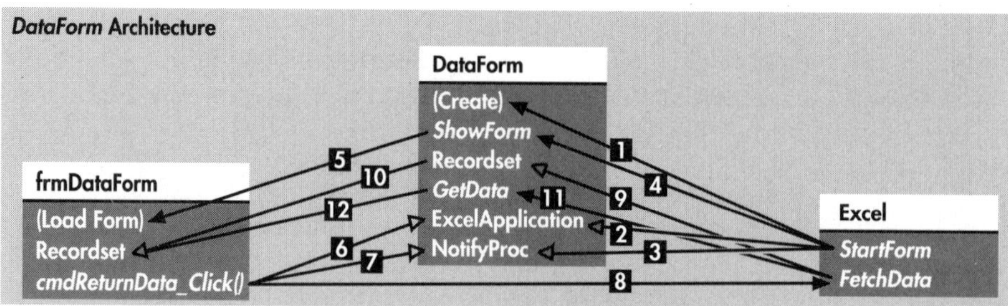

Figure 11-5. *Calls among objects in the* DataForm *sample.*

The *DataForm* sample makes extensive use of the Biblio database that comes with VB4. We use two data controls, a data-bound textbox and a data-bound list box, along with several recordset variables to manipulate our data. All of the database code is included and copiously commented on the sample CD, but we've omitted it from the source listings in the text so that you can concentrate on the task of effective communication between VB and Excel, which is the point of this sample.

Let's look briefly at each of the numbered calls in Figure 11-5.

0. You're right. There's no 0 in the diagram. Step 0 occurs when the user clicks the toolbar button, which calls the *StartForm* macro.

1. If Excel hasn't created a DataForm object yet, the *StartForm* macro uses *CreateObject* to get an object from the DataForm.Exe object server.

2. The ExcelApplication property of the new DataForm object is set so that the VB part of the program can call the *Application.Run* method.

3. The NotifyProc property is set to point to the *FetchData* macro. Just as in the *ExcelTimer* sample, we'll call the macro specified in the NotifyProc property when an event is fired on the VB form.

4. Now that the required properties are set to correctly run the *cmdReturnData_Click()* event procedure, we're ready to show the form.

5. The *ShowForm* method loads the form. The user is now free to select the set of data to return to Excel. There's no communication between the VB form and Excel until the user clicks the Return Data button.

6., 7., 8. The *cmdReturnData_Click()* event procedure uses the ExcelApplication and NotifyProc properties on the parent object to call the *FetchData* macro. We could have put a public *ReturnData* method on the DataForm object, but this would also have enabled Excel to force a return of data. Since data isn't always available, we decided against exposing *ReturnData* to Excel directly.

9., 10. The *FetchData* macro calls the Recordset property in the DataForm object, which in turn calls the Recordset property of frmDataForm to retrieve a reference to the current Recordset object. A Recordset object is used to hold a set of data. The *FetchData* macro extracts the names of all columns in the returned Recordset object. Note that each call to a method or property of the returned Recordset object is a cross-process call, but the number of calls we actually have to make is limited to the number of columns of data returned, so the cost is acceptable.

11., 12. The *FetchData* macro calls *GetData* to retrieve all of the data with one cross-process call. Although we've just noted that the number of cross-process calls required to retrieve the column headers using the

Recordset object from steps 9 and 10 is acceptable, retrieving all rows of data from the Excel side of the boundary can be costly, so we delegate all calls to the Recordset object to the VB side of the process boundary. Of course, all of the code to put the data in the current worksheet is done on the Excel side in the *FetchData* macro.

Now that you have some idea of how the macros and objects in the *DataForm* sample work together, it's time to look at the actual code.

The DataForm class

The DataForm class is a public, creatable class that can be created by means of

```
CreateObject("FormDemo.DataForm")
```

in Microsoft Excel. A Visual Basic form can't be made public, so a wrapper object is required to control a VB form from an external application. As with the ExcelTimer class and the frmExcelTimer form in our previous example, the DataForm class establishes itself as the parent object of the frmDataForm form. Here are the public properties and methods of the DataForm class.

ExcelApplication property The property Excel assigns an Application instance to so that VB can call the *Application.Run* method. (The "Miscellaneous Gotchas" sidebar in Chapter 9, pages 234 through 236, explains the bug.)

```
'BUG: As Excel.Application creates an early-bound
'type mismatch in Excel.
Public ExcelApplication As Object
```

NotifyProc property The property Excel sets to the name of the macro to be run. The macro name assigned to this property must be qualified by the name of the workbook that contains the macro. The *StartForm* macro sets this property to *DataForm.Xla!FetchData.*

```
Public NotifyProc As String
```

Recordset property A read only property called by Excel to retrieve a Recordset object containing the data. (See the "Miscellaneous Gotchas" sidebar in Chapter 9, pages 234 through 236.)

```
'BUG: As Recordset fails in Excel when the object
'is running in the VB environment. It does fine in
'EXE or DLL servers.
Public Property Get Recordset() As Object
    Set Recordset = m_frmDataForm.Recordset
End Property
```

ReturnDataToActiveSheet property A Boolean property of the DataForm class that corresponds to the currently selected option button. The form provides two option buttons to specify whether data should be returned to the top of the active worksheet in Excel or put on a new sheet.

```
Public Property Get ReturnDataToActiveSheet() As Boolean
    ReturnDataToActiveSheet = m_frmDataForm.optReturn(0).Value
End Property
```

***ShowForm* method** The method that shows the form. The *ShowForm* method has two optional parameters, ParentHandle and FloatingWindow, which specify a parent window (Excel's main window, for example) and whether the form should be contained in the parent window or float above it. (See the "Floating and Contained Windows" section in "DataForm Support Topics," later in this chapter, on page 297.)

```
Public Sub ShowForm(Optional ParentHandle, Optional FloatingWindow)
    If IsMissing(ParentHandle) Then ParentHandle = 0
    If IsMissing(FloatingWindow) Then FloatingWindow = False
    With m_frmDataForm
        Select Case .LoadState
            'We haven't tried to show the form yet.
            Case 0
                'This is the first time through.
                If ParentHandle Then
                    'ChangeParentWindow will load the form
                    'when it calls the hWnd property.
                    .ParentWindowHandler. _
                            ChangeParentWindow ParentHandle, _
                                            CBool(FloatingWindow)
                Else
                    .Visible = True
                End If

                'If the load is successful, the form will
                'have set its LoadState property to True.
                'Give the form the input focus.
                If .LoadState = 2 Then .SetFocus

            'We tried previously to show the form, but the
            'Form_Load() event procedure didn't run to completion.
            Case 1
                .Form_Load
                If .LoadState = 2 Then
                    .Refresh
                    .SetFocus
                End If
```

(continued)

```
                'The Form_Load() event procedure has already
                'run to completion.
                Case 2
                    .Visible = True
                    .WindowState = vbNormal
                    .Refresh
                    .SetFocus
            End Select
        End With
End Sub
```

***HideForm* method** The method that hides the form. The form is just hidden. It isn't unloaded until the DataForm object is destroyed, so the current position and properties of the form and all controls on the form are preserved.

```
Public Sub HideForm()
    'If the child form has been created, then hide
    'the child form.
    If Not m_frmDataForm Is Nothing Then
        m_frmDataForm.Visible = False
    End If
End Sub
```

***GetData* method** The method that retrieves data from the current Recordset object. Since the Recordset property returns an object owned by VB, not by Excel, manipulating the object directly in Excel would be too slow. *GetData* returns a Variant array that holds all of the data in the current recordset.

```
Public Function GetData() As Variant
    With m_frmDataForm.Recordset
        'RecordCount isn't accurate until all rows in
        'the recordset have been fetched. Use MoveLast
        'to fetch all records and then MoveFirst to get
        'back to the first row.
        .MoveLast
        .MoveFirst
        GetData = .GetRows(.RecordCount)
    End With
End Function
```

The rest Here's the rest of the code from the DataForm class module.

```
Private m_frmDataForm As frmDataForm
Private Sub Class_Initialize()
    'Create the child object, and establish the
    'parent-child relationship.
```

```
    Set m_frmDataForm = New frmDataForm
    SetChildObject m_frmDataForm, Me
End Sub

Private Sub Class_Terminate()
    'Unload the form.
    Unload m_frmDataForm
    'Correctly release the child object.
    ReleaseChildObject m_frmDataForm
End Sub
```

The frmDataForm form

Most of the code for the *DataForm* sample is contained in the frmDataForm form module. The DataForm class is the parent of this form and is used to facilitate communication between the form and Excel. Here are the public properties and methods of frmDataForm.

Parent property The standard Parent property of a child class as described earlier in this chapter in "The Parent Object Dilemma."

```
'The DataForm class is used as the parent of this form.
Public Parent As DataForm
```

ParentWindowHandler property An instance of the ParentWindowHandler class that forces the form to float over Excel. See "Floating and Contained Windows" in "DataForm Support Topics," later in this chapter.

```
'The ParentWindowHandler class makes this form a floating
'or contained window in Excel.
Public ParentWindowHandler As ParentWindowHandler
```

LoadState property The property that's *0* if the form has never been loaded—that is, if *DataForm.ShowForm* has never been called; *1* if loading the form failed, which happens if the database can't be found; and *2* if the form has been successfully loaded at least once.

```
'Load states
'0 = Haven't Tried
'1 = Failed
'2 = Succeeded
Public LoadState As Byte
```

Recordset property A read only property returning the current set of data.

```
'Variables used to cache the recordset returned to Excel
'so that we don't have to repopulate the recordset
'every time.
Private m_Recordset As Recordset
Private m_fHaveRecordset As Boolean
:
:
Public Property Get Recordset() As Recordset
Dim SQL As String
Dim i%
    'If we aren't in a state to return anything, or if the
    'recordset in m_Recordset is still valid, then don't
    'do anything.
    If cmdReturnData.Enabled And Not m_fHaveRecordset Then
        'Database manipulation code omitted.
        :
        :
        m_fHaveRecordset = True
    End If
    Set Recordset = m_Recordset
End Property
```

***Form_Load* method** When LoadState is *1*, called as a method of the form instead of being fired as an event procedure. If the initial *Form_Load()* event procedure doesn't run to completion, the LoadState property is set to *1*, which tells the DataForm class to retry *Form_Load* from the *ShowForm* method. (See "Persistent Program Settings" in "DataForm Support Topics" later in this chapter.)

```
'The default Private attribute on this event procedure
'has been changed to Public so that we can call the
'procedure as a method of the frmDataForm class from
'the parent object.
Public Sub Form_Load()
Dim strDBPath As String
Dim Field As Field
    'Indicate that we've tried to load the form.
    LoadState = 1
    'See if our database path is listed in the registry.
    strDBPath = GetSetting("FormDemo", "StartUp", "MDBPath", "")
    'Code omitted.
    :
    :
    'Database code omitted.
    :
    :
    'Synchronize all controls on the form.
    SyncControls
    'A LoadState of 2 indicates a successful load.
```

```
    LoadState = 2
    'Change the Visible property of the form to True.
    Me.Visible = True
End Sub
```

The rest Here's the remainder of the code from the frmDataForm module, which manages creating the current recordset and communicating with the DataForm class and Excel.

```
Private Sub cmdReturnData_Click()
Dim XLApp As Excel.Application
RetryNotify:
    On Error Resume Next
    With Parent
        'The Excel macro that created this object should
        'provide a macro to run when this button is clicked.
        'Run the macro to do Range object manipulation on
        'the Excel side of the process boundary. The Excel
        'macro will call GetData on the parent DataForm object
        'to get the current recordset.
        Set XLApp = .ExcelApplication
        If Not XLApp Is Nothing Then
            'The option buttons determine if the data is
            'returned to a new sheet or the active sheet.
            'If the active sheet in Excel isn't a worksheet,
            'then allow only the New Sheet option.
            If optReturn(0).Value Then
                If Not TypeOf XLApp.ActiveSheet Is _
                           Excel.Worksheet Then
                    MsgBox "Activate a worksheet, or choose " & _
                           "the 'New Sheet' option.", _
                           vbInformation
                    Exit Sub
                End If
            End If
            'If a notification procedure has been provided,
            'then run the notification macro now.
            If Len(.NotifyProc) Then
                XLApp.Run .NotifyProc
            End If
        End If
    End With
    'If something goes wrong (Excel might be busy), then
    'give the user the option of trying again.
    If Err Then
        Select Case MsgBox("Excel Update Notification Failed", _
                           vbExclamation Or vbRetryCancel)
```

(continued)

```
                Case vbRetry
                    GoTo RetryNotify
            End Select
        End If
    End Sub

    Private Sub SyncControls()
        'Database code omitted.
        :
        'See if we can return data at this point.
        SetReturnStatus
    End Sub

    Private Sub dblstPublishers_Click()
        'Use the DBList control to move the current position
        'of the hidden data control.
        datPublishers.Recordset.Bookmark = dblstPublishers.SelectedItem
        'Synchronize on the new publisher.
        SyncControls
    End Sub

    Private Sub lstFields_Click()
        'Update the current state.
        SetReturnStatus
    End Sub

    Private Sub SetReturnStatus()
        'We can return data only if there is data in the
        'recordset, there are fields selected to return,
        'and the Parent is set.
        cmdReturnData.Enabled = lstFields.SelCount And _
                                Not datResults.Recordset.BOF And _
                                Not Parent Is Nothing
        'Indicate that the cached recordset is no longer valid.
        m_fHaveRecordset = False
    End Sub

    Private Sub Form_Initialize()
        'Create a ParentWindowHandler object to prepare for
        'an external call to ParentWindowHandler.ChangeParentWindow.
        Set ParentWindowHandler = New ParentWindowHandler
        Set ParentWindowHandler.Form = Me
    End Sub

    Private Sub Form_QueryUnload(Cancel As Integer, _
                                 UnloadMode As Integer)
```

```
    'If the user is trying to close the form, using Alt-F4,
    'the system menu, or the close button, then prevent the
    'form from actually unloading. The form can be unloaded
    'only by the Unload method, which is called in the
    'Class_Terminate() event procedure of the parent object.
    If Not Parent Is Nothing Then
        If UnloadMode <> vbFormCode Then
            Me.Hide
            Cancel = True
        End If
    End If
End Sub

Private Sub Form_Unload(Cancel As Integer)
    'Hide the form before changing the parent window back
    'to avoid flashing.
    Me.Visible = False
    'If necessary, change the parent window of this form
    'back to its original window.
    ParentWindowHandler.ResetParentWindow
    'Destroy the ParentWindowHandler object.
    Set ParentWindowHandler = Nothing
End Sub
```

The DataForm driver (Excel module)

The DataForm object is created by a Microsoft Excel add-in, DataForm.Xla. After the *StartForm* macro has been called once, any subsequent calls to *StartForm* will show the form with the same settings it had the last time it was visible. All information on the form persists. The only way to release the server and, hence, the only way to reset the form, is to unload the add-in. This module contains only the *StartForm*, *HideForm*, and *FetchData* macros. Macros that are used only as support routines and that shouldn't be visible to an add-in user are in the Support Procedures module, which has *Option Private Module* set. Here are the DataForm driver macros.

StartForm The procedure used to launch the form. The toolbar button provided with the add-in calls this macro.

```
Private DataForm As DataForm

Sub StartForm()
    'If we haven't created the object yet, then create it.
    If DataForm Is Nothing Then
        Set DataForm = CreateObject("FormDemo.DataForm")
    End If
    With DataForm
```

(continued)

```
        'Be prepared for an abnormal shutdown of the
        'server.
        On Error Resume Next
        Set .ExcelApplication = Application
        If Err Then
            Select Case MsgBox("Something happened to our server.", _
                        vbExclamation Or vbRetryCancel)
                Case vbRetry
                    Set DataForm = Nothing
                    StartForm
            End Select
            Exit Sub
        End If
        On Error GoTo 0
        'Assign the notification procedure.
        .NotifyProc = ThisWorkbook.Name & "!FetchData"
        'Show the form as a floating window.
        'Note: to show the form as a contained window,
        'use ShowForm ExcelDeskWindow, False.
        .ShowForm ExcelMainWindow, True
    End With
End Sub
```

HideForm Not called but made available for completeness.

```
Sub HideForm()
    If DataForm Is Nothing Then Exit Sub
    'If something happened to our server, then ignore
    'it and deal with the problem in ShowForm.
    On Error Resume Next
    DataForm.HideForm
End Sub
```

FetchData The notification procedure called when the user clicks the Return Data button on the VB form. The *ShowForm* macro assigns the name of this procedure to the NotifyProc property of the DataForm object.

```
'The notification procedure. FetchData is called when
'the Return Data button on the DataForm is clicked.
Sub FetchData()
Dim WB As Workbook
Dim WS As Worksheet
Dim WorkRange As Range
Dim DataArray As Variant
Dim RS As Recordset
Dim Field As Field
Dim i%
```

```
'Unhandled errors in this routine are fatal to
'the DataForm server. Make sure we don't have any
'unhandled errors.
On Error GoTo GetDataTrap
If DataForm Is Nothing Then Exit Sub
If DataForm.ReturnDataToActiveSheet Then
    'Get the ActiveSheet. ReturnDataToActiveSheet
    'can be True only if a worksheet is active.
    Set WS = ActiveSheet
    'Clear the current contents.
    WS.Cells(1, 1).CurrentRegion.ClearContents
Else
    Set WB = ActiveWorkbook
    If WB Is Nothing Then
        'If we don't have an active workbook, then
        'open one and get the first worksheet.
        Set WS = Workbooks.Add.Worksheets(1)
    Else
        'If we have an active workbook, then just
        'add a worksheet.
        Set WS = WB.Worksheets.Add
    End If
End If
With WS
    'Use the field names for column headers on the
    'first row.
    i% = 0
    Set RS = DataForm.Recordset
    For Each Field In RS.Fields
        i% = i% + 1
        .Cells(i%) = Field.Name
    Next

    'Retrieve the data from the DataForm object.
    DataArray = DataForm.GetData
    'Set up a range to receive the data array.
    'The data array comes in transposed, so we use
    'the second dimension for the row count and the
    'first dimension for the column count.
    Set WorkRange = .Range(.Cells(2, 1), _
                   .Cells(UBound(DataArray, 2) + 2, _
                          UBound(DataArray, 1) + 1))
    'Transpose the array to assign it to the range.
    'The TransposeVariantArray function is in the
    'Support Procedures module.
    WorkRange.Value = TransposeVariantArray(DataArray)
    'Get the current region.
```

(continued)

```
        Set WorkRange = .Cells(1).CurrentRegion
        With WorkRange
            'Bold the first row (column headers).
            .Rows(1).Font.Bold = True
            'Size the columns for a best fit.
            .Columns.AutoFit
        End With
    End With
    Exit Sub
GetDataTrap:
    MsgBox "Error retrieving data", vbExclamation
End Sub
```

Support procedures (Excel module)

Not all procedures in an add-in should be exposed. If a macro or a function is included only to support an exposed macro and shouldn't be called directly, the macro can be placed in a *private module,* which means that other procedures in the project can call the procedure but VBA code outside the project can't see or call the internal procedure. Here are the functions in the *DataForm* sample Support Procedures module.

Module-level code Module-level options and declares.

```
Option Private Module   'Don't show these routines in the add-in.
Option Explicit
Option Compare Text
Private Declare Function GetActiveWindow Lib "user32" () As Long
Private Declare Function GetWindow Lib "user32" (ByVal hWnd As Long, _
                                                 ByVal wCmd As Long) _
                                                 As Long
Private Declare Function GetClassName Lib "user32" Alias _
                              "GetClassNameA" _
                              (ByVal hWnd As Long, _
                               ByVal lpClassName As String, _
                               ByVal nMaxCount As Long) As Long
Private Const GW_HWNDNEXT = 2
Private Const GW_CHILD = 5
```

***ExcelMainWindow* function** The function that returns a window handle for Excel's main window. *ExcelMainWindow* provides the window handle passed to the *DataForm.ShowForm* method to make the VB form float over Excel. (See "Floating and Contained Windows" in the "DataForm Support Topics" section later in this chapter.)

```
Function ExcelMainWindow() As Long
    'GetActiveWindow always returns the top-level window.
    ExcelMainWindow = GetActiveWindow
End Function
```

***ExcelDeskWindow* function** If a VB form is to be used as a contained child window instead of a floating window, the window handle for the parent window should be retrieved by means of this function.

```
Function ExcelDeskWindow() As Long
'Rely on the DefLng H at the beginning of the module for
'the type of hWnd.
Dim hWnd As Long
Dim strClassName As String
Dim iLen As Integer
    'The desk window is a child of the main window.
    'Cycle through the children of the main window.
    hWnd = GetWindow(GetActiveWindow, GW_CHILD)
    strClassName = String$(128, 0)
    Do While hWnd
        hWnd = GetWindow(hWnd, GW_HWNDNEXT)
        If hWnd Then
            iLen = GetClassName(hWnd, strClassName, 128)
            If iLen Then
                'Option Compare Text is in effect, so we don't
                'have to worry about case.
                If Left$(strClassName, iLen) = "XLDESK" Then Exit Do
            End If
        Else
            Exit Do
        End If
    Loop
    ExcelDeskWindow = hWnd
End Function
```

***TransposeVariantArray* function** The function used by the *FetchData* macro in place of *Application.Transpose* to flip the array returned by the *DataForm.GetData* method. The *GetRows* method of a Recordset object returns an array that's transposed. If the array is to be assigned to a Range object in Excel, it must be un-transposed. The built-in function *Application.Transpose* can be used sometimes but fails miserably if the array contains any entry that's Null. Also, assigning a Variant array that contains Null data to a range fails, so we would have to write our own routine even if *Application.Transpose* succeeded.

```
'Support function to transpose a variant array.
'Application.Transpose fails if an array contains
'Null values.
Function TransposeVariantArray(Source As Variant) As Variant
Dim LBound1 As Integer, UBound1 As Integer
Dim LBound2 As Integer, UBound2 As Integer
Dim i%, j%
```

(continued)

```
Dim Destination As Variant
    LBound1 = LBound(Source, 1)
    UBound1 = UBound(Source, 1)
    LBound2 = LBound(Source, 2)
    UBound2 = UBound(Source, 2)
    ReDim Destination(LBound2 To UBound2, _
                        LBound1 To UBound1) As Variant
    For i% = LBound1 To UBound1
        For j% = LBound2 To UBound2
            'If the value is Null, just leave it empty.
            'Assigning an array containing a Null value
            'to a range fails.
            If Not IsNull(Source(i%, j%)) Then
                Destination(j%, i%) = Source(i%, j%)
            End If
        Next j%
    Next i%
    TransposeVariantArray = Destination
End Function
```

If you've stuck with the *DataForm* sample this far, we have good news. The worst is over. You've made it through the most complicated sample program in this book. The architecture used to facilitate effective communication between VB and Excel is complicated, but it provides for very fast integration across the process boundary. When you run the finished sample, you'll see that there isn't any noticeable delay when the Return Data button is clicked. If we had made more cross-process calls, the delay would have been very noticeable. For larger applications, the delays caused by excessive numbers of cross-process calls in a poorly integrated custom solution can make a program unbearably slow. With skillful integration, however, your end user won't even notice that you're not running all your code in the same process.

At this point, you can jump to the *DllDataForm* sample to see how we implemented this sample in a DLL as opposed to an EXE. You'll find the architecture and the code much simpler, but the DataForm form itself will be modal. If you'd like to see how we constructed the user interface part of the DataForm form, read the "DataForm Support Topics," next.

DataForm Support Topics

The *DataForm* sample was designed to demonstrate how to communicate between a Visual Basic form and Microsoft Excel. The next four issues—"Floating and Contained Windows," "Resource Files," "Drag and Drop," and "Persistent Program Settings"—all bear on the *DataForm* sample code but are not central to our communication topic.

Floating and Contained Windows

Windows-based programs frequently require one or more windows that appear to be floating above a main window. Toolbars in Microsoft Excel, for example, can be dragged to an area outside Excel's client area but can't be obscured by Excel—that is, the toolbars float above Excel. When Excel is minimized, so is the toolbar window. Excel is said to be the *parent window* of each of its toolbars, which are *floating child windows*. A floating window is a requirement of the *DataForm* sample, so we need to make Excel's main window the parent window of the DataForm form.

Not all child windows are floating. A child window can also be contained within its parent window. An MDI (multiple document interface) child window—of which an Excel workbook window is a good example—never extends beyond the client area of its parent window. Any part of the window that would be drawn outside the client area of the parent window is clipped by Windows. When a contained child window is minimized, it's put within the client area of the parent window, not on the Windows 95 task bar.

Creating floating and child windows is similar to establishing a parent object in that your program must clean up after itself before it terminates. If you omit any of the directions below—or if you click the End button in the development environment—when a Visual Basic form is being used as a floating window, your program will crash.

As we've done in the code for creating parent-child object relationships, we've put all of the code for changing the parent window of a child form in a single file so that you have to add only a few lines of code to a form module to support changing the parent window. The ParentWindowHandler class has two methods, *ChangeParentWindow* and *ResetParentWindow*, and one property, Form. As an introduction to using this class, let's walk through an example of making a VB form float over another form. (The ParentWindowHandler class is implemented in the ParentWindow.Cls file in the Chapter 11\DataForm directory on the companion CD.)

1. Open a new VB project.
2. Add the ParentWindow.Cls file to the project.
3. Add a form to the project.
4. In the property sheet, change the Name property of the form to *frmChildWindow* and the BorderStyle property to *4 - Fixed ToolWindow*. Reduce the form to the size of a floating toolbar window.
5. Add the code shown on the next page to the frmChildWindow code module.

```
Public ParentWindowHandler As ParentWindowHandler
Private Sub Form_Initialize()
    Set ParentWindowHandler = New ParentWindowHandler
    Set ParentWindowHandler.Form = Me
End Sub

Private Sub Form_Unload(Cancel As Integer)
    'These lines must be executed at all
    'costs. Clicking the End button in the development
    'environment skips all Form_Unload events.
    ParentWindowHandler.ResetParentWindow
    Set ParentWindowHandler = Nothing
End Sub
```

6. Add another form to the project.

7. In the property sheet, change the Name property of the form to *frmParentWindow.*

8. Add the following code to the frmParentWindow code module:

```
Private m_frmChildWindow As frmChildWindow
Private Sub Form_Load()
    Set m_frmChildWindow = New frmChildWindow
    With m_frmChildWindow
        .ParentWindowHandler.ChangeParentWindow _
            hWndNewParent:=Me.hWnd, _
            FloatingWindow:=True
        .Show
    End With
End Sub

Private Sub Form_Unload(Cancel As Integer)
    'This line must be executed. m_frmChildWindow
    'is explicitly set to Nothing when this form
    'is unloaded, so there's no need to do it here.
    Unload m_frmChildWindow
End Sub
```

9. On the Project tab of the Options dialog, change the Startup Form: to frmParentWindow.

10. Run the project. Refer to Figure 11-6. Note that the ChildWindow form floats above the ParentWindow form. As indicated by the active title bar, the ParentWindow form has the focus, but the ChildWindow form isn't obscured by the ParentWindow form.

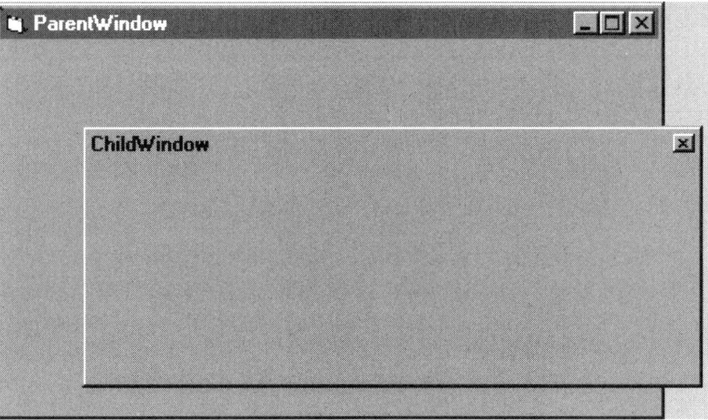

Figure 11-6. *The* ParentWindow *sample program.*

The completed code for this project can be found on the companion CD in the Chapter11\ParentWindow directory. Open the ParentWin.Vbp file. Let's go over the rules for using the ParentWindowHandler class.

- The form that is to have its parent window changed (the child form) should have a public or private module-level object variable of type ParentWindowHandler. The ParentWindowHandler variable shouldn't be declared with the *New* keyword. See the code in step 5 above.
- In the *Form_Initialize()* event procedure of the child form, the ParentWindowHandler object variable should be created and the Form property set to *Me*. See the code in step 5.
- In the *Form_Unload()* event procedure of the child form, *ResetParentWindow* must be called—essential for stopping the program from crashing. The parent window must be reset to its initial value before the new parent window is destroyed. The ParentWindowHandler object variable should be set to *Nothing* at this time to release the reference to the form object in the ParentWindowHandler class. See the code in step 5.
- The *ChangeParentWindow* method can be called at any time after the Form property of the ParentWindowHandler class has been set. See the code under step 8. The first parameter (hWndNewParent) is the new window handle, the second (FloatingWindow) is a Boolean value indicating whether to make the form a floating window or a contained window of the new parent. If the parent window is another VB form, the hWndNewParent parameter should be set to the hWnd property of the parent form, as in our example.
- The parent form must unload the child form before the parent form terminates. This is usually done in the *Form_Unload()* event procedure of the parent form. See the code in step 8.

NOTE In the development environment, clicking the End button on the VB toolbar immediately stops your program. *Form_Unload()*, *Form_Terminate()*, and *Class_Terminate()* event procedures won't execute. The parent of the child form won't be reset, and VB may crash.

ParentWindowHandler code listing

As with the *SetChildObject* and *ReleaseChildObject* support routines, you don't really need to know the details of the internal implementation of the ParentWindowHandler class, but you might be curious. This file is contained on the companion CD, Chapter11\ParentWindow\ParentWindow.Cls.

```
'Make sure all hWnd variables are declared as Long.
DefLng H
'API constant and declare to create a floating window
Private Const GWW_HWNDPARENT = -8
Private Declare Function SetWindowWord Lib "user32" Alias _
                           "SetWindowLongA" _
                           (ByVal hWnd As Long, _
                            ByVal nIndex As Long, _
                            ByVal wNewWord As Long) As Long
'API declare to create a contained window
Private Declare Function SetParent Lib "user32" _
                           (ByVal hWndChild As Long, _
                            ByVal hWndNewParent As Long) As Long
'Win16 declares are on the companion CD.

'The handle of the original parent window
Private hm_hWndOldParent
'The handle of the last window set as the parent
Private hm_hWndLastParent
'Whether the window was shown floating or contained
Private m_fFloatingWindow As Boolean

'The Form object we are modifying
Public Form As Form

Public Sub ChangeParentWindow(ByVal hWndNewParent, _
                              FloatingWindow As Boolean)
    'Don't do anything for a null parent window.
    If hWndNewParent = 0 Then Exit Sub

    'If we're already in the requested state, then just exit.
    If FloatingWindow = m_fFloatingWindow Then
        If hm_hWndLastParent = hWndNewParent Then Exit Sub
    End If
```

```
    'Make sure we always return to the original parent window.
    ResetParentWindow

    'Set the new parent, and keep the hWnd of the old parent.
    If FloatingWindow Then
        hm_hWndOldParent = SetWindowWord(Form.hWnd, _
                                         GWW_HWNDPARENT, _
                                         hWndNewParent)
    Else
        hm_hWndOldParent = SetParent(Form.hWnd, hWndNewParent)
    End If

    'Keep the current settings for future reference.
    m_fFloatingWindow = FloatingWindow
    hm_hWndLastParent = hWndNewParent
End Sub

Public Sub ResetParentWindow()
    'Reset if the parent window has been changed.
    If hm_hWndOldParent Then
        If m_fFloatingWindow Then
            SetWindowWord Form.hWnd, GWW_HWNDPARENT, hm_hWndOldParent
        Else
            SetParent Form.hWnd, hm_hWndOldParent
        End If
        hm_hWndOldParent = 0
        hm_hWndLastParent = 0
    End If
End Sub
```

Resource Files

Visual Basic 4 allows you to attach a resource file (.Res) to your project. The concept of a resource file is old hat to anyone who has written Windows-based programs in C or C++ but is a new feature for VB programmers. So what's in a resource file? A resource file is a binary description of many of the user interface elements you see in a Windows program. For example, icons, cursors, bitmaps, sound and video binaries, and string tables can all be stored in a resource file. Descriptions of dialogs and menus, accelerator tables (which define, for example, what Ctrl-C does in a program), version information, and type libraries can also be stored in a resource file, but the functionality provided by these resource types is built into VB programs, so you'll rarely use these types of resources in a VB project. In fact, VB won't let you add a resource file that contains some of these advanced types to your project. To add a resource file to your project, choose Add File from the File menu and select the .Res file you want to add. The file must have a .Res extension, and you can have only one resource file per project.

NOTE A .Res file is a compiled version of an .Rc file, which is a text file describing resources. Both 16- and 32-bit versions of the resource compiler (RC.Exe) are available on the Visual Basic 4 CD in the Tools\Resource\Rc16 and Tools\Resource\Rc32 directories to help you make a .Res file from an .Rc file. However, if you prefer using a GUI to type in the .Rc file in a text editor, you'll need another tool. Look in Tools\Resource\Resource.Txt for more information.

Why would you want to use a resource file? A resource file allows you to put all of the data for your program into one file and to load that data into your program as it's needed instead of loading all of the data when your program is first loaded. If you centralize string data in a resource file, for instance, you'll have a much easier time localizing your program for non-English-speaking markets. You might have the following line of code in a form module, for example:

```
MsgBox "You can't do that.", vbExclamation
```

For a German release of your product, you'd have to change the line of code to

```
MsgBox "Aktion nicht erlaubt.", vbExclamation
```

Then you'd have to change the code again for the French release, and so on. Resource files help you avoid this localization nightmare. If you rely on strings in a resource file, you can just plug a different resource file into your project and keep your code the same:

```
Private Const STRING_ID_NOCANDO = 200
:
MsgBox LoadResString(STRING_ID_NOCANDO), vbExclamation
```

A resource file has an ID associated with each piece of binary data in the file. In order to use a specific resource in your VB code, you must know the ID for the resource. You define constants in your VB project that correspond to the resource IDs in the .Res file. For example, here's the .Rc file for the *DataForm* sample, followed by the associated constants from the frmDataForm form module:

```
#define CURSOR_NODROP    100
#define CURSOR_DRAGMOVE 101
#define CURSOR_DRAGCOPY 102
CURSOR_NODROP      CURSOR     DISCARDABLE     "NODROP01.CUR"
CURSOR_DRAGMOVE    CURSOR     DISCARDABLE     "DRAGMOVE.CUR"
CURSOR_DRAGCOPY    CURSOR     DISCARDABLE     "DRAGCOPY.CUR"
```

```
'Constants corresponding to the cursors in the
'resource file attached to this project
Private Const CURSOR_NODROP = 100
Private Const CURSOR_DRAGMOVE = 101
Private Const CURSOR_DRAGCOPY = 102
```

NOTE The cursor files for the *DataForm* project were copied from the Tools\Graphics\Cursors directory on the Visual Basic 4 CD.

Visual Basic provides three functions for loading resources: *LoadResString* for strings; *LoadResPicture* for loading bitmaps, icons, and cursors; and *LoadResData* for loading everything else. *LoadResString* takes the resource ID as a parameter and returns the corresponding string. *LoadResPicture* takes a resource ID as the first parameter and *vbBitmap*, *vbIcon*, or *vbCursor* as the second parameter. The return value from *LoadResPicture* can be assigned directly to a picture type property (for example, Picture, MouseIcon, and DragIcon properties). The *DataForm* sample uses *LoadResPicture* to set the mouse cursor during a drag and drop operation. See VB's help file for more information on *LoadResData*.

Drag and Drop

The drag and drop user interface paradigm is a familiar, powerful feature of Windows. The *DataForm* sample uses drag and drop to enable the user to change the order of the items in the Fields: list box and to set the Preview: field. Any drag and drop operation has three main elements:

1. The user starts dragging by clicking and holding the mouse button on a user interface object.
2. The cursor changes as the user moves the mouse over different areas of the screen.
3. The program responds to the drop, which occurs when the user releases the mouse button.

In this section, we'll deal first with drag and drop in general and then move on to the more specific case of dragging from a list box using code from the *DataForm* sample application.

The *Drag* method

There are two ways to enable drag mode on a control. The first, which we'll mention only in passing, is to set the DragMode property of the control to *1 - Automatic* on the property sheet. In automatic drag mode, a control will go into drag mode whenever the left mouse button is pressed while the cursor is over the control. For a control in automatic drag mode, the *MouseDown* and *MouseUp* events won't be fired for the left mouse button, and the *Click* event will never be fired. Using automatic drag mode gives you very little control over starting the drag because no event is fired when the drag is started—your program just suddenly finds itself in drag mode.

For our sample, we'll leave the DragMode property set to *0 - Manual*, which is the default setting. When drag mode is set to manual, you must write your own code to start a drag and drop operation. Every type of Visual Basic control (except Line, Shape, and Timer) has a *Drag* method that's used to start dragging in manual mode. The *Drag* method is usually called in the *MouseDown* event when the left mouse button is pressed, as follows:

```
Private Sub AnyControl_MouseDown(Button As Integer, _
                                Shift As Integer, _
                                X As Single, Y As Single)
    If Button = vbLeftButton Then
        AnyControl.Drag vbBeginDrag
    End If
End Sub
```

Your program will now be in drag mode until a drop occurs—either because the user releases the mouse button or because the drag and drop operation is canceled in your code. Although you can call the *Drag* method with the vbEndDrag or vbCancel constant at any time to end the drag with a drop (vbEndDrag) or without a drop (vbCancel), ending the drag in code is rarely needed because most users don't like to hold down the mouse button any longer than they have to.

The *DragOver* Event

Once you've placed your control in drag mode in the *MouseDown* event, you won't receive the *MouseMove* events. Instead, each control or form the mouse cursor passes over will receive a *DragOver* event. If you've written code in the *control_DragOver()* event procedure, your code will be executed at that time. The *control_DragOver()* event procedure has four parameters:

- **Source** The control from which the *Drag* method was called.
- **X** The X coordinate, in twips, of the mouse position in the target form or control.
- **Y** The Y coordinate, in twips, of the mouse position in the target form or control.
- **State** *vbEnter*, *vbOver*, or *vbLeave*. This parameter indicates whether your user has just dragged over the control, has been there for a while, or has just started to drag over another control or over the form.

Since a *DragOver* event is fired for every mouse movement over any area of your form, your code should pay attention to the State parameter. If you're providing user feedback such as setting text in a status bar or changing the mouse cursor and you change the text in your status bar for every *Drag* event, your status bar will end up flickering badly. To avoid flickering, have your program check the State parameter before making any UI changes. Given hypothetical TrashCan and lblStatus controls, for example, you'd write

```
Private Sub TrashCan_DragOver(Source As Control, X As Single, _
                              Y As Single, State As Integer)
    If State = vbEnter Then lblStatus.Caption = "Incinerate it!"
End Sub
```

The *DragDrop* Event

When the mouse button is released in drag mode, VB fires the *DragDrop* event for whatever form or control the mouse cursor is over. The parameters for the *DragDrop* method are the same as for the *DragOver* method except that the State parameter is omitted. Any action associated with a drag operation, such as deleting a file or launching a program, should occur in the *DragDrop* event. The *DragDrop* event should also remove any visual indication of drag mode from the form. Here's the *DragDrop* code for our hypothetical TrashCan and lblStatus controls:

```
Private Sub TrashCan_DragDrop(Source As Control, X As Single, _
                              Y As Single)
    'Do some action.
    Incinerate Source
    'Turn off any visual indication of drag mode.
    lblStatus.Caption = ""
End Sub
```

The DragIcon Property

The DragIcon property is an essential piece of the user feedback puzzle for a program that uses drag and drop. When a program isn't in drag mode, the appearance of the mouse cursor over any given control is determined by the MouseIcon and MousePointer properties of the control. In drag mode, the mouse cursor is determined by the DragIcon property of the control that's being dragged, not by the MouseIcon pointer of the controls that are being dragged over.

The "Icon" part of the property names DragIcon and MouseIcon is a bit of a misnomer. Both of these properties can be set to either icons or cursors, but cursors provide much smoother dragging. Using an icon in the DragIcon and MouseIcon properties produces a mouse cursor that flashes badly whenever the mouse is moved.

During a drag operation, the DragIcon property of the source control will usually need to be changed repeatedly. The easiest way to support multiple drag cursors is to place them in a resource file, which is what we've done for the *DataForm* sample. For example, if no action results from dropping a control on the form, the *Form_DragOver()* event procedure could load a no-drop cursor (a circle with a line through it) from the project's resource file. Assume that the CURSOR_NODROP constant is defined and is a valid cursor identifier for the resource file:

```
Private Sub Form_DragOver(Source As Control, X As Single, _
                          Y As Single, State As Integer)
    Set Source.DragIcon = LoadResPicture(CURSOR_NODROP, vbResCursor)
End Sub
```

Dragging from a list box

A drag and drop operation in a list box poses two problems: how to allow a click, a double-click, and a drag to happen in the same list box; and how to figure out which item in the list box the mouse cursor is over. Let's start with the first problem.

If a user clicks on an item in a list box, the expected behavior is for the item to be selected. If a list box immediately enters drag mode when an item in the list is clicked, the user will be confused. Since the list box shouldn't go into drag mode immediately, calling the *Drag* method in the *MouseDown* event is ruled out. However, we do need to support putting the list box into drag mode, which means that the *Drag* method must be called at some point. But when? The trick lies in delaying the call to *Drag*. By activating a timer in the *MouseDown* event procedure instead of calling *Drag*, we give the user the chance he or she needs to complete a normal click before we put the list box into drag mode. If the *MouseUp* event procedure is fired before the *Timer* event, the timer is turned off and the *Drag* method is never called.

For an example of initiating drag mode in a *Timer* event, let's look at some code from the *DataForm* sample—the following procedures aren't complete, but they do demonstrate this concept. The Interval property of the timerStartDrag timer control has been set at design time to 150 milliseconds, which is plenty of time for the user to complete a normal mouse click but not enough time for the user to get impatient waiting for drag mode to start.

```
Private Sub lstFields_MouseDown(Button As Integer, _
                                Shift As Integer, _
                                X As Single, Y As Single)
    If Button = vbLeftButton Then
        'Don't do anything now. Just enable the timer.
        timerStartDrag.Enabled = True
```

```
    End If
End Sub

Private Sub lstFields_MouseUp(Button As Integer, Shift As Integer, _
                              X As Single, Y As Single)
    'If we got a MouseUp, the timer didn't fire, so turn
    'it off. If the timer is fired, we'll go into drag
    'mode and the MouseUp event will never be fired.
    timerStartDrag.Enabled = False
End Sub
Private Sub timerStartDrag_Timer()
    timerStartDrag.Enabled = False
    lstFields.Drag vbBeginDrag
End Sub
```

The second problem with drag and drop in a list box is determining which item in the list box the mouse cursor is over. To figure out where the mouse cursor is, we need to know the height of each item in the list box. VB's list box control doesn't have a built-in property that gives us this information, so we have to use the SendMessage call from the Windows API with the LB_GETITEMHEIGHT message to get the height of a single item in the list box. The *ListIndexFromMousePosition* function, shown here with the necessary API declarations, will determine which item is under the cursor for any list box.

```
'Module level declarations
Private Declare Function SendMessage Lib "user32" Alias _
                        "SendMessageA" _
                          (ByVal hWnd As Long, _
                           ByVal wMsg As Long, _
                           ByVal wParam As Integer, _
                           lParam As Any) As Long
Private Const LB_GETITEMHEIGHT = &H1A1
'Win16 declares are included on the companion CD.

'In MouseDown, MouseUp, MouseMove, DragOver, and
'DragDrop events, the ListIndex property can't be used
'to determine which list item is under the mouse. Use
'ListIndexFromMousePosition instead.
Private Function ListIndexFromMousePosition(LB As ListBox, _
                                            Y As Single)
Dim iItemHeight As Integer
Dim iIndex As Integer
    With LB
        'Get the item height.
        iItemHeight = _
           SendMessage(.hWnd, LB_GETITEMHEIGHT, 0, ByVal 0&)
```

(continued)

```
        'If TopIndex is -1, then there aren't any items in the
        'list box.
        If .TopIndex = -1 Then
            ListIndexFromMousePosition = -1
        Else
            'Calculate the index. iItemHeight is in pixels, so
            'we need to convert from twips. The X and Y arguments
            'passed by Visual Basic to Mouse and Drag events are
            'always in twips, regardless of the settings of the
            'ScaleMode property, so Y is in twips.
            iIndex = .TopIndex + 0.5 + _
                     ScaleY(Y, vbTwips, vbPixels) / iItemHeight

            'If we're below the last item in the list, just use
            'the last item.
            If iIndex > .ListCount Then iIndex = .ListCount

            'Our calculation ended up one-based. ListIndex is always
            'zero-based, so subtract 1 from iIndex and return.
            ListIndexFromMousePosition = iIndex - 1
        End If
    End With
End Function
```

NOTE List boxes in Windows 95 respond to an LB_ITEMFROMPOINT message, which does all of the work in ListIndexFromMousePosition (except for converting from twips to pixels) with a single line of code. LB_ITEMFROMPOINT isn't supported in Windows NT 3.51, however.

DataForm drag and drop code

The remainder of the code for the drag and drop operations in the *DataForm* sample is shown in this section. Let's review a few design considerations you should keep in mind as you look over the drag and drop code:

- The list item under the mouse cursor in the *lstFields_MouseDown* event is saved in the m_iDragStartIndex variable. We use this variable extensively in the code.
- When we enter drag mode, we set the caption of the status label (lblDragStatus.Caption) to indicate which item is being dragged.
- Since the selected state of an item in a simple multiselect list box is changed when the *MouseDown* event occurs, we change the selected state to the item's pre-MouseDown setting before we start dragging so that it will be dropped in its original state of either selected or not selected.

- When we drag over a list box item, we use the ListIndex property of the ListBox control to move the marquee (the dotted rectangle) to the item under the mouse cursor.
- To avoid defining *DragOver* event procedures for all controls on the form, we change the DragIcon property to indicate no drop when we leave the controls that are valid drop targets instead of when we enter the controls that aren't valid drop targets. *DragDrop* event procedures are provided for all controls.

Here's the drag and drop code from frmDataForm in the *DataForm* sample application:

```
'Constants corresponding to the cursors in the resource
'file attached to this project
Private Const CURSOR_NODROP = 100
Private Const CURSOR_DRAGMOVE = 101
Private Const CURSOR_DRAGCOPY = 102

'Module-level variables used in drag and drop operations
Private m_iDragStartIndex As Integer
Private m_fInDrag As Boolean

Private Sub DragOff()
    If m_fInDrag Then
        'Turn off the module-level flag.
        m_fInDrag = False
        'Don't show any drag status.
        lblDragStatus.Caption = vbNullString
        'Free the cursor from the DragIcon picture object.
        Set lstFields.DragIcon = Nothing
    End If
End Sub

Private Sub DragOn()
    'Turn on the module-level flag.
    m_fInDrag = True
    'Set the drag status to indicate which field is
    'being dragged.
    lblDragStatus.Caption = "Dragging: " & _
                            lstFields.List(m_iDragStartIndex)
End Sub

Private Sub lstFields_MouseUp(Button As Integer, Shift As Integer, _
                              X As Single, Y As Single)
    'This event will fire only if the Timer event didn't fire.
```

(continued)

```
        'In this case, the item was clicked and released immediately.
        'Be sure we don't go into drag mode.
        timerStartDrag.Enabled = False
    End Sub

    Private Sub timerStartDrag_Timer()
        'DragOn displays the item that's being dragged.
        DragOn
        'Turn the timer off so that this event procedure isn't
        'called again.
        timerStartDrag.Enabled = False
        With lstFields
            'Load the correct drag cursor.
            Set .DragIcon = LoadResPicture(CURSOR_DRAGMOVE, vbResCursor)
            'The selected state of a list box is changed before
            'the MouseDown event is received. Change it back.
            .Selected(m_iDragStartIndex) = Not _
                                    .Selected(m_iDragStartIndex)
            'Start dragging.
            .Drag vbBeginDrag
        End With
    End Sub

    Private Sub lstFields_DragDrop(Source As Control, X As Single, _
                                    Y As Single)
    Dim strItemName As String
    Dim fItemSelected As Boolean
    Dim iTargetIndex As Integer
        'The ListIndex is set to the item under the mouse cursor in
        'the DragOver event. Therefore, we can just use ListIndex
        'instead of calling ListIndexFromMousePosition.
        With lstFields
            iTargetIndex = .ListIndex
            'Check if we have a valid item in the list.
            If Not iTargetIndex Then
                'If the ListIndex is the same as the starting index,
                'then don't do anything.
                If iTargetIndex <> m_iDragStartIndex Then
                    'Store the string for the starting item and its
                    'selected state.
                    strItemName = .List(m_iDragStartIndex)
                    fItemSelected = .Selected(m_iDragStartIndex)
                    'Remove and re-add the item in its new position
                    'in the list. Be sure the item is active.
                    .RemoveItem m_iDragStartIndex
                    .AddItem strItemName, iTargetIndex
                    .Selected(iTargetIndex) = fItemSelected
```

```
                .ListIndex = iTargetIndex
            End If
        End If
    End With
    DragOff
End Sub

Private Sub lstFields_DragOver(Source As Control, X As Single, _
                              Y As Single, State As Integer)
Dim iTargetIndex As Integer
    'Update the mouse cursor to be the correct cursor.
    'Change the cursor only on vbEnter and vbLeave states.
    'Changing the cursor on a vbOver state is a wasted effort.
    'By using vbLeave in the DragOver event procedures for
    'the controls that accept dragging, we avoid creating
    'DragOver procedures for the forms and controls that
    'don't respond to the DragOver event.
    If State = vbEnter Then
        Set Source.DragIcon = LoadResPicture(CURSOR_DRAGMOVE, _
                                             vbResCursor)
    ElseIf State = vbLeave Then
        Set Source.DragIcon = LoadResPicture(CURSOR_NODROP, _
                                             vbResCursor)
    End If
    'Figure out which list item we are dragging over.
    iTargetIndex = ListIndexFromMousePosition(lstFields, Y)
    'Check if we are over a valid list item.
    If Not iTargetIndex Then
        With lstFields
            'If we are over a new list item, then move the
            'marquee in the list box to indicate the new item.
            If .ListIndex <> iTargetIndex Then _
               .ListIndex = iTargetIndex
        End With
    End If
End Sub

Private Sub txtPreview_DragOver(Source As Control, X As Single, _
                               Y As Single, State As Integer)
    'Dropping an item from the list box onto the
    'txtPreview control changes the field that shows in
    'the preview list. Indicate that the drop operation
    'does something by changing the mouse cursor.
    If State = vbEnter Then
        Set Source.DragIcon = LoadResPicture(CURSOR_DRAGCOPY, _
                                             vbResCursor)
```

(continued)

```
        ElseIf State = vbLeave Then
            Set Source.DragIcon = LoadResPicture(CURSOR_NODROP, _
                                                 vbResCursor)
        End If
    End Sub

    Private Sub txtPreview_DragDrop(Source As Control, X As Single, _
                                    Y As Single)
        With lstFields
            'Set the DataField property of the bound txtPreview
            'control to automatically show the new value.
            txtPreview.DataField = .List(m_iDragStartIndex)
            'Update the header label to indicate which field
            'is being previewed.
            lblPreviewHeader.Caption = "Preview: " & _
                                       .List(m_iDragStartIndex)
        End With
        'Turn off all drag settings.
        DragOff
    End Sub

    'To make it easier for the user to find the drop target,
    'the lblPreviewHeader control should have the same
    'drag/drop behavior as the txtPreview control. Just call
    'the txtPreview event procedures. Note that X and Y aren't
    'used, so we can pass anything we want.
    Private Sub lblPreviewHeader_DragOver(Source As Control, _
                                          X As Single, _
                                          Y As Single, _
                                          State As Integer)
        txtPreview_DragOver Source, X, Y, State
    End Sub
    Private Sub lblPreviewHeader_DragDrop(Source As Control, _
                                          X As Single, _
                                          Y As Single)
        txtPreview_DragDrop Source, X, Y
    End Sub

    'If the mouse button is released outside the form, we don't
    'get a DragDrop event. Turn off all drag settings the
    'next time the mouse is moved over the form.
    Private Sub Form_MouseMove(Button As Integer, Shift As Integer, _
                               X As Single, Y As Single)
        DragOff
    End Sub

    'For the form and all remaining controls, turn off
    'dragging on a DragDrop event by calling DragOff.
```

```
Private Sub Form_DragDrop(Source As Control, X As Single, _
                          Y As Single)
    DragOff
End Sub
:
'The DragDrop events for the dblstPublishers, lblPublishers,
'lblFields, lblDragStatus, cmdReturnData, and datResults
'controls all look like the Form_DragDrop() event procedure--
'they just call DragOff.
```

Persistent Program Settings

An end user expects any serious Windows-based program to have a good memory—even when the program is no longer running. Having your program remember its settings from one session to another requires writing data to the disk when the program is terminated and reading it back in when the program starts up again. Older versions of Windows relied on .Ini files in the Windows directory to retain application-specific settings when an application was no longer running. In Windows 95 and Windows NT, the system registry has taken over the task of retaining application settings.

Although application-specific settings are stored in a new location in Windows 95, the principles involved are still the same. Each application has one or more sections in which to store its settings. Each section has one or more keys, and each key has one or more values. VBA provides four built-in functions to help you write persistent program settings to the registry and read them back out when you need them.

NOTE The four persistent program settings functions aren't available in Excel-VBA. 16-bit VB4 writes settings to an .Ini file instead of to the system registry. However, where the data is actually saved is completely transparent to any code that uses the functions.

The first registry function you'll use is *SaveSetting*, which writes a value to the registry. In the *DataForm* sample, the user is prompted for the location of the Biblio.Mdb file the first time the application is loaded. Since Biblio.Mdb doesn't move around much, *DataForm* uses *SaveSetting* to make the location of Biblio-.Mdb persist in the system registry:

```
Dim strDBPath As String
:
SaveSetting "FormDemo", "StartUp", "MDBPath", strDBPath
```

This code creates a key in the registry that stores the value of strDBPath. Figure 11-7 below shows the corresponding section of the system registry and its path contents.

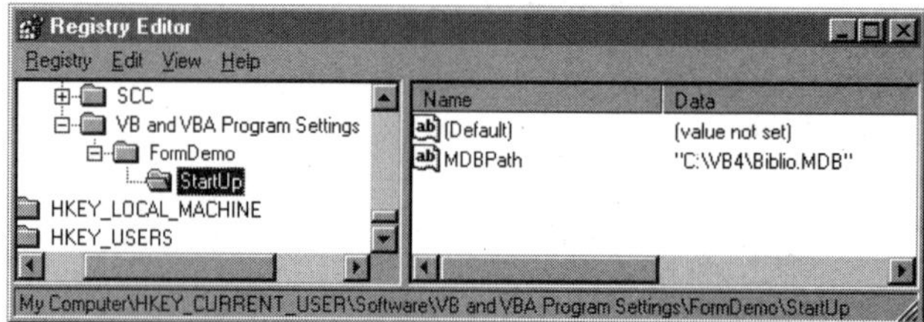

Figure 11-7. *The MDBPath key for the FormDemoVB project.*

To get the value back out of the registry, use the *GetSetting* function.

```
strDBPath = GetSetting("FormDemo", "StartUp", "MDBPath", "Not Found")
```

The last parameter of the *GetSetting* function is a default value for the setting. If the requested key isn't found in the registry, the default value is returned. If the Default parameter is omitted, an empty string is returned.

If you want to get all keys for the same setting at once, you can use the *GetAllSettings* function, which returns a variant containing a two-dimensional array of registry key names and values:

```
Dim strDBPath As String
Dim Settings As Variant
:
strDBPath = "C:\VB4\Biblio.Mdb"
SaveSetting "FormDemo", "StartUp", "MDBPath", strDBPath
:
Settings = GetAllSettings("FormDemo", "StartUp")
Debug.Print Settings (0, 0) & " = " & Settings(0, 1)

Output: MDBPath = C:\VB4\Biblio.Mdb
```

To delete a single key, a section, or even the settings for a whole application from the system registry, use *DeleteSetting*:

```
'Delete the MDBPath key.
DeleteSetting "FormDemo", "StartUp", "MDBPath"

'Delete the StartUp section.
DeleteSetting "FormDemo", "StartUp"
```

```
'Delete all settings for the FormDemo application.
DeleteSetting "FormDemo"
```

NOTE The VBA registry functions store all of their information under the *HKEY_CURRENT_USER\Software\VB and VBA Program Settings* key in the registry. The registry functions we've just reviewed can't be used to read or write values from other parts of the system registry.

In-Process *DataForm*

Now that we've gone to all the trouble to make *DataForm* a floating window in a cross-process OLE server, let's look at an in-process version of *DataForm* that contains the same functionality. We originally implemented *DataForm* as a cross-process server because we wanted a non-modal form. A form in a Visual Basic DLL in-process server must be shown modally. Therefore, unlike the cross-process *DataForm* sample, the in-process sample (we'll call it *DllDataForm*) won't allow any interaction with Microsoft Excel while the form is visible.

As you can see in Figure 11-8, the diagram for the *DllDataForm* architecture is significantly less complex than the same diagram (Figure 11-5 on page 282) for the cross-process server. We could have built the cross-process sample with this same architecture, but it would have been a very slow program because of the number of cross-process calls required. With an in-process server, there's no process boundary to cross, so we don't have to worry about whether, for example, the *Cells* method is called from code running in VB or from code in an Excel macro. Since there are no performance constraints forcing us to split up our code between VB and Excel, we'll put all of the code in our VB form module.

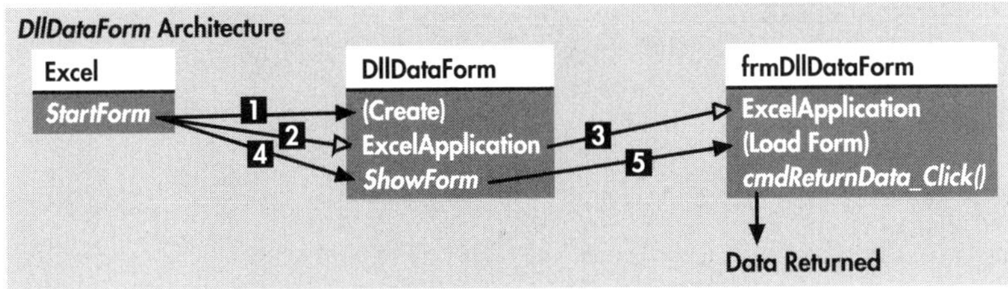

Figure 11-8. *Calls between objects in the* DllDataForm *sample.*

As in Figure 11-5, an open-head arrow represents setting or reading a property and a solid-head arrow represents calling a method. Let's look briefly at each of the numbered calls in Figure 11-8.

0. Step 0 (not shown) occurs when the user clicks the toolbar button that calls the *StartForm* macro.
1. The first time it's called, the *StartForm* macro creates a new instance of the DllDataForm class.
2. The ExcelApplication property of the DllDataForm object is set.
3. DllDataForm.ExcelApplication is actually a Property Set procedure that sets frmDllDataForm.ExcelApplication. Although the *Application.Run* method is no longer used, the ExcelApplication property is still needed to determine whether or not a worksheet is active.
4. *DllDataForm.ShowForm* is called. Since the form is shown modally, the *ShowForm* method won't be completed until the form is hidden by the user.
5. The *ShowForm* method shows the actual form. The form remains visible until the user clicks the Return Data button.

Figure 11-9 shows the *DllDataForm* window. Whereas in the original *DataForm* sample (Figure 11-4) Excel was active, note that the VB form, not Excel, is active here. In fact, the form must be closed before Excel can be activated. Also note that the Show DllDataForm toolbar button remains pressed until after the form is closed. Let's look at the differences between *DataForm* and *DllDataForm*.

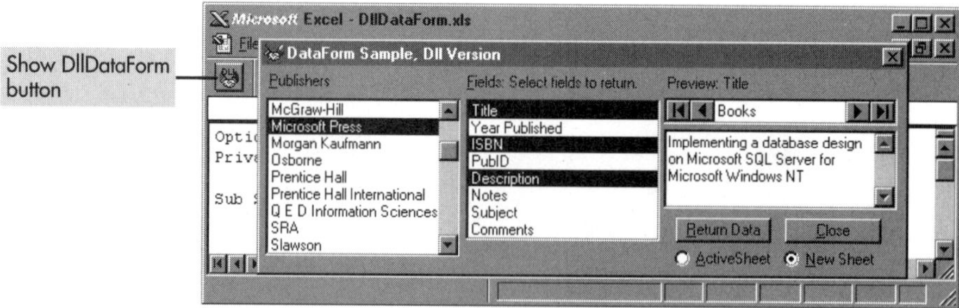

Figure 11-9. *The running* DllDataForm *sample.*

- The DataForm class has been renamed DllDataForm, and frmDataForm has been renamed (you guessed it) frmDllDataForm.
- frmDllDataForm doesn't have the ParentWindowHandler property. A modal VB form is always shown on top of all other windows in its task, so there's no reason to create a floating window. Since the *Form_Initialize()* and *Form_Unload()* event procedures were used only to manage the ParentWindowHandler class, these procedures have been eliminated, too.

- We've eliminated the Parent property of the form, so there's no way for frmDllDataForm to call properties or methods of the DllDataForm class. Instead of having the form read the ExcelApplication property from the parent object, we'll just pass the reference through the DllDataForm class and store it in an object variable in the form module as follows:

```
'Code in the DllDataForm class module
Public Property Set ExcelApplication(XLApp As Object)
    Set m_frmDllDataForm.ExcelApplication = XLApp
End Property

'Code in the frmDllDataForm code module
Public ExcelApplication As Excel.Application
```

- Since all of the data retrieval code has been moved from Excel's *FetchData* macro into frmDllDataForm, there's no longer a need to use *Application.Run* from VB to call an Excel macro. We've eliminated NotifyProc, Recordset, and *GetData* from DllDataForm. The Recordset property of frmDllDataForm has changed from public to private and has been renamed ResetRecordset. Code from the *FetchData* macro has been moved from Excel to the *FetchData* sub in frmDllDataForm.

- The form appearance has been changed slightly. We've added a Close button to hide the form and set the MinButton property to *False* at design-time so that the modal form can't be minimized.

- Instead of using a variant array to put the data in a specified range, the *FetchData* subroutine (which has moved from Excel to frmDllDataForm) uses Excel's built-in *CopyFromRecordset* method. The *CopyFromRecordset* method fails if the recordset object is owned by a cross-process server, which eliminated its use earlier and forced us to use a Variant array assignment. If you try to debug the *DllDataForm* sample in the VB environment, the *CopyFromRecordset* method will fail.

- At the end of the *Form_Load* procedure, we no longer set the Visible property of the form to *True*. Setting this property raises run-time error 400, "Form already displayed; can't show modally," on the m_frmDllDataForm.Show vbModal line in the *ShowForm* procedure.

The macro code from the DllDataForm Driver module in DllDataForm.Xls is shown on the next page. The *HideForm* and *FetchData* macros have been eliminated, and the Support Procedures module is no longer needed. Yes, this is all of the *StartForm* macro code!

```
Private DataForm As DllDataForm

Sub StartDllForm()
    'If we haven't created the object yet, then create it.
    If DataForm Is Nothing Then
        Set DataForm = CreateObject("FormDemo.DllDataForm")
        Set DataForm.ExcelApplication = Application
    End If
    DataForm.ShowForm
End Sub
```

Here's the DllDataForm class module. Like the code in the Excel module, this code is greatly simplified compared to the cross-process version.

```
Private m_frmDllDataForm As frmDllDataForm

'BUG: As Excel.Application creates an early-bound type
'mismatch in Excel, so we have to use As Object.
Public Property Set ExcelApplication(XLApp As Object)
    Set m_frmDllDataForm.ExcelApplication = XLApp
End Property

Private Sub Class_Initialize()
    Set m_frmDllDataForm = New frmDllDataForm
End Sub

Private Sub Class_Terminate()
    'Don't omit this line. Leaving a loaded, hidden form
    'in a DLL can cause termination problems.
    Unload m_frmDllDataForm
End Sub

Public Sub ShowForm()
    With m_frmDllDataForm
        Select Case .LoadState
            Case 0
                'We haven't tried to show the form yet.
                .Show vbModal
            Case 1
                'The load failed; try it again.
                .Form_Load
                If .LoadState = 2 Then .Show vbModal
            Case 2
                'The Form_Load() event procedure has already
                'run to completion.
                .Show vbModal
        End Select
```

```
    End With
End Sub
```

Here's the code from frmDllDataForm for new procedures and for *DataForm* procedures that have been modified.

```
'The new event procedure for the Close button we've added
Private Sub cmdClose_Click()
    Me.Hide
End Sub

'The modified cmdReturnData_Click procedure. All error-checking
'has been eliminated from this procedure. There's no chance
'of failure or of Excel's being busy as there is with the
'cross-process case.
Private Sub cmdReturnData_Click()
    If Not ExcelApplication Is Nothing Then
        'The option buttons determine if the data is returned
        'to a new sheet or to the active sheet. If the active
        'sheet in Excel isn't a worksheet, then allow
        'only the New Sheet option.
        If optReturn(0).Value Then
            If Not TypeOf ExcelApplication.ActiveSheet Is _
                          Excel.Worksheet Then
                MsgBox "Activate a worksheet, or choose " & _
                       "the 'New Sheet' option.", vbInformation
                Exit Sub
            End If
        End If
        'Return data to Excel.
        FetchData
    End If
End Sub

'The new FetchData routine
Private Sub FetchData()
Dim WB As Excel.Workbook
Dim WS As Excel.Worksheet
Dim WorkRange As Excel.Range
Dim Field As Field
Dim i%
    If optReturn(0).Value Then
        'Get the ActiveSheet.
        Set WS = ExcelApplication.ActiveSheet
        'Clear the current contents.
        WS.Cells(1, 1).CurrentRegion.ClearContents
    Else
```

(continued)

```
            Set WB = ExcelApplication.ActiveWorkbook
            If WB Is Nothing Then
                'If we don't have an active workbook, then open
                'one and get the first worksheet.
                Set WS = ExcelApplication.Workbooks.Add.Worksheets(1)
            Else
                'If we have an active workbook, then just add
                'a worksheet.
                Set WS = WB.Worksheets.Add
            End If
        End If

        'Make sure the m_Recordset variable is set.
        ResetRecordset

        With WS
            'Use the field names for column headers on the
            'first row.
            i% = 0
            For Each Field In m_Recordset.Fields
                i% = i% + 1
                .Cells(i%).Value = Field.Name
            Next

            'Use the CopyRecordset method to put the whole
            'recordset on the worksheet.
            m_Recordset.MoveFirst
            .Cells(2, 1).CopyFromRecordset m_Recordset

            'Get the current region.
            Set WorkRange = .Cells(1).CurrentRegion
            With WorkRange
                'Bold the first row (Column headers).
                .Rows(1).Font.Bold = True
                'Size the columns for a best fit.
                .Columns.AutoFit
            End With
        End With
    End Sub

    'The following sub used to be Public Property Get Recordset.
    'Now it just resets the m_Recordset object variable for
    'internal use. The body of the code hasn't changed, so
    'comments have been omitted.
    Private Sub ResetRecordset()
    Dim SQL As String
    Dim i%
```

```
    If cmdReturnData.Enabled And Not m_fHaveRecordset Then
        'Database manipulation code omitted.
        :
        m_fHaveRecordset = True
    End If
End Sub
```

XLCallBack Sample

Sometimes it takes a long time for a macro to run. After all, in real-world applications some tasks involve data-retrieval and calculations that just can't be completed in less than a second—or even less than a minute. In the old world of 16-bit Windows 3.1, the operating system made it difficult to continue working while a slow task was executing. The computer was completely tied up, working away while the user was left throwing wads of paper at the recycle bin.

With the Windows 95 and Windows NT 32-bit operating systems, programmers now have many more options to help the computer user keep working while the computer is busy. After all, there are more efficient ways to recycle paper.

The *XLCallBack* sample, whose window is shown in Figure 11-10, is a simple program that demonstrates how to execute a long Microsoft Excel macro from a Visual Basic program without interrupting the user of the VB program. In the *XLCallBack* sample, the Excel macro just waits around for 10 seconds before it decides it's done. In the meantime, you can type in the text box to see that the Excel macro is not interrupting your work. If VB didn't put a message on the form saying "Excel Finished," you wouldn't even notice when the Excel macro has finished processing. Of course, your programs will be a little more useful, but the techniques will be the same as in the *XLCallBack* sample.

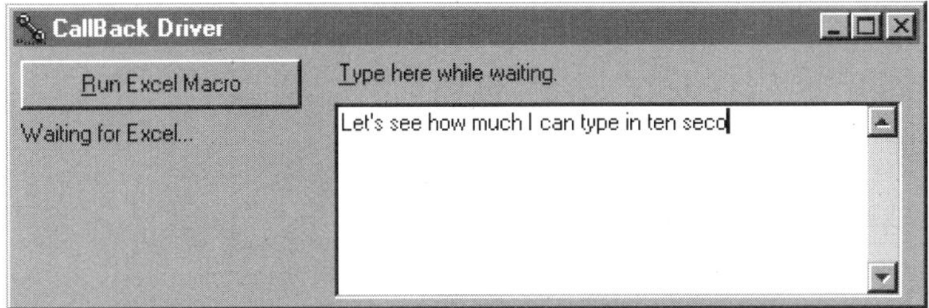

Figure 11-10. *Our boring CallBack Driver form, in which the user can continue to type while Microsoft Excel is running in the background.*

Asynchronous Processing

Windows 95 and Windows NT are multitasking operating systems, which means that several applications can use the system processor at the same time. The application currently receiving user input is said to be the *foreground* process, and all other applications are said to be *background* processes. The Microsoft 32-bit operating systems use processor time for background processing when the foreground application doesn't use all of the processor time. A well-known example of background processing is background printing, which allows a user to continue working while the computer is printing a document—instead of having to wait for the print job to finish.

NOTE Background printing is usually run on a different *thread* in the same process instead of in a separate process. Think of a thread as a sub-application running in the same process as your application. Visual Basic programs don't support multithreading.

Background processing allows an application that uses OLE Automation to easily do *asynchronous* processing. Let's define asynchronous processing by looking at synchronous processing, which is what we've done up to this point with object servers. Synchronous processing with an OLE Automation object proceeds as follows:

1. The client calls a method of the object server.
2. The object server finishes executing the method.
3. The object server returns control to the client.
4. The client continues with the next line of code.

Asynchronous processing takes a slightly different course:

1. The client calls a method of the object server.
2. The object server immediately returns control to the client without executing the assigned task.
3. The client continues with the next line of code.
4. In the background, the object server executes the requested method.
5. When execution of the method is completed, the object server notifies the client that processing is completed and returns any required data.

The final step of notifying the client that a background task has been completed is known as a *callback*. The notification part of a callback is usually accomplished by calling a method on an object provided by the client application. We'll use the term *callback object* to refer to the object provided by the client as a notification vehicle. If you use a callback architecture between two Visual Basic applications, providing the server with a callback object is easy because the client can pass a callback object to the server directly.

If Microsoft Excel is being used for background processing, passing a callback object directly isn't possible because there's no way to pass an object to the *Application.Run* method. (We mentioned this limitation of the *Run* method in Chapter 9.) Without a callback object, asynchronous processing becomes much more difficult because there's no good way to notify the client that background processing has been completed. Let's figure out a way to work around this limitation of the *Run* method.

XLCallBack Architecture

The goal of the *XLCallBack* sample is to perform background processing in Microsoft Excel. In order to launch an Excel macro asynchronously from a Visual Basic program, we need to answer two questions:

Q1. How can we make an Excel macro launch a background task and immediately return control to a calling program?

Q2. How can Excel get the callback object it will use to notify the VB program that background processing has been completed?

Storing and retrieving a callback object

Since there's no way to pass an object reference from a Visual Basic program to Microsoft Excel using the *Application.Run* method, we need to take a different approach, the one shown in Figure 11-11 on the next page. We go ahead and create a callback object before we start background processing in Excel, but instead of passing the object reference to Excel, we store the object and pass a token to Excel. When Excel is ready to use the callback object, it uses *CreateObject* to create an object that's owned by our VB program. Excel passes a method of this object the token it has been saving and in return receives a reference to the callback object.

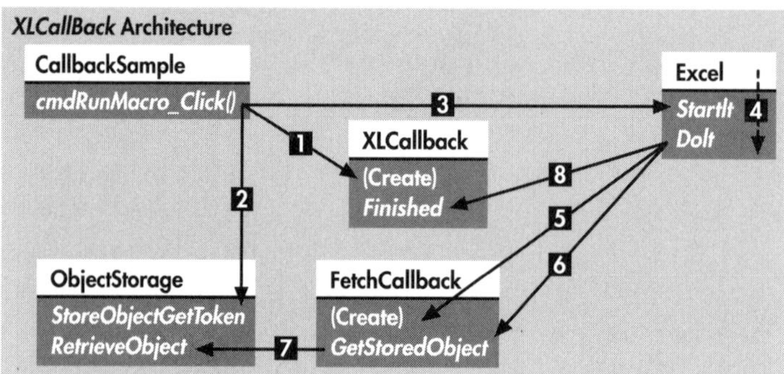

Figure 11-11. *Calls between objects in the* XLCallBack *sample.*

Let's walk through the steps shown in Figure 11-11. Along the way, we'll see how we've answered the two questions posed on the previous page.

0. The user starts the VB program and clicks the Run Excel Macro button.

1. A new XLCallback object is created.

2. The callback object is put into storage by a call to *StoreObjectGetToken*, and a token value is returned for retrieving the object later.

3. The *StartIt* macro is called in Excel. The token for the stored callback object is passed to Excel as an argument to the *StartIt* macro.

4. The *Application.OnTime* method is called from inside the *StartIt* macro to start the *DoIt* macro with a slight delay. (See the dotted line that represents the call by means of *Application.OnTime.*) The token is passed by building a single-quote delimited string containing the *DoIt* macro name and the token value. (Step 4 answers Question 1.)

5. After the *DoIt* macro runs to completion, it creates a FetchCallback object in the VB server.

6., 7. The *DoIt* macro passes the token to the *GetStoredObject* method, which retrieves the stored callback object using the *RetrieveObject* method. The actual callback object we created in step 1 is returned to Excel. (Question 2 has been satisfied.)

8. The *DoIt* macro calls the *Finished* method of the XLCallback class, returning data to the form.

The *XLCallBack* sample implements two different classes to manage storing and fetching objects. The ObjectStorage class has two methods, *StoreObject-GetToken* and *RetrieveObject. StoreObjectGetToken* takes an object parameter and returns an integer token that's used to retrieve the object using the

RetrieveObject method. Once a token has been used to retrieve an object, the token is no longer valid. The FetchCallback class is a public and creatable wrapper class that's used to retrieve an object from a global ObjectStorage instance in the VB program. *GetStoredObject* is the only method of the FetchCallback class. Let's look at code fragments that use the ObjectStorage and FetchCallback classes in both VB and Excel, and at code listings for the class modules themselves.

Here's some hypothetical code in VB to pass a callback object to Excel:

```
Dim XLApp As Excel.Application
Dim XLWorkbook As Excel.Workbook
Dim CallbackObj As New XLCallback
:
XLApp.Run XLWorkbook.Name & "!StartIt", _
            g_ObjectStorage.StoreObjectGetToken(CallbackObj)
```

This code in Excel retrieves the callback object from VB:

```
Dim FetchCallback As Object
Dim Callback As Object

Set FetchCallback = CreateObject("CallbackSample.FetchCallback")
Set Callback = FetchCallback.GetStoredObject(Token)
```

The XLCallbackModule module (XLCallBack.Bas) is needed to provide an ObjectStorage instance that can be used anywhere in the *XLCallBack* sample code:

```
Public g_ObjectStorage As New ObjectStorage
```

The following code in the FetchCallback module (FetchCallBack.Cls) is needed to access the internal g_ObjectStorage collection from Excel:

```
Public Property Get GetStoredObject(Token As Integer) As Object
    Set GetStoredObject = g_ObjectStorage.RetrieveObject(Token)
End Property
```

Cross-Reference

The ObjectStorage class uses the VBA.Collection object and an IntegerStack class. For more information on VBA's Collection object, see "VBA Language Concepts: Collections" in Appendix A. For the code listing of the IntegerStack class, see "An Integer Stack" in the "*XLCallBack* Support Topics" section, later in this chapter.

Here's the ObjectStorage class module code (ObjectStorage.Cls):

```
Private m_ObjectStorage As VBA.Collection
Private m_TokenStack As IntegerStack

Private Sub Class_Initialize()
    Set m_ObjectStorage = New VBA.Collection
    Set m_TokenStack = New IntegerStack
    'To avoid confusion with an uninitialized integer,
    'make sure m_TokenStack.Pop always returns a positive
    'value.
    m_TokenStack.Init StackBase:=1
End Sub

Public Function StoreObjectGetToken(StoredObject As Object) _
                                        As Integer
Dim iToken As Integer
    'Get an available token number from the stack.
    iToken = m_TokenStack.Pop
    'Add the object to the collection with the key of
    'the given token.
    m_ObjectStorage.Add StoredObject, CStr(iToken)
    StoreObjectGetToken = iToken
End Function

Public Function RetrieveObject(Token As Integer) As Object
    'If the token is bogus, the first line will cause
    'an error and RetrieveObject will error out. This
    'means that a bogus token will never get pushed onto
    'the stack.
    Set RetrieveObject = m_ObjectStorage(CStr(Token))
    m_ObjectStorage.Remove CStr(Token)
    m_TokenStack.Push Token
End Function

Public Property Get Count() As Integer
    Count = m_ObjectStorage.Count
End Property
```

Launching a background macro

For a macro to run in the background, the macro must be called after control has been returned to the calling program. How is this possible? The trick lies in using a timer to launch the actual macro code. In Microsoft Excel, this can be done with the *Application.OnTime* method. In a Visual Basic callback server, a timer control can be used to initiate background processing.

Here is the code from *XLCallBack* used to launch the background macro. This code doesn't actually do anything. It just waits for 10 seconds before calling back into the VB part of the program to notify the caller that the background macro is finished. The VB code calls the *StartIt* macro, which returns immediately after telling Excel to call the *DoIt* macro as soon as possible.

Here's the VBA code from the XLCode.Txt file. For our bare-bones sample, this code is dynamically loaded in Excel at run-time:

```
Sub StartIt(Token As Integer)
    'Call the OnTime macro to do the actual work. Starting
    'Now actually means as soon as possible. The token is
    'passed in as part of the macro name. Since it's possible
    'to call StartIt again before DoIt is finished, storing
    'the token in a single module-level variable isn't safe,
    'so we let Excel keep the value for us.
    Application.OnTime Now, "'DoIt " & CStr(Token) & "'"
End Sub

Sub DoIt(Token As Integer)
Dim StartTime As Double
Dim FetchCallback As Object
Dim Callback As Object
    'Replace the next four lines of code with something
    'useful. Remember to call DoEvents occasionally to help
    'the foreground process run smoothly.
    StartTime = Timer
    While Timer < StartTime + 10
        DoEvents
    Wend
    'In case of abnormal CallbackSample, shut down.
    On Error Resume Next
    Set FetchCallback = CreateObject("CallbackSample.FetchCallback")
    Set Callback = FetchCallback.GetStoredObject(Token)
    Callback.Finished "Excel Finished"
End Sub
```

Putting it all together

Now that we have all of the necessary tools for storing and retrieving a callback object, we're ready to actually create one. For our simple sample, our XLCallback class acts as the callback object. The XLCallback class has a *Finished* method that will be called by Excel when it has finished doing nothing for 10 seconds. To launch Excel, we'll use the ExcelLaunch class we created in Chapter 8.

The XLCallback class module is in XLCallBack.Cls. For a real program, you can modify this class without touching the ObjectStorage or FetchCallback classes. This class is public but not creatable.

```
Public Sub Finished(Status As String)
    frmDriver.lblStatus = Status
End Sub
```

The frmDriver code module is in XLCallBack.Frm. Omitted code is covered in "Activating a Previous Instance" in the "*XLCallBack* Support Topics" section, on the facing page.

```
Private m_XLLaunch As New ExcelLaunch
Private m_MacroWorkbook As Excel.Workbook

Private Sub Form_Load()
    'Code omitted.

    'Get a reference to Excel and load our macro into a
    'workbook. This is just a placeholder for loading an
    'existing Excel workbook or add-in that actually does
    'something.
    Set m_MacroWorkbook = m_XLLaunch.XLApplication.Workbooks.Add
    With m_MacroWorkbook
        .Windows(1).Visible = False
        .Modules.Add.InsertFile App.Path & "\XLCode.Txt"
        .Saved = True
    End With
End Sub

Private Sub Form_QueryUnload(Cancel As Integer, _
                            UnloadMode As Integer)
    If g_ObjectStorage.Count Then
        MsgBox "Can't terminate. " & _
               " Not all Callbacks have been retrieved."
        Cancel = True
    End If
End Sub

Private Sub Form_Unload(Cancel As Integer)
    'Code Omitted.

    'Close the workbook. If we started Excel, it will
    'close when m_XLLaunch goes out of scope.
    m_MacroWorkbook.Close
End Sub

Private Sub cmdRunMacro_Click()
Dim CallbackObj As New XLCallback
    lblStatus.Caption = "Waiting for Excel..."
    m_XLLaunch.XLApplication.Run _
               m_MacroWorkbook.Name & "!StartIt", _
               g_ObjectStorage.StoreObjectGetToken(CallbackObj)
End Sub
```

XLCallBack Support Topics

As with the *DataForm* sample, we used a couple of techniques as we wrote the *XLCallBack* sample code that are useful and worthy of mention but that aren't central to using an Excel macro for background processing. The first technique is for forcing a Visual Basic application to start only one instance of itself. By default, you can launch multiple instances of the same VB program at one time. We needed to block this functionality and limit the *XLCallBack* sample program to a single instance. The second useful technique was using a stack object to create and recycle tokens to be used as identifiers for the ObjectStorage class. Let's take a look at these techniques now.

Activating a Previous Instance

In our example, Microsoft Excel must use *CreateObject* to retrieve a callback object in order to notify the client (*XLCallBack*) that background processing is complete. *CreateObject* and the *New* keyword will always create a new object, but the object server that creates the object is impossible to specify or determine if more than a single instance of the server is running. If we follow the default behavior of Visual Basic and allow more than one instance of the *XLCallBack* sample program to successfully launch, it will be impossible for Excel to guarantee that *CreateObject* is returning a FetchCallback object from the correct instance of the object server.

To guarantee that only a single instance of the *XLCallBack* program will be running at any given time, we need to add code at the beginning of the program to check for a previously running instance of the program. VB's built-in App object has a PrevInstance property we can use to determine whether an instance of the application is already running. Let's look first at the code for activating a previous instance and then look at the steps we took in the code to accomplish the task of activating a previous instance. This code is pulled directly from the *XLCallBack* sample sources, but we've omitted anything that doesn't apply to activating the previous instance.

```
DefLng H
Private Declare Function ShowWindow Lib "user32" _
                        (ByVal hWnd As Long, nCmdShow As Long) As Long
Private Declare Function IsIconic Lib "user32" _
                         (ByVal hWnd As Long) As Long
Private Const SW_RESTORE = 9
'Win16 declares are included on the companion CD.

Private Sub Form_Load()
Dim strOldCaption As String
Dim hWndRestore
```

(continued)

```
    'To ensure that Excel creates a callback instance with
    'the right object server, we need to make sure that only
    'one instance of this application is running. Don't let
    'a second instance start.
    If App.PrevInstance Then
        strOldCaption = Me.Caption
        Me.Caption = "Hide Me"
        AppActivate strOldCaption

        'AppActivate will activate the application but not
        'restore it if it is iconized. Get the hWnd of the
        'running app from the program settings in the registry
        'and restore it if it's iconized.
        hWndRestore = GetSetting("CallbackSample", _
                                 "RunningInstance", _
                                 "hWnd", "0")
        If IsIconic(hWndRestore) Then _
            ShowWindow hWndRestore, SW_RESTORE

        'Just end. We don't want Form_Unload to run and delete
        'the program settings.
        End
    Else
        'Save the hWnd of this instance in the registry so
        'that other instances of this application can activate
        'this one without starting up a new application.
        SaveSetting "CallbackSample", "RunningInstance", "hWnd", _
                    Me.hWnd
    End If
End Sub

Private Sub Form_Unload(Cancel As Integer)
    'Clear all settings from the registry.
    DeleteSetting "CallbackSample"
End Sub
```

Let's go over the steps we took to activate the previous instance:

1. When the first instance of our application starts, we put the window handle (hWnd) of the form in the system registry:

   ```
   SaveSetting "CallbackSample", "RunningInstance", "hWnd", _
               Me.hWnd
   ```

   If the initial form is minimized when a later instance of the application tries to start up, this value is used to restore the form to a normal state.

2. If a previous instance is running when a new instance tries to start, use *AppActivate* to activate the previous instance. *AppActivate* activates a window by its caption, so we need to change the caption of the new instance to a new value before looking for the existing window—so that AppActivate won't find our current window:

```
strOldCaption = Me.Caption
Me.Caption = "Hide Me"
AppActivate strOldCaption
```

NOTE If your single-instance program changes its caption when it loads a new document, you should immediately write that new caption to the registry.

3. *AppActivate* will activate a minimized program, but it won't restore it. To restore the program from a minimized state, we use the *Show Window* API call. The hWnd value is pulled from the system registry.

```
hWndRestore = GetSetting (...)
If IsIconic(hWndRestore) Then _
    ShowWindow hWndRestore, SW_RESTORE
```

4. After the previous instance is activated, we terminate the program immediately with the *End* statement.

5. When the startup form for the original instance is unloaded, all of the program settings are deleted from the system registry by means of DeleteSetting:

```
DeleteSetting "CallbackSample"
```

Apart from the names used in the *SaveSetting* and *DeleteSetting* calls, you can simply copy and paste this code into the *Form_Load()* and *Form_Unload()* event procedures of the startup form for any of your applications that must be single-instance apps.

An Integer Stack

The *XLCallBack* sample program uses tokens to uniquely identify each object in the object storage collection. Each token in use must have a unique value, and each token should be reusable. Just think of a token as a room key: the key will work for only one patron at a time but can be given to another patron after the first has checked out. In the *XLCallBack* sample program, we've contained the functionality of handing out, retrieving, and recycling token values in a class module whose design is based on a very simple stack model.

A stack is a common programming concept. Stacks store values on a last-in, first-out basis—that is, the last value pushed onto the stack must be popped off the stack before any earlier values can be retrieved. Every stack supports a *Push* method to store a value and a *Pop* method to retrieve the value. The stack class itself is responsible for making sure it has enough memory allocated to store all of the values pushed onto the stack.

We've modified the stack concept a bit to suit our token requirements. Normally, popping a method off a stack will fail if a value hasn't been pushed onto the stack. In our IntegerStack class, however, we'll never raise an error when we pop a value from an empty stack. If the *Pop* method is called when a value hasn't been pushed onto the stack, we just return an initial value and then increment that value so that repeated *Pop* calls to the empty stack will return a different value. If we've lost you, follow the code below to see what's happening:

```
Dim Stack As New IntegerStack
Dim Token1 As Integer, Token2 As Integer, Token3 As Integer
'Initialize the stack so that the first value retrieved
'from an empty stack will be 1.
Stack.Init StackBase:=1
Token1 = Stack.Pop     'Token1 is now 1.
Token2 = Stack.Pop     'Token2 is now 2.
Stack.Push Token1      'Token1 is no longer in use; push its
                       'value onto the stack.
Token3 = Stack.Pop     'Token3 is now 1; the stack is empty again.
Token1 = Stack.Pop     'Token 1 is now 3.
```

Stacks can be useful for many programming problems. The IntegerStack class is provided as an example for creating your own stack class. With minor modifications to the IntegerStack class module, the stack can hold variants, doubles, or any data type you like. Here's the code for the Integer-Stack class:

```
'm_Stack: the array that holds the stack values
Private m_Stack() As Integer
'm_StackChunk: the number of elements to grow the
'array when more space is required
Private m_StackChunk As Integer
'm_StackTop: the size of the array
Private m_StackTop As Integer
'm_StackPointer: the current position on the stack
Private m_StackPointer As Integer

Sub Init(Optional StackChunk As Variant, _
        Optional StackBase As Variant)
    If IsMissing(StackChunk) Then StackChunk = 5
    If IsMissing(StackBase) Then StackBase = 0
    m_StackChunk = StackChunk
```

```
    m_StackTop = m_StackChunk
    ReDim m_Stack(m_StackTop)
    m_Stack(0) = StackBase
End Sub

Sub Push(NewValue As Integer)
    'Make sure we have enough space in the m_Stack array
    'to save the new value.
    If m_StackPointer Mod m_StackChunk = 0 Then
        m_StackTop = m_StackPointer + m_StackChunk
        ReDim Preserve m_Stack(m_StackTop)
    End If

    'Increment the stack pointer, and save the value.
    m_StackPointer = m_StackPointer + 1
    m_Stack(m_StackPointer) = NewValue
End Sub

Function Pop() As Integer
    'Get the value at the current position in the stack.
    Pop = m_Stack(m_StackPointer)
    If m_StackPointer Then
        'If we aren't at the bottom of the stack, then
        'decrement the stack pointer.
        m_StackPointer = m_StackPointer - 1

        'If we can shrink the stack array, then do so.
        If m_StackPointer = m_StackTop - m_StackChunk Then
            'To avoid constantly regrowing the array, don't
            'shrink the stack array down to nothing.
            If m_StackPointer Then
                ReDim Preserve m_Stack(m_StackTop - m_StackChunk)
            End If
        End If
    Else
        'There isn't anything on the stack. Increment the base
        'of the stack to the next available numeric value.
        m_Stack(m_StackPointer) = m_Stack(m_StackPointer) + 1
    End If
End Function
```

SUMMARY

- If two objects must retain a reference to each other, additional code is required to force the objects to terminate normally. Modifying the internal reference count of an object enables objects linked by a parent-child relationship to terminate correctly.
- By means of OLE Automation, Visual Basic forms and classes can be used by Microsoft Excel to create friendly user interfaces in VB that can be tightly integrated into Excel-based programs.
- It's much easier to use an in-process Visual Basic object server with Microsoft Excel than a cross-process server. An application designed around an in-process server doesn't need to worry about the number of calls between application components.
- A hidden Visual Basic form in an in-process server can be used to receive *Timer* events, which can be relayed back to Microsoft Excel. A form in a VB DLL must be hidden or modal.
- If a non-modal Visual Basic form is required, you must use a cross-process server.
- To maintain acceptable performance with a cross-process server, a custom application must minimize the number of cross-process calls. The vast majority of calls to all objects in the application should be made from the process that owns the object.
- A Visual Basic form can be made to float over any other application's window.
- Using callbacks, an application can take advantage of the multitasking properties of Windows 95 and Windows NT to enable background processing of time-intensive tasks.
- A stack-type class can be used to provide and recycle tokens to retrieve callback objects.

We've come to the end of our consideration of integrating Microsoft Excel and Visual Basic. Of course, many of the techniques you've learned along the way are applicable to any VB program you write that exposes classes or creates objects in cross-process servers. Let's move on to using VB4 with another popular Microsoft Office for Windows 95 application: Microsoft Word.

PART FOUR

The Kitchen Sink

IN THIS PART

You'd think Visual Basic 4 and Microsoft Excel were the only topics covered in this book! Not hardly. Microsoft Word and PowerPoint also integrate nicely with Visual Basic, and we'll cover those two applications in Part Four. In Chapters 12 and 13, we'll show you how to manipulate the Word and the PowerPoint object models, respectively, from Visual Basic for Applications. Be sure to check out Appendix C, which lays out the Microsoft Excel, Microsoft Word, and Microsoft PowerPoint object models.

Chapter 12 - Programming in Microsoft Word

The Microsoft Word object model hasn't changed all that much with version 7.0—you still have just one object from which you run WordBasic macros. Even so, you can do some powerful maneuvering of Word from within a VBA program—things that haven't really been addressed comprehensively before. Have fun with this chapter—and with this version of Word. We hope we'll get a nice juicy set of objects to play with in the next version of Word.

Chapter 13 - The Point Is Power

And powerful it is! PowerPoint has a spanking new object model that enables you to manipulate presentations and multimedia applications from your VBA applications. In this chapter, we'll cover creating, modifying, and running PowerPoint presentations using VBA and the PowerPoint OLE Automation server. Dig into the PowerPoint object model: it's an especially good example of how an OLE Automation server should work.

12

Programming in Microsoft Word

OK, we've programmed in Visual Basic, and we've programmed in Microsoft Excel. Both use versions of Visual Basic for Applications that are almost identical. Consequently, most of the code you write is easily ported from one host to the other. Programming in Microsoft Word is a different story. Word for Windows was the first Microsoft productivity application to use a macro language based on Basic. Unfortunately, the Word flavor of Basic, WordBasic, isn't completely compatible with VBA, so you can't just cut and paste WordBasic code into a Visual Basic program and make a few modifications to get it to work.

Starting with version 6.0, Word for Windows does expose an OLE Automation object, however, which makes Word programmable from any application that hosts VBA. This object isn't as rich as the objects exposed by Microsoft Excel, but it will still allow you to use word processing functionality in your VBA projects. In this chapter, we'll write WordBasic macros and port those macros to work in Visual Basic projects. We'll look at the WordBasic object in detail, and at the end of the chapter we'll consider some tips on programming efficiently with the WordBasic object from Visual Basic.

WordBasic

Let's start off by taking a look at WordBasic. Like Microsoft Excel, Word has a Record Macro option. If you select Record Macro from the Tools menu, Word will begin recording each action you take and will translate those actions into a WordBasic macro. Let's try it.

1. Start Word.
2. Select Tools-Macro to open the Macro dialog. (See Figure 12-1 on the next page.)

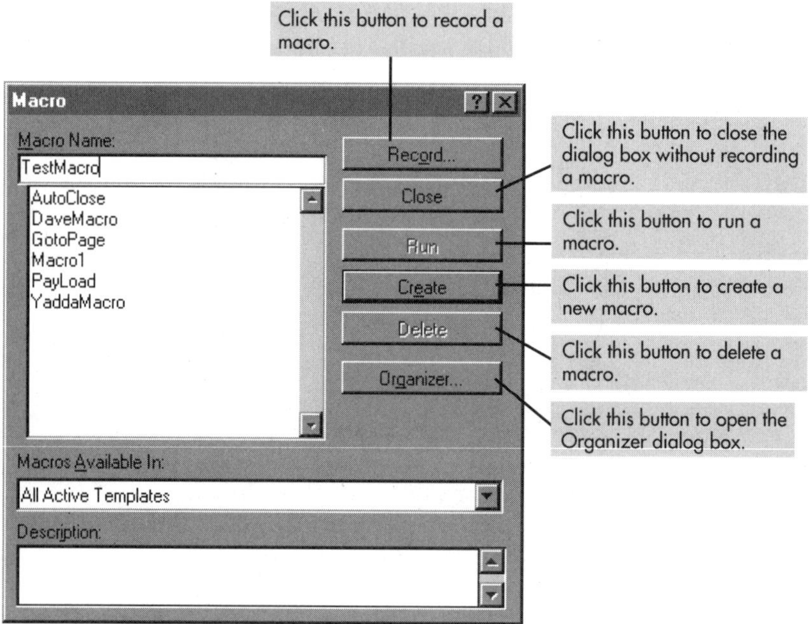

Figure 12-1. *The Microsoft Word Macro dialog box.*

3. Type *TestMacro* in the Macro Name: box, and click the Record button. You'll see a Record Macro dialog like the one shown in Figure 12-2.

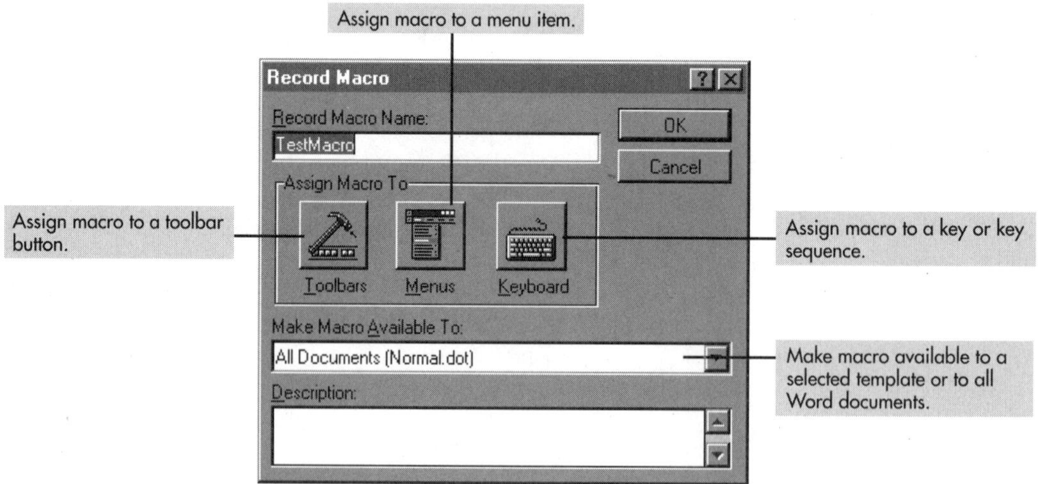

Figure 12-2. *The Microsoft Word Record Macro dialog box.*

4. The Record Macro dialog enables you to assign your macro to a toolbar button, a menu item, or a key (or key sequence). But for this example, we'll record a macro without assigning it to anything. Click the OK button. You'll see a button bar like the one shown in Figure 12-3.

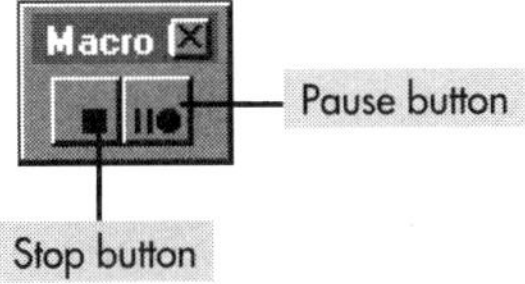

Figure 12-3. *The Record Macro button bar.*

Now you can perform the set of actions you'd like to record. Then when you click the *stop* button, Word will translate the steps you took into WordBasic code. This code will be stored in the form of a WordBasic macro you can attach to specific files or make available to all of your Word files.

Now let's take the steps we want to record in our macro.

1. Select File-New.
2. From the General tab, select Blank Document.
3. Type *This is a bold test.*
4. Using the Shift and arrow keys, select the word *bold* and then click the *bold* button on your toolbar (or select Format-Font, and under Font Style select Bold). Notice that we didn't use the mouse to select the word *bold.* You can't record mouse movements in Word macros.
5. From the File menu, select Save As. Save the file as *Yadda.Doc.*
6. Stop recording by clicking the *stop* button. (See Figure 12-3.)

You've just recorded a WordBasic macro. You can run this macro at any time by selecting Tools-Macro, clicking TestMacro, and then clicking the Run button. Word will perform the exact steps you performed when you recorded *TestMacro.*

To see the code for the *TestMacro* macro,

1. Select Tools-Macro, and then select TestMacro.
2. Click the Edit button.

You'll see the following code:

```
Sub MAIN
FileNew .Template = "C:\MSOffice\Templates\Normal.dot",
.NewTemplate = 0
Insert "This is a bold test."
WordLeft 3
WordRight 1, 1
Bold
FileSaveAs .Name = "yadda.doc", .Format = 0, .LockAnnot = 0, .Password
= "", .AddToMru = 1, .WritePassword = "", .RecommendReadOnly = 0,
.EmbedFonts = 0, .NativePictureFormat = 0, .FormsData = 0,
.SaveAsAOCELetter = 0
End Sub
```

Your macro may differ slightly from the one shown here. If you used single cursor movements instead of Ctrl-cursor to move one word at a time, your macro might include CharLeft and CharRight instead of WordLeft and WordRight.

NOTE Notice that with WordBasic macros, a code phrase can continue to the next line without the continuation character (_) VBA requires. WordBasic looks for an end-of-line character (hidden from the programmer) to determine when a line ends. You can toggle the Show/Hide ¶ toolbar button to view the end of line characters.

If you want to find out how to write the code for a specific Word operation, you can use the Edit button from Tools-Macro to see the code itself after you've recorded a macro for the operation. As you'll see, you'll have to modify the code a little—jump through some hoops to make it work right—if you plan to use it in Visual Basic projects.

Using the WordBasic Object

So what now? You've seen WordBasic macros. Now let's see how to use the WordBasic object and look at the changes we need to make to our WordBasic code to make it run in a Visual Basic project.

Creating the WordBasic Object

To manipulate Word from a Visual Basic project, we'll first declare an object variable and then use the *CreateObject* function to fill that object with an instance of the WordBasic object.

1. Open a new project in VB.
2. Drop a button on the default VB form, and double-click the button.

3. Create the following *Command1_Click()* event procedure:

```
Private Sub Command1_Click()
Dim wordObj As Object
    Set wordObj = CreateObject("Word.Basic")
    'The WordBasic object will come up invisible
    'by default, whereas in Word 6, it used to
    'come up visible.
    'Use .AppShow to make it visible.
    wordObj.AppShow
    With wordObj
        .FileNew _
        template:="C:\MSOffice\Templates\Normal.dot"
        .INSERT "This is a bold test."
        .WordLeft 3
        .WordRight 1, 1
        .Bold
        .FileSaveAs "yadda.doc"
    End With
    End Sub
```

Now press F5 to run our program, and click the Command1 button. The code we just wrote does the same thing as the WordBasic macro—*TestMacro*—that we recorded earlier.

Notice any differences in the code? The most immediate change you'll notice is the way in which arguments are passed. We'll discuss passing arguments to the WordBasic object in the next section. The point here is that using the WordBasic object from within Visual Basic is very similar to using WordBasic macros from within Word. Make a few changes in the code, and you can do most of the same things!

References

Notice that we used *CreateObject* to create the WordBasic object. We could also have used *GetObject* for essentially the same results. The code would have looked like this:

```
Set wordObj = GetObject("","Word.Basic")
```

Notice also that if Word is already running when you start your program *Create-Object* returns a reference to the running copy of Word. When you've finished using Word from your program, it will keep running because there's still another OLE Automation client, or perhaps even Word itself, holding a reference to the object that controls Word.

If Word is not running when you create your Basic object, OLE will load Word, which will initially be invisible. You'll need to use the WordBasic *AppShow* method to make Word visible, as in our *Command1_Click()* event procedure listing on page 343. Word will shut down when you set the Basic object to *Nothing* or when the object variable goes out of scope.

If multiple instances of Word are running when your VB program starts, you can't be sure which reference will be returned when you use the VBA *CreateObject* function. Consequently, you should always clean up after yourself when you use Word in a program. For instance, you should save the status of toolbars and menu items at the beginning of your program if you plan to change them somewhere in your program. Save back the original toolbar and menu statuses before your program leaves Word. Users get a little irritated when a program makes unauthorized changes to customized menus and toolbars and then doesn't clean up after itself.

As an example of such status handling, here's a Visual Basic code snippet that determines what Word toolbars are available and whether or not they're active. The information is saved in a two-dimensional array. After this code runs, you can safely make programmatic changes to the toolbars because you'll have the data you need to restore them to their original states.

```
Dim wordObj As Object
'Create a variant you'll use to store the names
'of the toolbars and an integer that represents
'whether or not each one is visible.
Dim ToolbarArray() As Variant
Dim Name As String
Dim i As Integer

    Set wordObj = CreateObject("Word.Basic")
    With wordObj
        'Enumerate through each of the toolbars.
        For i = 1 To .CountToolbars
        'Reset the toolbarArray array to be able to hold
        'another entry.
        ReDim Preserve ToolbarArray(1, i)
            'Get the name of the toolbar in the 'i' position.
            Name = .[ToolbarName$](i)
            'Assign the name of the toolbar to the array.
            ToolbarArray(0, i) = Name
            'Assign the state of the toolbar to the array.
            ToolbarArray(1, i) = Str$(.ToolbarState(Name))
        Next i

        'Uncomment this code if you want to see the names
        'of the toolbars pop up in a message box.
        'For i = 1 To .CountToolbars
        '    MsgBox (ToolbarArray(0, i))
        'Next i
End With
```

Using the *WordBasic* Object Library

Microsoft has created an object (type) library for the WordBasic object that you'll find on the companion CD. Recall from Chapter 6 that a type library provides descriptions of and online Help for an object and that a type library enables VB to correct your programming syntax automatically. We'll use the *WordBasic* object library throughout this chapter, so make sure you add it to any VB projects you develop.

The principal change you'll see in the rest of the code samples in this chapter is the use of the declaration

```
Dim wordObj As WordBasic
```

instead of the declaration

```
Dim wordObj As Object
```

You'll also see some speed benefits from using the WordBasic type library, but apart from the declaration line difference, the code will be basically the same. The Microsoft WordBasic 95 Type Library is included on the companion CD in \TypeLib\wb70en32.tlb. See Chapter 6 if you need to review adding a reference to an object library to your VB projects.

WordBasic Methods

You can access about 900 methods that correspond to WordBasic functions through the WordBasic object. The methods deal with these categories of activity:

- Word processing—document creation, text manipulation, and text formatting
- Word-based solution building—Word forms, mail merge, and integration with other applications
- Word environment control—menu items and toolbars
- Data manipulation—string and date and time formatting

All of the WordBasic methods fall into categories. These categories are contained in four functional areas, as shown in the following lists.

Word processing Bookmarks, borders and frames, bullets and numbering, character formatting, documents, and templates; add-ins, drawing, editing, finding and replacing, footnotes, endnotes and annotations; moving the insertion point and selecting; outlining and master documents; paragraph formatting, section and document formatting, style formatting, and tables

Solution building Application control, DDE, forms, mail merge, and OLE

Environment control AutoCorrect, AutoText, customization, environment, fields, Help, macros, proofing, tools, viewing, and windows

Data manipulation Date and time, disk access and management, and strings and numbers

Some WordBasic statements and functions that are not accessible from Visual Basic—but that mostly have Visual Basic equivalents—include control structures such as *If . . . Then . . . Else*, declarations (*Dim*), statements associated with custom dialog boxes, the *FileExit* statement, and statements or functions that require array variables as arguments.

Here's a partial list of methods that are not exposed through the WordBasic object. (You can access equivalents to most of these methods from Visual Basic itself.)

File I/O *Close*, *Line Input*, *Name*, *Open*, *Print*, *Read*, and *Write*

Branching and looping *Call*, *For . . . Next*, *Goto*, *If . . . Then . . . Else*, *On Error*, *Select Case*, *Stop*, and *While . . . Wend*

Definitions, declarations, and assignments *Declare*, *Dim*, *Function . . . End Function*, *Let*, *Redim*, *Rem*, *Sub . . . End Sub*, *Err*, and *Error*

Dialog boxes *Begin Dialog . . . End Dialog*, *Dialog*, and *GetCurValues*

Proofing *ToolsGetSpelling* and *ToolsGetSynonyms*

Cross-Reference Refer to the "Language Summary" section of the *Microsoft Word Developer's Kit*, on which the list of methods above is based. See WordBasic Help for more information on WordBasic methods.

Named Arguments

In WordBasic, you use named arguments to pass arguments into a method. A *named argument* is an argument whose value is associated with a name (rather than with a position)—brilliant definition, we know, but it's true! For example, the following statement in WordBasic finds the first occurrence of the words "Visual Basic" in a document:

```
EditFind .Find = "Visual Basic"
```

The argument is "named" because the argument "Visual Basic" is prefaced by the argument name—.Find. (See Figure 12-4.) If you use named arguments, you don't have to worry about the position in which you pass an argument into a method.

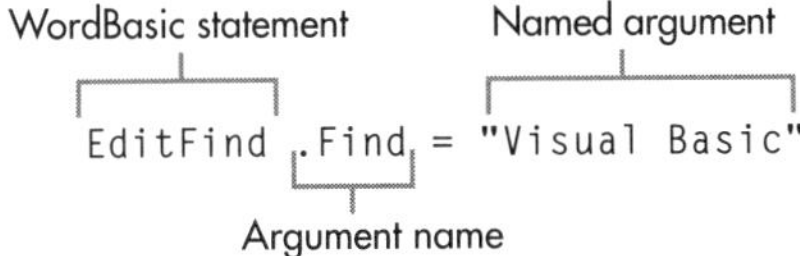

Figure 12-4. *Passing a named argument into a method.*

Remember from Chapter 2 that named arguments are syntactically a little different in VBA. For example, to call the WordBasic *EditFind* function from Visual Basic and find the word "Sabaki," you'd type the following:

```
wordObj.EditFind Name:="Sabaki"
```

You don't put a period before the argument name, and you follow the argument name directly with a colon and an equal sign and then the argument value.

Positional Arguments

You can also pass unnamed arguments from Visual Basic into WordBasic methods. From Visual Basic, you can leave the name off the arguments you pass into a WordBasic method if you pass the arguments in the order in which the WordBasic method is expecting them. An unnamed argument is called a *positional argument.*

To use a positional argument, you must first determine which arguments the method is expecting and in what order it is expecting them. You can find out by checking the WordBasic reference section in Help.

Here are the arguments for *EditFind* as they're listed in the WordBasic reference section in Help:

```
EditFind [.Find = text] [, .Replace = text] [, .Direction = number]
[, .WholeWord = number] [, .MatchCase = number] [, .PatternMatch =
number] [, .SoundsLike = number] [, .FindAllWordForms = number]
[, .Format = number] [, .Wrap = number]
```

To call *EditFind* using positional arguments, you pass the arguments in the expected order, using commas for the arguments you want to leave out. In the case we've been looking at, you'd use

```
wordObj.EditFind "Visual Basic", , , , , , , , ,
```

You can omit trailing commas, and since the only argument used in our example (.Find) is in the first position, you can rewrite the statement to say

```
wordObj.EditFind "Visual Basic"
```

Previous versions of Visual Basic didn't support named arguments, so you had to pass positional arguments into WordBasic methods. Now that Visual Basic supports named arguments, positional arguments will be used far less in programming Word from Visual Basic—keeping track of the commas that separate positional arguments can be hard.

Command Buttons

Some Word commands have corresponding WordBasic functions with which you can simulate making selections in a dialog box. For example, you use the *ToolsMacro* method to run a macro in WordBasic. The *ToolsMacro* method corresponds to the Macro dialog that comes up when a Word user selects Tools-Macro. (Figure 12-5 shows the Macro dialog box again.)

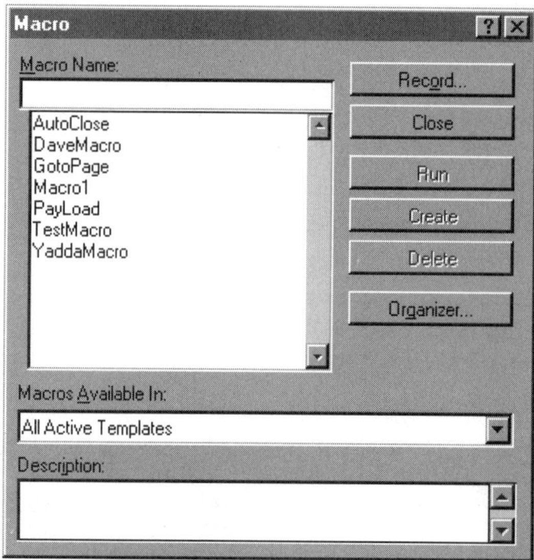

Figure 12-5. *The Microsoft Word Macro dialog box.*

You use the *ToolsMacro* method to get your program or macro to simulate pushing a command button in the Word Macro dialog. Take a look at the description of the *ToolsMacro* method in Word Help:

```
ToolsMacro .Name = text [, .Run] [, .Edit] [, .Show = number]
[, .Delete] [, .Rename] [, .Description = text] [, .NewName = text]
[, .SetDesc]
```

Notice that the second, third, fourth, and fifth arguments represent buttons on the dialog box. (The fourth argument, .Show, corresponds to the Macros Available In: dropdown.) To simulate using the dialog box, include one of these

ToolsMacro arguments in your WordBasic statement. For example, the following WordBasic statement uses the *ToolsMacro* method to run a macro called *CountOpenWindows*:

```
ToolsMacro .Name = "CountOpenWindows", .Run, .Show = 0, .Description
= "", .NewName = ""
```

We include .Run as a parameter because we want to simulate clicking the Run button in the Macro dialog. We could also leave off the empty arguments:

```
ToolsMacro .Name = "CountOpenWindows", .Run
```

If we wanted to simulate editing the *CountOpenWindows* macro instead of running it, we would write the following statement:

```
ToolsMacro .Name = "CountOpenWindows", .Edit
```

Notice that all we're doing is including a named parameter—.Run or .Edit—to represent the button we want to simulate clicking.

We'd use the following VBA code to accomplish the same thing:

```
wordObj.ToolsMacro Name:="CountOpenWindows", Run:=True
```

Notice that we used a Boolean value—*True* or *False*—in the position in which the command button argument would have been in WordBasic. A *True* value is equivalent to choosing a command button, and *False* is equivalent to not choosing it. Omitting a command button argument is equivalent to giving it a value of *False*.

What if we wanted to select a different button—say, the Edit button? Once again, we'd just use named arguments to set the Edit value to *True*:

```
wordObj.ToolsMacro Name:="CountOpenWindows", Edit:=True
```

NOTE If the macro you run with *ToolsMacro* opens a dialog box for some reason, you'll get an OLE Automation error unless Word is the active application. To make Word the active application before running WordBasic macros, use the *AppActivate* method.

The *CurValues* Method

Often you'll want your program to get return values from WordBasic methods. Some of the WordBasic methods will return values to your program, but others will only display information in dialog boxes. The *CurValues* method allows your program to get at the information that shows up in dialog boxes.

To use the *CurValues* method, you must call the method from *CurValues* that corresponds to the dialog for which you need information for your program. This information would normally be displayed only in a dialog box, but when you use the *CurValues* method Word will store the information in internal variables. You can then pull the information in the variables into a previously declared object. For example, the Word Help listing for the *ToolsWordCount* statement that corresponds to the Word Count dialog describes the Pages, Words, Characters, Paragraphs, and Lines variables:

```
ToolsWordCount [.CountFootnotes = number] [, .Pages = text]
[, .Words = text] [, .Characters = text] [, .Paragraphs = text]
[, .Lines = text]
```

Once you've declared a WordBasic object and called the *ToolsWordCount* dialog method, the values in these variables are accessible to your program.

Let's look at an example. The Tools-Word Count menu selection, as we've observed, results in a count of the number of pages, words, characters, paragraphs, and lines in a document or a selected section of a document and lists the results in a dialog box. WordBasic doesn't have a function that returns values for these variables to a VB program, so we have to use the *CurValues* method along with the *ToolsWordCount* method to get the information back to our VB program. The following code gets all of the information about the current paragraph in a Word document and displays that information in a Visual Basic message box:

```
Dim wordObj As WordBasic
Dim wordCount As Object

    Set wordObj = CreateObject("Word.Basic")
    With wordObj

        .ParaUp 1               'Go to beginning of paragraph
        .ParaDown 1, 1          'Select to end of paragraph

        'Count the pages, paragraphs, lines, words, and
        'characters in the selected paragraph, including
        'those found in the footnotes.
        'Call the ToolsWordCount method here to set the
        'CountFootnotes argument to True.
        .ToolsWordCount CountFootnotes:=True

        'Now call ToolsWordCount with CurValues to return
        'the information to the object variable.
        Set wordCount = .CurValues.ToolsWordCount
    End With
```

```
'You can access the internal variables for the
'ToolsWordCount dialog box.
'       .Pages
'       .Paragraphs
'       .Lines
'       .Words
'       .Characters
MsgBox "Pages:  " & wordCount.Pages & vbCrLf _
& "Paragraphs:  " & wordCount.Paragraphs & vbCr _
& "Lines:  " & wordCount.Lines & vbCrLf _
& "Words:  " & wordCount.Words & vbCrLf _
& "Characters:  " & wordCount.Characters
```

Quitting Word

To quit Word from a Visual Basic program, you have to let the Word object instance go out of scope or explicitly set the object variable to *Nothing*. Unlike Excel and the *Application.Quit* method, Word doesn't allow Visual Basic to access the *FileExit* WordBasic method so that errant programs won't be able to close Word when other programs or users are using Word.

If you accidentally allow your VB program's Word object instance to go out of scope, the Word document you are manipulating will close without asking the program (and consequently the user) to save work done on the document since the last save. Very impolite. One way to avoid being rude is to declare the Word object globally so that you must explicitly set the variable to *Nothing* or terminate your program to release your reference to Word's Basic object.

Embedded Objects

In Chapter 7 we looked at using in-place OLE objects in our VB4 programs. Now let's see how to embed a Word object in a VB4 application.

You can embed a Word object such as a Word document in your VB application by means of the Visual Basic OLE container control. You use the VB Object property to access the Word document and to use WordBasic statements and functions to manipulate the document object from your VB program.

We start out by dropping an OLE container control object on a VB form. (See Figure 12-6 on the next page.) Then we embed a Word document in the container and size the container.

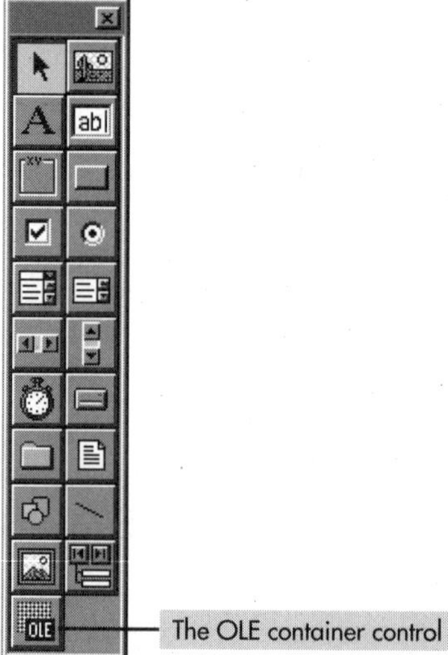

Figure 12-6. *The OLE container control on the VB toolbar. Use this control to embed OLE objects in your VB application.*

Next, we globally declare the wordObj variable as we normally would in a VB project. We then set that variable equal to the name of the OLE control in which the Word object will be embedded. For example, we could use the following code to access a document embedded in an OLE control called oleWordObj:

```
Public wordObj As WordBasic
Set wordObj = oleWordObj.Object.Application.WordBasic
```

The embedded object must be activated before it can be accessed by a VB program. We use the *DoVerb* method to activate an OLE control, as in

```
oleWordObj.DoVerb
```

The following code accesses a WordBasic object embedded in an OLE container through a command button on the form. Then it performs some simple WordBasic tasks. The *Command1.SetFocus* instruction deactivates the embedded Word object and returns the focus to the button on the form:

```
Dim wordObj As WordBasic
:
:
Private Sub Command1_Click()
    oleWordObj.DoVerb
    Set wordObj = oleWordObj.Object.Application.WordBasic
    wordObj.Insert "This is a very important document!"
    wordObj.EditSelectAll
```

```
    wordObj.Bold
    Command1.SetFocus
End Sub
```

See Chapter 7 for more information on using OLE container controls.

WordBasic Examples

Let's go through a couple of examples of manipulating the WordBasic object. You might find some of these code snippets useful as you write your programs. The first snippet finds each of the bookmarks in the current Word document and displays each bookmark's contents in a message box. Notice that we enclosed the *BookmarkName$* function in brackets. In certain circumstances, a Visual Basic program will fail if you don't include these brackets. You should get in the habit of using brackets to enclose the names of WordBasic functions that return strings—that is, whose function names end in a dollar sign ($).

Cross-Reference See VBA Language Concepts: Qualified Identifiers: Square Brackets

```
Dim wordObj as WordBasic
:
Set wordObj = CreateObject("Word.Basic")
Dim count as Integer
With wordObj
    For count = 1 To .CountBookmarks()
        MsgBox (.[BookmarkName$](count))
    Next count
End With
```

The following code changes the mouse pointer to an hourglass before creating the WordBasic object, and then changes the mouse pointer back to normal. If we don't set the pointer to an hourglass, the user won't have an indication that something is actually happening in the background and might just give our program the three-finger salute!

```
Dim wordObj As WordBasic
:
Screen.MousePointer = vbHourglass
Set wordObj = CreateObject("Word.Basic")
Screen.MousePointer = vbDefault
```

What if we want the user to see what's going on? The next code snippet uses the VB *AppActivate* statement to activate Word so that the user sees what's happening in Word while the VB program is running. The VB program then inserts text and pictures into a new Word document and formats them. Next, Visual Basic calls the VB *DoEvents* function to temporarily give control back to Windows to allow Word to take care of any events that are waiting. Finally, Visual Basic returns focus to Form1 using the *SetFocus* command.

```
Dim wordObj As WordBasic
:
Screen.MousePointer = vbHourglass
Set wordObj = CreateObject("Word.Basic")
AppActivate "Microsoft Word"
With wordObj
    .FileNewDefault
    .StartOfDocument
    .INSERT "This is "
    .Bold
    .INSERT "bold"
    .Bold
    .INSERT " and this is "
    .Underline
    .INSERT "underlined"
    .Underline
    .INSERT "."
    .InsertPara
    .InsertPara
    .RightPara
    .INSERT "And this is right aligned."
    .InsertPara
    .InsertPara
    .InsertPara
    .LeftPara
    'Insert the location of a metafile on your hard drive.
    .InsertPicture _
    "C:\Program Files\Microsoft Visual Basic\metafile\business\phone.wmf"
End With
DoEvents
Form1.SetFocus
Screen.MousePointer = vbDefault
```

In this code, we toggle on and off the blue screen option, which is available in Word on the General tab of the Options dialog. Select Tools-Options to open the dialog. Notice that we use the *Select Case* statement on the current BlueScreen value (*0* or *1*) and then toggle that value:

```
Dim wordObj As WordBasic
Dim dialogObj As Object
:
:
Set wordObj = CreateObject("Word.Basic")
With wordObj
    Set dialogObj = .CurValues.ToolsOptionsGeneral
    Select Case dialogObj.BlueScreen
        Case 0
            .ToolsOptionsGeneral , , , 1
        Case 1
            .ToolsOptionsGeneral , , , 0
    End Select
End With
```

Sample: *LetterMaker*

You'll never guess what the *LetterMaker* sample program does. That's right, it enables a user to put all of the information for a letter into one VB form and select a style, and then *LetterMaker* generates a letter—using Word, of course—and enables the user to save it. If you want to play with *LetterMaker*, just copy the code from the \Chapter12\LetterMaker directory onto your disk.

If you want to create the *LetterMaker* program from scratch, here's how to do it.

1. Create a VB form that looks like the one shown in Figure 12-7.

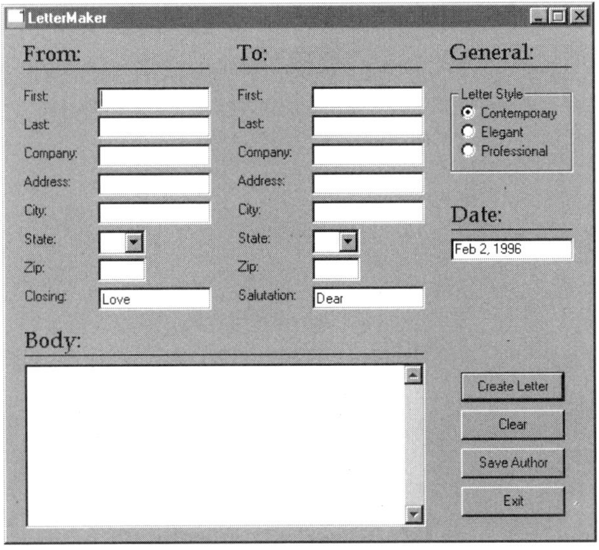

Figure 12-7. *frmLetterMaker, the main Visual Basic form for* LetterMaker.

The frmLetterMaker form uses the clsLetterMaker object, to do most of the work. If you saved clsLetterMaker as an OLE Automation server, you could actually create an application in another VBA application—say, Microsoft Excel—to perform the same functions as *LetterMaker*.

If your form looks like the one shown in Figure 12-7, it contains the controls shown in the table below.

Control Type	Control Names
Button	cmdCreateLetter, cmdClear, cmdSaveAuthor, cmdExit
ComboBox Array (2)	cmbState
CommonDialog	comDlg
OptionButton Array (3)	optTemplate
TextBox	txtClosing, txtSalutation, txtDate, txtBody
Two-Dimensional TextBox Array	txtFirstName, txtLastName, txtCompany, txtAddress, txtCity, txtZip

2. The list above doesn't show the control labels because they're not used in the code. Take a look at the form, and set the control labels however you want.
3. The code for each module for *LetterMaker*—containing two classes and one form—is listed below. Type in the code, and go for it! The code has lots of comments. Look them over and make sure you understand what's going on.

frmLetterMaker

```
Option Explicit
Private m_strFileName
Private m_Person(1) As clsPerson

Private m_Letter As clsLetterMaker
Public SaveFlag As Boolean
Dim AUTHOR As Integer
Dim RECIPIENT As Integer
Dim AuthorChanged As Integer

Private Sub Form_Load()

    'Initialize flags.
```

```
    AUTHOR = 0
    RECIPIENT = 1

    'Initialize variables.
    InitVariables

    'Uncomment TempInit to automatically fill in a
    'set of default information items. You can also
    'press Ctrl-Z when the form first loads.
    'TempInit

    Set m_Person(0) = New clsPerson
    Set m_Person(1) = New clsPerson
    Set m_Letter = New clsLetterMaker

End Sub

Private Sub Form_Unload(Cancel As Integer
    QuerySaveAuthor
End Sub

Private Sub txtAddress_Change(Index As Integer)
    If Index = 0 Then AuthorChanged = True
End Sub

Private Sub txtCity_Change(Index As Integer)
    If Index = 0 Then AuthorChanged = True
End Sub

Private Sub txtCompany_Change(Index As Integer)
    If Index = 0 Then AuthorChanged = True
End Sub

Private Sub txtFirstName_Change(Index As Integer)
    If Index = 0 Then AuthorChanged = True
End Sub

Private Sub txtFirstName_KeyDown(Index As Integer, KeyCode As Integer, _
                                Shift As Integer)
    'If the user presses Ctrl-Z, call TempInit to fill
    'in sample information.
    If (KeyCode = vbKeyZ) And (Shift And vbCtrlMask) Then TempInit
End Sub

Private Sub txtLastName_Change(Index As Integer)
    If Index = 0 Then AuthorChanged = True
```

(continued)

```
End Sub

Private Sub txtZip_Change(Index As Integer)
    If Index = 0 Then AuthorChanged = True
End Sub

Private Sub cmdSaveAuthor_Click()
    SaveAuthorInformation
    AuthorChanged = False
End Sub

Private Sub cmdExit_Click()
    Unload Me
End Sub

Private Sub cmdCreateLetter_Click()
Dim i As Integer
    If Not CheckFields Then Exit Sub
    Screen.MousePointer = vbHourglass
    If optTemplate(0) Then
        m_Letter.LetterTemplate = "Contemporary"
    ElseIf optTemplate(1) Then
        m_Letter.LetterTemplate = "Elegant"
    ElseIf optTemplate(2) Then
        m_Letter.LetterTemplate = "Professional"
    Else
        MsgBox "Please select a template.", vbExclamation
        Exit Sub
    End If

    'Fill in author and recipient information.
    For i = AUTHOR To RECIPIENT
        With m_Person(i)
            .FirstName = txtFirstName(i).Text
            .LastName = txtLastName(i).Text
            .Company = txtCompany(i).Text
            .Address = txtAddress(i).Text
            .City = txtCity(i).Text
            .State = cmbState(i).Text
            .Zip = txtZip(i).Text
        End With
    Next i

    'Set the properties of the m_Letter object.
    With m_Letter
        Set .LetterTo = m_Person(RECIPIENT)
        Set .LetterFrom = m_Person(AUTHOR)
```

```
        .LetterDate = txtDate.Text
        .LetterClosing = txtClosing.Text
        .LetterSalutation = txtSalutation.Text
        .LetterBody = txtBody.Text
        .CreateLetter
    End With

    'Grab focus back from the Word object.
    frmLetterMaker.SetFocus

    'Display dialog box that asks the user if he/she
    'wants to save the letter.

    Dim Msg As String, Title As String
    Dim Style As Integer
    'Define message.
    Msg = "Do you want to save the letter?"
    'Define buttons.
    Style = vbYesNo Or vbInformation Or vbDefaultButton2
    'Define title.
    Title = "Save Letter"
    If vbYes = MsgBox(Msg, Style, Title, 0, 0) Then     'User chose Yes.
        SaveIt
    Else                                                'User chose No.
        m_Letter.CloseDoc
    End If
        Screen.MousePointer = vbDefault

End Sub

Private Sub cmdClear_Click()
    QuerySaveAuthor
    ClearFields
    InitVariables
    Caption = "LetterMaker"
    SaveFlag = False
End Sub

Private Sub cmbState_Change(Index As Integer)
    If Index = 0 Then AuthorChanged = True
End Sub

Sub TempInit()
        txtFirstName(RECIPIENT).Text = "Nan"
        txtLastName(RECIPIENT).Text = "McCulloch"
        txtCompany(RECIPIENT).Text = "MomCo."
        txtAddress(RECIPIENT).Text = "31 Waterwood"
```

(continued)

```
        txtCity(RECIPIENT).Text = "Huntsville"
        cmbState(RECIPIENT).Text = "TX"
        txtZip(RECIPIENT).Text = "77340"

        txtFirstName(AUTHOR).Text = "Benjamin"
        txtLastName(AUTHOR).Text = "Dehlin"
        txtCompany(AUTHOR).Text = "BubbaJack Inc."
        txtAddress(AUTHOR).Text = "12843 NE 91st"
        txtCity(AUTHOR).Text = "Kirkland"
        cmbState(AUTHOR).Text = "WA"
        txtZip(AUTHOR).Text = "98033"

        txtBody.Text = "This is some sample text." & _
             " This is some sample text." & _
             " This is some sample text." & _
             " This is some sample text."
End Sub

Private Sub InitVariables()
Dim AuthorInformation As Variant
Dim i As Integer

    txtSalutation.Text = "Dear"
    txtClosing.Text = "Love"
    txtDate.Text = Format$(Now, "mmm dd, yyyy")
    optTemplate(0).Value = True
    If Len(GetSetting(appname:=App.Title, section:="AuthorInformation", _
                   Key:="LastName")) Then
        AuthorInformation = GetAllSettings(_
                             appname:=App.Title, section:="AuthorInformation")
        For i = 0 To 6

            Select Case AuthorInformation(i, 0)
                Case "FirstName"
                    txtFirstName(AUTHOR).Text = AuthorInformation(i, 1)
                Case "LastName"
                    txtLastName(AUTHOR).Text = AuthorInformation(i, 1)
                Case "Company"
                    txtCompany(AUTHOR).Text = AuthorInformation(i, 1)
                Case "Address"
                    txtAddress(AUTHOR).Text = AuthorInformation(i, 1)
                Case "ZipCode"
                    txtZip(AUTHOR).Text = AuthorInformation(i, 1)
                Case "City"
                    txtCity(AUTHOR).Text = AuthorInformation(i, 1)
                Case "State"
                    cmbState(AUTHOR).Text = AuthorInformation(i, 1)
            End Select
```

```
        Next i
    End If
    AuthorChanged = False
End Sub

Private Function SaveIt()
Dim tmpFileName As String
    On Error Resume Next
    m_strFileName = "Letter.doc"
    tmpFileName = m_strFileName
    With ComDlg
        'Provide an initial value for the file name.
        .filename = m_strFileName
        'These flags do the following:
        '1) cdlOFNPathMustExist--return file path exists.
        '2) cdlOFNOverwritePrompt--prompt for file overwrite.
        '3) cdlOFNNoReadOnlyReturn--file returned is writable.
        '4) cdlOFNHideReadOnly--no ReadOnly check box on dialog.
        .Flags = cdlOFNPathMustExist Or cdlOFNOverwritePrompt Or _
                 cdlOFNNoReadOnlyReturn Or cdlOFNHideReadOnly
        'CancelError property is true for ComDlg. This makes
        'ShowSave raise an error if no file was selected.
        .ShowSave
        If Err Then
            Exit Function
        Else
            m_Letter.SaveFile .filename
            frmLetterMaker.Caption = frmLetterMaker.Caption & _
                                     " - " & .filename
        End If
    End With
End Function

Sub SaveAuthorInformation()

Dim control As control

    'Cycle through all of the author information controls
    'and then Gosub to the RegisterStuff routine.
    Set control = txtLastName(0)
    Gosub RegisterStuff

    Set control = txtFirstName(0)
    Gosub RegisterStuff

    Set control = txtCompany(0)
    Gosub RegisterStuff
```

(continued)

```
    Set control = txtAddress(0)
    Gosub RegisterStuff

    Set control = txtCity(0)
    Gosub RegisterStuff

    Set control = cmbState(0)
    Gosub RegisterStuff

    Set control = txtZip(0)
    Gosub RegisterStuff

    Exit Sub

RegisterStuff:

            'Save the author information to the registry.
            'Example:
            '    [App name is:]
            '    LetterMaker
            '        [Pull key name from tag of each control.
            '        Pull value from control.text:]
            '        FirstName   = "Jonathon"
            '        LastName    = "Dehlin"
            '        Company     = "Kids Inc."
            '        Address     = "12843 NE 91st"
            '        City        = "Kirkland"
            '        State       = "WA"
            '        ZipCode     = "98033"

            SaveSetting appname:=App.Title, _
                         section:="AuthorInformation", _
                         Key:=control.Tag, _
                         Setting:=control.Text
            Return
End Sub

Sub QuerySaveAuthor()
Dim Msg As String, Title As String
Dim Style As Integer
    If AuthorChanged Then
        'Define message.
        Msg = "Would you like to save the author information?"
        Style = vbYesNo Or vbQuestion Or vbDefaultButton2   'Define buttons.
        Title = "Save Author?"                              'Define title.
        If vbYes = MsgBox(Msg, Style, Title) Then     'User chose Yes.
```

```
            SaveAuthorInformation     'Save author information to registry.
        End If
    End If
    'The user has either requested that we save the author
    'information or has decidedly not done it; so we can
    'reset the AuthorChanged flag to False.
    AuthorChanged = False
End Sub

Private Function CheckFields()

'Check to see if the fields in the form have been filled in.

Dim i As Integer
Dim strMsg As String

'We'll use this control as a variable to check the .text
'values of different text boxes.
Dim control As control

Dim WhichPerson(1) As String

    WhichPerson(0) = "author's"
    WhichPerson(1) = "recipient's"

    For i = AUTHOR To RECIPIENT

        Set control = txtFirstName(i)
        strMsg = "Please enter the " & WhichPerson(i) & " first name."
        Gosub CheckControl

        Set control = txtLastName(i)
        strMsg = "Please enter the " & WhichPerson(i) & " last name."
        Gosub CheckControl

        Set control = txtAddress(i)
        strMsg = "Please enter the " & WhichPerson(i) & " address."
        Gosub CheckControl

        Set control = txtCity(i)
        strMsg = "Please enter the " & WhichPerson(i) & " city."
        Gosub CheckControl

        Set control = cmbState(i)
        strMsg = "Please enter the " & WhichPerson(i) & " state."
        Gosub CheckControl
```

(continued)

```
        Set control = txtZip(i)
        strMsg = "Please enter the " & WhichPerson(i) & " zip code."
        Gosub CheckControl

    Next i

    Set control = txtClosing
    strMsg = "Please enter a closing (such as 'Sincerely,')."
    Gosub CheckControl

    Set control = txtSalutation
    strMsg = "Please enter a salutation (such as 'Dear')."
    Gosub CheckControl

    Set control = txtBody
    strMsg = "Please enter the body of your letter."
    Gosub CheckControl

    CheckFields = True
    Exit Function

CheckControl:
    With control
        'If the text property of this control is empty,
        'pop up a message box and then exit the function.
        If Len(.Text) = 0 Then
            MsgBox strMsg, vbExclamation
            .SetFocus
            CheckFields = False
            Exit Function
        End If
    End With
    Return
End Function

Private Sub ClearFields()
Dim control As control
    'This will clear the Text property of all controls that
    'have a text property (TextBox and ComboBox controls).
    On Error Resume Next
    For Each control In Controls
        control.Text = vbNullString
    Next
End Sub
```

clsLetterMaker

```
Option Explicit
Private m_WordObj As WordBasic
Public LetterTo As clsPerson
Public LetterFrom As clsPerson
Public LetterDate As String
Public LetterClosing As String
Public LetterSalutation As String
Public LetterTemplate As String
Public LetterBody As String

Public Sub CloseDoc()

    'The DocClose WordBasic method closes the current Word document.

    '   DocClose [Save]

    '   Save              Determines whether or not to save the document.

    '   0 or omitted      Prompts the user to save if changes have been
    '                     made in the document since the last time
    '                     it was saved.
    '   1                 Saves the document without prompting before
    '                     closing it.
    '   2                 Closes the window but does not save the document.

    '   The Save argument also controls whether a prompt appears if
    '   the document has a routing slip. A prompt appears if Save is
    '   0 (zero) or omitted; otherwise, the document is closed without
    '   being routed.

    m_WordObj.DocClose 2

End Sub

Public Function CreateLetter()

    Dim templateDir As String

    'This line will make Word active so that you can see what's going on.
    m_WordObj.AppShow
    AppActivate "Microsoft Word"

    'We're going to perform several steps on the Word object,
    'so we use a With here.
    With m_WordObj
```

(continued)

```
'Get the directory in which the Office for Windows 95
'templates are stored.
templateDir = .[GetPrivateProfileString$] _
("HKEY_CURRENT_USER\Software\Microsoft\MicrosoftOffice\95\FileNew\LocalTemplates", "", ""
'Use the FileNew method in Word to create a new file
'based on the template stored in LetterTemplate. In
'this app, the choices are Contemporary, Elegant, and
'Professional because those letter templates come with
'Word for Windows 95.

'Method Definition
'FileNew [.Template = text] [, .NewTemplate = number]

'   Creates a new document or template based on the
'   template you specify, or runs a wizard. The arguments
'   for the FileNew statement correspond to the options
'   in the New dialog box (File menu).

'Argument Explanation
'   .Template       The name of the template or document on
'                   which to base the new document or template,
'                   or the name of the wizard to run.
'   .NewTemplate    Specifies whether to create a new document
'                   or a new template.
'   0 or omitted    Create a new document.
'   1               Create a new template.

.FileNew Template:=templateDir & "\Letters & Faxes\" & _
                   LetterTemplate & " Letter.dot"

'Go to the beginning of the document.
.StartOfDocument

'Use EditFindStyle and EditFind methods to find the first
'occurrence of a word that has the style Return Address.

'Method Definition
'EditFindStyle .Style = TEXT

'   When followed by an EditFind or EditReplace instruction
'   in which .Format is set to 1, specifies the style of the
'   text you want to find. If the specified style does not
'   exist in the active document, or if the capitalization
'   does not match that of the actual style name, an error
'   occurs.
```

```
'Argument Explanation
'   .Style  The name of the style you want to find; to remove
'           a style from the specification, use an empty string ("").

'Method Definition
'EditFind [.Find = text] [, .Replace = text] [, .Direction = number]
'[, .WholeWord = number] [, .MatchCase = number] [, .PatternMatch =
'number] [, .SoundsLike = number] [, .FindAllWordForms = number]
'[, .SoundsLike = number] [, .FindAllWordForms = number]
'[, .Format = 'number] [, .Wrap = number]

'   Finds the next instance of the specified text, formatting,
'   or both. The arguments for the EditFind statement correspond
'   to the options in the Find dialog box (Edit menu). Used in a
'   While...Wend loop, EditFind can be extremely useful when
'   you need to repeat a series of instructions each time a
'   certain piece of text or formatting is found in your document.
'   Many examples in WordBasic Help illustrate this common use of
'   EditFind.

.EditFindStyle "Return Address"
.EditFind Find:=""

'Use the LineDown WordBasic method to select the entire line.

'Method Definition
'LineDown([Count] [, Select])

'   The LineDown statement moves down the insertion point or
'   the active end of the selection (the end that moves when
'   you press Shift+down arrow) by the specified number of lines.

'Argument Explanation
'   Count   The number of lines to move down; if omitted, 1 is
'           assumed. Negative values move up the insertion point
'           or the active end of the selection.
'   Select  Specifies whether to select text: 0 (zero) or omitted,
'           text is not selected. If there is already a selection,
'           LineDown moves the insertion point Count lines below
'           the selection.
'   Nonzero Text is selected. If there is already a selection,
'           LineDown moves the active end of the selection toward
'           the end of the document. In a typical selection made
'           from left to right, where the active end of the selection
'           is closer to the end of the document, LineDown extends
'           the selection. In a selection made from right to left,
'           LineDown shrinks the selection.
```

(continued)

```
'Return Values

'   VALUE Explanation
'   0 (zero)    The insertion point or the active end of the
'               selection can't be moved down.
'   -1          The insertion point or the active end of the
'               selection is moved down by any number of lines,
'               even if less than Count. For example, LineDown(10)
'               returns -1 even if the insertion point is only
'               three lines above the end of the document.

.LineDown 1, 1

'Use the Insert and InsertPara WordBasic methods to
'insert and format text in the new letter.

'Method Definition
'INSERT TEXT$

'   Inserts the specified text at the insertion point. You can
'   insert characters such as quotation marks, tab characters,
'   nonbreaking hyphens, and newline characters using the Chr$()
'   function with Insert. You can insert numbers by first
'   converting them to text with the Str$() function.

'Method Definition
'InsertPara

'   Inserts a paragraph mark at the insertion point.

.Insert LetterFrom.FullName
.InsertPara
.Insert LetterFrom.Address
.InsertPara
.Insert LetterFrom.Address2

'Repeat the process for information in the rest of the letter.
'Notice that we go to the start of the document each time before
'changing each style. We do this in case the styles we're using
'in a given template follow a different order. This is a little
'inefficient, but it makes our code able to handle different
'templates as they come along.

.StartOfDocument
.EditFindStyle "Date"
.EditFind ""
.Insert LetterDate
```

```
        .StartOfDocument
        .EditFindStyle "Company Name"
        .EditFind Find:=""
        If Len(LetterFrom.Company) Then
            .Insert LetterFrom.Company
        Else
            .Insert LetterFrom.FullName
        End If
        .StartOfDocument
        .EditFindStyle "Inside Address"
        .EditFind ""
        .Insert LetterTo.Company
        .InsertPara
        .Insert LetterTo.FullName
        .InsertPara
        .Insert LetterTo.Address
        .InsertPara
        .Insert LetterTo.Address2
        .StartOfDocument
        .EditFindStyle "Salutation"
        .EditFind ""
        .Insert LetterSalutation & " " & LetterTo.FirstName & ":"
        .StartOfDocument
        .EditFindStyle "Body Text"
        .EditFind ""
        .Insert LetterBody
        .StartOfDocument
        .EditFindStyle "Closing"
        .EditFind ""
        .Insert LetterClosing & ","
        .StartOfDocument
        .EditFindStyle "Signature Name"
        .EditFind ""
        .Insert LetterFrom.FullName
        .StartOfDocument
        .EditFindStyle "Signature Job Title"
        .EditFind ""
        .EditClear
    End With
End Function

Public Sub SaveFile(ByVal txtFileName As String)

    'Use the WordBasic Save File function. The argument
    'we pass in here (txtFileName) is the new file name.
    m_WordObj.FileSaveAs txtFileName
```

(continued)

```
    'Call the CloseDoc method.
    CloseDoc

End Sub

Private Sub Class_Initialize()
    'Upon object initialization, create an instance of the
    'Word object. Because we declared this object in the
    'General Declarations section, it won't go out of scope
    'until we set m_WordObj = Nothing (which we do in the
    'Terminate() event procedure).

    Set m_WordObj = CreateObject("Word.Basic")
End Sub

Private Sub Class_Terminate()
    Set m_WordObj = Nothing
End Sub
```

clsPerson

```
Option Explicit
Public LastName As String
Public FirstName As String
Public Address As String
Public City As String
Public State As String
Public Zip As String
Public Company As String

Public Property Get FullName() As String
    FullName = FirstName & " " & LastName
End Property

Public Property Get Address2() As String
    Address2 = City & ", " & State & " " & Zip
End Property
```

SUMMARY

- Use the Microsoft Word macro recorder to quickly spit out WordBasic code for functions you want to access from a Visual Basic project. You'll have to modify the code if you want to use it in Visual Basic.
- To declare a WordBasic object when your project has a reference to the *Word* type library, use the following line:

  ```
  Dim wordObj As WordBasic
  ```

- You can use either named or positional arguments when calling WordBasic methods from Visual Basic for Applications. Named arguments are usually better as they are more readable because the actual argument names are listed.
- Use *CreateObject* or *GetObject* to create a WordBasic object from Visual Basic for Applications code.
- Some methods—*ToolsMacro* is one—enable you to programmatically simulate clicking buttons in a dialog box.
- You should always record the status of Word toolbars and menus before you make changes in them because you'll need to restore them before your program ends in case Word was already open when your program started.
- Use *CurValues* to make the values from a Word dialog box accessible to a VB program.
- Use the OLE container control if you want to embed a Word object in a VB form.

13

The Point Is Power

If you've ever used a presentation package or created a multimedia application, you're going to love what you can do with Visual Basic and Microsoft PowerPoint. If you haven't, play around with PowerPoint a little before continuing with this chapter.

Introduction to PowerPoint

Remember when your Uncle Jim and Aunt Polly used to come over and show you slides of their trip to Niagara Falls? PowerPoint gives you the ability to create and show presentations just like that, only they're electronic presentations. And you can make your presentations much more exciting than Uncle Jim and Aunt Polly's were by using animation, color, pictures, and the other elements of PowerPoint presentations we'll take a look at in this chapter.

The basic unit of PowerPoint is the *slide*. You use PowerPoint to construct individual slides, and then you show the slides on your computer screen. You can choose from a variety of different kinds of objects as you construct your slides. (See Figure 13-1.)

When you string slides together, you create a *presentation* you can display to customers, business partners, students, seminar attendees, people you want to brainwash—whomever you want to communicate with.

Canned presentations are a thing of the past, however. Visual Basic and PowerPoint now enable you to programmatically customize and display your presentations. "Who cares?" you say? Well, that capability means that now you can do things such as pulling a customer name from a database and inserting it into a title slide on the fly, writing a program that automatically builds a presentation based on how much time the presenter has, and adjusting the size of a presentation window to fit into a Visual Basic multimedia application.

In this chapter, we'll look at the new classes PowerPoint exposes for your use in VB programs. After that, we'll create and modify a presentation. Finally, we'll see how to show a presentation in an exciting way.

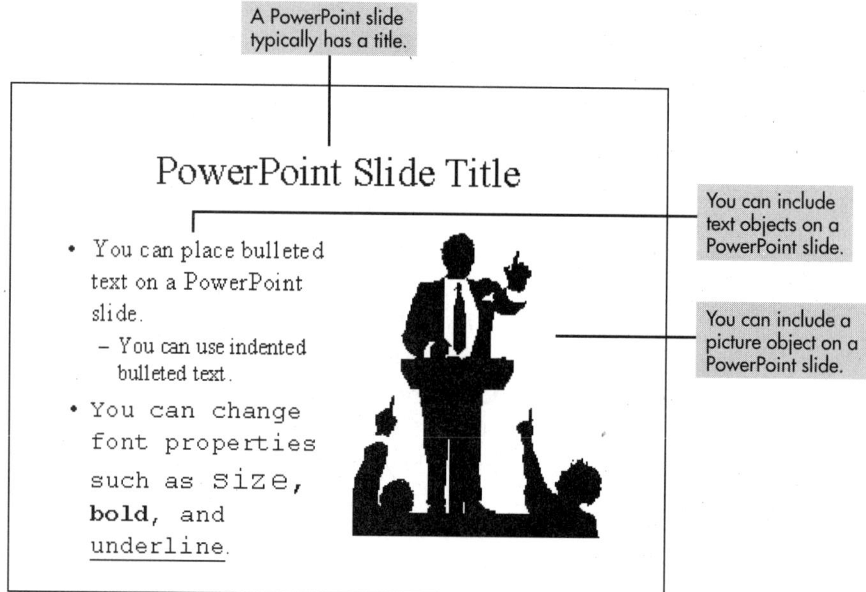

Figure 13-1. *A sample PowerPoint slide. You can include all kinds of objects—text, pictures, graphs, OLE objects, and so on—on a PowerPoint slide.*

Accessing PowerPoint Objects

PowerPoint's object model allows you to programmatically manipulate presentations, slides, and the objects you put on your slides. PowerPoint's object model is similar to Microsoft Excel's: Excel has *worksheets* that are contained in *workbooks*; in PowerPoint's object model, *slides* are contained in *presentations.*

PowerPoint exposes over 70 classes that collectively contain over 600 methods and properties. These classes make customizing presentations a breeze. Not all is bliss, however. The 1995 version of PowerPoint doesn't include Visual Basic for Applications as the 1995 version of Microsoft Excel does. To access PowerPoint classes, you'll need to use Visual Basic, Microsoft Excel, Visual C++, or some other application that will allow you to manipulate an OLE Automation server, which PowerPoint became in 1995. In this chapter, we'll explore programming PowerPoint from VB projects.

Cross-Reference Refer back to Chapter 8 for more information on Microsoft Excel's object model. And see Appendix C for a chart that shows the PowerPoint object model.

Using the PowerPoint Object Library

PowerPoint comes with a library of PowerPoint classes. Recall from Chapter 6 that an object library provides descriptions of and online Help for a group of classes and that an object library enables VBA to early-bind methods and properties to object variables and case your code as you type. We'll use the PowerPoint object library throughout this chapter, so make sure you add it to any VB projects you create.

Cross-Reference The file name of the *PowerPoint object library* is Powerpnt.Tlb. The file is in the MSOffice\PowerPnt directory of a default Microsoft Office for Windows 95 installation. See Chapter 6 for information on adding object library references to your VB projects.

PowerPoint objects are extremely easy to use. You can use them to open and modify presentations or to create completely new ones on the fly. In this section, we'll investigate declaring a Presentation object variable, making PowerPoint visible, creating the Presentation object, and opening and modifying presentations.

Declaring PowerPoint Variables

PowerPoint has a well-behaved application object: You never have to use *New* or *CreateObject* to create PowerPoint's application. You also never need to declare any variable as *PowerPoint.Application*. For example, the following code will start PowerPoint if it isn't running already and get a reference to the active presentation.

```
Dim ppPresentation As PowerPoint.Presentation
Set ppPresentation = PowerPoint.ActivePresentation
```

Making PowerPoint visible

PowerPoint will start automatically—if it isn't already running—when we reference it in our VB programs, but it will be hidden. That's OK if we don't want the user to see PowerPoint in action. Otherwise, we can make PowerPoint visible with the following statement:

```
'This statement makes PowerPoint visible.
'If PowerPoint isn't already running, this statement
'will also load PowerPoint.
PowerPoint.AppWindow.Visible = True
```

We would want PowerPoint to be visible if we wanted the user of our VB program to view the editing our program does or if we needed to have the user actually take some action by means of PowerPoint itself while our program was running. Otherwise, we can edit and display a presentation without ever making the PowerPoint application visible, as you'll see later.

Creating a Presentation Object

We've declared a PowerPoint Presentation object variable, ppPresentation. To actually use the variable in our VB program, we need to assign an object reference to it. To create a presentation object, we use a *Presentations.Add* statement in our code. *Presentations.Add* creates a new presentation and returns a reference to the new presentation. We can either cache this reference by assigning it to an object variable—in this case a hard-typed presentation object variable—or just create the presentation without maing use of the returned reference.

```
'This statement loads PowerPoint if it isn't
'already loaded, creates a new presentation,
'and assigns a reference to the presentation
'to the ppPresentation object variable.
Set ppPresentation = PowerPoint.Presentations.Add
```

This statement does the same but ignores the returned reference.

```
PowerPoint.Presentations.Add
```

Using the returned reference is a more elegant way to go because in that case we have an object variable—ppPresentation—that represents a specific PowerPoint presentation and from which we can access properties and methods directly.

Opening a Presentation

You're not always going to want to construct PowerPoint presentations from scratch. You might want to write a program that opens up an existing presentation and rearranges or selects certain slides.

To open up an existing PowerPoint presentation we use this syntax:

```
Set ppPresentation = PowerPoint.Presentations.Open([filename])
```

If PowerPoint isn't visible, we'll get an error with this line. We should use the following line instead if we want to open an existing presentation but keep the PowerPoint presentation invisible:

```
Set ppPresentation = _
    PowerPoint.Presentations.Open(FileName:=[filename], _
    WithWindow:=False)
```

Sample VB presentation program

Let's take it from the top now.

1. Put the following code into the declarations section of the code module of the default form in a new VB project:

```
Dim ppPresentation As PowerPoint.Presentation
```

2. Drag a button onto a blank VB form, and insert code into the *Command1_Click()* event procedure so that it looks like this:

```
Private Sub Command1_Click()
    'Make PowerPoint visible.
    PowerPoint.AppWindow.Visible = True
    'Add a new presentation.
    Set ppPresentation = PowerPoint.Presentations.Add
End Sub
```

3. Press F5 to start the program, and click the Command1 button. You should see PowerPoint come up with a new presentation. (If PowerPoint was already running and was minimized, it will remain minimized. You must maximize PowerPoint to see that it comes up with a new presentation.)

Now let's try opening up an existing presentation from a VB program.

1. Go into PowerPoint and manually create and save a simple PowerPoint presentation as C:\ObjProg\Chapter13\Ch13.Ppt.
2. Change this line in the code we wrote earlier

```
'Add a new presentation.
Set ppPresentation = PowerPoint.Presentations.Add
```

to say

```
'Open an existing presentation.
Set ppPresentation = _
    PowerPoint.Presentations.Open _
    ("C:\ObjProg\Chapter13\Chapter13.Ppt")
```

3. Press F5, and click the Command1 button to run the program again. This time you should see PowerPoint come up with our Chapter13.Ppt presentation.

Modifying a Presentation

In the ability to modify presentations from within VB programs lies the real power of the new PowerPoint object model. In this section, we'll discuss how to create new slides for an existing presentation, manipulate the slides, and make use of the PowerPoint Slide Master from within a VB project.

Adding a Slide to a Presentation

Once we've created or opened a presentation, we'll want to start adding slides to it. Adding a slide to a Presentation object and adding a presentation to a Presentations collection object, which we did earlier in our sample program with the statement *PowerPoint.Presentations.Add*, are similar operations.

Both kinds of classes, the Slide class and the Presentations class, have an *Add* method. The *Slide.Add* method has two input parameters. The first represents the position in the presentation in which the slide should be added. The second represents the layout of the slide.

To understand exactly what the second parameter is, let's take a look at PowerPoint itself. When you create a new slide from within PowerPoint, you see the dialog shown in Figure 13-2, which gives you a choice of AutoLayout types.

Each of the layouts in the dialog in Figure 13-2 has a corresponding AutoLayout enumeration type you can use to define a new slide programmatically.

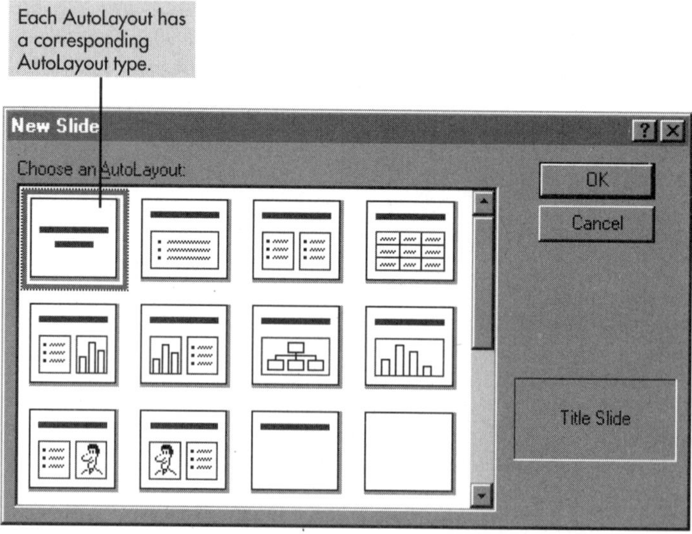

Figure 13-2. *The PowerPoint* AutoLayout *New Slide dialog box. This dialog allows you to select an AutoLayout for a new slide.*

Here are the constant values for the AutoLayout property:

ppLayoutBigObject
ppLayoutText
ppLayoutBlank
ppLayoutTextAndClipart
ppLayoutClipartAndText
ppLayoutTextAndGraph
ppLayoutClipartAndVerticalText
ppLayoutTextAndMediaClip
ppLayoutFourObjects
ppLayoutTextAndObject
ppLayoutGraph
ppLayoutTextAndTwoObjects
ppLayoutGraphAndText
ppLayoutTextOverObject
ppLayoutMediaClipAndText
ppLayoutTitle
ppLayoutMixed
ppLayoutTitleOnly
ppLayoutObject
ppLayoutTwoColumnText
ppLayoutObjectAndText
ppLayoutTwoObjectsAndText
ppLayoutObjectOverText
ppLayoutTwoObjectsOverText
ppLayoutOrgchart
ppLayoutVerticalText
ppLayoutTable
ppLayoutVerticalTitleAndText
ppLayoutVerticalTitleAndTextOverGraph

The AutoLayout constants are self-explanatory. For example, ppLayoutTitle creates a slide with only a title on it, ppLayoutBlank creates a slide with nothing on it, and ppTwoObjectsOverText creates a slide containing two OLE objects positioned side by side above a text object.

The syntax for creating a new slide would be as follows:

```
Dim ppSlide As PowerPoint.Slide
:
Set ppSlide = _
    ppPresentation.Slides.Add([PositionNumber],[Slide Type])
```

To insert a slide in a specific position, we'd use this code:

```
Dim ppSlide As PowerPoint.Slide
:
'Insert a new slide in the third position in the
'presentation. The slide will have a place automatically
'set aside for one OLE object.
Set ppSlide = ppPresentation.Slides.Add(3, ppLayoutObject)
```

Then we could use the ppSlide object variable to refer to the third slide in ppPresentation.

Let's try some real code. In the last section, we saw how to create a new presentation or open an existing one. Let's add a slide to a presentation.

1. Insert the following code into the declarations section of the code module of the default form in a new Visual Basic project (or add the second line below to the declaration code we wrote previously):

```
Dim ppPresentation As PowerPoint.Presentation
Dim ppSlide As PowerPoint.Slide
```

2. Insert a button into a blank form, and insert code into the *Command1_Click()* event procedure so that it looks like this:

```
Private Sub Command1_Click()
    'Make PowerPoint visible.
    PowerPoint.AppWindow.Visible = True
    'Add a new presentation.
    Set ppPresentation = PowerPoint.Presentations.Add
    'Add a new slide with two objects and one text box.
    Set ppSlide = ppPresentation.Slides.Add(1, _
        ppLayoutTwoObjectsAndText)
End Sub
```

3. Press F5 to start the program, and click the Command1 button. PowerPoint should come up with a fresh presentation and a brand new slide like the one shown in Figure 13-3.

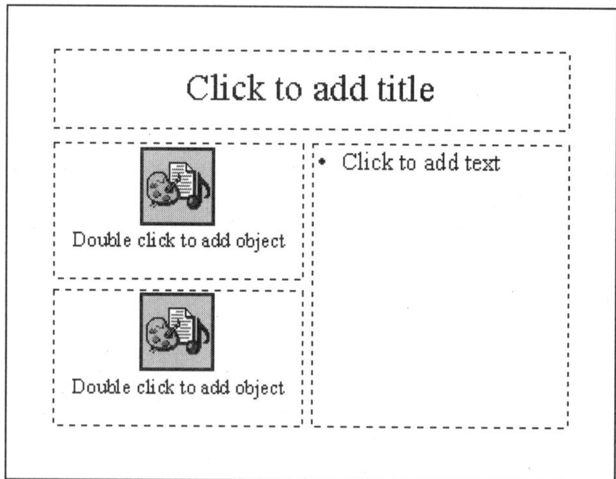

Figure 13-3. *A PowerPoint slide with a layout for a title, two objects, and some text.*

Finding a Slide in a Presentation

What if you don't want to create all new slides? What if you just want to open an existing presentation and find a particular slide? No problem. You can just use the Slides collection. Check out the following code, which opens a PowerPoint presentation file called Yadda.Ppt and prints the title from slide #3. To run the code, go ahead and create a presentation called Yadda.Ppt in your C:\ObjProg\Chapter13\ directory, and make sure it has a third slide with some text in the title placeholder.

```
Dim ppPresentation As PowerPoint.Presentation
Dim ppSlide As PowerPoint.Slide
:
:
Private Sub Command1_Click()
    'Make the PowerPoint window visible.
    PowerPoint.AppWindow.Visible = True
    'Open Yadda.Ppt at C:\, and assign it to the
    'ppPresentation object.
    Set ppPresentation = _
        PowerPoint.Presentations.Open _
        ("C:\ObjProg\Chapter13\Yadda.Ppt")
    'Set the ppSlide object equal to the third slide
    'in the presentation.
    Set ppSlide = ppPresentation.Slides(3)
    'Print the contents of the title of the current
    'slide (slide #3) to the screen.
    MsgBox ppSlide.Objects(1).Text
End Sub
```

Modifying a Slide

We know how to create a PowerPoint presentation, open a presentation, create slides, and find slides in PowerPoint from a VB project. Now let's talk about how to manipulate slides and slide objects.

Anything on a slide—text, a title, a picture, an OLE object, and so on—is considered an object. We know, we know. Haven't we used that word enough already? Well, we can't get around it here. We actually use a slide's Objects collection to create and modify the objects on the slide.

Collecting objects

All of the objects on a slide are created or modified through the Objects collection. The objects on the slide are indexed according to the order in which they were put on the slide. If you programmatically create a slide using an AutoType constant value, each of the objects on that slide is automatically part of that slide's Objects collection.

To access the first object on such a slide, you'd say:

```
ppSlide.Objects(1)
```

Here are four examples of AutoLayout types and the objects that initially correspond to index numbers 1, 2, and 3 for the Objects collection:

AutoLayout Type	Index #1	Index #2	Index #3
ppLayoutTitle	Title	Subtitle	NA
ppLayoutText	Title	Text	NA
ppLayoutTextOverObject	Title	Text	OLE Object
ppLayoutBlank	NA	NA	NA

Accessing objects

If you wanted to change the text of the title and the subtitle on a slide created with the ppLayoutTitle AutoLayout type, you could access the objects from a VB program by means of their index numbers in the Objects collection:

```
'Index #1 is Title for ppLayoutTitle.
ppSlide.Objects(1).Text = "New Title"
'Index #2 is subtitle for ppLayoutTitle.
ppSlide.Objects(2).Text = "New Subtitle"
```

You can do lots of other things to objects in a slide by means of their index numbers as well. You can copy, crop, and duplicate an object in a slide; check whether an object in a slide contains text; flip an object in a slide vertically or horizontally; and so on—all from a VB program.

You can change the order of the objects in the Objects collection by changing the order of the objects in the slide with the Draw menu's Bring to Front, Send to Back, Bring Forward, and Send Backward commands. For this reason, the PowerPoint object model provides for a Title alias and placeholders to help you refer to the objects on a slide in your VB program.

Title alias A special title textbox object serves as a placeholder for a title on a slide. (See the title textbox shown in Figure 13-4.) A programmer who wants an easy way to get to the text of the title textbox without having to keep track of its object index number can use *Objects.Title.Text* to point to the title of a slide—if the slide has a title textbox.

For example, *Objects(1).Text* on a slide created with the ppLayoutTitle AutoLayout type could also be referred to as *Objects.Title.Text.* In other words, the following line

```
ppSlide.Objects(1).Text = "New Title"
```

could be replaced with the line

```
ppSlide.Title.Text = "New Title"
```

Even if we changed the order of the objects so that *Objects(1)* became *Objects(2)*, *Title.Text* would still refer to the title textbox.

Placeholders Let's say we've created a two-column text slide (AutoLayout type ppLayoutTwoColumnText). We'd have a slide like the one shown in Figure 13-4.

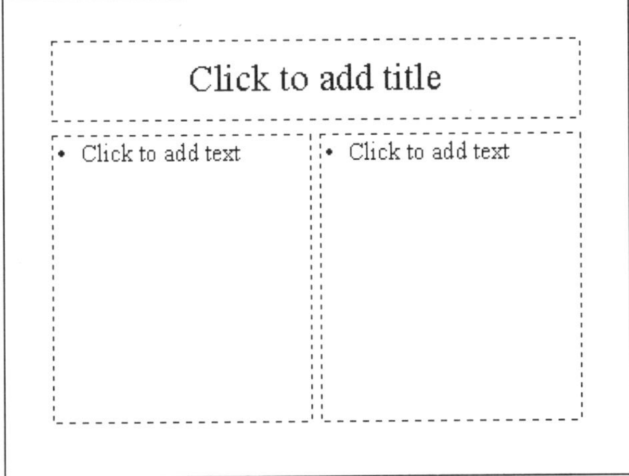

Figure 13-4. *A new two-column text slide.*

This slide contains three boxes made up of dashed lines. The top box will hold the title, and the other two boxes are text placeholders, one for each text column. Placeholders make it easy to keep track of where the original objects on a slide are located, regardless of object additions, object order changes, or other changes that affect the Objects collection index numbers.

As a user of PowerPoint, you could click on the title box or either of the two text placeholders to add information to one of the already created textboxes. The two placeholders point to programmable objects, so they can also be programmatically accessed just as the title textbox can. The difference is that instead of using the Title alias, you use the Placeholders collection.

Placeholders vs. additional objects If you wanted to, you could add a new object to the slide, but the new object would not have a placeholder pointing to it. Placeholders—whether text objects (other than the title object), drawing objects, OLE objects, or picture objects—are set up when a slide is first created to represent the standard objects that initially come with the type of AutoLayout slide you create. All placeholders are objects, but not all objects are placeholders.

Any object you create after the initial creation of a slide won't have a corresponding placeholder.

The Placeholders collection is thus a subset of the Objects collection because you can programmatically add objects to a slide that won't have corresponding placeholders.

Placeholders are handy because you can delete objects, move objects, change object index numbers in the Objects collection, and always get back to the initial objects on the slide by means of placeholders. Let's check out how to use the Placeholders collection. You can use the following line in your VB program to tell you how many objects are in a slide's Placeholders collection:

```
ppSlide.Objects.Placeholders.Count
```

To access the contents of the first placeholder—which would be the left text column in our earlier example of a two-column text slide—you'd use the following line:

```
ppSlide.Objects.Placeholders(1).Text
```

NOTE *Placeholders(1)* usually refers to the Body textbox. *Body* is the textbox on a slide that will contain the main text for the slide.

Even if the initial Objects collection has been rearranged, you can always get back to the first-column textbox by means of the *Placeholders(1)* designation.

Adding objects to a slide's Objects collection

The Objects collection has methods that allow you to add lots of different types of objects to the collection—and hence to the slide. Each kind of object that can go on a slide has a corresponding *Add* method you use to add an instance of the class to a slide's Objects collection. Examples of some of the common *Add* methods are shown in the table below.

Add **METHODS FOR OBJECTS COLLECTION**

Method	*Example*
AddArc	.AddArc 4000, 4000, 4000, 2000
AddLine	.AddLine 4000, 4000, 4000, 2000
AddPicture	.AddPicture "c:\data\barney.bmp", 500, 500, 2000, 2000
AddShape	.AddShape ppShapeTrapezoid, 500, 4500, 4000, 2000
AddTextFrame	.AddTextFrame 700, 700, 900
AddTitle	.AddTitle

AddTitle is useful only if the slide has a Title placeholder and the title has been deleted. You'll get an error message if the title still exists.

Cross-Reference For a complete listing as well as a full description of all of the arguments for each method, see the *Microsoft Solutions Development Kit 2.0*. You can also use the Object Navigator on the companion CD that comes with this book to see the syntax—including arguments—for each of these methods. See Appendix B for information on using the Object Navigator.

The following code would take care of error checking as you added a title object to a slide:

```
With ppSlide.Objects
    'Check if the .Objects collection has a Title
    'placeholder. If not, add one.
    If Not .HasTitle Then
        .AddTitle
    End If
    'Add the text to the title, using the .Title alias
    'to locate the title on the slide, now that you're
    'sure the .Objects collection has a title placeholder.
    .Title.Text = "This is the new title."
End With
```

Adding a text object to a slide's Objects collection Let's check out *AddTextFrame* to see how you might add an object to the Objects collection.

To add a text frame object to a slide, use the following syntax:

```
Set <variable> = ppSlide.Objects.AddTextFrame(X:=, Y:=, Width:=)
```

X and Y represent the position on the slide screen at which the text frame will be inserted. X is the number of twips from the left side of the slide, and Y is the number of twips from the top.

NOTE PowerPoint uses *twips* as its unit of measurement. In VB, you can use *Screen.TwipsPerPixelX* and *Screen.TwipsPerPixelY* to convert twips to pixel counts.

Here's a real example. The following code would add a text frame to ppSlide:

```
Dim ppTextObj As SlideObject
:
Set ppTextObj = ppSlide.Objects.AddTextFrame(700, 700, 900)
```

Until you actually add text to ppTextObj, the three positional arguments are irrelevant. The text frame will sit in the middle of the slide until you add code like the following:

```
ppTextObj.Text = "yadda"
```

At this point the text frame will assume the position and size you designated in the *AddTextFrame* arguments.

Adding multi-level text (bullets) to a slide's text object You can add multi-level text —bulleted text—to a textbox on a slide using code like this statement:

```
'vbCr is the VBA constant for carriage return.
ppSlide.Objects.Placeholders(1).Text = "Bullet #1" & vbCr & _
    "Bullet #2" & vbCr & "Bullet #3"
```

Formatting a slide's text objects You know how to add, find, and access objects. Now, let's look into formatting text objects.

You use the Font member object for most changes to text formatting. In the object model hierarchy, the Font member hangs off the Text member, which hangs off an object. The whole shebang looks like this:

```
ppSlide.Objects.Placeholders(1).Text.Font
```

NOTE *Placeholders(1)* doesn't necessarily need to point to a text object. If *Placeholders(1)* were pointing to a rectangle, *Text* would refer to text centered in the middle of the rectangle.

You can hard type an object variable to hold the reference returned by the *Font* method with the CharFormat class as follows:

```
Dim ppFont As CharFormat
:
Set ppFont = ppSlide.Objects.Placeholders(1).Text.Font
```

There are lots of text properties you can change through the Font member. Some examples of text properties and their settings are shown in the table on the next page.

Text Properties	Property Settings
Baseline	ppFont.Baseline = –.25 Sets the superscript offset if a positive percentage or the subscript offset if a negative percentage.
Bold	ppFont.Bold = ppTriStateToggle ppTrue is *1*, ppFalse is *0*, and ppTriStateToggle means toggle to whatever the current value isn't. (If Bold is set to *True*, setting Bold to ppTriStateToggle will set Bold to *False*, and vice versa.)
Color	ppFont.Color.RGB = 210
Embossed	ppFont.Embossed = ppTrue Embossed and Shadow are mutually exclusive.
Font	ppFont.Font = "Times New Roman"
Italic	ppFont.Italic = ppTrue
Points	ppFont.Points = 14
Shadow	ppFont.Shadow = ppTrue Embossed and Shadow are mutually exclusive.
Size	ppFont.Size = 14 * 20 Take the font size in points, in this case 14, and multiply it by 20 to get PowerPoint twips. Size must be set in twips.
Underline	ppFont.Underline = ppTrue

Text formatting practice Let's try it. We're going to create a form with some buttons that make use of many of the methods we've discussed above.

1. Enter the following code into the declarations section of a new VB form:

```
Dim ppPresentation As PowerPoint.Presentation
Dim ppSlide As PowerPoint.Slide
Dim ppFont As PowerPoint.CharFormat
```

2. Edit the *Form_Load()* event procedure to look like this:

```
Private Sub Form_Load()
    PowerPoint.AppWindow.Visible = True
    Set ppPresentation = PowerPoint.Presentations.Add
    Set ppSlide = _
        ppPresentation.Slides.Add(1, ppLayoutTitle)
    Set ppFont = ppSlide.Objects.Placeholders(1).Text.Font
    'Title is a unique placeholder you can address directly.
    ppSlide.Objects.Title.Text = "Awesome Presentation"
End Sub
```

3. Create buttons with the following names, and place the line of code listed for each under the *Click* event procedure for each button:

Button	Code
btnBold	ppFont.Bold = ppTriStateToggle
btnColor	ppFont.Color.RGB = 210
btnEmbossed	ppFont.Embossed = ppTrue
btnFont	ppFont.Font = "Arial"
btnItalic	ppFont.Italic = ppTriStateToggle
btnPoints	ppFont.Points = 44
btnShadow	ppFont.Shadow = ppTriStateToggle
btnSize	ppFont.Size = 44 * 20 (44 points * 20 twips per point = 880 twips)
btnSubscript	ppFont.Baseline = –.25
btnSuperscript	ppFont.Baseline = .3
btnUnderline	ppFont.Underline = ppTriStateToggle

4. Press F5 to run your program, and click the buttons to see the changes occur to the title slide. Try making a few changes to the code to get a feel for how the CharFormat object works. Notice when errors occur, and make sure you understand why you got an error. For example, you can't emboss text that has been shadowed, and vice versa.

Making changes to a TextStyles object You won't often change the font style of a single text object in your presentation. Usually, you'll want to change the font style of all the text objects so that your presentation will be internally consistent. The Presentation object has an associated object called TextStyles. Changes you make to the TextStyles object apply to text objects throughout the slides in your presentation.

The code to make a change to a TextStyles object might look like this:

```
ppPresentation.TextStyles(ppBodyStyle).Levels(1).Font.Underline = _
    ppTrue
```

ppBodyStyle refers to the type of text that is being changed. Besides ppBody-Style, you can change other types of text objects. See the full list of TextStyle types in the following table.

TextStyle Type	Denotation
ppBodyStyle	All of the Body textboxes in your presentation
ppDefaultStyle	Textboxes other than the placeholders
ppNotesStyle	Text in the notes pages
ppTitleStyle	Text in slide titles

NOTE Changing TextStyles(ppBodyStyle).Levels(1) changes the text style of only the first level of bulleted text. To change the text style of all bulleted text in a placeholder, you need to set up a *For* loop to go through each of the levels.

Editing text ranges You can break a textbox down into subunits, specifically paragraphs, sentences, lines, words, and characters. To get the first word of the first sentence of the first paragraph, you'd use the following statement:

```
strTemp = _
   ppSlide.Objects(2).Text.Paragraphs(1).Sentences(1).Words(1)
```

Adding a shape to a slide's Objects collection We've been looking at text objects. Now let's see how to manipulate *drawing objects* such as circles, squares, and triangles. You already know that you use the *AddShape* method to add a shape to a slide. You specify which shape to add to the slide by selecting one from the following shape types:

ppShapeBalloon
ppShapeCube
ppShapeDiamond
ppShapeEllipse
ppShapeFivePointStar
ppShapeHexagon
ppShapeHomePlate
ppShapeMediumArrowDown
ppShapeMediumArrowLeft
ppShapeMediumArrowRight
ppShapeMediumArrowUp
ppShapeMixed
ppShapeOctagon
ppShapeParallelogram
ppShapePlusSign
ppShapeRect
ppShapeRightTriangle
ppShapeRoundRect
ppShapeSixteenPointStar
ppShapeThickArrowDown
ppShapeThickArrowLeft
ppShapeThickArrowRight
ppShapeThickArrowUp
ppShapeTrapezoid
ppShapeTriangle

Here's an example of the code you'd use to add a shape to a slide:

```
ppSlide.Objects.AddShape ppShapeHomePlate, 2000, 2000, 2000, 2000
```

How do you know the index number of the shape object you just inserted? An object on a slide is given an index number based on the order in which it was added to a slide. So if your slide starts with three placeholders and you add a rectangle, that rectangle has an index number of 4. If next you add a circle, the circle's index number is 5. You can use *Objects.Count* to find out how many objects are currently on the slide. The object you add will have an index of Objects.Count + 1.

Changing the background of a slide or an object

Changing the background of a slide or an object is the easiest way to alter its appearance. You can fill the background with a single color, a blend of colors, a texture, a pattern, or even a picture. These properties all hang off the Graphic-Format object. Use *Background.Fill* with an appropriate fill format to change the background of a slide and *GraphicFormat.Fill* with an appropriate fill format to change the background of an object on a slide.

Changing the background of a slide Let's look at changing the background of a single slide first. You'd use the following syntax:

```
ppSlide.Background.Fill.<Fill Format> <argument>
```

To set the background for all slides in your presentation, you'd use the following syntax:

```
ppPresentation.SlideMaster.Background.Fill.<Fill Format> <argument>
```

Cross-Reference See "The Slide Master," coming up, for more on the SlideMaster object.

The fill format represents *how* the slide will be filled. For example, to fill the slide background with a single color, you'd use the ForeColor fill format. To fill the slide background with an oak texture, you'd use the PresetTextured fill format as follows:

```
ppSlide.Background.Fill.PresetTextured ppPresetTextureOak
```

NOTE For a complete list of all the fill format methods and properties, activate the PowerPoint library in the Object Browser in VB and select FillFormat from the Classes/Modules: list box.

The fill formats are listed in the table below:

Property	Fill Format
BackColor	.BackColor.RGB = RGB(255, 255, 255) Changing the BackColor fill format of a slide changes only the second color of a two-color slide background. To change the background of a slide with a single-color background or to change the first color on a two-color background, use ForeColor.
ForeColor	.ForeColor.RGB = RGB(0, 0, 0)
OneColorShaded	.OneColorShaded ppShadeHorizontal, 1, .5
Patterned	.Patterned 10
PresetShaded	.PresetShaded ppShadeVertical, 1, .5
PresetTextured	.PresetTextured ppPresetTextureOak
TwoColorShaded	.TwoColorShaded ppShadeHorizontal, 1, .5
UserTextured	.UserTextured "C:\MyTexture.Bmp"
WithPicture	.WithPicture "C:\MyPicture.Bmp"

Changing the background of an object You use the GraphicFormat object to change the backgrounds of specific objects on a slide. The code is essentially the same as the code for changing the background of a slide. It looks like this:

```
ppSlide.Objects(2).GraphicFormat.Fill.Patterned 10
```

To change the fill pattern of the third slide object—assuming the third object is a drawing object or a text placeholder—to an oak pattern, you would type:

```
ppSlide.Objects(3).GraphicFormat.Fill.PresetTextured _
    ppPresetTextureOak
```

The Slide Master

PowerPoint has a powerful feature called the Slide Master. (See Figure 13-5 on the next page.) The Slide Master is a slide to which you can make changes that affect all of the slides in the presentation to which it belongs. You can insert a bitmap into the slide's background, for example, or change the color of the background, or change the title font, or insert a footer/header, and have all of the slides change. Using the Slide Master to change slides is a valuable timesaving trick.

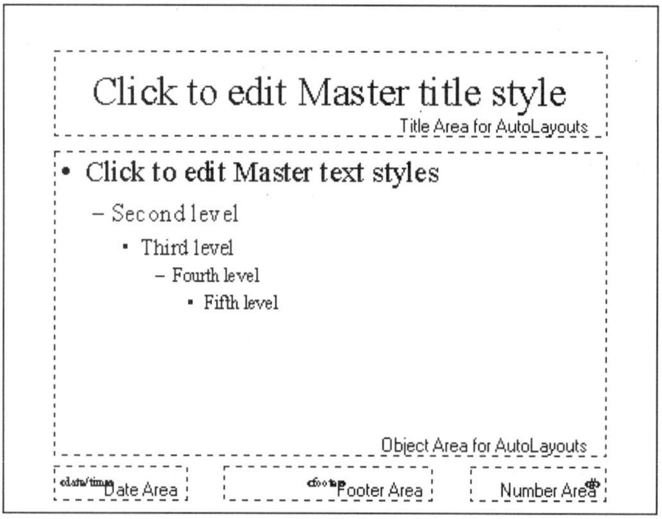

Figure 13-5. *The PowerPoint Slide Master.*

To make changes programmatically by means of the Slide Master, replace the specific slide—*Slides(1)* in the code below—with *SlideMaster*. So this code

```
ppPresentation.Slides(1).Background.Fill.Shade
```

is replaced by

```
ppPresentation.SlideMaster.Background.Fill.Shade
```

Other interesting PowerPoint operations

You can perform some interesting miscellaneous operations with the PowerPoint object model, too.

Pasting from the clipboard You can use the *Paste* method to paste objects from the clipboard to a PowerPoint slide. Let's say you used the following code to copy a bitmap from a PictureBox control declared as Picture1 to the clipboard in VB:

```
Clipboard.SetData  Picture1.Picture
```

You could use this code to paste the graphic into a PowerPoint slide:

```
PowerPoint.ActiveWindow.View.Paste
```

NOTE *Paste* works only in PowerPoint's Slide View and NotePages View.

Using the Tags object What if you want to customize your slides by adding a new property that isn't contained in the object model? No problem. You can create custom properties with the Tags object. You create a new property and set its value with this line:

```
ppSlide.Tags.Add <Property Name>, <Value>
```

NOTE Value is a string. Thus, when you want to use the value of a tag as an integer, you'll have to type something like the following:

```
CInt(ppSlide.Tags("TimeRequired"))
```

Let's say you want to associate a TimeRequired value with each slide in a presentation so that you can automatically create presentations on the fly based on the time available to show your presentation. You'd type

```
'The TimeRequired property for this particular slide
'is set at 5 minutes. Another slide might have a
'TimeRequired property of 2 minutes. If you had a
'total of 7 minutes to show your presentation,
'adding together the TimeRequired properties would
'tell you that you can show only these two slides.
ppSlide.Tags.Add "TimeRequired", "5"
```

To retrieve data from a custom property such as TimeRequired, use the following syntax:

```
<variable> = ppSlide.Tags("TimeRequired")
```

To change the value of an already-created property such as TimeRequired, use the property-setting syntax with a new value:

```
ppSlide.Tags.Add "TimeRequired", "10"
```

To delete a property, use an empty string:

```
ppSlide.Tags.Add "TimeRequired", vbNullString
```

Saving Your Presentation

Once you've created or modified a presentation, you need to save it using the *SaveAs* method of the Presentation object. Here's the syntax:

```
ppPresentation.SaveAs <filename>, <SaveAsFileType>
```

You can specify what type of file you'd like to save using one of the file constants shown in the table on the next page.

File Type Constant	Denotation
ppSaveAsPowerPoint4	Save as a PowerPoint 4 presentation
ppSaveAsPresentation	Save as a PowerPoint 95 presentation
ppSaveAsRTF	Save as a Windows Rich Text File
ppSaveAsTemplate	Save as a PowerPoint template
ppSaveAsWindowsMetafile	Save as a Windows metafile

Showing Your Presentation

OK. We're finally going to put all of this stuff we've learned to good use. We'll show slides, and then we'll look into sprucing up a presentation.

Presenting Your Slides

Once you've opened or created a presentation, running it is easy. You simply use the *Run* method on the SlideShow object. You can run the presentation in either a window or a full screen. The following line will show a full screen presentation:

```
ppPresentation.SlideShow.Run(ppSlideShowFullScreen)
```

Showing a presentation in a window is a little different because you set up a window reference so that you can easily change the window size and maximize, minimize, and do other things to the presentation. To create the reference, use these statements:

```
Dim ppWindow As PowerPoint.SlideShowWindow
Set ppWindow = ppPresentation.SlideShow.Run(ppSlideShowWindow)
```

The *Run* method returns a reference to a SlideShowWindow object, which can be used to control the window of the running presentation.

To change the location of the window on the screen, you'd use the Top, Left, Height, and Width properties. Here's an example:

```
With ppWindow
    .Top = 2000
    .Left = 2000
    .Height = 4500
    .Width = 4000
End With
```

Going to a slide in presentation mode

What if we want to go to a certain slide during a presentation? In this case, we're using the *GotoSlide* method:

```
ppWindow.View.GotoSlide 7
```

Sprucing Up

PowerPoint gives us lots of nifty ways to modulate and polish our presentations. In this section, we'll talk about making use of hidden slides, transitions, and animations.

You use the SlideShowEffects object that hangs off the Slide object to set the effects on your slides. The "Hidden slides" and "Slide transitions" sections that follow discuss properties of the SlideShowEffects object.

Hidden slides

The Hidden attribute lets you hide a slide you don't want to show up in your presentation. Hiding a slide is useful when you want to shorten the length of a presentation or if the presentation audience is different from the original target audience and might not be interested in a certain slide. The code to hide a slide looks like this:

```
ppSlide.SlideShowEffects.Hidden = ppTrue
```

Slide transitions

Good transitions will set your presentation apart from more run-of-the-mill presentations. Interesting transitions will hold the viewer's attention and can spice up a dry presentation.

AdvanceTime The AdvanceTime attribute is the number of seconds PowerPoint will wait before automatically advancing a slide.

```
'You must first set the slide transition advance
'mode to ppSlideShowUseSlideTimings, which tells
'PowerPoint to use the AdvanceTime settings.
Presentations(1).SlideShow.AdvanceMode = ppSlideShowUseSlideTimings

'During presentations, the slide will advance
'itself after 3 seconds.
ppSlide.SlideShowEffects.AdvanceTime = 3
```

EntryEffect If you haven't seen the entry effects available in PowerPoint, you should open PowerPoint and play with them now. (From the Tools menu, select SlideTransition.) The effects include checkerboards, boxes, covers, wipes, and dozens of other kinds of cool transitions. To see a list of the possible entry effects, select Effect from the Classes/Modules: list box in the Object Browser. They're also shown on the next page, for your convenience.

ppEffectBlindsHorizontal
ppEffectBlindsVertical
ppEffectBoxIn
ppEffectBoxOut
ppEffectCheckerboardAcross
ppEffectCheckerboardDown
ppEffectCoverDown
ppEffectCoverLeft
ppEffectCoverLeftDown
ppEffectCoverLeftUp
ppEffectCoverRight
ppEffectCoverRightDown
ppEffectCoverRightUp
ppEffectCoverUp
ppEffectCut
ppEffectCutThroughBlack
ppEffectDissolve
ppEffectFade
ppEffectFlashOnceFast
ppEffectFlashOnceMedium
ppEffectFlashOnceSlow
ppEffectFlyFromBottom
ppEffectFlyFromBottomLeft
ppEffectFlyFromBottomRight
ppEffectFlyFromLeft
ppEffectFlyFromRight
ppEffectFlyFromTop
ppEffectFlyFromTopLeft
ppEffectFlyFromTopRight
ppEffectMixed
ppEffectNone
ppEffectRandom
ppEffectRandomBarsHorizontal
ppEffectRandomBarsVertical
ppEffectSplitHorizontalIn
ppEffectSplitHorizontalOut
ppEffectSplitVerticalIn
ppEffectSplitVerticalOut
ppEffectStripsDownLeft
ppEffectStripsDownRight
ppEffectStripsLeftDown
ppEffectStripsLeftUp
ppEffectStripsRightDown
ppEffectStripsRightUp
ppEffectStripsUpLeft
ppEffectStripsUpRight
ppEffectUncoverDown
ppEffectUncoverLeft
ppEffectUncoverLeftDown
ppEffectUncoverLeftUp
ppEffectUncoverRight
ppEffectUncoverRightDown
ppEffectUncoverRightUp
ppEffectUncoverUp
ppEffectWipeDown
ppEffectWipeLeft
ppEffectWipeRight
ppEffectWipeUp

You can programmatically set the transition—the EntryEffect—for each slide.

```
ppSlide.SlideShowEffects.EntryEffect = ppEffectBoxIn
```

EntryTime Unlike AdvanceTime, which sets the amount of time in seconds that a particular slide is displayed, EntryTime gets/sets the speed of the slide transition—in other words, how fast you want to go from one slide to another. In PowerPoint, you have a choice among slow, medium, and fast values, and you must use only the following values. (These are just numeric values, not times in seconds as the AdvanceTime attribute's values are.) Currently there is no enumeration for these values:

Speed	Value
Slow	*0.5*
Medium	*1.0*
Fast	*1.5*

Here are example statements that set EntryTime to slow, medium, and fast.

```
ppSlide.SlideShowEffects.EntryTime = 0.5     'Slow

ppSlide.SlideShowEffects.EntryTime = 1.0     'Medium

ppSlide.SlideShowEffects.EntryTime = 1.5     'Fast
```

Setting EntryTime has no effect if an EntryEffect has not been set.

Sound The Sound attribute allows you to associate a .Wav file with a slide transition. So, for example, you could create a .Wav file of a trumpet call and play it whenever you move from one slide to another. The code might look like this:

```
'Play a .Wav whenever PowerPoint transitions away from this slide.
ppSlide.SlideShowEffects.Sound.FromFile("C:\Data\Waves\Trumpet.Wav")
```

Animations of text and other objects

One of the really neat new features of PowerPoint for Windows 95 is its ability to assign build effects to specific objects—and even to specific levels of text objects—on a slide. To assign a build effect to an object, you start out by telling PowerPoint how many levels of the object you want to build.

Animating a nontext object With nontext objects, you'd build the whole thing:

```
'This line tells PowerPoint to build the whole object.
ppSlide.Objects(2).BuildEffects.Type = ppBuildTypeAllLevels
```

Then you'd assign a build effect to the object from the list of entry effects on page 396. Here's an example of assigning a fade effect to the second item in a collection of objects on a slide:

```
ppSlide.Objects(2).BuildEffects.Effect = ppEffectFade
```

Animating a text object by level If the object is a textbox, you can build one level of the text at a time. Think of the levels of text in a textbox in terms of an outline. (See Figure 13-6.)

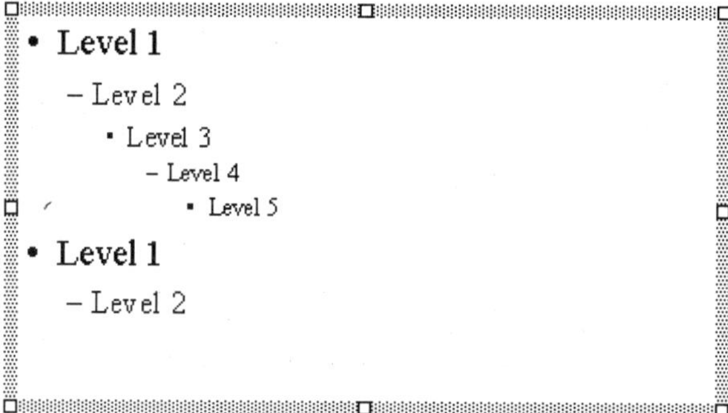

Figure 13-6. *A textbox containing multiple levels of text.*

The value assigned to BuildEffects.Type from the following list designates at which level(s) the build will take place:

ppBuildTypeAllLevel
ppBuildTypeFifthLevel
ppBuildTypeForthLevel*
ppBuildTypeThirdLevel
ppBuildTypeSecondLevel
ppBuildTypeFirstLevel
ppBuildTypeNone

In a textbox, the build effect builds top to bottom one level at a time down to the level specified by the build type. As an example, let's say you set the build effect to ppEffectFade. If you set the build type to ppBuildTypeFirstLevel, the first bullet and all levels of bullets under it would fade in at once and then the next first-level bullet would fade in with all of its sublevel bullets and so on. Since the build type was ppBuildTypeFirstLevel, no level under level 1 was built separately—levels 2 and following faded in with level 1.

Now let's use the same build effect but set the build type to ppBuildType-SecondLevel. In this case, the first level would fade in and then the second level and all levels under it would fade in at once. Then the next first level would fade in, followed by its second level and all levels under that, and so on. Since in this case the build type was ppBuildTypeSecondLevel, level 1 faded in by itself, but levels 2 and on were built together. This is what the code to fade in text from the second level of bullets would look like:

```
With ppslide.Objects(2).BuildEffects
    .Type = ppBuildTypeSecondLevel
    .Effect = ppEffectFade
End With
```

* Yes, that's the PowerPoint spelling!

SUMMARY

- The PowerPoint object model contains many objects—including presentations, slides, and fonts—you can access through applications that support OLE Automation.
- You can start PowerPoint running and make it visible with the following code:

```
PowerPoint.AppWindow.Visible = True
```

- You create a new slide based on a PowerPoint AutoLayout slide using the appropriate AutoLayout constant value.
- You can access and manipulate text objects programmatically. Some text objects also have corresponding placeholders.
- You can add objects to a slide by adding them to the slide's Objects collection.
- You use the Font object to change text properties such as bold, font size, and underline.
- You use GraphicFormat to change the backgrounds of slides and of objects on a slide.
- You change elements of all the slides in a presentation by means of the SlideMaster object.
- You use the Tags object to add custom properties to a slide.
- You use *SlideShow.Run* to show a presentation either in a window (ppSlideShowWindow) or in full screen mode (ppSlideShowFullScreen).
- You use the SlideShowEffects object to adjust slide and object build effects and timings.

Appendix A

Visual Basic Language Concepts

Arrays in Variants

The Variant data type is incredibly flexible. In addition to being able to hold a single element of any Visual Basic for Applications intrinsic type, a variant can also hold an array of any intrinsic type. In this topic, we'll look at three different ways to assign arrays to variants, and then we'll look at identifying variants containing arrays and at retrieving elements from those arrays.

Creating arrays in variants

The three ways to place an array in a variant are direct assignment, direct assignment with the *Array* function, and allocation with the *ReDim* statement.

Direct assignment The easiest way to place an array in a variant is by direct assignment. Given any array, assigning it to a variant will place a copy of the array in the variant:

```
Dim Var As Variant
ReDim strArray(10) As String
Var = strArray
```

Var will now contain a copy of the strArray array.

NOTE In general, you can't place an array on the left side of an assignment statement, so you can't assign a variant containing an array to an array. The exception to this rule is arrays of type Byte, which are allowed on the left of the equal sign. The expression to the right of the equal sign must evaluate to a String or Byte array type.

Direct assignment with the *Array* function The VBA *Array* function provides a quick and dirty way to place an array in a variant. The *Array* function parameters are simply a list of the elements you'd like in your array, as in the following:

```
Dim Var As Variant
Var = Array(1, "Hello", Null)
```

Although the *Array* function is easy to use, it isn't very flexible. You can create only 1-dimensional arrays, and the number of elements in your array is fixed when you define the array. An array created with the *Array* statement contains elements of the Variant type, which take up a huge amount of memory. In fact, the memory requirement for Var in the code snippet above is a whopping 92 bytes. See the Visual Basic "Data Type Summary" help topic for more information on the sizes of data types.

In Microsoft Excel and the initial release of Visual Basic 4.0, the base of the array returned by the *Array* function depends on the *Option Base* setting for the current module. However, in release 4.0a the *Array* function always returns a 0-based array. (If your Visual Basic CD contains any 1996 files, you have version 4.0a.)

Allocation with the *ReDim* statement Once you explicitly declare a variable as type Variant, you can use the *ReDim* statement with the variable directly to place an array of any type in the variant:

```
Dim Var As Variant
ReDim Var(10) As String
```

Note that both the *Dim* and the *ReDim* statements are required. Without the *Dim* statement, Var becomes a String array instead of a variant containing a String array.

Manipulating arrays in variants

Before you try to pull any values from an array in a variant, you might want to verify first that the variant actually contains an array. You can make this check using either the *IsArray* or *VarType* function:

```
'Using the IsArray function
If IsArray(MyVariant) Then MsgBox "It's an array!"
'Using the VarType function
If VarType(MyVariant) And vbArray Then MsgBox "It's an array!"
```

A variant will never have a VarType exactly equivalent to vbArray. The vbArray constant—which has the value *8192*, or hexadecimal 2000—is always combined with another VarType constant, such as vbString or vbInteger, to indicate the type of the contained array. You can use the Xor Boolean operator to strip the vbArray bit and read the underlying VarType as follows:

```
If VarType(MyVariant) And vbArray Then
    Select Case VarType(MyVariant) Xor vbArray
        Case vbString
        .
        .
        .
        Case vbInteger
        .
        .
        .
    End Select
End If
```

Once you've determined that a variant actually contains an array, you retrieve individual elements of the array exactly as you would the elements of a normal array. You can also use the *LBound* and *UBound* functions to get the upper and lower bounds of the array, just as you would the bounds of a normal array:

```
For i% = LBound(MyVariant) To UBound(MyVariant)
    Debug.Print MyVariant(i%)
Next i%
```

If your array contains an array of variants, one of the variants contained in the array may also contain a variant. These nested variant arrays are indexed using multiple sets of parentheses as follows:

```
MyVariant = Array(Array(1, 2, 3), Array(4, 5, 6), Array(7, 8, 9))
Debug.Print MyVariant(0)(0), MyVariant(1)(2)
```

Output:

```
1        6
```

Don't confuse nested variants containing arrays with a variant containing a multidimensional array. A multidimensional array is indexed using one value for each dimension in a comma-delimited list in the same set of parentheses, not in multiple parentheses:

```
Dim Var As Variant
ReDim Var(10, 10) As String
Var(0, 0) = "The first element"
```

Unfortunately, VBA doesn't have a function to tell you the number of dimensions of an array. The *Dims* function shown on the next page will return the number of dimensions of an array in a variant—or in any normal array.

```
Function Dims(AnyArray As Variant) As Integer
Dim i As Integer
Dim iTmp As Integer
    On Error Resume Next
    Do
        iTmp = LBound(AnyArray, i + 1)
        If Err Then Exit Do
        i = i + 1
    Loop
    Dims = i
    Err.Clear
End Function
```

Advanced: Extracting arrays from variants

If you're a C/C++ programmer, this discussion will give you some insight into the inner workings of VBA arrays and arrays in variants and point you in the right direction for writing your own C/C++ DLLs. This discussion is not meant to be a comprehensive explanation of the topic, but it should get you started.

Assigning an array to a variant results in a deep copy of the array, meaning that a copy of each element of the array is made. When the assignment operation is completed, you will have two separate copies of each array. For a large array, the deep copy can be very expensive—unnecessarily so if you won't be using the source array later in your code. And there's no way to assign a variant containing an array to an array. To help you optimize your programs that use arrays in variants, here's a C++ code snippet that extracts an array from a variant and places it in an intrinsic string array. For more information on creating C/C++ DLLs for use with Visual Basic, look in Vb4dll.Txt in the root directory of your Visual Basic installation.

```
//Listing in a module section in an .Odl file. An .Odl file is
//processed by the MkTypLib utility, which comes with Microsoft Visual
//C++, to create a .Tlb, which is the stand-alone version of a type
//library. You can include the type library as a resource in your DLL
//with the line 1 typelib MyTlb.Tlb in a resource file (.Rc) for your
//project. Note: The [out] flag on the DestArray parameter stops VBA
//from compiling your code if you try to call ExtractStringArray with
//a fixed-size string array. VBA doesn't handle static or fixed-size
//arrays in variants.
[entry(1), helpstring("Extract string array from Variant")]
HRESULT __stdcall ExtractStringArray
                  ([in, out] VARIANT *SourceVariant,
                  [out] SAFEARRAY (BSTR) *DestArray);

//A line from the EXPORTS section of the DEF file in your C project
ExtractStringArray        @1
```

```
//The ExtractStringArray code listing
extern "C" HRESULT WINAPI ExtractStringArray
                          (VARIANT FAR* SourceVariant,
                          SAFEARRAY FAR* FAR* DestArray)
{
    HRESULT hr = NOERROR;
    if (SourceVariant->vt == VT_ARRAY | VT_BSTR) {
      *DestArray = SourceVariant->parray;
      SourceVariant->vt = VT_EMPTY;
    }
    else {
      hr = 0x800A000D;      //Raises a type-mismatch error in basic.
    }
    return hr;
}
```

Boolean Comparison

In Visual Basic for Applications, *0* is False and *−1* is True; however, all other non-zero numeric values also evaluate to True when they're used in a conditional expression. The Boolean type is used to coerce any non-zero expression to True. A Boolean variable can contain only the values True and False, and assigning any numeric value of any other type to a Boolean will automatically coerce to one of these two values.

The hard part of using Boolean values in Visual Basic for Applications doesn't lie in evaluating a single operator but in evaluating expressions that use logical operators. For a complete list of the logical operators, refer to Visual Basic Help. All VBA logical operators are strictly binary in nature, meaning that evaluation is always done on a bit-by-bit basis according to the tables listed in the help file. Let's review using three of the most common operators: Not, And, and Or.

Not

Not is probably the most commonly used operator—and one of the operators most prone to errors. The difficulty lies in the underlying bits of integer types. In binary, *0* is represented as (surprise) all 0s, 00000000, and *−1* is represented as all 1s, 11111111. The Not operator changes all 0s to 1s and all 1s to 0s, so *Not −1* (the same as Not True) is *0* (False). However, *Not 1* is *−2* (in binary notation, Not 00000001 = 11111110). Hence, if i% is an integer that evaluates to True, Not i% does not necessarily evaluate to False.

If you're unsure of the outcome of a Not operation that should return True or False, use the *CBool* function to make sure it works correctly. *Not CBool(1)* will return *0* instead of *−2*, which is the result you want. This line of code, for example, will beep only if i% is *0*:

```
If Not CBool(i%) Then Beep
```

You can take advantage of the Not operator to check for the number −1. *Not −1* is False, whereas *Not <any other integer>* is True. One useful application of the Not operator is with the ListIndex property of a ListBox. If ListIndex is *−1*, then there is no current selection in the list box.

```
With List1
    If Not .ListIndex Then      'Verify we have a valid selection.
        Debug.Print .List(.ListIndex)
    End If
End With
```

And

Like the Not operator, And is a binary operator. The bit-level binary And operation means that the expression *A And B* might be False even though *expression A* is True and *expression B* is True. Getting down to the binary basics: the And operator returns a *1* in the nth bit if the nth bit of both arguments is *1*; otherwise, the And operator returns *0*. Hence, *1 And 2* is False (1 = 00000001, and 2 = 00000010). This bug can bite you in a seemingly random fashion. After all, *1 And 3* evaluates to *3*, which is True. As with the Not operator, you can use the *CBool* function on one of the arguments to force proper logical evaluation. *CBool(1) And 2* evaluates to *−1*, which is True.

Or

Or is probably the easiest of the three common operators to use because *A Or B* will always evaluate to True if either A or B evaluates to true. Or returns a *1* in the nth bit if the nth bit of either of its arguments is *1*; otherwise, it returns *0*.

The Or operator should also be used to combine bit fields. In the text of the book, we frequently use Or to combine MsgBox fields:

```
MsgBox "We have a problem.", vbYesNoCancel Or vbExclamation
```

We recommend using Or in these scenarios instead of the plus (+) operator. Most of the time, the two operators are functionally interchangeable when they're used to combine bit fields. However, the + operator will give a bogus result when a given bit is listed twice in an expression. Let's use the values *3* (00000011) and *5* (00000101) in an example:

```
3 + 5 = 8   '00001000
3 Or 5 = 7  '00000111
```

Note that 3 + 5 ended up with the fourth bit set—but not the first three, which was the desired result.

Redundant Boolean Evaluation

It's all too common to see the following code:

```
Dim fFlag As Boolean
     :
     :
If fFlag = True Then Beep
```

In this expression, the = *True* is completely redundant. The code

```
If fFlag Then Beep
```

works just as well and saves VBA a bit of work.

Flipping Bits

In some cases, you'll want to use an integer to hold bit fields. A bit field is used to hold several related *0* and *1* values without using a lot of memory. Each bit from the bit field in the integer represents a different flag. You can create your flags using constants. Each constant should be a power of 2 (that is, *1*, *2*, *4*, *8*, *16*, and so on). You can use the VBA logical operators to maintain your bit fields as follows:

```
'Here are some bit flags.
Const STATUS_FILEFOUND = 1
Const STATUS_FILEOPEN = 2
Const STATUS_FILEDIRTY = 4

'Use these two procedures to manipulate your bits.
Sub TurnBitOn(BitField As Integer, Mask As Integer)
    BitField = BitField Or Mask
End Sub
Sub TurnBitOff(BitField As Integer, Mask As Integer)
    BitField = Not (BitField Imp Mask)
End Sub

'Here are some examples of using TurnBitOn and TurnBitOff.
'Turn on one bit.
TurnBitOn FileStatus, STATUS_FILEFOUND
'Turn on two bits.
TurnBitOn FileStatus, STATUS_FILEFOUND Or STATUS_FILEOPEN
'Turn a bit off.
TurnBitOff FileStatus, STATUS_FILEDIRTY
'Check if a bit is on.
If FileStatus And STATUS_FILEDIRTY Then Cancel = True
```

Branching and Looping

Branching, which is jumping forward or backward several lines of code without executing intervening statements, and looping, which is executing the same code multiple times, are essential capabilities of any programming language. The Visual Basic for Applications language has four branching constructs: *If...Then*, *GoTo*, *GoSub*, and *Select Case*. VBA has two looping constructs: *For* loops and *Do* loops.

If...Then

We'll start with the most common branching construct. *If...Then* statements form the decision-making core of any program. All but the most trivial programs must make constant decisions about which code needs to be run at any given time.

If...Then statements come in two varieties: single-line and multi-line. A single-line *If...Then* statement combines a conditional expression with a statement to be executed if the conditional expression evaluates to True:

```
If CashOnHand < 10 Then MsgBox "Please make a deposit."
```

You can execute multiple statements in a single-line *If...Then* statement by separating the statements to be executed with a colon:

```
If CashOnHand < 10 Then MsgBox "Please make a deposit.": MsgBox "Now!"
```

If you end up with more than one statement to be executed in a single-line *If...Then* statement, though, you probably have too many. For multiple statements to be executed, it's easier to use a multi-line *If...Then* statement (a block), and your code will be much easier to read:

```
If CashOnHand < 10 Then
    MsgBox "Please make a deposit."
    MsgBox "Now!"
End If
```

In both the single-line *If...Then* statement and the multi-line *If...Then...End If* block we just saw, the statements to be executed will be executed only if the conditional expression evaluates to True. If you want to execute a different set of statements when the conditional expression evaluates to False, add an *Else* statement. Depending on the truth value of the conditional expression, either one block of code will be executed or the other. The two blocks of code will never both be executed.

```
If CashOnHand < 10 Then
    MsgBox "Please make a deposit."
```

```
Else
    MsgBox "Hang tight."
End If
```

The last piece in the puzzle is to provide for even more logic by inserting one or more *ElseIf...Then* statements after the *If...Then* statement and before the *Else* and *End If* statements. If the initial conditional expression evaluates to false, then VBA keeps evaluating the conditional expressions in succeeding *ElseIf...Then* statements until an expression that evaluates to True is found, at which point VBA executes the block of code after that *ElseIf* statement. If all conditional expressions evaluate to False, then the code in the *Else* block is executed if an *Else* block is provided:

```
If CashOnHand < 10 Then
    MsgBox "Please make a deposit."
ElseIf CashOnHand > 2000 Then
    MsgBox "Invest."
Else
    MsgBox "Hang tight."
End If
```

Unlike C and some other programming languages, the Basic language does not short-circuit conditional expressions. All sub-expressions in a conditional expression will always be evaluated—even if not all sub-expressions are required to determine the truth value for the whole expression. For example, in C you could write

```
if ((base != 0) && (value / base > 10)) {...}
```

without ever dividing by zero because the second sub-expression will be evaluated only if the first sub-expression is true. To safeguard against division by zero in VBA, you'd have to write code with two nested *If...Then* statements:

```
If base <> 0 Then
    If value / base > 10 Then
        :
        :
    End If
End If
```

GoTo

A *GoTo* statement is the simplest kind of branching statement. A *GoTo* statement simply tells your code to jump to a line by number or name. You can jump only to lines in the same procedure. For example:

```
Sub GoToDemo
    GoTo 10
GoToLabel:
    MsgBox "Code"
    Exit Sub
10 MsgBox "Spaghetti"
    GoTo GoToLabel
End Sub
```

As the preceding code snippet has gone out of its way to demonstrate, *GoTo* statements have a reputation for resulting in spaghetti code, that is, code that's almost impossible to read and maintain. However, *GoTo* statements can be very useful for breaking out of deeply nested branching or looping constructs. But if you find yourself using more than one *GoTo* statement per procedure, you're probably using too many.

```
    If...Then
        If...Then
            :
            If...Then
                :
                If fProblem Then GoTo BailOut
            End If
            :
        End If
        :
    End If
BailOut:
```

NOTE In Visual Basic 3, line numbers and label names must be unique within a module. In VBA, however, line numbers and label names have the same scope as local variables. You can use the same line number or label name in as many procedures as you like.

GoSub

A *GoSub* statement is a homesick *GoTo* statement. After you've completed code in the block your *GoSub* sent you to, you call *Return* to jump back to where you were before the jump to the label specified in the *GoSub* statement. A *GoSub* statement is similar to a procedure call, but, instead of passing arguments, you simply use local variables. As with *GoTo* statements, extensive use of *GoSub* statements isn't encouraged.

The *ShowForms* procedure shown below needs to center and show two different forms. Instead of repeating the *Move* and *Show* methods for each individual form, a *GoSub* statement is used so that the code has to be written only once. Note the use of a local variable inside the *GoSub...Return* block and the placement of the *Exit Sub* statement.

```
Sub ShowForms()
'Set this local variable before jumping to ShowCenterForm.
Dim frmCurrent As Form
    Set frmCurrent = Form1
    GoSub ShowCenterForm
    Set frmCurrent = Form2
    GoSub ShowCenterForm
    'Exit the procedure now to avoid rerunning ShowCenterForm.
    Exit Sub
ShowCenterForm:
    With frmCurrent
        .Move (Screen.Width - .Width) / 2, _
              (Screen.Height - .Height) / 2
        .Show
    End With
    Return
End Sub
```

Select Case

Select Case statements provide a fast solution for a conditional branch that pivots on a single value. Any *Select Case* statement can be duplicated with an *If...Then* conditional block, but *Select Case* is usually much cleaner. Let's compare a simple *Select Case* block with the equivalent *If...Then* block.

```
'Match ProductType using Select Case.
Select Case ProductType
    Case 1
    Case 5
    Case Else
End Select

'Match ProductType using If.
If ProductType = 1 Then
ElseIf ProductType = 5 Then
Else
End If
```

You can see that the *Select Case* statement makes for much cleaner code. The *Select Case* statement is evaluated just as the *If* clause is—the expression in each *Case* statement is compared to the test expression in the *Select Case* statement until a match is found. The code after the matching *Case* statement is then executed, with control branching to the *End Select* statement immediately before another *Case* statement is evaluated. If a match isn't found and a *Case Else* block is specified, the code in the *Case Else* block is executed.

Select Case statements are most often used for direct comparison, but they also support more complicated expressions. Let's look at some more complex *Case* statements and the equivalent *If* clause.

```
Case 1, 2, 3
If TestExpression = 1 Or TestExpression = 2 Or TestExpression = 3 Then

Case Is < 3
If TestExpression < 3 Then

Case 1 To 2
If TestExpression >= 1 And TestExpression <= 2 Then

Case Is < 0, Is >= 100
If TestExpression < 0 Or TestExpression >= 100 Then
```

As you can see, *Case* statements can be complicated. Any number of comma-delimited expressions are allowed in a *Case* statement. The multi-expression *Case* statements shown above are actually smarter than their equivalent *If* statements because a *Case* statement will evaluate sub-expressions only until a match is found, whereas an *If* statement will evaluate every sub-expression.

Any numeric or string data type can be used as the test expression, and any comparison operator except *Like* or *Is* can be used after the *Is* keyword in a *Case* statement. Don't confuse the *Is* keyword in a *Case* statement with the *Is* operator.

Do Loops

The *Do* loop, which has several variations, is used to repeatedly execute a single block of code. The simplest *Do* loop uses a *Do* statement to mark the beginning of the code block and a *Loop* statement to mark the end. The code in between the *Do* and the *Loop* will continue to execute until the program executes an *Exit Do* statement. If you forget the *Exit Do* statement, your program will go into an infinite loop and never execute code after the *Loop* statement. Such a program can terminate only with an *End* statement. (This use of a *Do* loop is strongly discouraged.)

```
Do
    :
    Exit Do
    :
Loop
```

You can make your *Do* loop smarter by evaluating a conditional expression in every iteration of the loop with a *While* or *Until* keyword. There are four types of *Do* loops with *While* and *Until*.

Do While *TestExpression*...Loop If *TestExpression* is true, then execute one iteration of the code block and return to the *Do* statement. If *TestExpression* is false, then continue execution after the *Loop* statement.

Do Until *TestExpression*...Loop If *TestExpression* is false, then execute one iteration of the code block and return to the *Do* statement. If *TestExpression* is true, continue execution after the *Loop* statement.

Do...Loop While *TestExpression* If *TestExpression* is true, then jump back to the line after the *Do* statement. If *TestExpression* is false, continue with the next line of code.

Do...Loop Until *TestExpression* If *TestExpression* is false, then jump back to the line after the *Do* statement. If *TestExpression* is true, continue with the next line of code.

Let's use a *Do* loop to read all the lines from a file:

```
Dim fNum As Integer
Dim strLine As String
fNum = FreeFile
Open "MyFile.txt" For Input As fNum
'EOF will return True if all lines have been read from the file.
Do Until EOF(fNum)
    Line Input #fNum, strLine
    Debug.Print strLine
Loop
Close #fNum
```

NOTE A *Do While StartExpression...Loop* block can also be written *While StartExpression...Wend*. The two constructs are functionally equivalent.

For Loops

The *For...Next* loop lets you execute the same block of code multiple times while incrementing and testing a counter value. In a quick example, let's print all values in a three-element array.

```
Dim iCounter As Integer
Dim VarArray As Variant
VarArray = Array("First", "Second", "Third")
For iCounter = 0 To 2
    Debug.Print VarArray(iCounter)
Next iCounter
```

The syntax of the *For* statement is:

```
For Counter = StartExpression To StopExpression [Step StepExpression]
```

Let's go over each part of the *For* statement.

- *Counter* The variable to increment. *Counter* is set to *StartExpression* at the beginning of the loop, compared to *StopExpression* to determine when to end the loop, and incremented by *StepExpression* at the end of each loop iteration. *Counter* can be a variable of any numeric type, but the Integer type will give you the fastest loop iteration. For performance reasons, you should avoid Variant, Single, and Double counters.
- *StartExpression* The initial value for *Counter*.
- *StopExpression* The limiting value. When *Counter* reaches or passes the *StopExpression* value, execution continues at the line of code immediately after the *For* block.
- *StepExpression* An optional value specifying the increment that should be added to *Counter* at the end of each loop iteration. If the *Step* clause is omitted, the default increment value is *1*. A step of *0* is allowed but isn't very useful unless you like infinite loops.

To see what VBA is doing under the covers, let's look at the *Do* loop equivalent of a *For...Next* loop. Here are two things to look for in the *Do* loop code snippet, both of which apply to the *For...Next* loop as well:

- *StartExpression*, *StopExpression*, and *StepExpression* are evaluated once and stored in temporary variables. If the value of any of these expressions changes during execution of the loop, it has no effect on the counter value or on termination of the loop.
- If the starting value is greater than the stop value (or less than the stop value when the step is negative), then the code in the *For...Next* block is never executed.

```
'The For...Next loop we're emulating
Dim iCounter As Integer
For iCounter = StartExpression To StopExpression Step StepExpression
    :
Next iCounter

'The Do Loop equivalent
Dim iCounter As Integer
Dim iStartVal As Integer
```

```
Dim iStopVal As Integer
Dim iStepVal As Integer
iStartVal = StartExpression
iStopVal = StopExpression
iStepVal = StepExpression
iCounter = StartVal
Do
    If iStepVal < 0 Then
        If iCounter < iStopVal Then Exit Do
    Else
        If iCounter > iStopVal Then Exit Do
    End If
    :
    iCounter = iCounter + iStepVal
Loop
```

You can jump out of a *For* loop at any time with the *Exit For* statement. Let's use a *For* loop to find a matching value in an array. We'll use *Exit For* to jump out of the loop as soon as a match is found.

```
For iCounter = LBound(MyArray) To UBound(MyArray)
    If MyArray(iCounter) = TestValue Then Exit For
Next iCounter
'If the counter is bigger than the termination value
'of the For loop, then we didn't jump out of the loop
'with an Exit For.
If iCounter > UBound(MyArray) Then MsgBox "No Match"
```

Cross-Reference See "Collections: *For Each... Next*" in this appendix for a description of *For Each* loops.

Collections

Collections play a central role in object programming with Visual Basic. A *collection* is a set of related objects or values. Each member of the collection has a *key* associated with it that is unique in the collection. A member of a collection can be retrieved either by its key value or by its *index*, meaning the numerical position of the member in the collection. In this topic, we'll look at retrieving values from collections and at a description of the Visual Basic for Applications built-in Collection object.

Collection lookup

An item is retrieved from a collection using the *Item* method. The *Item* method takes one argument, which can be set to either the *key* or the *positional index* of the item. *Item* is also the default method of most collections, so you can type *collection*(*Index*) instead of *collection*.Item(*Index*) to retrieve an item from a collection.

By key A *key* can be any string value. A key name isn't always required. The VBA collection object, for example, doesn't require keys for its items. A key can be associated with one and only one item in a collection. To retrieve an item from a collection using its key, you simply specify the string for the key value. The following line of code uses a key ("Sheet1") to retrieve an item from the Sheets collection.

```
ThisWorkbook.Sheets("Sheet1").Visible = xlHidden
```

By positional index Retrieving an item from a collection by positional index is the fastest lookup method available. However, there are also disadvantages to retrieving items by index. Unlike the key of an item in a collection, the numerical position of an item in a collection can change with time. If your code doesn't have full control of a collection object, you should always use the key instead of the index to retrieve an item from the collection.

Let's look to Microsoft Excel for our second example of collection lookup. If a workbook has two tabs, *Sheet1* and *Sheet2*, and the user drags the tab for *Sheet2* to the left of *Sheet1*, the contents of the Sheets collection haven't changed but the order of the items in the Sheets collection has changed. Before the drag, *Sheets(1)* returned a Worksheet object that referred to *Sheet1*. After the drag, *Sheets(1)* refers to *Sheet2*, not *Sheet1*. However, Sheets("Sheet1") will always return the Worksheet object corresponding to *Sheet1*.

When accessing items in collections by index, you'll need to know the base index for the collection. Excel collections and the VBA Collection object are both base 1, so valid indexes for those collections are in the range 1 to *collection*.Count. Collections in the DAO object library (Workspaces, Databases, Fields, TableDefs, and so on) are 0-based, so valid indexes fall in the range 0 to *collection*.Count −1.

The bang (!) operator

The ! symbol, also known as the *bang* operator, can be used to look up items in a collection. The bang operator is followed by the key name *without* quotes. The following lines of code are all equivalent:

```
Debug.Print MyColl.Item("MyKey")
Debug.Print MyColl("MyKey")
Debug.Print MyColl!MyKey
```

If the key contains a space, you need to enclose the key name in square brackets:

```
Debug.Print MyColl![Another Key]
```

ForEach... Next

A *For Each...Next* loop can be used to iterate through each element in a collection. The syntax is

```
For Each iterator In collection
    :
Next [iterator]
```

where *collection* is a Collection object and *iterator* is a variable of type object or type variant. The *For Each* syntax is roughly equivalent to the following *For...Next* loop:

```
For i% = 1 To collection.Count
    Set iterator = collection.Item(i%)
    :
Next i%
```

We recommend using the *For Each* syntax to iterate collections. Most collections (including VBA's Collection object) are implemented as doubly linked lists. To look up an item in the collection by either key value or index, you need to walk the entire list until the matching item is found. Using a *For Each...Next* loop instead of a *For...Next* loop to walk through all elements in a collection lets the internal implementation of the Collection object maintain its position in the list and move one item forward for each call instead of having to completely reset its position for every item in the list.

Using a *For Each...Next* loop to remove items from a collection is generally a bad idea. When an item is removed from a collection, the current position maintained by the object during a *For Each* iteration is no longer well-defined. Continuing to iterate through the collection will have unpredictable results. If you must remove some items from a collection in a loop, use *For...Next* to walk the collection backwards. Removing items while walking the collection backwards doesn't affect previous items in the collection.

```
For i% = collection.Count To 1 Step -1
    Set iterator = collection.Item(i%)
    :
Next i%
```

VBA's Collection object

VBA has a built-in Collection object for your programming pleasure. Unfortunately, there is no way to create a custom Collection object with a class module that supports *For Each* iteration, so you'll have to rely on VBA's implementation. *VBA.Collection* is a creatable class, so you can create a Collection object at any time with the *New* keyword:

```
Dim MyColl As VBA.Collection
:
Set MyColl = New VBA.Collection
```

Let's go over the methods and properties of the Collection object.

Add(item, [key, [before, [after]]]) The *Add* method is used to add a new item to a collection. The only required parameter is *item*. The *key* parameter is optional but must be specified if you want to support retrieving the item by means of a key name. The following code snippet adds and retrieves an item from a Collection object:

```
Dim MyColl As New VBA.Collection
MyColl.Add 10, "Ten"
Debug.Print MyColl!Ten 'Output: 10
```

By default, the *Add* method puts the new item at the end of the collection. If you want to put the item in the middle of a collection, you can set either the *before* or the *after* parameter to the key or index of an existing item in the collection. Adding items to a collection slows down drastically if you set the *before* or *after* parameters to items in the middle of the collection; hence, the use of these parameters isn't recommend.

Item(index) *Item* is the standard method used to retrieve an item from the Collection object. The *index* parameter can be either a key or a positional index. *Item* is the default method of any collection-type object.

Remove(index) The *Remove* method deletes an item from the Collection object. As with the *Item* method, the *index* parameter can be either a key or a positional index.

```
MyColl.Remove "Ten"
```

Count The Count property returns the number of items currently in the Collection object. A newly created Collection object always has 0 elements.

Clear While the Collection object doesn't have a *Clear* method, it should. In order to remove all items from a collection, simply assign a new instance of the Collection object to your Collection object variable instead of calling the *Remove* method for each individual item in the collection.

For Each alternatives

In order to use a *For Each* loop with a VB-created class, a VBA Collection object must be returned from a public method of that class:

```
'In the class module
Public Things As VBA.Collection

'In a calling routine
For Each Thing In ThingClass.Things
:
Next
```

Unfortunately, a major security problem accompanies using a public collection. A carefully conceived collection fundamental to the inner workings of a class module has just been exposed for any client of the class to modify. Nothing stops code outside the class module from modifying the collection:

```
ThingClass.Things.Clear
```

There's no way to ensure the security of a public collection in a class module. If security is required, the *For Each* statement can't be used. You'll need to use some other means of iterating through the members of an internal collection. The approach you choose depends on whether or not you know the number of elements in a collection when you start iteration. If you always know the number of items in your collection, set up your class module(s) to support the following code:

```
Dim iIterator As Integer
Dim SomeThing As Thing    'Thing is a hypothetical object type.
:
With ThingClass.Things
    For iIterator = 1 To .Count
        Set SomeThing = .Item(iIterator)
        :
    Next iIterator
End With
```

Using a *For...Next* statement works very well if a Count property is available, but an accurate count of items in a collection isn't always available. If your Thing object happens to be a line in a file, for example, there's no way to get an accurate count until the end of the file has been reached. It doesn't make any sense to read the whole file one time through to get an accurate line count, then a second time to actually read the data. In this type of situation, you can use a method on your class to retrieve the next available item in a collection as shown on the next page.

```
'Hypothetical client code to get Thing objects from
'a collection
Dim SomeThing As Thing
:
With ThingClass
    .ResetThings
    'SomeThing will contain the next Thing object in
    'the collection if GetThing returns True.
    Do While GetThing(SomeThing)
        :
    Loop
End With
'Code from the class module that owns a collection of Thing objects
Public Function GetThing(SomeThing As Thing) As Boolean
Dim fGotThing As Boolean
    :
    'Return False if there are no more Thing objects available.
    If Not fGotThing Then Set SomeThing = Nothing
    GetThing = fGotThing
End Function
```

DoEvents

A polite Windows program should always assume that it isn't the only program running on the system. If a program needs to perform a complicated, slow operation, such as file copying or extensive calculations, it should turn over system processing time to other programs that might be running on the system. Visual Basic for Applications provides the *DoEvents* function to enable a program to release control of the processor to other programs.

In addition to releasing processor control to other applications, the *DoEvents* function makes sure that all events in your own program can be fired. For example, *DoEvents* can be used to provide a Cancel button to enable the user to terminate a long operation before it is completed. Assume that the following code snippet is contained in the code module of a form with two command buttons, cmdGo and cmdCancel:

```
Private m_fFinished As Boolean
Private Sub cmdGo_Click()
    cmdCancel.Enabled = True
    'Make sure we don't call this event procedure until we're done.
    cmdGo.Enabled = False
    m_fFinished = False
    Do Until m_fFinished
```

```
        .
        .
        .
        'Allow the user to click the Cancel button.
        DoEvents
    Loop
    cmdGo.Enabled = True
    cmdCancel.Enabled = False
End Sub
Private Sub cmdCancel_Click()
    'Allow the processing loop to terminate.
    m_fFinished = True
End Sub
```

Reentrancy

The biggest problem with using *DoEvents* is reentrancy. An event procedure without a *DoEvents* statement is guaranteed to run to completion before the event procedure is called again by Visual Basic. However, if your program calls *DoEvents* and the user has caused the event that fired the event procedure code to be fired a second time (for example, if the user clicks a button a second time before the event procedure for the first button click has completed execution), your program can quickly get confused. In fact, the processing for the second button click will always be completed before the processing for the first button click.

If you decide to use *DoEvents*, your code should block reentrancy. In the code snippet above, we blocked reentrancy by disabling cmdGo using the Enabled property. With cmdGo disabled, the user is blocked from firing another click event. The other way to block reentrancy is with a static local variable in the event procedure that needs to finish processing before it is called a second time:

```
Private Sub cmdGo_Click()
Static fStayOut As Boolean
    If fStayOut Then Exit Sub
    fStayOut = True
    .
    .
    .
    DoEvents
    .
    .
    .
    fStayOut = False
End Sub
```

Open forms

In Visual Basic, the return value from the *DoEvents* function is the number of visible forms in the currently running program. If the return value is *0*, then there are no visible forms in your program. The number of visible forms can be useful information if your VB program doesn't implement public class modules. In a program that doesn't act as an object server, the lack of a visible form indicates that there's no way for the user or another program to run any code in the program. In other words, a *0* return value from *DoEvents* indicates that it's a good time to programmatically terminate your program if it's stuck in a loop because there's no other way to stop it. If your program is an object server, a *0* return value from *DoEvents* doesn't imply that your program is no longer in use because a client of your exposed objects might still be holding a reference to a running object.

Sleep API alternative to *DoEvents*

The *Sleep* API call is similar to *DoEvents*, but it doesn't do as much and doesn't have the reentrancy side effects *DoEvents* does. *Sleep* simply releases the system processor to other programs for a given amount of time. Your program will receive no processor cycles until that specified time has elapsed. *Sleep 0* will release the processor, but processing will return to your program right away if no other programs are in need of CPU cycles. Because calling the *Sleep* API won't process queued events in your program, there is no reentrancy danger with *Sleep*. Here is the declaration for the *Sleep* API call. (*Sleep* is available only on 32-bit systems.)

```
Declare Sub Sleep Lib "kernel32" (ByVal dwMilliseconds As Long)
```

Error Trapping

Error trapping is an important capability of any programming language. In a perfect world, errors would never occur, but in our imperfect world, users enter invalid dates, disks fill up, files are accidentally deleted, and systems crash—sorry, there's no way to trap a system crash error in VBA. Anticipating and being prepared for the worst case scenario is an essential function of any program.

In Visual Basic for Applications, any code executing while an error trap is active is able to survive a run-time error without immediately terminating execution of the current procedure. If an error trap isn't active in the current procedure when an error is raised, control is returned to the calling procedure. If that procedure doesn't have an active error trap, it, too, is terminated. Procedures in the call stack are terminated one by one until a procedure with an active error trap is reached. If VBA runs out of calling procedures without finding an active error trap, the error is fatal and the program terminates. Untrapped run-time errors in event procedures, including the *Class_Initialize()* and *Class_Terminate()* event procedures, are fatal because event procedures are called by events, not by other procedures.

If there's no chance that a chunk of code will fail, don't activate an error trap. Error trapping isn't free. Every line of code executed inside an error trap runs slightly slower than the same code outside an error trap and takes up a bit more space in the executable file. And using an error trap to continue to execute in spite of legitimate errors hides logic errors and makes debugging difficult in the long run. If something in your program is going drastically wrong, it's best to find out before your users do.

So how do you activate an error trap in a procedure properly? Visual Basic offers two main error trapping constructs: *On Error GoTo* and *On Error Resume Next.* You activate one of these error traps when an *On Error...* statement is executed. The error trap is deactivated when the procedure terminates or when you execute an *On Error GoTo 0* statement, which deactivates the current error trap (if any) and clears any current error information.

NOTE The following code snippets make use of the Err object, which isn't available in Excel VBA. Refer to the "Rich Error Information" topic in this appendix for equivalent Excel-VBA constructs.

On Error GoTo

If you're familiar with the *GoTo labelname* statement, you won't have any trouble understanding the *On Error GoTo labelname* error trapping construct. If code executed after the *On Error GoTo* statement causes a run-time error, VBA will automatically execute a *GoTo labelname* statement instead of continuing normal code execution or terminating the procedure. The pending *GoTo,* which will never be executed if no run-time error is raised, remains in effect until the procedure is finished or until another *On Error...* statement is executed. The code after the *labelname* label is referred to as an *error handler.*

```
Sub AnySub()
    On Error GoTo ErrorTrap
    :
    :
    Exit Sub
ErrorTrap:
    Select Case Err
        'Figure out how to handle the error.
    End Select
End Sub
```

If a run-time error occurs, code execution moves immediately to the code in the error trap, where the error can be dealt with. To return to normal code execution, your program can make one of three calls:

Resume All error information is cleared, and execution returns to the line of code that initially caused the error. You should use the *Resume* statement with caution. If whatever caused the initial error hasn't been taken care of when you call *Resume,* the line of code that caused the error will execute and raise another error. If the error condition persists, the chances for an infinite loop are very high because each subsequent error will return control to the error trap, which will repeatedly return control to the same misbehaving line of code.

Resume Next All current error information is cleared, and control is returned to the line of code after the offending line so that normal execution can resume.

[End | Exit][Sub | Function | Property] Any of these statements terminates code execution in the current procedure. All error information is cleared before the procedure terminates, and normal execution proceeds in the calling procedure (if there is one).

A run-time error in an error trap itself is considered to be an untrapped error. The error will be propagated back up the call chain to the next calling procedure that has an active error trap. Generally, you'll want to put an *Exit procedure* statement before the label marking the start of your error trap to avoid running unnecessary code and because calling *Resume* or *Resume Next* without a corresponding jump into an error trap is illegal.

On Error Resume Next

The *On Error GoTo* philosophy of error trapping is "if there's a problem, go away and fix it and come back when it's cleared up." *On Error Resume Next* lets you employ a fundamentally different error trapping philosophy: "ignore any problems for now, but keep the error information for later." If a line of code generates a run-time error when *On Error Resume Next* is active, VBA proceeds with the next line of code. All the error information has been set and is available in the Err object, but the error isn't raised.

By using *On Error Resume Next*, you can avoid writing complicated error traps. This construct lets you move your error handling code inline to be executed right where the error is generated, not two pages of code later. Inline error trapping is particularly useful for handling expected errors. Let's look at a code snippet that determines if a collection object recognizes a key name:

```
Dim coll As VBA.Collection
  .
  .
  .
On Error Resume Next
coll.Item strKeyName
If Err Then
    'This item isn't in the collection.
End If
'Clear the Err object, and turn off error trapping.
On Error GoTo 0
```

Clearing the error When *On Error Resume Next* is active, be sure that you call *Err.Clear* or *On Error GoTo 0* after checking the value of *Err.Number* and handling the error that occurred. The current error information won't be cleared unless you clear it explicitly, and the error values will propagate over the procedure boundaries. And if a calling procedure is relying on an *On Error Resume Next* error trapping construct, that procedure will get a false positive reading when it runs *If Err Then* to see if an error needs to be handled. Both procedures will end up handling the error. Bugs resulting from this type of dangling error can be difficult to track down.

Custom object errors

VBA provides a large set of run-time error values, but no set of error values can be considered comprehensive—covering all situations. As you define custom class modules, you'll find that you want to specify, document, and return custom error values specific to your application. For example, if you're writing a class to make telephone calls, you might return an error number meaning "The number is busy"—a concept not covered by the predefined set of VBA errors.

To specify an error specific to your class without using an error value already defined by VBA, VBA provides a base *object error number* defined by the constant vbObjectError. By adding your error value to this base number, you can create and return errors specific to your object without trespassing on VBA's personal error space. Let's say your object defines the following custom errors:

```
Public Const PHONE_ERR_BUSY = 513
Public Const PHONE_ERR_INVALID_NUMBER = 514
```

In the *Dial* method, your class would then raise an error,

```
Err.Raise vbObjectError + PHONE_ERR_BUSY
```

and the calling procedure would respond with

```
On Error Resume Next
PhoneClass.Dial strPhoneNumber
If Err Then
    If Err And vbObjectError Then
        Select Case Err Xor vbObjectError
            Case PHONE_ERR_BUSY
                'Try again later.
            Case PHONE_ERR_INVALID_NUMBER
                'Update the database.
        End Select
    Else
        'Standard VBA error
    End If
End If
On Error GoTo 0
```

NOTE vbObjectError has a hexadecimal value of 80040000. The values in the top two bytes (the 8004 part) of any error code have special meaning to OLE Automation and shouldn't be modified. Consequently, custom error numbers added to vbObjectError should be restricted to the range 0-65535. Furthermore, you should avoid numbers below 512 because VBA maps some of these numbers to other errors. For example, Err.Raise vbObjectError + 483 comes through as run-time error 429, "OLE Automation server can't create object."

An object doesn't have to return a vbObjectError error value for every run-time error. If the error is generic and well-defined by a standard VBA error value, go ahead and return the standard error number. For example, defining a custom object error for "Out of memory" (error 7) or for "Subscript out of range" (error 9) would be excessive. However, just because you use the standard error number doesn't mean that the text description of the error needs to be standard. See the "Rich Error Information" topic for information on custom error descriptions.

Library Constants

With the proliferation of object libraries resulting from the increasing number of OLE Automation object servers, you, the programmer, face an increasing challenge: you need to keep straight not only objects, with their associated properties and methods, but also the values to use with the methods and properties. For example, you can assign any of these three different values to the WindowState property of Excel's Window object: *-4143*, *-4140*, or *-4137*. Luckily, you don't have to remember those three numbers. Instead, you just have to remember *xlNormal*, *xlMinimized*, and *xlMaximized*. These three constant values, along with many others, are defined for you in Excel's object library.

When you commit a line of code, VBA will case any known constants the same way it cases object, method, property, and variable names. You'll know right away whether the constant value you've entered is valid. Extensive use of constants also makes your code more readable. Although you may know that assigning the MousePointer property a value of *11* results in an hourglass cursor, you may not remember what that value means the next time you read your code. However, you—or another programmer maintaining your code—won't have any problem deciphering this line of code:

```
Screen.MousePointer = vbHourglass
```

Many object libraries keep constants for the entire library in one group called (surprise!) *Constants*, but it's also possible (and it's the current trend) to put related constants in separate groups, as in the *AlignmentConstants* and *CheckBoxConstants* groups in the *Visual Basic objects and procedures* library. It's customary for all constants in an object library to have the same prefix—xl for Excel, for example, and vb for Visual Basic or for Visual Basic for Applications.

An unqualified constant name is generally sufficient to uniquely identify the constant in a given project, but there are occasional conflicts when a project contains references to two or more libraries that define a constant with the same name. If there is a conflict, the value from the referenced library with the highest priority is used. You can be more precise about which constant value you want to use by qualifying the name of the constant with the name of the library and/or the group that contains it. All three of the following lines of code have the same end result. Assume that chkRequired is a CheckBox control:

```
chkRequired.Value = vbChecked
chkRequired.Value = CheckBoxConstants.vbChecked
chkRequired.Value = VB.CheckBoxConstants.vbChecked
```

NOTE If you have a hard time remembering the name of a particular constant, the Object Navigator tool on the book's companion CD can help you find it.

Option Base

When you use the *Dim* or *ReDim* statement to dimension an array in Visual Basic for Applications, the default lower bound for each dimension of the array is 0. For example, the following statement creates a 1-dimensional array with a lower bound of 0 and an upper bound of 10:

```
Dim strArray(10) As String
```

Note that you can also explicitly specify the lower bound of your array:

```
Dim strArray(0 To 10) As String
```

By placing the *Option Base 1* statement at the top of your code module, you tell VBA to use a default lower bound of 1 instead of 0 for your arrays. *Option Base 0* is the default. The default base options are pretty limited—you can specify only 0 or 1. For example,

```
Option Base 1
:
Dim strArray(10) As String
```

is equivalent to

```
Dim strArray(1 To 10) As String
```

Since all of Microsoft Excel's collections are 1 based, including the Range object, it's a good idea to use *Option Base 1* in Excel modules that make extensive use of array manipulation.

Option Compare

By default, string comparisons in Visual Basic for Applications are case-sensitive. The expression

```
"a" = "A"
```

returns False. This type of string comparison, which is very fast, is known as *Binary* comparison. Case-insensitive comparison, which considers upper and lower case letters to be equivalent, is known as *Text* comparison.

If you want all string comparisons in a given module to be case-insensitive, put *Option Compare Text* at the top of your module. (You can also use the default *Option Compare Binary* if you want to be explicit.)

The string comparison mode affects all string comparison expressions in the module, all *Select Case* statements in the module that use strings, the Like operator throughout the module, and the *InStr* and *StrComp* run-time functions in the module. The *InStr* and *StrComp* functions default to the comparison mode of the module, but they can also take an optional parameter to override the module's default comparison mode setting. For string comparison expressions, *Select Case* statements, and Like operations, there's no way to override the comparison mode on a line by line basis. See Visual Basic Help for more information on Like, *InStr*, and *StrComp*.

Option Compare Text is particularly useful anytime you're evaluating data the user types in. Suppose you had a program that asked the user to enter the abbreviation for a state name. You'd want "wa," "Wa," and "WA" to be equivalent, so you'd use the following code:

```
Option Compare Text
Private strStates(0 To 49) As String
:
'Compare the two left characters to known states.
For i% = 0 To 49
    If strStates(i%) = Left$(strInputState, 2) Then
        strInputState = strStates(i%) 'Synchronize casing.
        Exit For
    End If
Next i%
If i% = 50 Then Beep 'Not a valid state.
```

Of course, you could also write the code without *Option Compare Text*. Here are two options:

```
'Case the search value before comparing. Assume strStates
'is upper case.
If strStates(i%) = UCase$(Left$(strInputState, 2)) Then

'Use the StrComp function to force text-based comparison.
If 0 = StrComp(strStates(i%), Left$(strInputState, 2), 1) Then
```

The two alternative lines of code are functional, but they're much harder to read than the *Option Compare Text* module's code. You also stand a much higher chance of introducing a bug if your code must be case-insensitive and you rely on *StrComp* or *UCase$* to do your comparisons. Although text comparison isn't quite as fast as binary comparison, it saves a lot of coding and a lot of bugs if your code relies heavily on case-insensitive string comparisons.

Option Explicit

Putting *Option Explicit* at the top of a module, that is at the top of the General Declarations area in the Code pane, forces Visual Basic for Applications to require a declaration (*Dim*, *Static*, *Public*, or *Private* statement) for every variable used in the module. To automatically add this line of code to every new module, class, and form, check the Require Variable Declaration option on the Environment tab of the Options dialog.

By default, variables in VBA code don't have to be declared. Hence the following code will compile and run correctly:

```
Private Sub Command1_Click()
    Open Text1 For Output As fnum%
    For i% = 0 To List1.ListCount - 1
        Print #fnum%, List1.List(i%)
    Next i%
    Close fnum%
End Sub
```

Since this is so simple, why would a programmer want to require a declaration for each variable? A declaration for every variable requires a few extra lines of code but is well worth the effort. In the preceding example, a typo in the *Print* line, *List1.List(j%)*, would result in repeated printing of the first element of List1 to the file because j% would have remained *0* no matter what happened to i%. You can easily avoid this kind of typo bug by using *Option Explicit*. With *Option Explicit* turned on, the buggy code simply wouldn't compile.

Here's the same code with *Option Explicit* turned on:

```
Private Sub Command1_Click()
Dim fnum%, i%
    Open Text1 For Output As fnum%
    For i% = 0 To List1.ListCount - 1
        Print #fnum%, List1.List(i%)
    Next i%
    Close fnum%
End Sub
```

Here's a summary of the advantages of using *Option Explicit*:

- You avoid typos. If a variable isn't declared, VBA assigns it a type Variant unless a *DefXXX* statement is in effect or a type character (%, &, !, #, @, $) is used. Variants are assigned an *Empty* value by default, which evaluates to *0* in a numeric expression. Hence, any variable name that's incorrectly typed will have the value *0*. This kind of bug can be difficult to track.
- You will receive immediate feedback from the editor in the design environment about whether a variable or a constant has been typed correctly. If you declare a variable Foo, anytime you type in *foo*, it will change to Foo when you commit the line of code. The case of a variable provides instant feedback while you're writing code and can help you remember long variable, method, property, and constant names. If a variable name isn't defined, the case of all occurrences of that variable will match the case of the version of the variable name last typed. Hence, an earlier Foo will change to foo. If you see the case of a previously typed variable change, it's a good indication that the variable hasn't been declared.
- You end up using fewer variables. A programmer who must declare all variables is more aware of the number of variables in use and tends to use one temporary variable for several tasks in a procedure.
- It can be easier to decipher and maintain someone else's code if you can see the variables declared up front.

Qualified Identifiers: Square Brackets

Occasionally you'll need to use the name of an object, a method, or a property that doesn't comply with basic syntax rules. In most of these cases, the name will have a leading underscore or, if you're using the WordBasic object, a trailing $. Visual Basic for Applications allows you to use an invalid name, but you must enclose the name in square brackets. VBA will case a name in square brackets just as it will any other recognized name. The default property of a ListBox control, for example, is called _Default, and its value corresponds to the value of the currently selected item in the list. Square brackets allow you to use the _Default property directly in a *With* statement:

```
With MyListBox
    'If the list has a selection, then print the current value.
    If Not .ListIndex Then Debug.Print .[_Default]
End With
```

The three objects in Microsoft Excel that can be created with the *New* keyword (_ExcelApplication, _ExcelSheet, and _ExcelChart) are invalid VBA names. However, with square brackets, you can use these names in your VBA code.

```
'Declare an implicitly created Worksheet object.
Dim XLSheet As New [_ExcelSheet]
```

Let's look at objects in Excel to see two more uses for square brackets. The first use is with the collection lookup, or bang (!), operator. If a collection key name includes a space, you must put the name in square brackets. The other use of square brackets is for setting off a *qualified identifier*, a name that can't be resolved by VBA at compile-time but that can be resolved by the host at run-time.

Let's look at a code example that illustrates both uses of square brackets. When run in an Excel macro, the following code will put the values *1*, *2*, *3*, and *4* in the first four cells of the *Data Sheet* worksheet in the active workbook:

```
Sub NotSoCommonCode()
    Sheets![Data Sheet].[a1:b2] = Array(Array(1, 2), Array(3, 4))
End Sub
```

Let's look more closely at this code's second use of square brackets. The expression *a1:b2* is clearly not in Excel's object library, so VBA can do nothing with it—but Excel knows exactly what the code is talking about and resolves the expression at run-time as a cell address. In fact, Excel will even resolve the expression *a1:b2* to the active sheet if you don't specify a sheet:

```
Sub EvenWeirderCode()
    [a1:b2] = Array(Array(1, 2), Array(3, 4))
End Sub
```

NOTE In Visual Basic 3, any method or property name that uses the same name as a basic keyword's name has to be enclosed in square brackets. The most common conflicting name was Close. In Visual Basic 4, this restriction no longer applies.

Rich Error Information

In Visual Basic 3 and Excel-VBA, error information is very limited. The *Err* function returns the value of the current error, and the *Error$()* function returns the description of the current error. There's no way to set descriptions for user-defined error values. VBA 2.0 has support for *rich error information,* which allows your objects to provide customized information about an error instead of just an uninformative number. In VB4, this additional error information can be read and set by means of properties and methods of the Err object. (If you're unfamiliar with error trapping constructs in VBA, refer to the "Error Trapping" topic in this appendix.)

Before we examine the properties and methods of the Err object in detail, let's work up a small case study of using rich error information. Suppose you have a Documents class with an *Open* method, which takes a FileName parameter. If the file isn't valid, the method should return run-time error 53 (File not found) or 76 (Path not found). We'll write two versions of the routine: the first raises an error with default information, and the second raises an error with rich error information.

```
'The Open method with default error information
Public Sub Open(FileName As String)
    .
    .
    .
    'Let any error propagate back to the calling
    'procedure with default error information.
    m_fNum = FreeFile
    Open FileName For Input As m_fNum
    .
    .
    .
End Sub

'The Open method with rich error information
Public Sub Open(FileName As String)
    .
    .
    .
    On Error GoTo ErrorTrap
    m_fNum = FreeFile
    Open FileName For Input As m_fNum
    .
    .
    .
    Exit Sub
ErrorTrap:
    With Err
        Select Case .Number
            'File not found and Path not found
            Case 53, 76
```

```
                'Raise the error again. Override the default
                'Source and Description fields, but use the
                'same error number.
                .Raise .Number, "Documents", _
                       "Path or file not found, '" & FileName & "'"
            Case Else
                'Raise the error again. Override just the
                'Source field.
                .Raise .Number, "Documents"
        End Select
    End With
End Sub
```

Although the second version of the *Open* method is more complex than the first, it returns useful information to the caller. Instead of an error description that says "File not found," we get the error description, "Path or file not found 'C:\SomeDir\Bogus.Doc' " The rich error description is ready for display to an end user. Displaying the default VBA error description to an end user is likely to lead to frustration at best—and it just might attract a large magnet to your distribution disks.

Now for those Err object details. A reference to the Err object is obtained by calling the VBA *Err* function. There is only one Err object: there is no support for creating new instances of the Err object; you can retrieve only the instance maintained by VBA.

Err object properties

Number The default property of the Err object. If you use Err in your code (without a dot after it), you are reading or setting the Number property. This default behavior allows VBA 2.0 to interpret code ported from Visual Basic 3 or Excel-VBA to Visual Basic 4.

Source A name identifying the object that raised the error. By default, the Source property is set to the name of the project (Project1, for example) as soon as an error is raised. See "Setting the Source property" on the next page.

Description A string describing the error. By default, the Description value is set to the VBA description of the current error number. Description is the field most commonly modified when you're using rich error information. The current value of *Err.Description* in VB4 is equivalent to the return value of the *Error$()* function in Excel. In VB4, *Error$()* is still supported, but it won't reliably return all user-defined error descriptions.

HelpFile and HelpContext If you're distributing a VB object server designed as a tool for use by third parties, you'll probably provide a help file as well. If the HelpFile and HelpContext fields of the Err object are set when an error is raised, the Help button in the VBA error notification dialog will be enabled and will provide information to your clients that will help them figure out what went wrong.

LastDllError This read only property is useful only if you're using API calls in your program. When they fail, many of the calls in the Win32 API set an error value that must be retrieved with another API function call to *GetLastError*. One error value is maintained for each thread on the system, and the error value may potentially be reset by any API call. Calling *GetLastError* directly from VBA code is useless because VB is likely to make API calls that reset the thread's error value before you are able to call the *GetLastError* API from your VBA code. *GetLastError* is called for you immediately after an API call has been completed, and the LastDllError property of the Err object saves the information returned from *GetLastError* until you make another API call from your VBA code.

Err object methods

Raise(Number, [Source, [Description, [HelpFile, [HelpContext]]]]) The *Raise* method is used to raise an error. Setting properties of the Err object, including the Number property, won't actually raise an error until the *Raise* method is called explicitly. The parameters of the *Raise* method correspond to the settable properties of the Err object. Only the Number parameter is required. The *Err.Raise <ErrorNumber>* is equivalent to the now obsolete statement *Error <ErrorNumber>*.

Clear The *Clear* method, as the name implies, reinitializes all properties of the Err object. *Err.Clear* is equivalent to *Err = 0* in older VB versions and in VBA 1.0.

Setting the Source property

The default value for the Source field of the Err object is the name of your Visual Basic project, which can be specified in the Options dialog. Unfortunately, ProjectName isn't a property of VB's App object, so there's no easy way to programmatically determine the default Source value and, hence, whether the Source property is currently set to its default value. The *DefaultErrSource* function shown below raises a trapped error to use the Source field of the Err object to determine the project name at run-time. The value is then cached in a static variable, so only the first call to *DefaultErrSource* will affect the current state of the Err object.

```
Public Function DefaultErrSource() As String
Static strSource As String
    If Len(strSource) Then
        DefaultErrSource = strSource
        Exit Function
    End If
    On Error GoTo ErrorTrap
```

```
    Err.Raise 0
ErrorTrap:
    strSource = Err.Source
    DefaultErrSource = strSource
End Function
```

Now that you know how to get the default string for the Source property, let's look at when you might use this information. If you implement a class in VB that creates an instance of Excel (or any other class of object) internally, you want to avoid overwriting rich error information returned by Excel.

```
Private Sub Class_Initialize()
    'Make sure the data in the DefaultErrSource
    'function is initialized.
    DefaultErrSource
End Sub

Public Sub SomeMethod()
    :

ErrorTrap:
    With Err
        If .Source = DefaultErrSource Then
            'The error was raised locally. Rich error
            'information hasn't been set yet.
            .Raise .Number, "ThisClass"
        Else
            'Raise the error again without disturbing
            'any of the current rich error information.
            .Raise .Number
        End If
    End With
End Sub
```

If rich error information has been set by a dependent call, you're doing yourself and your user a disservice if you overwrite the information. The object that first raises an error is best equipped to give the most descriptive information about it. If the error number returned by a dependent object isn't a number you've documented as a potential error return from your object, you should re-raise the error with a different number, but you shouldn't change the Source and Description fields. All of the Err object fields except Number are intended for user information. Only Number should be relied upon programmatically to determine which error was raised.

Scoping

Variable and procedure scoping is an integral part of programming with Visual Basic. The scope of a variable or a procedure determines which modules and procedures can access it. We'll look at five different levels of scoping: local, module-level, global, project-level, and library-level. Then we'll look at how Visual Basic for Applications resolves name conflicts among these various scoping levels.

Local scope If your program is well-designed, most of your variables will have local scope. A local variable can be declared anywhere inside a procedure—the fact that it's declared there makes it local—and is accessible only within the procedure in which it's declared.

```
Sub MyProc()
Dim iCounter As Integer
    For iCounter = 0 To ...
End Sub
```

A local variable is very inexpensive in that it doesn't take up any permanent memory in your program. When a procedure is called, all of its local variables are pushed onto the stack. When the procedure terminates, its locals are pulled off the stack. No permanent memory is allocated.

If you declare a local variable with the *Static* keyword instead of with *Dim,* the variable is put in a permanent memory space instead of on the stack. A static local variable retains its value between calls to its procedure. A static local variable in a procedure in a class module does *not* retain its value across different class instances. A separate static local variable is maintained in memory for each instance of the class. A common use for a static local variable is stopping an event procedure from recursing:

```
Private Sub List1_Click()
Static fStayOut As Boolean
    If fStayOut Then Exit Sub
    fStayOut = True
    :

    'This line fires another List1_Click event, which
    'will exit immediately because of the immutable
    'value of the fStayOut variable.
    List1.ListIndex = 0
    :

    fStayOut = False
End Sub
```

Module-level scope A module-level variable is declared with the *Dim* or the *Private* keyword before any procedure declarations in the module. A module-level variable maintains its value until the program terminates (for a module) or until the class instance is destroyed (for a form or class module). A module-level variable is available to all procedures in the module, but it can't be accessed from outside the module.

```
'A module-level variable
Private m_strStatus As String
'A private procedure to set the m_strStatus variable
Private Sub SetStatus(NewStatus As String)
    m_strStatus = NewStatus
End Sub
'A public procedure to display the m_strStatus variable
Public Sub ShowStatus()
    If Len(m_strStatus) Then
        MsgBox m_strStatus
        m_strStatus = vbNullString
    End If
End Sub
```

A module-level procedure is declared with the *Private* keyword. In the preceding code snippet, the private *SetStatus* procedure is available only to procedures inside its module. The *ShowStatus* procedure is declared as public, and we'll look at the significance of that next.

Global scope To make a variable visible or a procedure callable from outside the module, you simply declare it as you would at module-level but set its declaration keyword to *Public* instead of *Private.* A public variable or procedure in an ordinary module is available from anywhere in your project. A public variable in a form or class module becomes a property of the object, and the property's scope is confined to use with the object. It doesn't get global scope. In a form or class module, a public procedure becomes a method—and, in the case of a public property procedure, a property—of an instance of the class.

```
Public Status As String
```

Project-level scope With local, module-level, and global scope, you have full control over all of your variable and procedure declarations. However, since you can't write code at project-level scope, VBA declares project-level variables for you. One project-level variable is declared for each application object in a referenced object library, and one project-level variable is declared for each form in your project.

If your program contains a reference to the Microsoft Excel object library and contains one form called frmMain, VBA will provide the following lines of code for you. You can't see or edit these implicit variables, but you can access them from code anywhere in your project.

```
Public [_ExcelApplication] As New [_ExcelApplication]
Public frmMain As New frmMain
```

Many Visual Basic programs make extensive use of these pre-declared variables. For example, calling *frmMain.Show* in any procedure makes use of the implicit frmMain variable.

Library-level scope Library-level scope doesn't involve variables at all. Any procedure, constant, or object declared in an object library lives at this scoping level and is available to any procedure in your project when the project references the library.

In all of the scoping levels below library level, name conflicts aren't allowed within the same level. For example, you can't have two local iCounter variables in the same procedure. However, at the library level, it's perfectly valid to have two different procedures with the same name in different libraries. VBA provides a priority value for each of the reference libraries. The highest-priority library that can resolve the name gets chosen. Hiding a procedure name in a lower-priority library is known as *name shadowing*. Refer to "Library Constants" in this appendix for more information on resolving name shadowing problems.

Name conflict resolution

So what happens when you have the same variable or procedure name declared at two different scoping levels? VBA resolves the name to the variable or procedure with the lowest scope—local scope is lowest for variables, and module-level scope is lowest for procedures. In the following code snippet, the message box in the *SetStatus1* procedure will always display an empty string because the assignment statement in *SetStatus2* sets a local strStatus variable instead of the module-level variable with the same name.

```
Private strStatus As String
Sub SetStatus1()
    strStatus = vbNullString
    SetStatus2
    MsgBox strStatus
End Sub
Sub SetStatus2()
Dim strStatus As String
    strStatus = "This will set the local variable"
End Sub
```

If you need to call a procedure at global scope that has the same name as a procedure at module-level scope, you can qualify the global procedure name with the name of the module or project that contains the procedure and avoid name conflicts. Look closely at the following code snippets for examples of calling like-named procedures in several modules. Assume that all of these modules are contained in a project called *Project1*.

Module1 code module

```
Public Sub DoLoad()
End Sub
Public Sub NotifyLoaded()
End Sub
```

Module2 code module

```
Public Sub DoLoad()
End Sub
```

Form1 code module

```
Private Sub Form_Load()

    'Call this module's DoLoad.
    DoLoad

    'Call Module1's DoLoad.
    Module1.DoLoad

    'Call Module2's DoLoad.
    Module2.DoLoad

    'Call DoLoad at project level. Won't compile; two
    'public DoLoad procedures therefore have global
    'scope in this project, so VBA can't resolve the
    'procedure name.
    'Project1.DoLoad

    'Will compile at module level with project specified.
    Project1.Module1.DoLoad

    'Call NotifyLoaded in this module.
    NotifyLoaded

    'Call NotifyLoaded in Module1. Since only one
    'NotifyLoaded procedure has global scope, this
    'code calls Module1.NotifyLoaded.
    Project1.NotifyLoaded
End Sub
Private Sub DoLoad()
End Sub
```

(continued)

```
Private Sub NotifyLoaded()
End Sub
```

Overriding project- and library-level variables and procedures

Suppose, for debugging purposes, that you want to keep a log of every call to the *MsgBox* function but that you don't want to modify very much code. All you have to do is add your own *MsgBox* function at global scope in an ordinary module. Since VBA's *MsgBox* function is at library-level scope, which is at a higher level than global scope, any unqualified call to *MsgBox* will call your lower-level global function instead of VBA's library-level function. Your *MsgBox* function, in turn, can call *VBA.MsgBox* after writing to your log file. The rest of your program will behave exactly as it did before you introduced the custom *MsgBox* function.

```
Public Function MsgBox(Prompt As Variant, _
                Optional Buttons As Variant, _
                Optional Title As Variant, _
                Optional HelpFile As Variant, _
                Optional Context As Variant) As Integer
Dim fNum As Integer
    fNum = FreeFile
    Open "MsgBox.Log" For Append As fNum
    Print #fNum, Prompt
    Close #fNum
    MsgBox = VBA.MsgBox(Prompt, Buttons, Title, HelpFile, Context)
End Function
```

Similarly, you can override a project-level variable by declaring a variable of the same name at global scope. For example, if you have a form called frmMain and want to disable the implicit project-level frmMain variable, you can use the following code at global scope:

```
Public frmMain As frmMain
```

Now you'll get a run-time error if you call

```
frmMain.Show
```

Instead, you'll have to explicitly create the frmMain object:

```
Set frmMain = New frmMain
frmMain.Show
```

These examples of manipulating library, project, and global-level variables and functions aren't meant to encourage you to make such procedure and variable overriding a common programming practice. They're here in the spirit of For Your Information.

Server Registration

If a Visual Basic application is to create an object that's implemented in an external object server application, the external application must be correctly registered. In general, all server registration is taken care of at setup: the Setup Wizard application that ships with VB will correctly register dependent-object servers with the system. However, it's always a good idea to have a safety net. If the *New* or *CreateObject* keywords fail to create an object, your program can try to register the object server at run-time.

Any OLE DLL created with Visual Basic has two entry points to register and unregister the server with the system. If creation of an object fails at run-time but the object's DLL is on the system in the current path, then the *DllRegisterServer* entry point can be called to force the DLL to register itself. You'll rarely find a need to use the *DllUnregisterServer* entry point. The following code snippet demonstrates how to call the *DllRegisterServer* entry point to register the MyObject object implemented in MyServer.Dll.

```
Private Declare Function RegisterMyObject Lib "MyServer.Dll" _
                Alias "DllRegisterServer" () As Long
Function VerifyMyObjectRegistered() As Boolean
Dim MyObject As MyServer.MyObject
    'Default to successful creation.
    VerifyMyObjectRegistered = True
    On Error Resume Next
    'Try to create the object.
    Set MyObject = New MyServer.MyObject
    If Err Then
        'Creating the object failed; try to register its server.
        RegisterMyObject
        'Clear any errors.
        Err.Clear
        'Try a second time to create a MyObject instance.
        Set MyObject = New MyServer.MyObject
        'If object creation still fails, then we're stuck.
        If Err Then
            MsgBox "Can't find MyServer.Dll, quitting.", vbCritical
            VerifyMyObjectRegistered = False
        End If
    End If
End Function
```

If you need to register an object that's implemented in a VB .Exe file instead of a DLL, you can use the Shell function to force the .Exe to self-register. All of the VB .Exe files that are object servers support the command line switches *Regserver* and *Unregserver*. To register an EXE instead of a DLL server in the previous code snippet, replace the *RegisterMyObject* line inside the *VerifyMyObjectRegistered* function with this:

```
Shell "MyServer.Exe /Regserver"
```

Browsing with the References dialog

In Visual Basic's design mode, you use the References dialog to add and remove references from your project. If an object library isn't in the Available References: list, you can click the Browse button and find the file containing the type library yourself. At this point, you'll find that you can program to your heart's content, but you won't be able to create an object from the referenced library when you actually run your program. What's happened?

The Browse button has successfully registered the object library with the system under the *Typelib* key in the register, but it hasn't registered the CLSID of the server. Recall from Chapter 6 that the CLSID is the value added to the registry for each creatable object exposed by an OLE Automation object server. A CLSID must be registered before an object can be created. If you find yourself with a partially registered server, you'll have to do one of the following:

- If your server is a VB .Exe file, run the .Exe once with the /Regserver command line.
- If your server is a VB .Dll file, use the RegSvr32.Exe utility from the \Tools\Pss directory of the Visual Basic CD. Run *RegSvr32 MyServer.Dll.*

If you still can't get your server application to run correctly, rerun the application's setup program.

With Statement

A *With* statement is a convenience of Visual Basic for Applications syntax that enables you to make multiple property and method calls to the same object:

```
With <Object variable or Expression returning an object>
    .<Method>
    .<Property> =...
End With
```

If the expression after the *With* keyword is a simple object variable, *With MyObject* can act as shorthand—repeatedly typing *MyObject* can get tedious. If the *With* expression is more than a simple variable, the expression will be evaluated only once instead of several times. Compare the following code snippets to center the active form on the screen:

```
'Snippet without With
Screen.ActiveForm.Move (Screen.Width - Screen.ActiveForm.Width) / 2, _
      (Screen.Height - Screen.ActiveForm.Height) / 2

'Snippet with With
With Screen.ActiveForm
    .Move (Screen.Width - .Width) / 2, (Screen.Height - .Height) / 2
End With
```

The first code snippet evaluates the expression *Screen.ActiveForm* three times. Using the *With* statement in the second snippet reduces the number of evaluations to one.

At the first line of a *With* statement, VBA assigns a reference to the object specified after the *With* keyword to a temporary object variable. VBA implicitly puts this hidden object variable in front of all unqualified dots inside the *With* block. The same binding rules apply to the hidden object variable as to an ordinary object variable. If the expression used in the *With* statement returns a Variant type or an Object type, every call in the *With* block that uses the unqualified dot syntax will be late bound. To ensure optimal performance in a *With* block, be sure that the variable or expression used in the *With* statement returns a hard-typed object. Here's an example that uses Microsoft Excel objects.

```
Dim xlSheet As Excel.Worksheet
Dim xlWindow As Excel.Window
:

'Stop displaying headings, tabs, and gridlines.
Set xlWindow = xlSheet.Parent.Windows(1)
With xlWindow
    .DisplayHeadings = False
    .DisplayWorkbookTabs = False
    .DisplayGridlines = False
End With
```

With statements can also be nested. Any unqualified dot refers to the nearest enclosing *With* expression. A nested *With* expression can refer to the containing *With* statement, but this isn't required.

```
Set xlWindow = xlSheet.Parent.Windows(1)
With xlWindow
    :
    With .ActiveCell      'Refers back to the outer With expression.
        .Value = 100
        .Font.Bold = True
    End With
```

(continued)

```
    With xlSheet     'Temporarily overrides the outer With expression.
        .ProtectContents = True
        .ProtectWindows = True
    End With
End With
```

Although it isn't as common as the dot operator, the ! (bang) collection lookup operator can also be used without qualification inside a *With* statement:

```
With Sheets
    !Sheet1.Activate
End With
```

With statements are particularly useful for optimizing and removing clutter from object-intensive code. But *With* statements leave you at a big disadvantage when it comes to debugging. VBA doesn't support instant or persistent watches on unqualified expressions that begin with a dot. To get the current value for *xlSheet.ProtectWindows*, for instance, you'd have to enter the full expression as a watch or in the Immediate pane. Trying to watch just *.ProtectWindows* will fail.

Appendix B

The Object Navigator

The Object Navigator application on the companion CD-ROM will help you find your way, easily and quickly, through the maze of objects described in any object library. The Navigator's primary service is to rapidly locate any object, any method or property *member*, or any constant value in one or more object libraries. Second, the Navigator is an expression builder. Using the Navigator, you can create code fragments, complete with parameter values, that are guaranteed to be valid object expressions.

Why Use the Navigator?

The standard Visual Basic for Applications Object Browser also shows you objects, members, and constants, but that's where its similarities to the Object Navigator end. The Object Browser has no way to indicate the structure of an object model, no search capability, no way to view objects from multiple libraries simultaneously, no way to view categories of objects, and no expression building capabilities. All of these needs have been addressed in the Object Navigator.

If you know exactly what you're looking for, or if you want to jump directly to a particular procedure in your own Visual Basic project, use the standard VBA Object Browser. But if you haven't memorized the hierarchical structures and contents of the myriad of object models available to the custom solutions developer, the Object Navigator is the way to go.

Cross-Reference See the developer's note at the end of this appendix for a brief discussion of the history and design of the Object Navigator.

Navigator Setup

The Object Navigator setup program is on the companion CD in the Object Navigator directory. The default installation directory on your hard drive is C:\Program Files\Object Navigator. If you already have Visual Basic 4 installed, the Navigator will take up less than 450K of additional disk space. After setup is completed, you can launch the Navigator by using the program group and icon provided by Setup or by running ObjNav.Exe from the command line.

Before you start making regular use of the Navigator, it's a good idea to give this appendix a thorough reading. It explains the features of the Navigator and the capabilities represented by the different user interface elements. You should read this appendix at the computer with the Navigator running. You might not end up using many of the Navigator's advanced features right away, but you'll know what's available.

Navigator User Interface

Throughout this appendix, we'll be focusing on Navigator user interface elements such as "lock buttons" and the "Browse pane." Refer to Figure B-1 at any time to identify these and the other Navigator user interface elements.

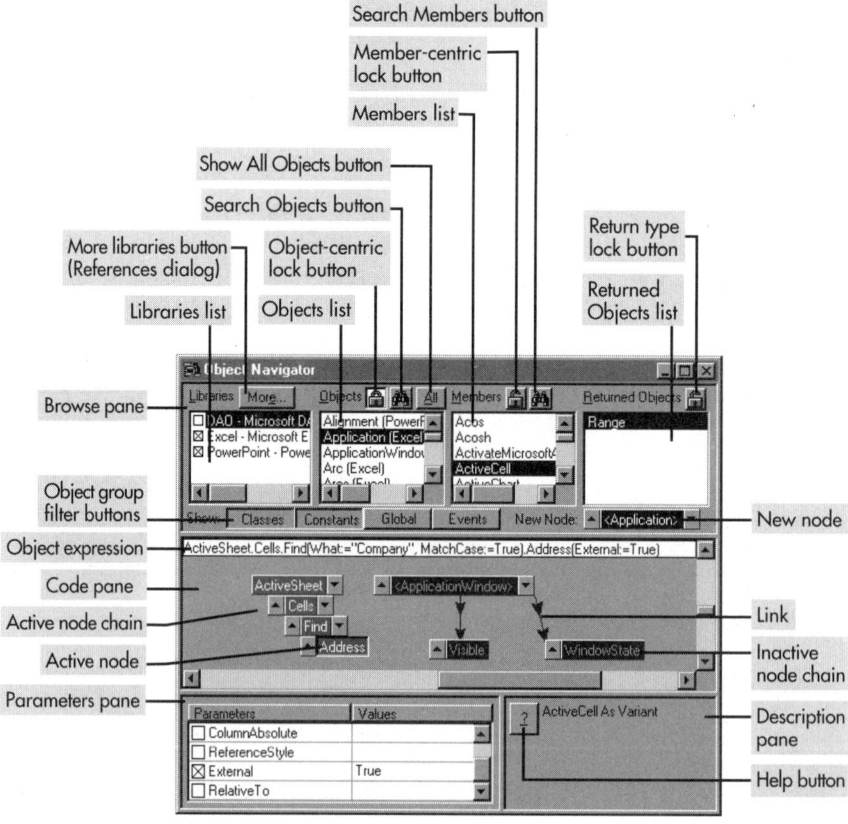

Figure B-1. *The Object Navigator user interface.*

Managing Libraries

An object browser of any type is useful only when it references libraries. The Object Navigator displays the list of currently loaded libraries in the Libraries list box in the left part of the Browse pane. An entry in the list contains the library name followed by the more descriptive library title: for example, PowerPoint - PowerPoint 7.0 Object Library. Unlike a Visual Basic for Applications project, the Navigator has no sense of library priority, so the libraries on the system are shown in alphabetical order.

The References Dialog

The Object Navigator References dialog, shown in Figure 3-2, should look familiar—it's based on the VBA References dialog and serves the same general purpose. To open the dialog, click the More button above the Libraries list. (If the Libraries list was empty when you last exited the Navigator—when the previous instance of the Navigator was shut down—the References dialog will be opened automatically when you launch the Navigator again.) You can use the Navigator References dialog to either add or remove entries in the Libraries list. When you first open the References dialog, the currently referenced libraries are grouped at the top of the Available References list, and all other valid object libraries on the system are displayed alphabetically below the current references.

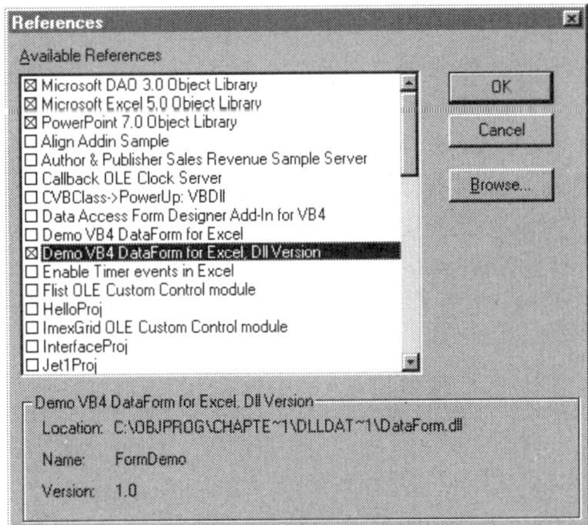

Figure B-2. *The Object Navigator References dialog box.*

To add or remove a library to or from the Navigator's Libraries list, simply check or uncheck the check box to the left of the library name. (You won't be able to check two libraries that use the same name.) If a library doesn't appear in the Available References list, you can use the Browse button to find the file containing the object library. Custom controls don't appear in the References dialog, so you'll have to use the Browse button to reference any custom controls you want to navigate. Once you've referenced a custom control, it will remain in the References dialog. Custom controls in your Visual Basic project will appear automatically when you open the Navigator as an add-in. (We'll look at the Navigator as an add-in in just a moment.)

When you've finished selecting your libraries, click the OK button. Current references that you've unchecked will be removed from the Libraries list, and any new libraries you've checked or located via the Browse button will be added. Or you can click Cancel to close the References dialog without saving any changes.

Activating Libraries

The Libraries list, like the Available References list in the References dialog, is a checked list box. Any library that's checked in the Libraries list is currently active—that is, it can be navigated. The Navigator's Browse pane completely ignores an inactive library. If more than one library is active, every object name shown in the Objects list will be followed by the name of the parent library in parentheses: for example, Range (Excel). To avoid repeating the obvious, the library name isn't shown if only one library is active.

The Navigator as a Visual Basic Add-In

The Object Navigator can be launched from the Visual Basic Add-Ins menu. Before launching the Navigator from the Add-Ins menu, you should save your project to disk. If your project hasn't been saved, references for a default project will be placed in the Navigator's Libraries list. When the Navigator is running as an add-in, the References dialog is unavailable. The More button that normally appears above the Libraries list changes to an Update button. After adding or removing references or custom controls to your project through the VB References dialog, you'll need to save your project and click the Update button in the Navigator to update the Libraries list to match the current state of your project.

Enhanced Browsing

The standard Visual Basic for Applications Object Browser displays the Classes/Modules: and Methods/Properties: list boxes. The corresponding list boxes in the Object Navigator are designated Objects and Members. In the VBA Object Browser, clicking in the Classes/Modules: list changes the contents of the Methods/Properties: list. Clicking in the Objects list to change the Members list is also the default behavior in the Object Navigator, but refinements are available. Let's take a look at the other options.

Object Groups

The Navigator lets you view objects and members by group. The four different groups described below can be selected one at a time or simultaneously. To toggle the selected state of a group, simply click the filter button associated with the group at the bottom of the Browse pane.

Classes The Classes group is the most common selection. It contains all object types that can appear after the *As* keyword in a *Dim* statement. The Returned Objects list is active only when the Classes group is selected. Members of an application object, which can be called without qualification, that is, members that don't require the dot (.) qualifier before their names, are listed under the <Unqualified> object name in the Classes group.

Constants Selecting the Constants category makes all library constants visible. For some libraries, such as Excel and DAO, all constants are grouped in a single object category called *Constants*. For other libraries, there are multiple constant groupings. Items added to the Objects list that belong to the Constants, Global, and Events groups aren't really objects because you can't declare an object variable with types from these groups. I'll call them *pseudo-objects*.

Global members Some object libraries—*Visual Basic for Applications*, for instance—contain declarations of direct calls to methods or properties that don't belong to an object proper. For example, VBA's DateTime pseudo-object, which appears in the Global category, has members such as *DateAdd*, *DateDiff*, and *WeekDay* that can be called directly in VBA code.

Events If an object is a control type, it may also have events associated with it. For example, VB's CommandButton object has a *Click* event. With the Events group selected, you'll usually see the same set of objects in the Objects list as you do with the Classes group selected, but event names will be shown in the Members list. If the Classes group is also active, events will appear in the Members list along with methods and properties.

Members list

The only thing noteworthy about the Members list is its use of a special item in the list called <Default>. The most commonly used property or method of an object is flagged in the object library as the default, and it's often useful to know what the default member is. When the <Default> entry in the Members list is selected, the description of the member in the lower right pane of the Navigator will reveal the identity of the default. Often, the default will also be listed elsewhere in the Members list, but this isn't always the case. For example, the default property of VB's ListBox object is called _Default and isn't normally visible in an object browser.

Returned Objects list

The Returned Objects list is the only Navigator list that doesn't have a counterpart in the VBA Object Browser. When the return type of a member is a class, that return type is shown in this list. In general, the list will contain zero or one entry. However, in two cases the Returned Objects list will contain more than one entry. If a member actually returns a value of a Variant or an Object type, the Navigator may show multiple returned object types for the member. (See "Link Files" on page 453.) In such a case, the return type entries in the Returned Objects list will be alphabetized.

The second case in which you might see multiple entries in the Returned Objects list is when the <Default> item is selected in the Members list. If the default member returns a value of an object type that has a default member that returns a value of an object type that has... Well, you get the picture. In such a case, all possible return types will be shown, with the return type of the current default object listed first. For example, DAO.DBEngine.<Default> has the following returned object types (in order): Workspaces, Workspace, Databases, Database, TableDefs, TableDef, Fields, and Field. As you can see from the following perfectly valid line of code, overuse of multiple levels of default types can be confusing, but the Navigator gives you the information you need if you want to use them. (See "Setting Parameters" on page 467 for more information on building expressions that contain multiple levels of default types.)

```
DBEngine(0)("MyDB")("Table1")("Name").AllowZeroLength = False
```

NOTE Object names in the Returned Objects list show the library name only if the returned object is contained in a different library than the library that contains the currently selected item in the Objects list. For example, selecting CheckBox (VB) in the Objects list and Font in the Members list will show Font (StdType) in the Returned Objects list because the Font object isn't contained in the *Visual Basic objects and procedures* object library.

Locking Lists

The Objects, Members, and Returned Objects lists in the Navigator are tightly linked. At any given time, at least one, and sometimes two, of these three lists are locked. What do I mean by *locked*? When one of these three browse lists is locked, clicking in either of the other two browse lists won't change the contents of the locked list. By default, the Objects list is locked and the other two lists are unlocked, which means that selecting an item in the Objects list might change the contents of the other two lists but clicking in the other two lists won't change the contents of the Objects list. I'll refer to this default behavior as the *object-centric mode.* A padlock button above each of the three lists indicates the locked state of the corresponding list. Figures B-3, B-4, and B-5 show the three list lock buttons in various states.

Object-centric mode

There are several ways to put the Navigator into object-centric mode.

- Click the right mouse button in the Objects or Returned Objects list to bring up the context menu. Select the Members of 'ObjectName' menu item.
- Double-click any item in the Objects or Returned Objects list. The selected item will become active in the Objects list.
- Click the lock button above the Objects list to close the padlock.
- Complete a successful search for an object name.
- Click the All button, located above the Objects list. The All button shows all objects and pseudo-objects from the active libraries in the selected groups (Classes, Constants, Global members, and Events).

Member-centric mode

In member-centric mode, clicking an item in the Members list shows all objects from the currently selected libraries and groups that have a member whose name matches the selected item in the Members list. Here are some ways to put the Navigator into member-centric mode.

- Click the right mouse button in the Members list to bring up the context menu. Select the Objects with 'MemberName' member menu item.
- Double-click any item (other than <Default>) in the Members list. The selected item will become active in the Members list.
- Click the lock button above the Members list to close the padlock.
- Complete a successful member search.

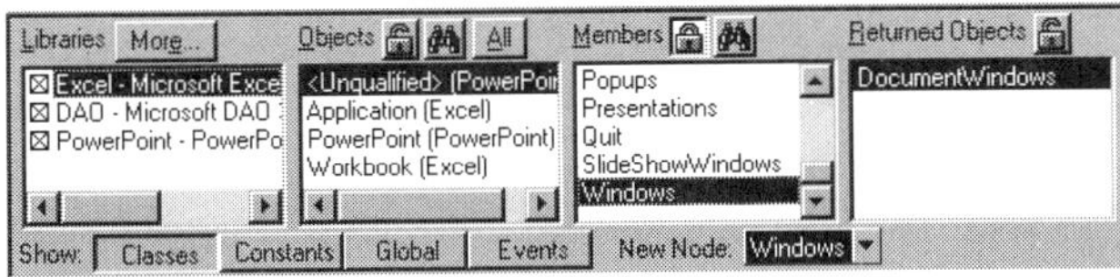

Figure B-3. *Member-centric mode. Note the state of the member-centric lock button.*

Locking the Return Type

Being able to quickly determine for you all methods and properties that return a given object type is one of the most powerful features of the Navigator. Locking the return type leaves a single item in the Returned Objects list. All members now listed in the Members list return an object of the type shown in the Returned Objects list.

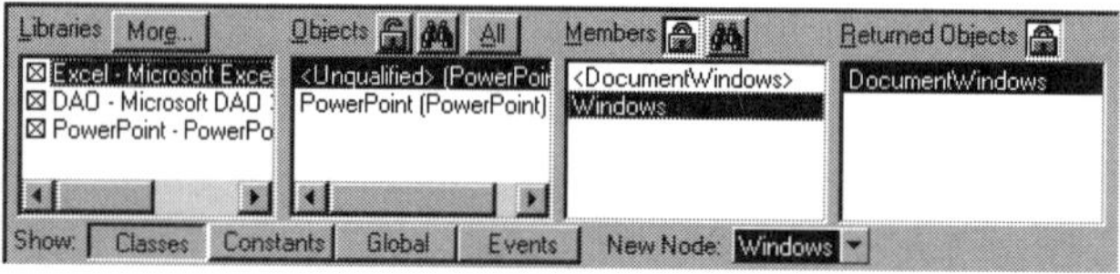

Figure B-4. *Member-centric mode with a locked return type. Note the states of the member-centric and return type lock buttons.*

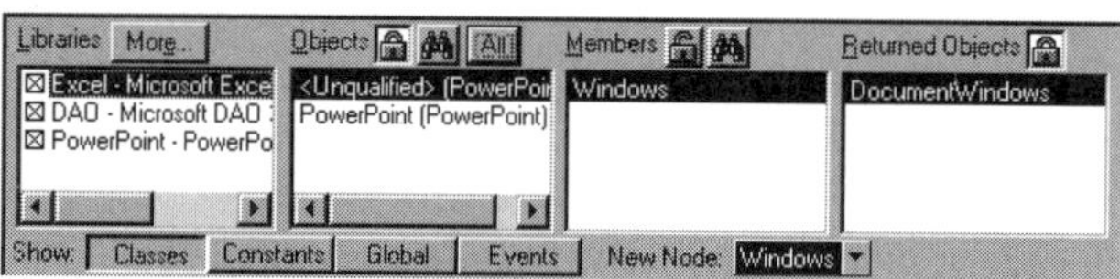

Figure B-5. *Object-centric mode with a locked return type. Note the states of the object-centric and return type lock buttons.*

With the Returned Objects list locked, you can still toggle between member-centric and object-centric modes. In member-centric mode, the Members list contains all members returning the given type, along with one additional item that has the format <ObjectName> representing an object variable of the returned type. We'll take up this special entry again and others like it in the "Nodes" section on page 458. Also, in member-centric mode, selecting an item from the Members list will fill the Objects list with all objects that contain a member that has the selected member name and that returns the corresponding return type. In object-centric mode with a locked return type, selecting an item in the Objects list fills the Members list with all members of the selected object that return the locked return type.

With the Returned Objects list locked, you need to use the lock button above the Objects or the Members list to set object- or member-centric mode. Double-clicking in any of the three lists produces the same behavior regardless of whether the return type is locked. There are several ways to lock the lists into return type mode:

- Click the right mouse button in the Returned Objects list to bring up the context menu. In object-centric mode, select the Objects containing

'ObjectName' menu item, which will be the second item in the context menu. In member-centric mode, the context menu item is called Members returning type 'ObjectName.'

- Ctrl-double-click any item in the Objects or Returned Objects list.
- Click the lock button above the Returned Objects list to close the padlock. If a valid return type is available from both the Objects and the Returned Objects lists, you'll see a context menu that will enable you to resolve the ambiguity and determine which type to use as your locked return type.

And there are several ways to unlock the Returned Objects list.

- Click the right mouse button in any list to bring up the context menu for that list and select a menu item.
- Double-click any item in any list. The selected item will become active in its list.
- Click the depressed lock button above the Returned Objects list to release the lock and switch to normal object-centric or member-centric mode. As with clicking the Returned Objects lock button to close the padlock, releasing the lock can be ambiguous, in which case a context menu will help you resolve the ambiguity.

You can't lock the return type for all object types. The following criteria allow an object type to be locked as a return type.

- The object is from the Classes group, that group is selected, and an event is not selected in the Members list.
- The object name isn't shown as qualified.
- A member of the class in one of the activated libraries actually returns the type.

NOTE The ToolTips for the lock buttons change dynamically to tell you what action will be performed if you select or deselect the lock button in the current context.

Link Files

While viewing return types, and later on while building expressions, you may notice that the display of the objects and members that return a given type is extremely fast. Finding all members that return a given type requires walking all methods of all objects of all activated object libraries, which, as you can imagine, could be a slow process for large libraries. Why is this operation so blindingly fast in Navigator? All of the hierarchical information for an object library is cached in an *Object Navigator Link* file (extension .Onl). A link file is loaded for each object library you add to the Libraries list.

All of the link files are saved in the Navigator installation directory. If an .Onl file for an object library doesn't exist when the library is first loaded, a new file is automatically generated. Thus, when you navigate a library for the first time, you may notice a delay the first time you reference the library. Don't worry. The next time you reference the library, you won't experience a delay because the .Onl file will need only to be read, not generated. Generating the .Onl file creates a delay because it's essentially equivalent to looking up and storing the information required to lock the Returned Objects list for each class in the object library.

You may recall from our lengthy consideration of Microsoft Excel's object model in Part Three that all methods and properties in Excel return values of the type Variant. An .Onl file that shows returned object types can't be auto-generated for Excel's object library, so the .Onl file for that library had to be enhanced to include the information about the object hierarchy that wasn't available. If a member of an object in an object library returns a Variant or an Object, the .Onl format allows multiple return types for the same member. For example, selecting Excel's *Application.Selection* method puts 73 different types in the Returned Objects list! For most cases, the auto-generated .Onl file is complete and doesn't require customization.

NOTE The MakeONL utility on the companion CD can be used to customize .Onl files. Copy MakeONL.Exe from the Object Navigator\Tools directory on the CD to the Object Navigation directory on your hard disk before you run it. This tool isn't as pretty as the Navigator itself, but it's the only way to customize an .Onl file—unless you want to figure out the format yourself.

Searching

The lack of a search capability is one deficiency of the Object Browser that the Object Navigator corrects. The Navigator lets you search either object names or member names for any substring—that is, search for a string that contains the search string. We'll focus here on searching member names. Searching object names works exactly the same way as searching member names.

Follow these steps to execute a member name search.

1. Click the Search Members button above the Members list to see the Search Members dialog shown in Figure B-6. The search dialog floats above the main Navigator window.

2. Type in the string to search for, or click the down-arrow button to make a selection from previous search strings.

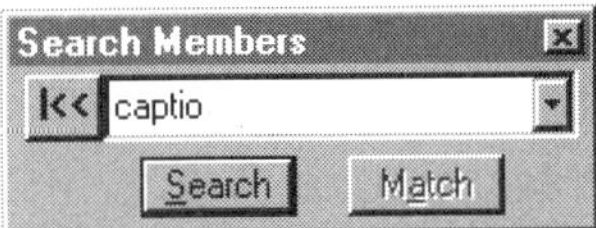

Figure B-6. *The Search Members dialog box. Note the state of the Match button.*

3. Click the Search button.

   If matching member names or matching substrings are found, the Members list will be filled with all matching member names and the Navigator will be put in member-centric mode.

That's all there is to it! You now have a list of matching member names in the Members list. Until you perform some other action, such as changing from member-centric to object-centric mode or conducting another search, your selecting or deselecting object groups or adding or removing libraries will cause the search to be reevaluated and updated. If deselecting a group or deactivating a library eliminates all of the matching members, the Navigator temporarily goes into object-centric mode with all objects showing until a group is selected or a library added that contains members matching the member name search string or substring.

Searching for members

As you type the search string in the Search Members dialog, the Navigator tries to match the name you're typing to a member name in the activated libraries. If a match is found, the string is cased according to the case of the member that was found and the Match button is activated, as shown in Figure B-7. If there is no match for the string you've typed in, the search text is forced into lower case and the Match button is disabled. If the search dialog is visible, you'll see the case of the name you've typed change as you add or remove groups and libraries. All items in the Search Members dialog dropdown list, which contains strings from previous successful searches, are also cased to match the current context when the dropdown is opened.

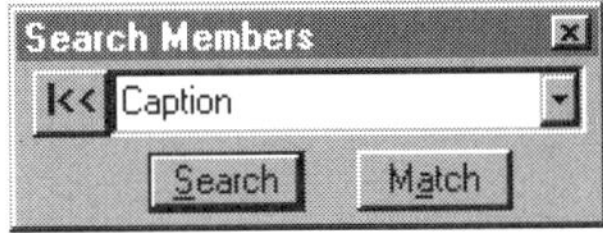

Figure B-7. *The Search Members dialog box with the Match button activated.*

When you click the Match button, the current contents of the Members list are cleared, the current search string is displayed as the only item in the list, and the Navigator is put into member-centric mode. If the search string is not a member name of the object selected in the Objects list, the appropriate object will be selected because the Navigator has moved into member-centric mode.

Search beginning of word only option By default, all searches are done on a substring basis, meaning that a name is considered a match if the string you've typed in is found anywhere in the member name string. By clicking the button to the left of the combo box in the Search Members dialog, as shown in Figure B-8, you can override the default and force the search engine to match a name only if the substring is found at the beginning of the word. This search option can make it easy to find related methods and properties.

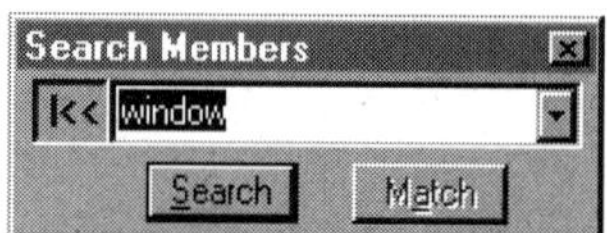

Figure B-8. *The Search Members dialog box with the Search beginning of word only button pressed.*

Searching for objects

As we've noted, searching for object names is similar to searching for member names, with one interesting difference. If a member name is found in more than one library during a member search, only one entry is placed in the Members list. If an object name is found in multiple libraries, one entry for each library is placed in the list. For example, if the Microsoft Excel and Microsoft PowerPoint libraries are active, the Classes button is selected, and the search text is *Menu*, clicking the Match button in the Search Objects dialog will put two items into the Objects list:

```
Menu (Excel)
Menu (PowerPoint)
```

NOTE The Navigator has only one search dialog, which is set to either Search Members or Search Objects. To change the search type, either click the appropriate search button in the Browse pane of the main Navigator window or use the context menu in the search dialog.

Searching in a browse list

The Objects, Members, and Returned Objects lists all support fast type searching. In any of the lists, you can jump to an item by clicking anywhere in the list to activate it and then quickly typing a sequence of characters contained in the target item. Once you've established your search characters, pressing Ctrl-up arrow or Ctrl-down arrow will move you to the next or previous matching item in the list. By default, the search is made at the beginning of each word. See the "Navigator Options" section on page 469 for information on overriding the default to use fast typing to force a substring search throughout each string in the active list.

FYI

Getting Help

As in the Visual Basic for Applications Object Browser, the question mark (?) button in the Description pane (the lower right pane) takes you to the help topic associated with the current item. You've probably noticed that pressing F1 on a VBA keyword will take you to different help files depending on whether you're using VB4-VBA or Excel-VBA. VBA relies on the host application—VB4, Excel, and so on—to determine which help file to use. The Navigator doesn't have a host application to fall back on, so it often can't determine which is the correct help file to bring up.

If the information read from the system registry isn't sufficient for the Navigator to find the correct help file, the Navigator will prompt you to locate the help file yourself. Don't worry—the information is cached, so you'll be prompted at most once for every library you request help for. To change the help file for the current item, right-click on the help button itself to get a context menu, from which you can open a file-open dialog.

Expression Building

Trying to visualize a hierarchical object model by looking at a single member of a single object at a time is very difficult. To understand how a hierarchy is structured, you need to view more than one level at a time and see how the different levels connect. The middle pane of the Object Navigator, the Code pane, is designed to help you construct object expressions from the currently referenced set of objects. Here's an example of an object expression from Microsoft Excel's object model:

```
ActiveSheet.Cells(RowIndex:=1). _
            Find(What:="Company", MatchCase:=True). _
            Address(External:=True)
```

An object expression is simply an ordered set of one or more method and property calls connected by dots.

By the end of this section, you'll be able to build this complete expression inside the Object Navigator and put it on the clipboard for use in your VBA project. As you learn to construct node chains in the next section, glance occasionally at the code you're generating. The object expression corresponding to the graphical depiction of the active chain is shown at the top of the Code pane.

Nodes

In the Code pane, each method or property is represented graphically by a single rectangular *node*. A series of linked nodes is called a *node chain*. By combining code from each of the nodes in a chain, the Navigator builds an object expression. Figure B-9 shows the graphical representation of the sample object expression listed on the previous page.

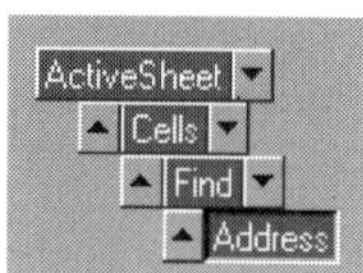

Figure B-9. *A node chain with default alignment.*

Before we actually create a node, let's take a minute to examine the four pieces of information that become available just from looking at a node:

- The caption on a node is the name of a method or property such as the ActiveSheet caption of the first node in the chain in Figure B-9. Back on page 452, we noted that locking the Returned Objects list in member-centric mode puts an extra, <ObjectName>, entry in the Members list that represents an object variable of the returned type. A node can have the caption <ObjectName> that represents a placeholder for an object variable type, too.
- On the left side of a node, you might see an up-arrow button. If the up-arrow is present, the member has parent objects. If the up-arrow isn't displayed, the member can be called from code without a dot (.) qualification. A node with no up-arrow corresponds to an entry in the Members list when the selected item in the Objects list reads <Unqualified>.
- On the right side of a node, you might see a down-arrow button. If the down-arrow is present, the member named in the node caption returns an object of a known Object type. If the member returns a non-object type, such as an Integer, the down-arrow is omitted.

- One more piece of information is available from the graphical node itself. If you move the mouse cursor over the node, you'll see a tooltip that identifies the type of object returned by the node member. Moving the mouse cursor over the Cells node in the example chain, for example, would bring up a Range tooltip. If a node doesn't represent a type of object, the tooltip will indicate the type of the node above it in the chain. The tooltip for the Address node, for instance, is Member of Range.

In addition to the information about a member available from the caption, arrow buttons, and tooltip of the node that represents it, the colors and rendering of the node help to indicate its state. The node states are represented by different colors and graphical treatments in the Code pane.

Active and inactive node chains The Navigator Code pane can contain multiple node chains, but only one chain can be active at a time. To distinguish the active node chain from the inactive chains, the Navigator displays the active chain in a different color. For information on setting the node foreground (text) and background (fill) colors, see "Color Options," in the "Navigator Options" section, on page 470.

Active node The active node is drawn with its caption sunken as if it were a depressed, and therefore selected, button. When a node is active, the Navigator lets you change parameter values for the node. See "Setting Parameters" on page 467. You activate a node by clicking in its caption area. (You don't click the node's up-arrow or down-arrow to activate it.) Refer back to the Address node in Figure B-9 on the facing page to compare the appearance of the active node to the other nodes in the chain.

Editable node An editable node is indicated by the highlight color of the system, which is the same color used to indicate the selected item in a list box. When a node is editable, the contents of the Objects, Members, and Returned Objects lists correspond to the objects and members that can be placed in the node and the members' return types, as determined by other nodes linked to it. Selecting items in the three main browser lists dynamically changes the contents of the editable node. If a node is linked to at least one other node, you can put it into the editable state at any time by double-clicking on its caption. The ChartTitle node shown on the next page in Figure B-10 in the system highlight color is an example of an editable node.

Freshly created, editable node If a node up-arrow or down-arrow is depressed, a node one step up or down from the node with the depressed button has just been created and is currently editable. The arrow will remain in the depressed position until you decide on the contents of the new node and put it out of the editable state by clicking anywhere in the Code pane or the Parameters pane. The depressed arrow state is too tricky to fully describe at this point, but you need to be familiar with the graphical expression of this new, editable node state. Refer to the ActiveChart node in Figure B-10 for an example of a depressed node arrow. See "Moving down" on the next page and "Moving up" on page 462 for more information on what happens when you click a node button.

Figure B-10. *An ActiveChart active node with its down-arrow button depressed to show its relationship to the new, editable ChartTitle node shown in the system highlight color.*

We've spent more than enough time examining nodes up close. Let's move on to actually creating them and placing them in the Code pane.

Creating Nodes

If you've started the Navigator and opened a library, you've already seen a node displayed in the Browse pane, which is updated whenever you change the selection in the Objects list. (Refer back to the new node in Figure B-1.) To put a node in the Code pane, the action that starts a new node chain, simply drag the node from New Node: in the Browse pane to anywhere in the Code pane. A copy of the new node will now be displayed in the Code pane.

NOTE Double-clicking the new node in the Browse pane produces the same result as dragging the new node to the middle of the Code pane.

Not all nodes are the same: a new node falls into one of three categories.

- A node with an <ObjectName> caption and both up-arrow and down-arrow buttons. This type of node is just a placeholder waiting to be replaced by a method or property that returns an object of type ObjectName. See "Moving up." To see how to get a new node of this type, activate the *Microsoft Excel 5.0 Object Library* and select Application from the Objects list.
- A node with an <ObjectName> caption and a down-arrow button, but no up-arrow button. The lack of an up-arrow button indicates that there are no methods or properties in the object model that return an object of this type. An <ObjectName> node without an up-arrow button represents an object variable of the specified type. To see an example of a new node of this type, activate the *Visual Basic objects and procedures* library and select CheckBox from the Objects list.

- A node with a valid member name caption and no up-arrow button. If any entry that reads <Unqualified> is selected in the Objects list, showing an object name in a new node makes no sense because the object is implied. In this case, we just display the member name. If the member returns an object type, the node has a down-arrow button; otherwise, the node has no arrow buttons. To see an example of a new node of this type, activate the *Microsoft Excel 5.0 Object Library* and select <Unqualified> (Excel) from the Objects list and ActiveCell from the Members list.

Once a permanent node has been created and moved to the Code pane (permanent node means any node other than an <ObjectName> placeholder node), the caption and return type of the node can't be changed. Therefore, if multiple choices are offered in the Returned Objects list, as with the *ActiveSheet* method in Excel, be sure that you select the correct return type (Chart, DialogSheet, Module, or Worksheet) in the Returned Objects list before placing the new node in the Code pane. The one exception to not allowing the return type of a node to change occurs with chaining to default members, which we'll get to later in this section.

Moving down

A single node isn't very exciting. Let's make use of the node arrow buttons to create a node chain and, hence, an object expression.

NOTE If the Recurse after new node option (the default) is set, the Navigator will automatically click the down-arrow button for you—if the down-arrow button is available—whenever you create a new node. See "Navigator Options" on page 469.

Once you've dragged a new node from the Browse pane to the Code pane, you can click the down-arrow button on the new node to add a second node to your chain. When you click the down-arrow button, the following things will happen:

1. A new, editable node will be displayed directly below the node on which you clicked the down-arrow button.
2. A single item, whose type will correspond to the object type of the node you're moving down from, will be placed in the Objects list. The Objects list will be disabled.
3. The Members and Returned Objects lists will work just as they normally do, except that selecting an item from either list will modify the editable node in the Code pane. The new node, which normally appears next to the New Node: label in the Browse pane, isn't displayed.

Your newest node will be in an editable state until you press Enter; double-click in the Libraries, Members, or Returned Objects list; check or uncheck a library in the Libraries list; add or remove a group filter; or click anywhere in the Code pane. When you leave editable mode, your node will become permanent. To cancel creation of the new node, just press Esc while the node is still editable. When you leave editable mode, the Browse pane will return to the same state it was in before you pressed the first node's down-button.

Moving up

Moving down from a node is only half the fun. Using the Object Navigator's ability to show all members that return a given object type, you can also move up the object chain from a given node—as long as there's a parent node to move up to. There is something to move up to when the object in the node is a member of another object. Moving up is similar to moving down. A new node is created and placed in editable mode, at which point you edit the node by clicking in the browse lists.

When you move up, a single item is placed in the Returned Objects list, the list is then disabled, and the Objects and Members lists remain available so that you can select the parent node. Note that the Objects list can't be modified while you're moving down and that the Returned Objects lists can't be modified while you're moving up.

We noted earlier that the new node you drag from the Browse pane is often just a placeholder node waiting to be replaced by a real node of the given type. If you click the up-arrow on a node directly below a placeholder node, or if you click the up-arrow on the placeholder node itself, the Navigator will replace the placeholder instead of creating a new node. Let's walk through a short example.

1. With *Microsoft Excel 5.0 Object Library* active, click the All button to place the Navigator in object-centric mode, and then select Range (Excel) from the Objects list.
2. Drag the new node, which will have the caption <Range> and both up-arrow and down-arrow buttons, from the Browse pane to the Code pane.
3. If the Recurse after new node option is active, the Navigator will automatically click the down-arrow button of the <Range> node for you. If that option isn't active, you should click the down-arrow button.
4. Double-click Address in the Members list to leave editable mode and permanently add an Address node to the active chain.
5. Click the up-arrow button of the <Range> node. <Unqualified> is now selected in the Objects list, ActiveCell is selected in the Members list, and ActiveCell has replaced <Range> in the node chain.

You'll now have a chain with two nodes, ActiveCell and Address. The temporary placeholder node will be gone.

Default properties

Default properties are an interesting variation on the Navigator's linked node paradigm because default properties are essentially invisible. A default property doesn't require a *.MemberName* in VBA code to be called, and it doesn't get its own node in the Navigator. If you click the down-arrow button of a node in the Code pane when the <Default> member is selected in the Members list, a new node isn't created. Instead, the node you're moving down from is modified directly. If the default property returns an object type, the return type of the node is modified. (Remember that each node can show a tooltip that indicates the current return type of the node.) If the default property doesn't return an object type, the down-arrow button is removed and the node tooltip reads Default of ObjectName instead of ObjectName.

Once you've modified a node to contain one or more default properties, there's no way to back out. The Parameters pane, which we'll take up in the "Setting Parameters" section on page 467, clearly displays the different default levels, as does the copy string at the top of the Code pane.

NOTE You can't double-click to activate a node that contains default levels.

Linking Nodes

The nodes we've created so far have been placed so that they touch each other, so we haven't seen any links between the nodes. However, nodes aren't confined to a fixed location. Any node in a chain can be moved around at will. When you start moving nodes, you'll come across some advanced features of the Object Navigator Code pane.

Moving nodes

To move a node, just click and hold down the left mouse button in the caption part of the node and drag it to a different location. It's that simple. If the node is linked to one or more other nodes, lines will be drawn between the nodes to indicate that the nodes are linked. If you separate the nodes a sufficient distance, two arrows will appear, one near each end of the link line. The arrowheads always point from the parent node to the child node—corresponding to the directions indicated by the up-arrow and down-arrow buttons. Refer to Figure B-11 on the next page to see a node chain that has physically separated nodes.

NOTE As you perform a drag operation in the Code pane, you'll see a single-pixel-wide drag line follow your mouse cursor around the Code pane. The line is anchored to the point at which you started dragging.

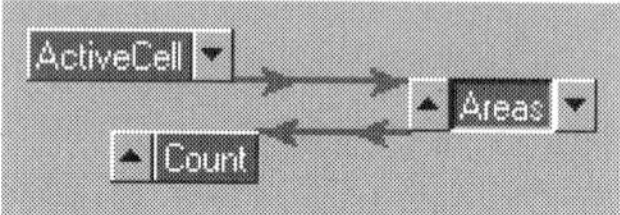

Figure B-11. *A node chain with physical distance between the nodes and the relationship among the three nodes indicated by link lines.*

Multiple nodes can be selected and moved together. When a node is selected, its appearance is modified by an inversion of its color. There are two ways to select multiple nodes. The first is to hold down the Ctrl key while clicking the nodes you want to select. The second is to use a selection rectangle, as shown in Figure B-12. These methods of selecting multiple graphical objects operate as they do in Visual Basic and many other Windows-based applications.

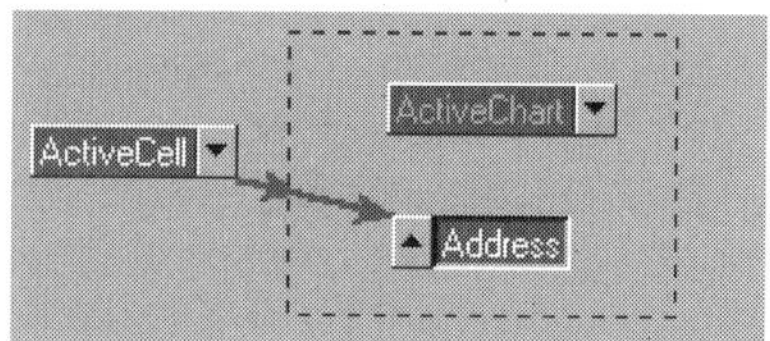

Figure B-12. *Selecting multiple nodes by means of a selection rectangle.*

Once you have selected multiple nodes, you can drag any of the selected nodes to move all selected nodes the same distance. Pressing the Del key will destroy all selected nodes (or the active node if no nodes are selected). Pressing Esc, clicking on the background of the Code pane, or clicking a node without pressing the Ctrl key will cancel the selection.

Dragging buttons

Clicking the up-arrow and down-arrow buttons on an existing node is only one way to create a new node. If you click and hold down the left mouse button on a node arrow button, you'll find yourself in drag mode.

NOTE To cancel the drag, either drop in the caption on the node you started with, or press Esc.

At this point, you can drag your arrow button around the Code pane. Several things can happen when you drop:

- If you drop on the Code pane background, you'll create a new node. This drag operation has the same effect as clicking the node arrow button and then moving the node.
- If you drop on another node, a new link will be established between the node you started dragging from and the node you dropped on. Of course, not all nodes can be linked. Refer to the Code Pane Drag Cursors table on the next page to see the cursor indicating that a link can't be made.
- If you drop on a node that's directly linked to the source node in the same direction (up or down) that you're dragging, that node and other nodes linked to it will be replaced by the newly dropped node. This replace action also has a special drag cursor

Cross-Reference By default, all linked nodes are replaced when a new node is created with a button click (as opposed to a drag-drop action). See "Code pane: Replace linked nodes with new node," in the "Navigator Options" section later in this appendix for a more detailed explanation of the replacement operation.

In the second bulleted item above, we saw how to create a new link between two existing nodes. The description didn't mention anything about first deleting existing links. That's because the Object Navigator supports multiple links to any given node. This support for multiple links allows you to use pieces of a node chain in more than one object expression without having to completely rebuild the chain for each expression.

Moving link lines

After you separate your nodes, expose the link lines and corresponding arrows, and maybe even add a few links by dragging node buttons, you may find that you want to move or delete a link. The link line arrows that indicate the directional relationship between two linked nodes can also be dragged to other nodes. When you drag a link line arrow over a node, you'll get the same mouse cursor verification you get when you drag a node up-arrow or down-arrow button. See the table on the next page for more information on cursors and their behavior.

CODE PANE DRAG CURSORS

Normal drag cursors for the up-arrow and down-arrow node buttons. These cursors appear while you're dragging an arrow button over the Code pane or, if a link can be added to the node, when you're dragging an arrow button over another node.

No-drop cursors for the up-arrow and down-arrow node buttons. When one of these cursors appears, an arrow node button is being dragged over a node that can't be linked to the source node.

Special cursors for the up-arrow and down-arrow node buttons. When such a button is being dragged over an adjacent node, a drop on the adjacent node will delete it and all nodes linked to it.

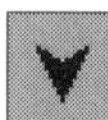

The cursor for dragging a link line arrow. This cursor appears over a node only when the end of the link line being dragged can be moved to the node under the mouse cursor

The "normal" look of the cursor when you're dragging a link line arrow. A link line arrow can't be dropped on the Code pane background, so this is the first cursor you'll see when you start to drag a link line arrow.

The link line arrow is being dragged over the node farthest from it on the link line. Dragging the opposite end of a link line back to its source node deletes the link, which is clearly indicated by this cursor.

Circular links

Generally, you have to work hard to link nodes in such a way that they create a circular node chain, but it is possible. When you do manage to create a circular node chain, as shown in Figure B-13, the Navigator will signal your "success" by highlighting the offending chain and putting a slashed-circle bitmap in the middle of each link in the chain. Most of the functionality in the Code pane will then be disabled until you click one of the special slashed-circle bitmaps, which will delete the link and break the circle. While a circular chain is active, you can move single or multiple nodes, but you can't delete nodes, use the up-arrow or down-arrow button, or move links.

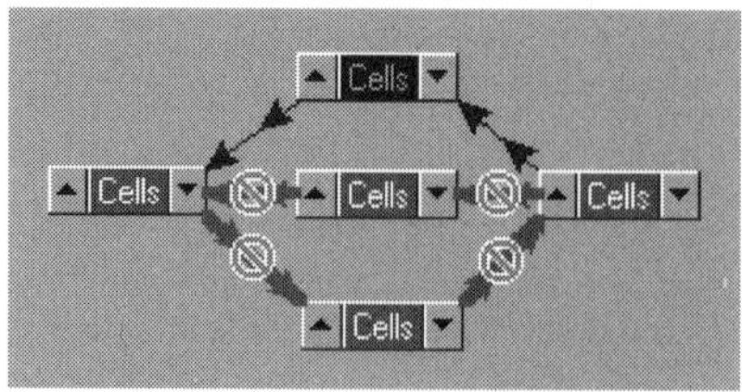

Figure B-13. *A circular node chain. This diagram actually contains two circles. Deleting one of the inner links will create a new circular chain consisting of the outer four nodes.*

Setting Parameters

Parameters are an important part of any object expression. The Parameters pane in the Navigator lets you modify the parameters of the method or property represented by the active node. The Parameters pane is arranged very much as the Visual Basic property sheet is, with parameter names on the left and values on the right. See Figure B-14 for an example of the Parameters pane in action.

Parameters	Values
Excel.Range.Find	
What	"Company"
☐ After	
☐ LookIn	
☐ LookAt	
☐ SearchOrder	
☐ SearchDirection	
☒ MatchCase	True
☐ MatchByte	

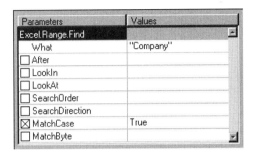

Figure B-14. *Setting parameters for the* Find *method of Excel's Range object. Note that a description of the active node is shown highlighted on the first line of the Parameters list.*

If a parameter is optional, you'll find a check box beside it. A parameter will be included in your final object expression only if the parameter name is checked in the Parameters list (in the case of an optional parameter) or if no check box is provided, which means that the parameter is required. Values for the parameters can be set in the Values column in the Parameters pane.

NOTE The values in the Values column will be pasted as is. No attempt is made to verify the data or to provide you with dropdown lists of acceptable parameter values. As with every software product, some Object Navigator features that would be really handy were scrapped in deference to a ship date.

We noted earlier that a node can be made to imply one or more default properties. Especially in cases in which multiple default property levels are in effect (as in the DBEngine case we observed earlier), some of the defaults will have required parameters. In the case shown in Figure B-15 on the next page, a Database object implies two default levels. One of the default properties of Database is TableDefs, which itself has a default property, Item, which has one required parameter, Index, that gets displayed in the Parameters pane. The other default level of DBEngine displayed in Figure B-15 is Fields, which has the same default property as TableDefs. The multiple default levels are clearly displayed in the Parameters window, and the parameters for each of the default properties implied by the node can be set. Each grayed-out line in the Values column indicates a new set of parentheses. The resulting object expression is similar to the DBEngine expression shown in the "Returned Objects list" section (back on page 450).

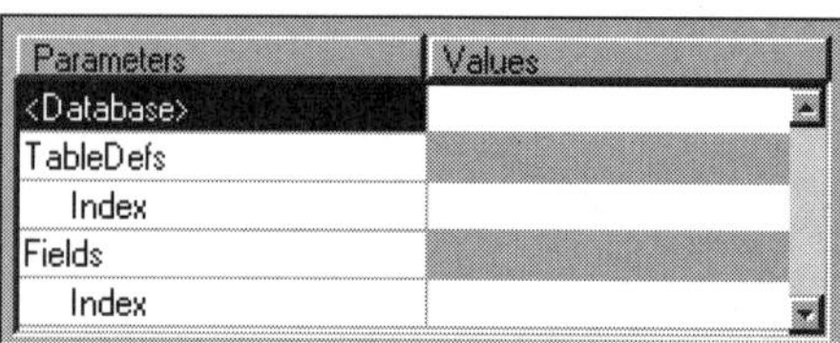

Figure B-15. *Setting parameters for a variable-name node with two default levels.*

In Figure B-14, the first line in the Values column is grayed out, which means that the entry is purely informational and you can't assign a value to it. However, the first value line in Figure B-15 isn't gray. If the active node has a caption of <ObjectName> and doesn't have an up-arrow button (meaning that it isn't just a placeholder node), the Parameters pane will allow you to type in a value for the represented object variable. The node display won't be affected, but your final object expression will include the name you specified for your object variable instead of <ObjectName>.

Copying Your Expression

The goal of this "Expression Building" section is to enable you to build an object expression that can be copied to the clipboard and pasted directly into your VBA code, so here's the final step. To copy the code expression you've been building—the expression displayed at the top of the Code pane—into the clipboard for pasting into your code, just click in the Code pane and press Ctrl-C or Ctrl-Ins. You can also double-click in the expression area at the top of the Code pane or choose Copy from the Code pane context menu.

Constant values can't be placed in the Code pane, but you can still copy them. The Description pane in the lower right corner of the Object Navigator screen, which is updated whenever you click a list item in the Browse pane, is implemented as a standard read only textbox. Just select any text you want to copy—the name of a constant, for instance—and press Ctrl-C.

Navigator Options

All Object Navigator options are set via the Options submenu on the system menu. Simply open the Options submenu, choose the option group you're interested in, and add or remove check marks to set the options. The three option groups are Browse Pane, Code Pane, and Search Window. All three option groups have a Show ToolTips option.

Browse pane: Substring search on fast typing The default behavior of the Objects, Members, and Returned Objects lists is to match rapidly typed text to the beginning of a word. For example, if you type *w-i-n* with less than half a second between characters, you might end up on the item Window in the active list box. If you want to end up on ActiveWindow instead, you should set the substring search on the fast typing option. Whether this option is on or off, once you've found your string, you can press Ctrl-down arrow and Ctrl-up arrow to jump to the next and previous list items that also match the string or substring.

Code pane: Recurse after new node When you place a new node in the Code pane, the default behavior of the Navigator is to create yet another new node by programmatically clicking the up-arrow or down-arrow button of the node you just created, if the appropriate button is available. Generally, this is the behavior you want. However, clicking the up-arrow or down-arrow button always puts the newest node in editable mode, so if you want a node to be placed in editable mode only when you explicitly click a node arrow button, turn off this option.

Code pane: Replace linked nodes with new node If this option is turned off, repeatedly clicking a node button will result in nodes piled on top of each other. If you leave this option on, which is the default setting, creating a new child or parent node with a button click will automatically delete any current child or parent nodes already linked to the node.

Code pane: Copy named/positional parameters This setting determines whether code with or without named parameters is generated in the Code pane. All of the figures in this appendix have shown screens with this option set to Copy named parameters. If Copy positional parameters is set, commas are inserted as needed to correctly position optional parameters. If a parameter value isn't supplied in the Values column, the string <ParameterName> is shown in the expression for that parameter.

Search window: Close on successful search If this option is turned on, the Search Members dialog will automatically close if a successful search has been executed or if the Match button is clicked. Of course, the Search Members dialog is easy to bring back up with the search buttons on the Objects and Members lists. This option is also available on the context menu in the Search Members dialog.

Color Options

For almost two years after its initial incarnation, the Navigator used a bright red background color to show that a node was active and a yellow background color for an inactive node. Many objections to that color combination have been voiced. If you don't like the default node colors, you can use the Color Options dialog to choose your own active and inactive node colors. Your choice of colors—and of all other options—is saved between Navigator sessions. The Color Options dialog, shown in Figure B-16, is available through the Colors item on the system menu. Its workings will be evident to you.

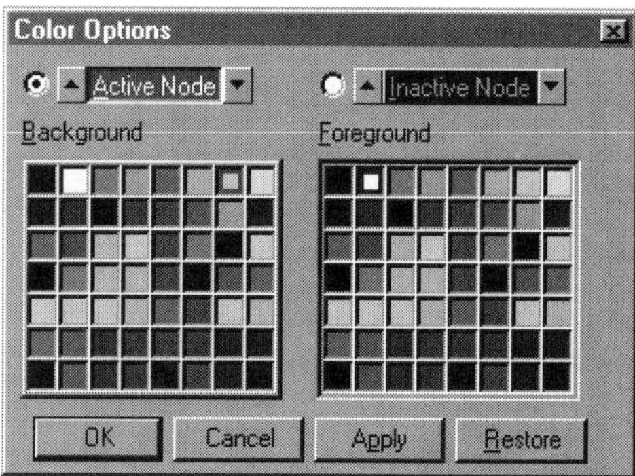

Figure B-16. *The Color Options dialog box. The raised edge of the box surrounding the blocks of color choices indicates that the Background color block has the current input focus. You can change the color with the arrow keys or with the mouse.*

FYI

Developer's Note: The Genesis of the Object Navigator

The Object Navigator in its current form is the culmination of a long, sporadic, and sometimes obsessive development cycle of more than two years. The major part of the work was done during the last four months of 1995. The Navigator originated in my reaction, along the lines of so many developers' reactions, to the complexities of programming Microsoft Excel's objects and the long time it takes to get up to speed with Excel's object model. My initial Object Model Browser was an Excel dialog that had all the hierarchical display and search capabilities of the current Navigator but none of the later incarnation's nifty UI features. The Object Model Browser was big and slow. It needed a 350K data worksheet and a 100K add-in to navigate Excel's objects. It couldn't read arbitrary object libraries dynamically, and only the most desperate user could figure out how to use it. Ironically, despite its greater number of capabilities, the Object Navigator application takes up less disk space than its early predecessor!

The Navigator is written in Microsoft Visual Basic 4 and Microsoft Visual C++. The engine DLL (TlbInf32.Dll) does all of the talking to the object libraries. The DLL is used to search, fill object and member lists, and retrieve other information from type libraries on the system. The DLL is written as an in-process OLE DLL server. For the sake of size—including the type library adds approximately 30K, or 80 percent, to the DLL—and security, the type library resource isn't included in TlbInf32.Dll. Among other things, this arrangement precludes using late binding to objects implemented in the DLL from Visual Basic code, so you can rest assured that all calls from the Object Navigator front end to the engine are early bound.

The entire Object Navigator front end is written in Visual Basic. The only custom control I used is the Common Dialog control (ComDlg32.Ocx) that ships with VB. I've made extensive use of control arrays, lightweight graphical controls (Image, Label, Line, and Shape), and class modules. Numerous calls go directly to the Windows API. All strings are in a resource file for easy localization. I used subclassing heavily to implement features such as the checked list boxes, the scroll bars, and the tooltips. Adding all the features without using custom controls supplied me with numerous personal challenges, some of which I barely met, but Visual Basic is a powerful programming tool and always came through for me in the end, generally with very elegant solutions.

I hope you'll enjoy using the Object Navigator. I've tried to combine a lot of capability with an aesthetically pleasing user interface to make your—and my own—object programming much more productive. Feel free to send me questions, comments, suggestions, and (gasp!) bug reports at MattCur@Microsoft.com. Happy navigating! I'm sleeping in tomorrow.

—Matt

Appendix C

Microsoft Office for Windows 95 Object Models

The best way to figure out the names of members—properties, methods, objects—that belong to an object, and what the object's relationship to other objects is, is to use the Object Navigator on the book's companion CD-ROM. However, sometimes it's nice to see a print representation of the whole shebang. This appendix features graphical representations of the object models we've considered in this book, as well as some others you might find interesting.

We've based this appendix on *Your "Un"Official Guide to Using OLE Automation with Microsoft Office and Microsoft BackOffice*, which is included in the Microsoft Solutions Development Kit (MSDK) version 2.0.

Cross-Reference The Microsoft Solutions Development Kit contains excellent information for people interested in developing applications with Microsoft products.

Conventions Used in This Appendix

The key below shows the types of items that appear in the object model diagrams in this appendix and how they are designated.

This type of item...	...is designated this way
object only	
object and collection	
metacollection	

Within the object models in this appendix, collections are referred to by singular names even though collections are actually plural elements. The Worksheets collection in Microsoft Excel, for example, is referred to in the object model as the Worksheet collection. And, by convention, a collection always contains an object of the same name. The Worksheet collection in Microsoft Excel contains a Worksheet object. A metacollection is a collection that can contain more than one type of object. DrawingObjects, in Microsoft Excel, is a metacollection that can contain Button objects, Rectangle objects, and many other object types.

When you view an application's object model in the Visual Basic Object Browser or with the Object Navigator on this book's companion CD, you're actually viewing that application's "type library." For example, when you see the Microsoft Excel object model in the Object Browser, you are really looking at Xl5en32.olb. (The "en" indicates that this is the English-language version of the type library.) Type library names and locations are provided for each application.

The Microsoft Access/DAO Object Model

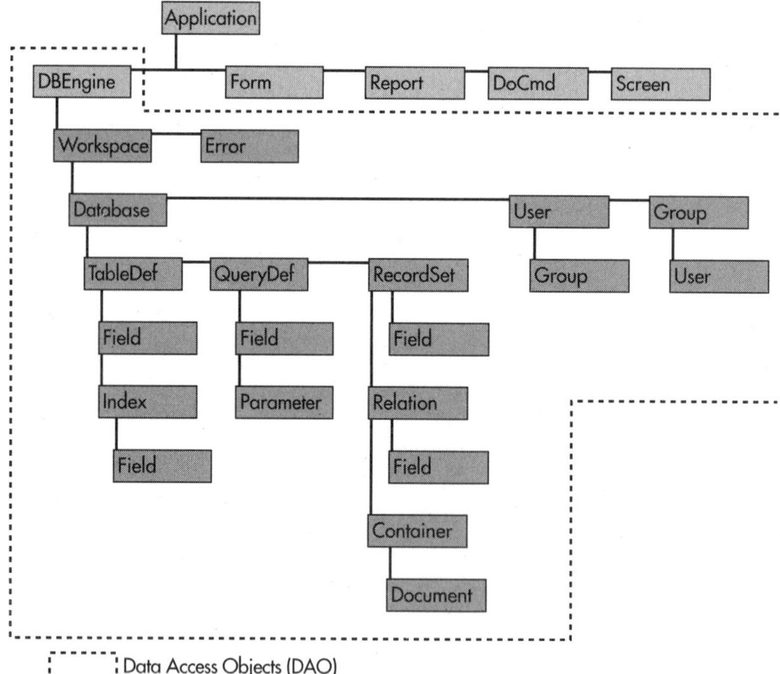

The Microsoft Access object model is provided by Msaccess.tlb, which is included when you install Microsoft Office Professional for Windows 95 or Microsoft Access for Windows 95. By default, Msaccess.tlb is installed in the

\MSOffice\Access subdirectory. Online help for this object model is available in Access.hlp.

The Microsoft DAO object model is provided by Dao3032.dll or Dao2516.dll (for DAO version 3.0 or 2.5, respectively), which is included when you install Microsoft Visual C++ version 4, Microsoft Excel for Windows 95, Microsoft Visual Basic version 4 (Professional and Enterprise editions), or Microsoft Access for Windows 95. By default, Dao3032.dll or Dao2516.dll is installed in the \Windows\MSAPPS\DAO subdirectory, the \Windows\System subdirectory, or the \Program Files\Common Files\Microsoft Shared\DAO subdirectory.

The Microsoft Excel Object Model

The Microsoft Excel object model shown on pages 476 and 477 is provided by Xl5en32.olb, which is included when you install Microsoft Office for Windows 95 Standard or Professional or Microsoft Excel for Windows 95. By default, Xl5en32.olb is installed in the \MSOffice\Excel subdirectory. Online help for this object model is available in Vba_xl.hlp.

The Microsoft Office Binder Object Model

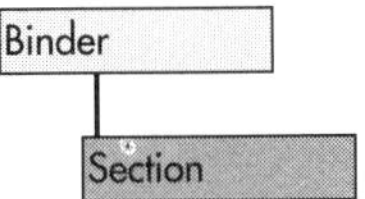

The Microsoft Office Binder object model is provided by Binder.tlb, which is included when you install Microsoft Office for Windows 95. By default, Binder.tlb is installed in the \MSoffice\Office subdirectory. Online help for the binder object model is available in Vba_bin.hlp.

There is a Microsoft Office Object Model (Mso5enu.dll) in the VB References dialog. Although you don't call this object directly, it provides functionality for the (Windows 95) Microsoft Excel, Microsoft Project, and Microsoft Office Binder document property collection used by the BuiltInDocumentProperties and CustomDocumentProperties collections. You should maintain a reference to this object in your Visual Basic projects. For more information about a consistent way to read and write document properties, see the Microsoft Solutions Development Kit version 2.0.

The Microsoft PowerPoint Object Model

For simplicity's sake, the Color object, which is used throughout the Microsoft PowerPoint object model, is not shown in the model on page 478. The Microsoft PowerPoint object model is provided by Powerpnt.tlb, which is included when you install Microsoft Office or Microsoft PowerPoint for Windows 95.

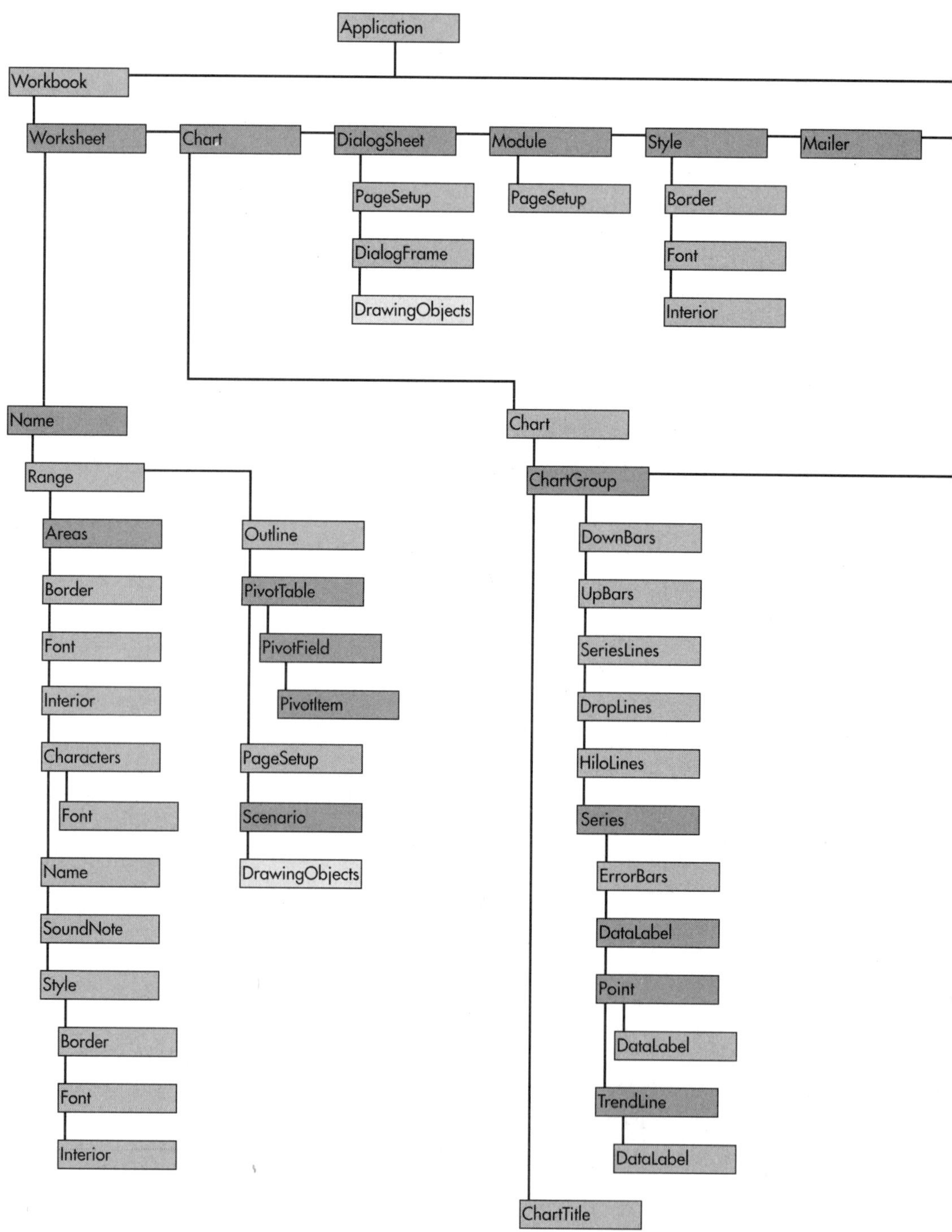
Application
Workbook
Worksheet
Chart
DialogSheet
Module
Style
Mailer
PageSetup
DialogFrame
DrawingObjects
PageSetup
Border
Font
Interior
Name
Range
Areas
Border
Font
Interior
Characters
Font
Name
SoundNote
Style
Border
Font
Interior
Outline
PivotTable
PivotField
PivotItem
PageSetup
Scenario
DrawingObjects
Chart
ChartGroup
DownBars
UpBars
SeriesLines
DropLines
HiloLines
Series
ErrorBars
DataLabel
Point
DataLabel
TrendLine
DataLabel
ChartTitle

The Microsoft Excel Object Model

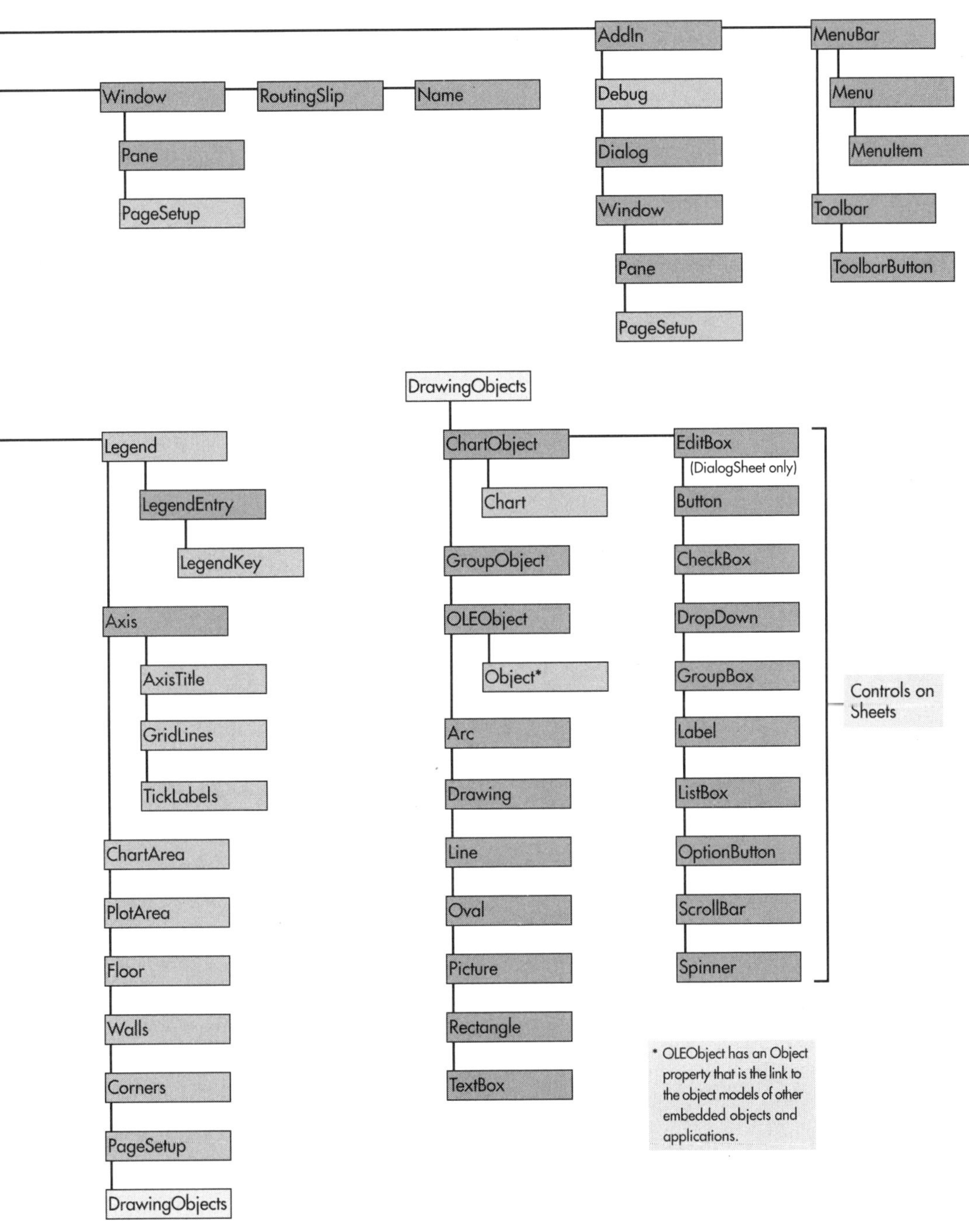

The Microsoft PowerPoint Object Model

- Application
  - ApplicationWindow
    - DocumentWindow
      - Selection
      - View
    - SlideShowWindow
      - SlideShowView
  - Presentation
    - ColorSchemes
      - DocSchemeColors
    - ExtraColors
    - FontInfo
    - GraphicFormat
      - FillFormat
      - LineFormat
      - ShadowFormat
    - PrintOptions
      - PrintRange
    - SlideShow
    - Sounds
    - TextStyle
      - FitText
      - Ruler
        - RulerLevel
        - TabStop
    - TextStyleLevel
      - CharFormat
      - ParaFormat
        - BulletFormat
        - LineSpacingSet
          - LineSpacing
    - Slide
      - GraphicFormat
        - FillFormat
        - LineFormat
        - ShadowFormat
      - HeaderFooter
        - SlideObject
      - SchemeColors
      - SlideObject
        - Placeholders
          - SlideObject
          - BuildEffects
            - SoundEffects
          - FitText
          - GraphicFormat
            - FillFormat
            - LineFormat
            - ShadowFormat
          - PlayOptions
            - SoundNotes
            - PlayOptionsVerbs
          - Text
            - CharFormat
            - ParaFormat
              - BulletFormat
              - LineSpacingSet
                - LineSpacing
            - Ruler
              - RulerLevel
              - TabStop
            - TextBounds
            - TextRange
              - CharFormat
              - ParaFormat
      - SlideShowEffects
        - SoundEffects

By default, Powerpnt.tlb is installed in the \MSOffice\Powerpnt subdirectory. Online Help for this object model is available in Vba_pp.hlp, which is included in the Microsoft Solutions Development Kit version 2.0.

The Microsoft Word Object Model

Word

The Microsoft Word object model consists of the WordBasic object. All of the Microsoft WordBasic macro commands are accessible through this object. To find out more about using WordBasic commands, see the online WordBasic help file, Wrdbasic.hlp, which you can choose to install when you set up Microsoft Word for Windows 95.

The Microsoft Word type library, Wb70en32.tlb, is on the book's companion CD. Copy it to your system \Windows\System directory, and add it to the VB References dialog (see page 475) by means of the Browse command button. Remember to distribute the type library to users of your solutions.

Appendix D

Hungarian Prefixes in Visual Basic

Internal groups at Microsoft have made an effort to establish standards for code written in Visual Basic. The tables in this appendix define standard naming prefixes used by Microsoft Consulting Services (MCS) for intrinsic types, controls, and database objects. A final table shows one-letter scope prefixes. The VB prefix conventions are loosely based on Charles Simonyi's Hungarian notation. The information in this appendix was taken from a document called *Visual Basic Standards,* which was produced by Microsoft's Internal Technology Group (ITG). These guidelines are flexible, but they'll give you an idea of the kinds of conventions you need to develop for your own programming.

VISUAL BASIC VARIABLE AND FUNCTION NAME PREFIXES

Tag	*Variable Use*	*Data Type*	*Suffix*
bln, f	Boolean flag	Boolean	
cur	Currency, 64 bits	Currency	@
dbl	Double, 64-bit signed quantity	Double	#
dtm	Date and time	Date	
err	Error		
sng	Float/Single, 32-bit signed, floating point	Single	!
hnd, h	Handle	Long (32-bit)	
idx	Index	Integer	%
lng, l	Long, 32-bit signed quantity	Long	&
int, i	Number/counter	Integer	%
str	String	String	$
uns	Unsigned, 32-bit unsigned quantity	Long	&
udt	User-defined type		
vnt	Variant	Variant	
ary	Array		

VISUAL BASIC CONTROL PREFIXES

Prefix	*Object Type*	*Example*
ani	Animation button	aniMailBox
bed	Pen Bedit control	bedFirstName
cbo	Combo box and dropdown list box	cboEnglish
chk	Check box	chkReadOnly
clp	Picture clip	clpToolbar
cmd (3d)	Command button (3D)	cmdOk (cmd3dOk)
com	Communications control	comFax
ctr	Control (when specific type unknown)	ctrCurrent
dat	Data control	datBiblio
dir	Directory list box	dirSource
dlg	Common Dialog control	dlgFileOpen
drv	Drive list box	drvTarget
fil	File list box	filSource
frm	Form	frmEntry
fra (3d)	Frame (3D)	fraStyle (fra3dStyle)
gau	Gauge control	gauStatus
gpb	Group push button	gpbChannel
gra	Graph control	graRevenue
grd	Grid control	grdPrices
hed	Pen Hedit control	hedSignature
hsb	Horizontal scroll bar	hsbVolume
img	Image	imgIcon
ink	Pen Ink	inkMap
key	Keyboard key status	keyCaps
lbl	Label	lblHelpMessage
lin	Line	linVertical
lst	List box	lstPolicyCodes
mdi	MDI child form	mdiNote
mpm	MAPI message	mpmSentMessage
mps	MAPI session	mpsSession
mci	MCI control	mciVideo
mnu	Menu	mnuFileOpen
opt (3d)	Option Button (3D)	optRed (opt3dRed)
ole	OLE control	oleWorksheet
out	Outline control	outOrgChart
pic	Picture	picVGA
pnl (3d)	Panel (3D)	pnl3d
rpt	Report control	rptQtr1Earnings

VISUAL BASIC CONTROL PREFIXES *continued*

Prefix	*Object Type*	*Example*
shp	Shape control	shpCircle
spn	Spin control	spnPages
txt	Textbox	txtLastName
tmr	Timer	tmrAlarm
vsb	Vertical scroll bar	vsbRate

VISUAL BASIC PREFIXES FOR DATABASE OBJECTS

Prefix	*Object Type*	*Example*
db	ODBC Database	dbAccounts
ds	ODBC Dynaset object	dsSalesByRegion
fdc	Field collection	fdcCustomer
fd	Field object	fdAddress
ix	Index object	ixAge
ixc	Index collection	ixcNewAge
qd	QueryDef object	qdSalesByRegion
qry (suffix)*	Query	SalesByRegionQry
tb	Table object	tbCustomer
td	TableDef object	tdCustomers

*Using a suffix for queries allows each query to be sorted with its associated table in Microsoft Access dialogs such as Add Table and List Tables Snapshot.

VISUAL BASIC SCOPE AND USAGE PREFIXES

Prefix	*Description*
g	Global
m	Local to module or form
st	Static variable
(no prefix)	Non-static variable, variable local to procedure
v	Variable passed by value (local to a routine)
r	Variable passed by reference (local to a routine)

We dealt with scoping variables in several of the chapters in this book. A letter at the beginning of a variable name can indicate its scope, the extent of its visibility, or accessibility. In other words, a variable's scope indicates how broadly it can be read or modified. A variable with module-level scope, for example, can be accessed only from routines in the same module.

INDEX

Note: An italic page-number reference indicates a figure, a table, or a program listing.

Special Characters and Numbers

A

D

E

N

O

P

Q

T

U

V

W

X

Joel Dehlin grew up in Katy, Texas, and attended Brigham Young University, where he studied accounting. He put himself through school by teaching economics and history and ran a small retail computer company on the side. Immediately out of school, he worked at Novell, Inc., supporting NetWare, and did a stint at Arthur Andersen & Co. in Chicago, where he worked in research and development, programming mostly in Visual Basic, C++, and Lotus Notes. Joel has written articles for *LAN Times* under the name Victor Madison. He is currently the manager of corporate marketing at Microsoft but says he would prefer a cushy job on a beach somewhere. Let him know if you've got something. Joel is married to Lani Dehlin—part-time speech pathologist and full-time mom—and has two children, Benjamin and Jonathon. He says that "this book stuff" is a hobby, that his real love is good music. Joel can be reached at JoelD@Microsoft.com.

Given a head start by the Early Entrance Program at the University of Washington, **Matthew Curland** graduated with distinction in 1988 at the ripe old age of 18 with a B.S. in mathematics. He has been making a living with Basic in one form or another since 1989. Matt's first stint at Microsoft was interning as a tester on the QuickBasic team, where he was introduced to life in the software industry with an assignment to write the matrix math sample library—which is still shipping with Visual Basic for MS-DOS. In 1992, Matt took one semester of piano performance at Brigham Young University before the BYU math department and, subsequently, Microsoft offered him jobs that actually produced income. He is currently a developer working on Microsoft's Visual Basic for Applications team. Matt is married to Lynn Curland, who is a published fiction writer and a musician. He can be reached at MattCur-@Microsoft.com.

Register Today!

Return this
Object Programming with Visual Basic® 4
registration card for a Microsoft Press® catalog

U.S. and Canada addresses only. Fill in information below and mail postage-free. Please mail only the bottom half of this page.

1-55615-899-8A ***OBJECT PROGRAMMING WITH VISUAL BASIC® 4*** ***Owner Registration Card***

NAME

INSTITUTION OR COMPANY NAME

ADDRESS

CITY STATE ZIP

NO POSTAGE
NECESSARY
IF MAILED
IN THE
UNITED STATES

BUSINESS REPLY MAIL
FIRST-CLASS MAIL PERMIT NO. 108 REDMOND, WA

POSTAGE WILL BE PAID BY ADDRESSEE

MICROSOFT PRESS REGISTRATION
OBJECT PROGRAMMING
WITH VISUAL BASIC 4
PO BOX 3019
BOTHELL WA 98041-9946